BOW VALLEY SPORT

BY DEREK GALLOWAY

BOW VALLEY SPORT

QUICKDRAW
PUBLICATIONS

POSTAL ADDRESS
PO Box 5313
Squamish, BC V8B OC2
Canada

CONTACT US
(604) 892-9271
info@quickdrawpublications.com
www.quickdrawpublications.com

Quickdraw Publications is constantly
expanding our range of guidebooks. If
you have a manuscript or an idea for a
book, or would like to find out more
about our company, please get in touch.

Designed and typeset in Canada;
printed and bound in China.

FIRST EDITION

INTERNATIONAL STANDARD BOOK NUMBER
ISBN 978-0-9732593-9-1

AUTHOR
Derek Galloway

PHOTOGRAPHY
All photography by the author unless otherwise noted. Front
cover photo: Greg Tos on *Buffet Royal* (5.13C) at the Lookout
by Gery Unterasinger. Page one photo: Marc Bourdon on *The
Convincer* (5.12B) at Heart Creek. Photo this page: Gery Unterasinger on *Dark Side of the Boom* (5.12A) at the Notch.

Give Us Your Feedback

Due to the changeable nature of rock climbing, guidebooks often become outdated soon after publication.
In an attempt to alleviate this problem, we post updates on our website, **Quickdrawpublications.com**.
To help improve everyone's climbing experience in the Bow Valley, we need your feedback! After using this
book, please help us by providing information about your experiences. We welcome suggestions and correc-
tions to the route information as well as changes to photographs or maps. And, of course, if you establish a
new climb, please let us know. Thank you for helping improve climbing in the Bow Valley.

Disclaimer

Read this before you use this book! Rock climbing is a sport with inherent risks. Participating in rock climbing may result in injury or death.

This guidebook is intended for climbers with a degree of ability and experience. The terrain described within
is dangerous and requires a high level of fitness and technical expertise to negotiate. This guidebook is a
compilation of information from several sources. As a result the author cannot confirm the accuracy of any
specific detail. Difficulty ratings are subjective and may vary depending on your own personal experience
and the conditions of the climb. There may be misinformation in regards to route descriptions, conditions,
difficulties or any other detail. This guidebook does not give the user the right to access any terrain described
within. The land owner or land manager may limit access to any part of an area at any time. It is your
responsibility to adhere to all closures.

This book belongs to:

_____

_____

ACKNOWLEDGEMENTS

I started this project in 2007 and in the following years spent copious amounts of time at the crags gathering the information necessary to write the book you now hold in your sweaty palms. Much of my work required psyched partners and, to my great relief, a core group of friends immediately stepped forward. I owe each of them countless belay hours and would like to individually acknowledge their efforts. Without Gery Unterasinger this book would still be years away from completion. Gery proved to be my most consistent partner and was always psyched (or at least pretended to be) to check out new walls in the name of "guide book work". Todd Guyn and Ryan Johnstone provided valuable feedback on drafts and also spent countless days gathering route information—belaying me—when I'm sure they would have preferred to be working on their own projects. A big thanks also goes to Zak McGurk for the endless belay sessions, especially the one that almost killed him! My publisher, Marc Bourdon, also deserves a nod for his patience and assistance. He somehow managed to turn my seventh grade writing skills into a manuscript an adult might have produced. Last but not least, I'd like to thank my longtime girlfriend Michelle Kollmuss for supporting me from start to finish. I know it wasn't easy when you had to go to your job and I was heading to the cliff, yet again, to "work".

Others that provided valuable assistance include: Takeshi Abe, Roger Chayer, Marc-Andre Cousineau, David Dornian, Andy Genereux, Jon Jones, Joel Labonte, JD LeBlanc, John Martin, Simon Meis, Scott Milton, Carsten Moldenhauer, Dung Nguyen, Chris Perry, Ian Perry, Lev Pinter, Brandon Pullman, Scott Semple, Greg Tos and Sonnie Trotter. If I missed you, slap me (gently) in the back of the head next time I see you so I won't forget next time!

Climbing pictures are truly worth a thousand words and I've got the following excellent photographers to thank for the use of their stunning images: Marc Bourdon, Andrew Burr (Andrewburr.com), Roger Chayer, Ryan Creary (Ryancreary.com), Nick Croken (Redlinephoto.ca), Sean Dougherty, Grzegorz Florek (Photoincline.com), Jon Jones, JD LeBlanc, Simon Meis, Matt Muller, Sandra Studer (Sandrastuder.com), Ross Suchy, Sonnie Trotter (Sonnietrotter.com), Gery Unterasinger and Tony Whitehouse. Finally, a big thanks goes to all the route developers. You make writing a guidebook possible. Keep up the great work!

PREFACE

So this is where the preface goes, right up here at the beginning of the book. It's where I'm supposed to tell you what you are about to read; and just in case you get overwhelmed by the quality and depth of the information held within the following pages, you can always refer back to this statement and it should set you straight: **This is a guidebook to the best sport climbing areas of the Bow Valley, written by one of the best climbers the Valley has produced to date.** Trust me, Derek knows where the good stuff is and he won't lead you astray. (Even though I told him not to put the good stuff in his book.)

For an area with a soul-crushingly short climbing season and a handful of hidden gems amongst seemingly endless miles of chossy rock, the Bow Valley has been the home base to a number of talented Canadian climbers. Speaking from personal experience, this success has been the result of combining a highly motivated and supportive climbing community with a rock type that generally forces you to apply good technique while pulling hard and getting pumped all at the same time. It's climbing pay dirt!

This pay dirt does come at a price though; many of us have hiked our asses off looking for the next great crag and we've only scratched the surface of what might be out there. This is where you come in: I hope this guidebook motivates you to climb at every crag within its pages, but more importantly I hope it opens your eyes to the potential waiting for you elsewhere in the valley.

Wait a minute, that was far too positive. I'm making it all sound too good. Let me wrap it up by summarizing with this: The climbing season is short—maybe two good weeks in August. The rock is chossy and wet most of the time. All the good crags have already been found. The approaches are monumental: 1–2 hours uphill at a minimum. The crags are super crowded and everyone is aggressive toward outsiders. Grizzly bears are everywhere and they are hungry, very hungry. There is one good crag, and it isn't in this book.

But don't tell anyone, it's our little secret.

–Scott Milton, 2011

METOLIUS

Super Chalk

TABLE OF CONTENTS

AREA MAP . . . . Cover
ACKNOWLEDGEMENTS 4
PREFACE 6

INTRODUCTION 10
The Lay of the Land 11
Geology 12
Flora and Fauna 13
Planning Your Trip 16
Hazards & Emergency Response 26
Rest Day Activities 28
Sport Climbing History 30
How to Use This Book 40
Where do You Want to Climb Today? 42
Top 100 Sport Climbs 44

THE CLIMBS 46

1. PRAIRIE CREEK 48

2. BARRIER MOUNTAIN 58
Salt and Pepper Wall 62
Barrier Wall 64

3. ACÉPHALE 70
The Lower Wall 76
The Upper Wall 81
Down Under 87

4. HEART CREEK 88
First Rock 92
Jupiter Rock 95
Amphitheatre Sector 98
Bunny Hill Sector 102
Bayon Sector 104

5. GROTTO CANYON 110
Water Wall 114
Hemingway Wall 118
Paintings Wall 121
The Right Wing 124
The Narrows 126
The Alley 130

6. BATAAN 133
First Cave 136
The Sweet Hereafter 138
The Slab 140
The Cheese Grater 142
The Eyes of Bataan 144

7. ECHO CANYON 150

The Hideaway 155
The Lookout 158
The Coliseum 165
The Notch 172

8. COUGAR CANYON 178
House of Cards Sector 182
Poolside Sector 196
Cosmology Sector 199
Canadian Forks Sector 202

9. GRASSI LAKES 211
Upper Grassi 215
Lower Grassi 221

10. CARROT CREEK 227
Raven's Nest Buttress 231
The Cave 240

11. BLACK FEATHER CANYON 246
Entrance Sector 251
Main Sector 253

12. TUNNEL MOUNTAIN 258
Black Band 262
Scoop Area 264
Industrial Playground 267

13. RAVEN'S CRAG 271

14. LAKE LOUISE 277
Outhouse Sector 281
Amphitheatre Sector 288
Blob Rock Sector 293

Index of Sport Routes by Grade 300
Notes 310
About the Author 312

ADVERTISERS

WELCOME TO THE BOW VALLEY

The Bow Valley is one of North Americas best kept sport climbing secrets, and it's been hiding in plain sight for almost three decades. The cragging potential of the area was long overlooked due to the chossy nature of the bands of mountain limestone, the often lengthy approaches and the unpredictable nature of the weather, but over time motivated locals stopped listening to the detractors and slowly started unearthing gems on hidden bands of pristine stone. Nowadays, an entire region of high-quality cliffs await visitors and anyone who has spent time climbing in the valley knows the truth: this is one of the most special climbing areas in all of Canada. Where else can you find stunning mountain scenery, endless rest day activities, a laid-back mountain town and a ridiculous number of climbing venues, all with perfect temperatures for climbing in the middle of summer?

For those that do treat themselves to a Bow Valley climbing holiday, a full gamut of climbing styles and crags will provide endless opportunities to get psyched. Whether you want a quick pump at the end of the day, spectacular views at a crag high above the valley floor, or a chance to dip your feet into a cool creek between burns on your latest project, you'll find it here. And it doesn't matter if you are just learning or putting endless winter hangboard sessions to the test on your first 5.14—once you've had a taste for the amazing experience the region has to offer, you'll be coming back again and again. Who knows? You might even decide to join the clan of lucky climbers who call the Bow Valley home.

I really hope you enjoy your time in the Bow Valley and look forward to seeing you out at the crags. And to help keep my favourite cliffs free of crowds, be sure to tell all your friends to stay home because the rock is too chossy, the approaches are too long and the weather is just too unpredictable!

SONNIE TROTTER (THE THREE SISTERS)

THE LAY OF THE LAND

The Bow Valley lies on the eastern edge of the jagged Canadian Rocky Mountains in the western province of Alberta. It is named for the Bow River, which originates in Bow Lake and flows eastward toward Calgary, eventually merging with the South Saskatchewan River.

At a glance...

Province: Alberta
Valley elevation: 1350–1750 m
Rock: Limestone & quartzite
Time zone: MST

The valley is comprised of three small, mountain communities, which are separated along 83 kilometres of the valley floor. The farthest west, Lake Louise, has a population of 1,000 and is known for pristine mountain lakes, rugged Alps-like scenery and a famous Canadian railway hotel, the Chateau Lake Louise. (It's also the community with the highest elevation in Canada.) The second town, Banff, has a population of 8,700 and is, understandably, the busiest of the three since it's a world-famous tourist destination where wild animals literally roam the city streets (it's a national park and all hunting is prohibited). The final community, Canmore, has 12,000 residents making it the largest of the three, but it's outside the park boundaries giving it a wonderful laid-back vibe. This makes it the perfect base camp for all outdoor sports-related activities in the Bow Valley corridor, including our favourite, sport climbing.

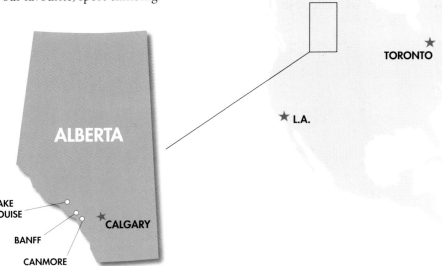

GEOLOGY

The beautiful and rugged mountains that surround the Bow Valley are, geologically speaking, a relatively young chain of peaks that were born approximately 700 million years ago when the Pacific Ocean covered most of the western provinces. Over the course of the next 500 million years, the ocean advanced and receded many times, depositing layers of sand and sediment, along with the remains of marine invertebrates and early crustaceans, along the ocean floor. With time, the immense weight of the upper sedimentary layers compressed the lower layers into shale, sandstone, quartzite and our beloved limestone.

From about 200 to 75 million years ago, in a process called Continental Drift, the true mountain building work began when the Pacific plate and the North American plate collided, forcing one to slowly surge above the other. The result was a lot of folding, twisting and squeezing, evidence of which can easily be seen in the layers of rock that line the valley to this day. During this process, giant slabs of older rock broke free and were forced on top of the younger rock, a process known as thrust faulting (a great local example is Mt. Yamnuska). All of this dramatic tectonic activity was followed by several ice ages that covered the Rocky Mountains with up to two kilometres of ice (photo 1) at a time. The glaciers ground down the mountains and carved broad, U-shaped valleys, a classic example of which is the Bow Valley (photo 2). After the glaciers retreated about 12,000 years ago, wind and rain began the final process of sculpting and buffing the mountain faces and canyons into the fine climbing crags that we enjoy climbing on today.

FLORA & FAUNA

The Bow Valley supports an amazing diversity of wildlife and vegetation—grasslands, alpine meadows and evergreen forests provide ample opportunities to appreciate all the living wonders the region has to offer. Rest days are perfect for exploration, and hiking in the valley is rarely very difficult as the forests contain minimal undergrowth and the trees are well spaced. Species of trees commonly encountered are Douglas fir, pine, white spruce, aspen, larch and balsam. The grasslands bloom with wildflowers from mid-July to mid-August and species you'll likely stumble upon are Indian paintbrush (page 100), common harebell, bunchberry, prickly rose, purple fleabane, yellow columbine and wood lily, amongst others.

Living in the forests and grasslands are some 53 species of mammals, and there's a good chance you will see something during your stay. The most common sightings are white tail and mule deer, elk and mountain sheep. Although not as likely, sightings of black bears, grizzly bears, moose, coyotes and mountain goats are also possible. And if you're really lucky, you might glimpse a cougar (mountain lion), but sightings of these solitary hunters are rare as they roam the forests with great stealth.

Local Examples – The wood lily (top) is a striking wildflower found in the forests of the Bow Valley. It grows to a height of 30 to 90 cm and produces red or orange blooms between June and August. A hoary marmot (middle) peaks out from between two boulders, used for protection from predators. It makes a high-pitched whistle when in danger. The prickly rose (bottom) is Alberta's provincial flower and is found throughout the valley. It grows from 1 to 3 m tall, the flowers are pink and the hips (fruit) are pear shaped and deep red in colour.

MARC BOURDON

Grizzly Bear – This solitary omnivore is easily identified by a pronounced, muscular hump on its back, which aids digging and running. Males may weigh up to 450 kg, and their range can be over 4,000 square kilometres. Females reproduce every other year and giver birth to 1 to 4 cubs, who typically weigh no more than one pound each.

Yellow Columbine – This is a wildflower native to mountain meadows, open woods and alpine slopes of the Rocky Mountains. The plant grows to 20 to 70 cm in height. While the most common flower color is yellow, portions of the flowers can also be yellow-pink, raspberry pink, white and cream. The flowers are edible raw and are quite sweet.

Mountain Goat – These large-hoofed herbivores sport spiked, black horns and woolly, white coats. They graze mainly on grasses and lichens, and spend most of their time at high elevations. They are sure footed, and live in cliff-like terrain to avoid predators. Males weigh up to 135 kg and females give birth to just a single offspring.

Common Harebell – This pretty wildflower is part of the bellflower family and is native to temperate regions of the Northern Hemisphere. Harebells are common in dry, nutrient-poor grasslands and also successfully colonize cracks on cliff faces. The flowers have five petals fused into a bell shape and bloom from late spring to autumn.

Purple Fleabane – This plant belongs to the genus *Erigeron* which consists of about 390 species of flowering plants in the family Asteraceae. The stems typically reach 25 to 30 cm in length and the plant flowers from July through September. It is very common in the Bow Valley and thrives in open woodlands and on moist banks.

Rocky Mountain Bighorn Sheep – Alberta's provincial mammal lives in cool, mountainous regions and, like the goat, prefers steep, cliff-like terrain to avoid predators. They are grazing herbivores and are easily identified by the males' prominent, curved horns, which can weigh up to 15 kg and are used in pre-rut fighting rituals.

Bunchberry – This plant is a member of the Dogwood family. It grows about 20 to 30 cm tall and bears tiny flowers in the centre of four, larger white petals. It is found in montane coniferous forests, where it grows along the margins of moist woods, on old tree stumps and in mossy areas. The small, reddish fruits are edible and taste somewhat like apples.

White-tailed Deer – These are some of the most common herbivores in the Bow Valley and are quickly identified by the white underside of their tails. The deers' coats are reddish-brown and the males have prominent horns with many points that are regrown each year. These mammals are generalists and can easily adapt to a variety of different habitats.

PLANNING YOUR TRIP

Canmore is the focal point of climbing activity in the Bow Valley and is located along the Trans-Canada Highway 110 km west of Calgary. This large city (population of around 1 million) has an international airport (YCC) and, if arriving by plane, car rentals may be obtained from a variety of companies at the airport or within the city. If you need to take the bus to Canmore from Calgary, Greyhound (www.greyhound.ca) offers service from a number of city locations. Direct airport shuttles to Canmore and Banff are available through Banff Airporter (www.banfairporter.com) and Sundog Tours (www.sundogtours.com).

To drive to Canmore from any location within Canada, it's as simple as navigating to the Trans-Canada Highway and heading either east or west depending on where you're travelling from. If you're travelling from the United States, there are a number of highway options depending on your location.

To take advantage of all the climbing possibilities in the Bow Valley, it's necessary to have access to a car. If that's not an option, Canmore and Banff each have two cragging areas within comfortable walking distance of the town centres. Finally, it's not too hard to find a partner while at the cliff. The locals are friendly, approachable and always on the lookout for fresh belayers.

Visitor Information

The Bow Valley in Alberta is a tourism hub, and there's no shortage of information or options to be found. The following three websites are great resources for planning a vacation:

www.visitcalgary.com
www.tourismcanmore.com
www.bannflakeouise.com

Once in Canmore, the best option for gathering information is the local tourism centre, open daily from 9:00 a.m. to 5:00 p.m. and located at 907A 7 Avenue.

When to Come

The climbing season in the Bow Valley usually begins sometime in April and lasts into early October, but for those traveling from afar, July through September is the warmest and most stable period, although a bit of snow, especially on the high peaks surrounding town, is not unheard of. Canmore's elevation ranges between 1,350 and 1,480 metres and the climate is *relatively* mild compared to most regions of Canada. January is the coldest month with an average high of –4.6, but the extremely low humidity makes it feel considerably warmer. Summers are short with daytime temperatures ranging from 18° to 22°C, and winters are usually sunny and dry. The area averages 330 days of sunshine annually, with a short wet season occurring from mid-May to early June.

Seven-day forecasts may be obtained on the Environment Canada website, Weatheroffice.gc.ca. Note that certain areas—Prairie Creek and Lake Louse especially—can have very different conditions than those occurring in Canmore. Webcams, useful for checking current conditions, may be found at www.canmorealberta.com and www.explorerockies.com/banff-webcam.

© RYAN CREARY (HA LING PEAK)

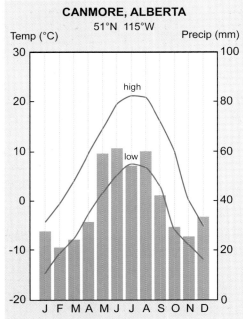

CANMORE, ALBERTA
51°N 115°W

Temp (°C)   Precip (mm)

Figure 1 *Average monthly precipitation and temperature (high and low) for the city of Canmore, Alberta, Canada.*

What to Bring

A sport climbing trip to Canmore requires the usual climbing essentials, but a number of items are worth special consideration. The limestone in the valley varies from severely overhanging to slabby and thin—make sure you have the proper shoes to handle the type of climbing you plan to focus on. A 60-metre rope will do for most routes, but a 70-metre rope is required for some of the newer zones, like Echo Canyon or Planet X at Cougar Canyon. A rack of 10 to 15 quickdraws is generally adequate, but up to 22 draws may be required for some of the newest rope stretchers. Some routes have been designed so that the first bolt needs to be pre-clipped—a portable stick clip can come in really handy to maximize options and safety. Your knees will thank you for packing hiking poles to use on the steep approaches and descents, and brining a helmet is never a bad idea,

© RYAN CREARY

either. Loose rock above the crags is always a concern in the Rockies, and can be rained down without warning by hikers, mountain sheep or simply through the normal process of natural erosion. When planning your day, pay attention to the weather. Just because it's the middle of summer doesn't mean you'll be hanging out in shorts and T-shirts at the north-facing crags. The weather can change quickly in the mountains and most locals pack parkas and hats, even in the middle of summer. Finally, carrying a can of bear spray may help you feel a tad more confident in some of the more remote areas, but it's no substitute for common sense.

If you need to purchase gear while in the area, you have a number of good options:

❑ Coast Mountain Sports – 817 10th Avenue SW (Calgary)

❑ Mountain Equipment Co-op – 830 10th Avenue SW (Calgary)

❑ Wicked Gravity Climbing Equipment – 4602 Bowness Road NW (Calgary)

❑ Valhalla Pure Outfitters – 726 8 Street (Canmore)

❑ Vertical Addiction – 100-1040 Railway Avenue (Canmore)

❑ Monod Sports – 129 Banff Avenue (Banff)

❑ Mountain Magic Equipment – 224 Bear Street (Banff)

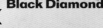

Accommodation

The Bow Valley is a popular year-round tourist destination and there is no shortage of accommodation options. Unfortunately, free camping typical of some climbing areas in North America isn't readily available around Canmore, but for those traveling in a van it's fairly easy to park and sleep on the street if you don't call attention to yourself and change locations often.

Park campgrounds are abundant and pleasant, but book early if travelling in the busy summer season. Use these websites to explore options:

- ❏ www.thehostelbear.com (Canmore hostel)
- ❏ www.alpineclubofcanada.ca (Canmore hostel)
- ❏ www.discovercanmore.com (Canmore hotel list)
- ❏ www.wapiticamping.com (Camping in Canmore)
- ❏ www.bowvalleycampgrounds.com (Camping near Canmore)
- ❏ www.bafflakelouise.com (Camping around Banff and Lake Louise)

Groceries

Canmore has a few well-stocked grocery stores to meet your shopping needs. Safeway (1200 Railway Avenue) and Sobeys (104-1040 Railway Avenue) offer a great selection of groceries, and if you prefer to buy bulk foods or want more natural food options, check out Nutter's Bulk and Natural Foods at 900 Railway Avenue.

Eating Out

For dining out, there is a large variety of options in the Bow Valley. Here's some local favourites in Canmore.

- ❏ Rocky Mountain Bagel Company (830 8 Street) – This laid back coffee shop specializes in bagels, has free Wi-Fi, and a sunny outdoor patio. It's a great rest day hangout as well as a good meeting place before heading to the crag.

CANMORE OVERVIEW

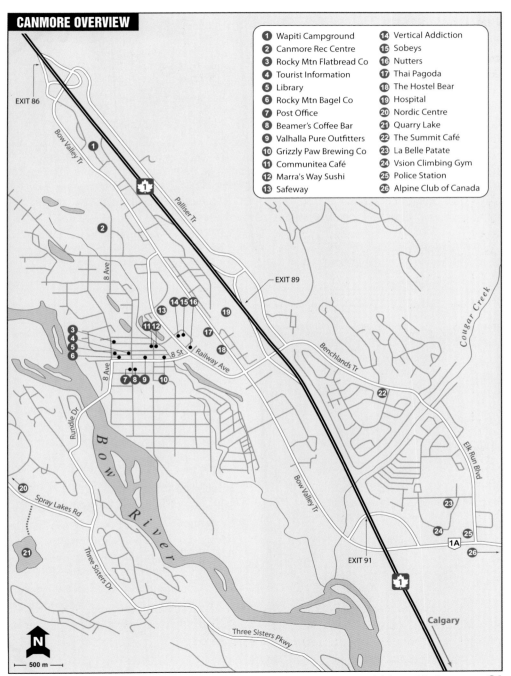

1. Wapiti Campground
2. Canmore Rec Centre
3. Rocky Mtn Flatbread Co
4. Tourist Information
5. Library
6. Rocky Mtn Bagel Co
7. Post Office
8. Beamer's Coffee Bar
9. Valhalla Pure Outfitters
10. Grizzly Paw Brewing Co
11. Communitea Café
12. Marra's Way Sushi
13. Safeway
14. Vertical Addiction
15. Sobeys
16. Nutters
17. Thai Pagoda
18. The Hostel Bear
19. Hospital
20. Nordic Centre
21. Quarry Lake
22. The Summit Café
23. La Belle Patate
24. Vsion Climbing Gym
25. Police Station
26. Alpine Club of Canada

EXIT 86

EXIT 89

EXIT 91

Bow Valley Tr

Palliser Tr

8 Ave

8 St

Railway Ave

8 Ave

Benchlands Tr

Cougar Creek

Rundle Dr

Bow River

Spray Lakes Rd

Three Sisters Dr

Bow Valley Tr

Elk Run Blvd

1A

Three Sisters Pkwy

Calgary

N

500 m

❑ Beamer's Coffee Bar (737 7 Avenue) – This is a nice little coffee shop that features great coffee, treats and free Wi-Fi.

❑ The Communitea Café (1001 6 Avenue) – If you prefer tea over coffee this is the place for you. Comfy chairs make it perfect for reading a book or a place to get some work done on a rest day. They also have a lot of live music happening in the evening. Ask the staff for up to date info.

❑ The Summit Café (102-1001 Cougar Creek Drive) – This is another great, small coffee shop that has yummy home-cooked breakfasts. This popular local's spot fills up fast.

❑ The Grizzly Paw Brewing Company (622 8 Street) – This bustling restaurant brews its own beer and makes sodas from scratch. It has a pleasant atmosphere and a large, sunny patio. This is a must-visit for any serious beer lover.

❑ Thai Pagoda (7A-1306 Bow Valley Trail) – This spot features good Thai food at a reasonable price and a beer selection that puts most larger restaurants to shame.

❑ Marra's Way Sushi (3-637 10 Street) – This is a great place for a quick bite. Pick and choose individual items to build your meal.

© MARC BOURDON (JOHNSTON CANYON)

❑ La Belle Patate (102 Boulder Crescent, Bay 4) – Montreal smoked meats and poutine at a reasonable price makes for a deadly combo.

❑ Rocky Mountain Flatbread Company (838 10 Street) – This place is renowned for flatbread pizzas cooked in a giant wood-fired oven.

Internet Access

Since many of us can hardly let a day go by without checking our email or updating our Facebook/8a.nu page, a list of local Wi-Fi locations becomes critical information. The Bagel Company, Beamer's Coffee and Communitea Café all have free Wi-Fi, as does Safeway. If you need access to a computer, go to the Canmore library, which offers free Wi-Fi as well.

Showers

There are two places in town where you can clean up when the funk builds to a critical level. The first is the Canmore Recreational Center at 1900 8 Avenue. It's open from 6:00 a.m. to 9:00 p.m. on weekdays and 9:00 a.m. to 5:00 p.m. on weekends. The swimming pool drop-in rate is $4.75. The second option is the Vsion Climbing Gym at 109 Boulder Crescent. Showers cost $3.00 and hours vary—check www.thevsion.com before dropping by.

If you're in Banff looking for a shower, the best option is the Sally Borden Recreation and Fitness at the Banff Centre, 107 Tunnel Mountain Drive. The swimming pool drop-in rate is $4.50.

Climbing Updates

The Association of Bow Valley Climbers (TABVAR) provides new route information as well as access updates. Check www.tabvar.org, for the latest beta.

Useful Books

The following list of books cover other Bow Valley climbing areas as well as local interest in the region. Find them in local gear and book stores.

❑ *Sport Climbs of the Canadian Rockies, 6th Edition* – The original sport climbing guide to the Rockies.

❑ *Yamnuska Rock: The Crown Jewel of Canadian Rockies Traditional Climbing* – The comprehensive guidebook to all the routes on Mount Yamnuska.

RYAN CREARY (THE NOTCH)

RYAN CREARY

- ❏ *Canmore Sport Climbs* – A small book that focuses on the Grassi Lakes area.

- ❏ *Ghost Rock, 3rd Edition* – A guidebook to the pristine rock of the Ghost River and Waiparous areas west of Calgary.

- ❏ *Bouldering in the Canadian Rockies, 2nd Edition* – Everything you need to know to go bouldering in the Canadian Rockies.

- ❏ *Scrambles in the Canadian Rockies, 3rd Edition* – Details 150 easy scrambles throughout the Canadian Rockies. Good for damp days.

- ❏ *More Scrambles in the Canadian Rockies* – Includes 60 new scrambles. A great compliment to the first book.

- ❏ *The Yam: 50 Years of Climbing History on Yamnuska* – A good read for those wanting to know a bit more about the traditional stomping grounds of Mt Yamnuska.

- ❏ *Handbook of the Canadian Rockies* – For those interested in their natural surroundings, this is the definitive guide to the Canadian Rockies. It's exhaustive.

- ❏ *Don't Waste Your Time in the Canadian Rockies* – This attractive guide covers the best hikes in the Canadian Rockies, and should keep you busy for quite a while.

Rainy Days

Unfortunately there aren't many options for rock climbing when the rain sets in. When it's storming, it's time to head indoors and pull on plastic. Fortunately there are lots of climbing gyms in the Bow Valley and close by in Calgary.

- ❏ The Vsion (109 Boulder Crescent, Canmore) – www.thevsion.com

- ❏ The Banff Center-Sally Borden Center (107 Tunnel Mountain Drive, Banff) – www.banffcentre.ca/sbb

- ❏ Calgary Climbing Center-Chinook (#6 7130 Fisher Road, SE Calgary) – www.calgaryclimbing.com

- ❏ Calgary Climbing Center-Stronghold (140 15th Avenue NW) – www.calgaryclimbing.com

- ❏ The Crux Climbing and Bouldering Bay (#9-1415 28th Street NE) – www.thecruxclimbing.com

HAZARDS & EMERGENCY RESPONSE

The Bow Valley is a relatively safe place to climb, and the hazards are mostly environmental (rock fall, severe mountain weather, etc.), but if you climb in the area long enough, you will undoubtedly come into contact with some form of wildlife. These encounters are worth special consideration, and a little caution and knowledge can go a long way toward minimizing the chance of a negative outcome. Obey all animal closures and warnings, and carry a cell phone, which is more or less mandatory from a safety standpoint these days. Understand that reception may be problematic in some areas, so come armed with a first aid kit and a back-up plan, just in case.

Bears

The Bow Valley is prime grizzly and black bear habitat, and although it's nice to spot one, it's best to do so from a safe distance. Avoidance is the primary strategy in bear country and, for sport climbers, surprise encounters along the approach trails are the main concern. Obey all trail closures and animal warnings, carry bear spray, and when you do hike, minimize surprise encounters by travelling in noisy groups. Watch for evidence of fresh bear activity (tracks, scat, diggings), walk your dog on a leash and if you smell a dead animal, leave the area immediately. Should you spot a bear, stay calm and walk away slowly—the bear may not notice you. If the bear does see you, make sure it has an escape route. Back away, speak calmly to the bear and resist the temptation to run, as this may trigger a chase. Attacks are extremely rare, but educating yourself about the best way to respond to an aggressive bear is the most sensible action you can take. Go to www.wildsmart.ca, click on "Learn" and then "Living Smart with Bears" to see the latest recommendations by professionals.

Cougars

The chances of running into a cougar while out climbing are extremely low, but if you do happen to encounter one, stay calm. Make sure there is room for the cougar to escape and don't turn your back or run away as this may trigger an attack. Make yourself appear as large as possible (hold an object like a backpack overhead) and back away slowly. If you are attacked, the recommended strategy is to fight back—aggressively. Again, www.wildsmart.ca has a great summary and the latest recommendations.

Elk

Being herbivores, you may think that elk (upper right photo) pose no threat to humans, but a surprise encounter with a 350-kilogram animal that sports antlers longer than your arm may quickly change your mind. If an elk feels threatened or

Important Phone Numbers

Emergencies	911
Canmore Hospital	(403) 678-5536
Banff Hospital	(403) 762-2222
Canmore RCMP	(403) 678-5516
Banff RCMP	(403) 762-2226

is protecting its young, it may attempt an attack. This is especially true during May and June when the females are calving and during September and October when the males are fighting for breeding rights. Give the animals a wide berth of at least 50 metres to stay out of harms' way.

© ALAN VERNON

Ticks (Rocky Mountain Wood Tick)

Ticks are common in the Bow Valley in springtime and look like small, flattened spiders with oval-shaped bodies and eight legs. They are generally 3 to 5 mm in length and are found on grassy, south-facing slopes. If they drop onto your clothing, they'll usually crawl around for a couple of hours looking for some tender skin to attach themselves to. For this reason, check your clothing, body and gear thoroughly at the end of each hike. If you do find an em-

© JERRY KIRKHART

bedded tick, grasp it firmly at the head and gently pull until it releases, being careful not to rip off the head. It's very important that the tick is entirely removed—anything left behind may cause an infection. If the tick is too deep to remove safely, see a doctor. Local ticks can carry Rocky Mountain spotted fever and Lyme disease, both of which are very serious illnesses. To learn more, visit www.canadatrails.ca/outdoors/lyme.htlm.

Rescue

If you find yourself in need of medical assistance while out climbing, dial 911 to initiate a rescue. The local search and rescue crews are well trained in mountain rescue, but in order to find you, they'll need very specific directions with street names, addresses and highway numbers—they will not know where "Acéphale" or "Black Feather Canyon" is (trust me, I speak from personal experience). Send a party member to the highway or parking lot to meet the crew, if in doubt. Also, it's important to note that cell phone coverage is patchy in the Bow Valley and reception will depend on your network and specific location. If you can't get a signal, it's probably best to send a party member toward the highway to make the call. Text messaging a friend to call 911 may also work where connections are poor.

Hospitals

There are two hospitals in the area with emergency services. The Canmore hospital is located at 1100 Hospital Place and Banff's is located at 305 Lynx Street.

REST DAY ACTIVITIES

The Bow Valley is a world-class outdoor tourist destination and rock climbing is just a fraction of what the area has to offer. Whether you want to work up a sweat bagging an alpine peak or find a comfy seat in a coffee shop to read a book, the area has plenty of options.

Hiking

The hiking possibilities really are endless in the Bow Valley, especially if you have access to a vehicle. Any of the peaks seen from Canmore or Banff are easily done in a day and offer amazing views, but a few local hikes are worthy of special mention. If you want a serious workout, check out Sulphur Mountain in Banff. This 5.5-kilometre hike on a well-manicured trail with a 655-metre elevation gain will certainly make you sweat, but the views from the observation deck up top are definitely worth the effort. Buy an ice cream and ride the gondola back down for an added kick. A much mellower, but equally interesting option is the highly popular hike through Johnston Canyon, about 20 minutes west of Banff. This predominantly flat walk follows boardwalks and walkways along a deep, limestone gorge en route to a couple of beautiful waterfalls. Finally, the hiking around Lake Louise and Moraine Lake is truly hard to beat. The views from Sentinel Pass are breathtaking and the hike to the Lake Agnus Teahouse is extremely popular and only moderately strenuous, perfect for a mellow rest day.

For more information or additional hiking options, check out www.banff.com or the Banff National Park section of the Parks Canada website, www.pc.gc.ca. Two excellent books also detail many popular local hikes: *Don't Waste Your Time In the Canadian Rockies* and *Where the Locals Hike In the Canadian Rockies*. Find them in local bookstores.

MARC BOURDON (JOHNSTON CANYON)

Mountain Biking

If you're a mountain biker, it's worth packing your bike because the local riding is almost as good as the climbing. The Nordic Center in Canmore has 80 kilometres of cross-country riding, and the benchlands above the Alpine Club of Canada is laced with great and varied trails. Give one of the local bike shops a call for more information or pick up the book, *Backcountry Biking in the Canadian Rockies*.

Movies

The Lux Cinema Centre in Banff has first-run films on three different screens. It's located at 229 Bear Street.

Libraries

The Canmore Public Library is located at 950 8 Avenue and offers free wireless Internet access. Check out the website www.canmorelibrary.ab.ca for hours and information. The Banff Public Library also offers free Wi-Fi. Find it at www.bannflibrary.ab.ca and 101 Bear Street.

Swimming

On a hot day there's nothing quite like a swim in a freshwater, mountain lake, but most of water in the Bow Valley is *beyond* cold. The exceptions are Quarry lake in Canmore and Cascade Pond/Johnson Lake in Banff, but save them for the hot days of summer.

Two-Day Trips

If the weather takes a turn for the worse, some slightly more far-flung sightseeing options are definitely worth checking out, and one of the best is the drive to Jasper along the Icefields Parkway. This is considered by many to be one of the most beautiful drives on the planet. The scenery is jaw dropping and there are dozens of spectacular hikes along the way if you want to stretch your legs. This four-hour journey (one way) really is a must-do for anyone vacationing in the Bow Valley. For more information, check out www.icefieldsparkway.ca. If this drive seems too long, try the 2.5-hour drive to Drumheller to check out the "Dinosaur Capital Of Canada" and the skeleton-filled Royal Tyrrell Museum. Visit www.traveldrumheller.com for more information.

MARC BOURDON (SULPHUR MTN)

RYAN CREARY (SENTINEL PASS)

GERY UNTERASINGER (LAKE LOUISE)

RYAN CREARY

SPORT CLIMBING HISTORY

Origins

Sport climbing in the Bow Valley didn't just materialize out of thin air. Instead, the steep, bolted limestone faces we enjoy today were the result of a constantly evolving climbing community that began 125 years ago when the Canadian Pacific Railway imported Swiss mountain guides to safely lead a surge of adventure hungry tourists attracted to the mountainous area by a newly completed rail line. The early guides and climbing pioneers were more focused on bagging summits than technical difficulty, but as the peaks got climbed, they turned their attention to more challenging lines, and this approach defined the evolution of climbing in the area for the next 85 years. By the 1950s, the technical standard had risen to a level that allowed climbers to turn their gaze to the vast rock faces of the surrounding peaks, such as Ha Ling, Mt. Rundle and Mt. Yamnuska. These striking mountains all bore a common characteristic: sheer limestone walls, hundreds of metres tall, with few slabs or ledges for respite. Climbs like *Diretissima* and *Belfry* (both 5.8+) on Mt. Yamnuska were huge leaps forward in terms of technical difficulty, especially considering the climbers lacked the high-tech equipment we take for granted today. This departure from the snow-covered flanks of the mountain faces was the birth of rock climbing in the Canadian Rockies.

As standards rose, style became a significant element of any new line—simply reaching the summit was no longer considered challenge enough—and climbers began attempting to free long routes from start to finish without grabbing the aid rack at the first sign of difficulty. Cutting-edge climbs were accomplished ground up, and utilized pitons and natural protection to protect obvious weaknesses that traced their way up the sheer, mountain walls. Aid moves remained mandatory on certain routes, but there was always a climber in the wings wondering if the moves could be freed. By the early 1980s, a group of young climbers shifted their attention away from the cracks and started focusing on smooth, single-pitch faces in areas such as Grotto Canyon, Heart Creek and Wasootch Slabs. These new lines sprouted sparingly-placed bolts, which were installed on lead from hands-free drilling stances or the support of a carefully placed hook, but were far from the current-day standard of safety for sport climbing. Although these lines received little attention and were considered mere practice for adventures on the big walls, the ball was set in motion and it wouldn't be long before the Bow Valley saw the arrival of its first, truly modern sport routes.

The Birth of a New Style

A number of factors brought about the first rappel bolted routes in the Bow Valley but, by far, the most influential was the nature of the rock. In certain areas, the compact stone offered few opportunities for natural protection or drilling stances, and in others, dirty and extremely loose sections meant that traditional ground-up methods were overly difficult or dangerous. Without the introduction of rappel cleaning and bolting, the progression of difficulty would have slowed considerably.

Likely the first use of pre-inspection, rappel cleaning and pre-placement of fixed hardware (pitons, in this case) can be traced back as early as 1973 to Crag X, a long-forgotten wall with horrific rock located near Grotto Canyon. The resulting route, *Sideline*, (5.9, but originally graded 5.10a, a first in the Bow Valley and the reason for the effort) was prepared on rappel—a big departure from the norm— before it was climbed ground up by Bugs McKeith and Chris Perry. A second route that played a pivotal role in a stylistic shift toward greater free climbing possibilities came with the opening of *The Maker* (5.10a), located on the Ripple Wall of the CMC Valley. In 1977, Bruce Keller and Jon Lachlan left the security of the gear-protected weaknesses and ventured onto a blank face where the thrifty use of hand-drilled bolts allowed them to protect the climbing. These watershed approaches and the resulting climbs provided inspiration that would lead certain Bow Valley climbers toward the new, sport climbing style.

John Martin

The climber most likely responsible for consolidating the top-down approach in the Bow Valley was John Martin, a Calgary native who suffered a brutal, 60-metre fall on Mt. Yamnuska's *Bottleneck* in late 1969. This event changed his philosophy regarding route development and he started experimenting with the new style between 1980 and 1983, a time when a staunch, ground-up ethic was still firmly in place. His first attempts were on somewhat obscure slabs that have slowly grown into obscurity, but all his work was done top down, a noteworthy shift in style. Bolts and anchors were drilled tediously by hand and a 30-metre route could easily have as few as three bolts, a far cry from today's well-protected lines. John would become a major player in years to come.

Andy Genereux

Around this time, Andy Genereux, a young climber built like a bulldog, but with the energy of a kid hopped up on sugar, started experimenting with ground-up bolting in the Ghost River and on the Mt. Norquay Slabs. His early routes were mostly short, multi-pitch affairs up vertical faces, but he'd become a major contributor to the single pitch sport climbing route pool in years to come. Dave Morgan and Sean Dougherty, two young and extremely talented expat Brits, also started to dabble in bolted face climbing around the same time. Multiple players showed that interest in bolted routes and the top-down approach was growing, but development in the Bow Valley was occurring in a vacuum. Few climbers travelled, and those that did frequented traditional bastions like Yosemite. The only source of outside influence came from French climbing magazines and the odd visiting European climber. Locals were stumbling around in the dark, trying to find a clear path to the future.

Let the Games Begin

As the addition of bolted face climbs started to become less contentious, Chas Yonge, Dave Morgan and Andy Skuce decided to give Grotto Canyon a second look late in 1984. By winter, two new routes materialized on the steep, smooth and previously-dismissed walls. These lines, *The Abluter* (5.10b) and *Across the River and Into the Trees* (5.11c), weren't the most aesthetically pleasing, but they did show what was possible when the new, top-down tactics were applied to the steeper and less-featured walls littered throughout the Valley.

Sean Dougherty

Word spread, and by the spring of 1985 the snow-covered canyon was laced with the tracks of climbers scoping for first ascents. When the snow finally melted, the canyon quickly filled with eager climbers, willing to hang from ropes and drill shiny new bolts by hand. Over fifty new sport routes quickly appeared and climbers from Calgary regularly made the hour-long drive to sample the new, highly-technical and fingery routes. Among the plums were Sean Dougherty's *Walk on the Wild Side* (5.11c), *Tower of Pisa* (5.11c) and the crimpy *Importance of Being Ernest* (5.12a), the Bow Valley's first 5.12. Other noteworthy climbs were Chas Yonge's *Spring Clean* (5.10a), Bill Rennie's *Falling From Heaven* (5.9), and Dave Morgan's *Farewell to Arms* (5.11a), a route that is still one of the most sought after 5.11s in Grotto Canyon. While some focused on

Bill Rennie

finding new test-pieces, Andy Genereux, Bill Rennie and Jon Jones spent much of this season establishing lots of moderate lines, a true gift to the growing community.

While the majority of the crowd was busy in Grotto Canyon, Lawrence Ostrander and David Dancer decided to focus on the sheer walls of Barrier Mountain in Kananaskis Country, and enjoyed solitude as they picked plum after plum. They established over a dozen bolted lines including *The Great Outdoors* (5.11a), *Age of Reason* (5.11c) and *In Us, Under Us* (5.11b), all of which were of good quality and solid technical difficulty.

It's safe to say that by the end of 1985, sport climbing had arrived in the Bow Valley. The bolt spacing was still generous, and the holes were all drilled by hand, but the idea of sport climbing as a legitimate style had taken hold and there was no putting the genie back in the bottle. The Calgary Mountain Club's 1985 newsletter summed it up: "Now that what's climbable has been discovered, there are ridiculous looking bits of rock getting close scrutiny. However, to be able to do these routes, a set of ethics has been adopted that promotes a safe climbing atmosphere. Cleaning and placing of bolts for protection on rappel has been taken up and, as a result, harder routes have been achieved safely, and more importantly, enjoyably."

Growing Pains

The momentum that began in 1985 continued into the next two seasons. The focus of development (and difficulty) remained firmly rooted within Grotto Canyon's narrow walls, but much of the low-hanging fruit had already been plucked so climbers had to get creative. Sean Dougherty obliged with the steep *Mr. Olympia* (5.11d), and Bruce Howatt, a visionary climber with a keen eye for a great line, jumped the standard a few notches by establishing the desperate *Tropicana* (5.12d). This was done with the help of a couple of manufactured edges, a precursor to what would soon occur across the river on the near-blank Water Wall. Meanwhile, a talented trio of climbers, Joe Buszowski, Marc Dube and Jim Sanford, discovered an excellent new wall lurking in the east fork of the canyon. The Alley eventually yielded a variety of high-quality climbs including *Barchetta* (5.11c), *Submission* (5.11d) and *Grace Under Pressure* (5.11d). For Jim, this was a modest beginning as he'd go on to establish Canada's first 5.14 (in Squamish) 15 years later.

Back at the front of the canyon, one of the Bow Valley's most contentious events was ramping up. A group of eager young climbers from Banff, interested in pushing standards in an arena without clearly defined "rules", rented a gas-powered generator and set to work manufacturing routes on the seemingly blank right-hand end of the Water Wall. (These actions were likely inspired by hold manufacturing—the long-term effects of which were not yet clearly understood—that was occurring concurrently in high profile climbing areas around the world.) Much drama ensued with the most forceful opposition coming from the expat Brits in the Calgary crowd and the locals who had been developing Grotto at the same time. The Calgary group reacted by stripping the wall of all gear (the studs remained intact) in an attempt to start a dialogue. Tense days followed, but in the end the gear was returned and the community more or less reached a consensus as to what was acceptable. This ethical line would occasionally get blurred in the future, but overall Bow Valley climbing grew from the experience. Interestingly, some of the routes remain popular to this day.

Jon Jones

While the chipping war played itself out in Grotto, Barrier Mountain saw over twenty routes go in with some of the most notable additions being Dave Dancer's amazing *Sisyphus Goes to Hollywood* (5.11c), Lawrence Ostrander's spooky *Double Clutch* (5.12a), and Keith Haberl and Todd Guyn's incredibly thin *Naked Teenage Girls* (5.12a). Heart Creek also saw a huge increase in interest with over forty new routes joining the line up. The main contributors were Jon Jones and Andy Genereux who added classics such as *Venus* (5.10a), *Puppet on a Chain* (5.10c) and *Heart of Darkness* (5.11b). Meanwhile, Bill Rennie and Andy Skuce went for a hike up the Carrot Creek drainage and found an entirely new area. They joined forces with Andy Genereux and Jon Jones to exploit the amazing potential of this water-polished canyon. When the dust had settled, the Raven's Nest Buttress was home to many slopey and classic pumpfests, including *The Sorcerer's Apprentice* (5.11c) and *The Wizard* (5.12a), routes which remain sought after to this day.

SEAN DOUGHERTY COLLECTION

Joe Buszowski

Hilti Comes to Town

Another major shift occurred in 1987 when Steve Stahl introduced the Bow Valley to the battery-powered Hilti TE-10A hammer drill. After witnessing its power, John Martin quickly made Steve a tempting offer and purchased the drill with the intention of putting it to great use. Envious of John's new acquisition, Jon Jones, Andy Genereux and Andy Skuce pooled their money to acquire their very own Hilti that same year. The following season, Jim Sanford won the first-ever Canadian National Climbing Championships, held at the Eric Harvey Theatre at the Banff Center. His prize? Another Hilti, which he also put to good use for years to come. Gone were the days of tedious and painful hand drilling in the Bow Valley.

MARC BOURDON

Todd Guyn

The Hilti really was a game changer. In the following years, John Martin set to work developing Cougar Canyon, a new drainage located right in the town of Canmore. By the time the early 1990s had arrived, he'd turned Cougar Canyon into a full-blown area with over 80 routes! This new zone was instantly popular, but Grotto Canyon remained the place to climb hard. Joe Buszowski focused his efforts on *Dr. No* (5.12b) and then teamed up with JD LeBlanc to produce *Cracked Rhythm* (5.12c). Around the corner, Simon Parboosingh struggled up *Tintin and Snowy get Psyched* (5.12d) and Marc Dube finished his *Crimes of Passion* (5.12d), routes that were at the top end of the difficulty scale at the time. Elsewhere, Keith Pike finished *Sword in the Stone* (5.12c) at Carrot Creek, Simon Parboosingh and Joe

Buszowski teamed up to establish the excellent *Lizard* (5.12b), and Keith Haberl managed to find a gem on the seemingly climbed out walls of Barrier Mountain when he scaled the desperately technical *Regatta de Blank* (5.12b). Finally, the development at Lake Louise, an immaculate quartzite crag where bolt holes took two hours to drill by hand, made a huge leap forward with the introduction of the hammer drill. First to fall prey to the Hilti were some, runout, gear-protected horror shows that had seen very few ascents. With drill in hand, Mark Whalen retrobolted lines including *Wicked Gravity* (5.11a), *Chocolate Bunnies From Hell* (5.11c) and *Liquid Sky* (5.11c), and watched as they became instant classics. New climbs were created as well, and lines such as *DEW Line* (5.11c), *Female Hands* (5.12b) and *Jason Lives* (5.12d) remain classic and highly popular to this day.

The Jump to 5.13

The first half of the '90s saw standards rocket into the elusive realm of 5.13, and the bulk of this rise can be credited to one man, Todd Guyn. He became adept at completing abandoned projects, and amassed a string of hard ascents in Grotto Canyon including *Cause and Affect* (5.13a), *Burn Hollywood Burn* (5.13b), and *The Resurrection* (5.13c), routes that consolidated the 5.13 grade in the area. Todd was not alone in this Water Wall rampage, though. Scott Milton, a lanky young climber with a very dry wit, journeyed from Calgary to redpoint *Shep's Diner* (5.13a), a harbinger of things to come as Scott's name would later become synonymous with high end difficulty in the Bow Valley. All of these 5.13s were by-products of the "generator incident", but Simon Parboosingh eventually proved that all-natural 5.13s existed on the Water Wall when he sent *Metabolica* (5.13b)—eyebrows were raised. This focus on difficulty overshadowed the fact that John Martin, Jon Jones, and Andy Genereux continued to open new routes at an incredible pace, including classic pitches such as *Tour de Force* (5.12a) and *Sidewinder* (5.11b).

Simon Parboosingh

Grotto wasn't the only home to high-end climbs. Carrot Creek continued to see aggressive development and 70 more pitches were added, including Todd Guyn's amazing test-piece, *American Standard* (5.13b). Confidence grew, and the previously-dismissed, too-steep Carrot Cave was revisited. Todd Guyn, JD LeBlanc and Joe Buszowski settled in and established a slew of wildly overhanging test-pieces with *Elmer Fudd* (5.12d), *Carnivore* (5.12d), *Doppio* (5.13b) and *Mouthful of Freddie* (5.13c) being the best.

At the same time, three new areas emerged in the Valley. Peter Arbic (PA) started by developing the small but steep Raven's Crag, perched above the townsite of Banff. This crag would eventually yield some long classics, such as *The Masque* (5.12d), and *Telltale Heart* (5.13a) and became PA's stomping grounds for a couple of seasons. Closer to

Canmore, Shep Steiner walked a distant cliff line that would eventually become Bataan. Richard Jagger, Keith Haberl and JD LeBlanc got work underway with *Nirvana* (5.13a) and *Jacob's Ladder* (5.13a), but soon discovered that even though the stone was amazing the hike was not, and securing partners was next to impossible. And then came the discovery of Acéphale. JD and Richard dropped everything at Bataan and immediately joined Shep Steiner, Todd Guyn, Daren Tremaine and Helmut Neswabda to establish a slew of new hard routes at this "crag of the future". Among the best lines from the first couple of seasons were *Deal With It* (5.12c), *Nemo* (5.12d), *The Dark Half* (5.13a) and *Sweet Thing* (5.13b), but most impressive was likely the addition of *Army Ants* (5.13c) by a 16-year-old "kid" from Calgary named Lev Pinter. This wouldn't be the last time Lev would leave an impression at Acéphale. The future had arrived.

While the boys were busy up at Acéphale, Mark Whalen made waves within the climbing community when he rappel bolted the five-pitch *True Grit* (5.10c) on the east end of Mt. Rundle (EEOR). Intense debate followed as to whether or not this style of multi-pitch route was acceptable, but in the end, this EEOR sport route saw more accents in a couple of weeks than all the traditional routes did in an entire season—proof enough. More climbs of this style followed, culminating with Roger Chayer, Hugh Lenney and Gennie Hill's 21-pitch *Sisyphus Summits* (5.10d) on the neighbouring Ha Ling peak. This was a monumental task and remained the longest bolted multi-pitch north of Mexico for many years to come.

New Crags and the Arrival of 5.14

By the mid '90s the Bow Valley had possibly the highest concentrations of 5.13 routes in Canada, and likely North America, but as the focus on pushing difficulty continued, so did interest in spreading out and finding new crags. Areas that had previously been dismissed as being too chossy or having too long an approach got second looks, and among the previously sidelined crags was Grassi Lakes. Grassi's location close to Canmore and short approach were appealing enough attributes for John Martin to take a harder look, and he was instantly convinced of its worthiness. He dove right in and began producing entire walls of soon-to-be classics. He was eventually joined by Roger Chayer, a man with an uncanny eye for picking out plums, and the hard-working mountain guide, Peter Arbic. Grassi's destiny as an ultra popular climbing arena was sealed, and Roger and Peter left the canyon with a long list of must-do climbs including *Voice of Fire* (5.12a), *No Tickee No Laundry* (5.12b) and *China Town* (5.12b).

Elsewhere in the Valley, other crags were getting a second going over. Bataan, previously dismissed as being just too far away, got renewed interest and Roger Chayer once

© ROGER CHAYER

JD LeBlanc

again led the charge by producing some classics, including *Culture of Fear* (5.12a) and *The Sweet Hereafter* (5.12a). Closer to Calgary, a new area, Prairie Creek, was discovered and Ryan Johnston, Daren Tremaine, and Jon Jones went to town establishing dozens of new routes in the 5.11 to 5.13 range. Prairie's unique, bulging pocketed walls made it a popular diversion from some of the more edge oriented climbing found in abundance throughout the Bow Valley.

Scott Milton, coming off a number of strong seasons climbing in Europe, was back and ready to take his place at the top of the heap. In 1997, up at Acéphale, he cleaned an abandoned project, removed all but one of the artificial edges, put his nose to the grindstone and produced *Existence*

Peter Arbic

© MARC BOURDON

Keith Haberl

© ROGER CHAYER

Mundane (5.14b), the first 5.14 in the Bow Valley and likely the first 5.14b in Canada. This ascent was quite impressive as Scott had managed to jump the local standard from 5.13d to 5.14b in one fell swoop. Shortly afterward, the route once again came into the limelight when visiting climber Sonnie Trotter hacked off the final "improved" edge. This move created great debate amongst local climbers—some felt that the existing route shouldn't have been altered while others felt that Sonnie's removal of the final glued edge was the next logical step, picking up from were Scott left off. Luckily a tiny edge revealed itself underneath the glue, and it allowed Sonnie to complete his ascent. The grade remained unchanged, though.

Bataan Fills In

The new millennium saw two new areas appear near Banff with the development of Black Feather Canyon and Tunnel Mountain. Black Feather Canyon featured high-quality stone, and Kelly MacLeod, Chris Miller, John martin and Peter Arbic all quickly contributed, producing a small canyon full of interesting lines like *Sister Ray* (5.10c), *Minor Threat* (5.11a), *Brain Dead* (5.11d) and *Carnal Prayer Mat* (5.12b). On the back of Tunnel Mountain, John Martin took over where Kelly MacLeod left off and, once again, single-handedly developed a raft of new climbs (40 this time), all 5.11 or below. In doing so, he created Banff's equivalent to Grassi Lakes—a quick access crag with a large spread of moderate climbs.

During this period, the word got out about the quality of Bataan and more and more people started making the grueling two-hour trek up to the crag. An increasing number of moderate routes were going up, allowing climbers of all abilities to enjoy the immaculate rock. The father and son duo of Ian and Chris Perry joined Jon Jones and Roger Chayer to truly fill out the area. By 2005 they had created countless new routes including classics such as *Significant Digits* (5.11b), *Goldfinger* (5.11c), *Welcome to the Fabulous Sky Lounge* (5.12b) and *Eyes Wide Shut* (5.12a). Other notable ascents were Ross Suchy's send of an abandoned project to create *Vishnu* (5.13b) and Scott Milton's redpoint of Roger Chayer's brilliant *Freedom in Chains* (5.13c). A small, steep sector at Heart Creek also started to see attention at this time. Daren Tremaine and Marcus Norman led the charge to produce The Bayon, one of the most

Scott Milton

Lev Pinter

powerful walls in the Valley. Routes like *Palm Sisters* (5.12b), *Salty* (5.13a) and *Old Timer* (5.13c) appealed greatly to boulderers looking for shorty, burly challenges. Up at Acéphale Scott Milton turned his attention to all the abandoned projects that littered the Upper Wall. When he finished, just about every bolted line was transformed into a new route. His efforts included *Whale Back* (5.13c), *Endless Summer* (5.13d) and *Leviathan* (5.14a).

Bunda De Fora, the Next Level

Despite the Acéphale sending spree, Scott was no longer alone in his quest to produce high-end routes. A new generation of young climbers was starting to assert themselves and the leader, Lev Pinter, a Calgary local with a physique chiseled out of stone, turned much of his attention to Acéphale. In 2006, and after a hard-fought three years, Lev finally battled up *Bunda de Fora* (5.14d), currently a contender for Canada's hardest rock climb. He originally graded the pitch a modest 5.14c, but when Dave Graham spent five days and over twenty tries on the second ascent, he proposed a grade of 5.14d—time will tell. While Lev was busy at Acéphale, Derek Galloway, a shy, scrawny climber from Vancouver Island with fingers of steel, was busy cleaning up old projects scattered around the Valley. Routes like *Above the Clouds* (5.13d) and *Forever Young* (5.13c) added to the Bow Valley's growing list of 5.13s, but Derek soon became distracted, helping to revive an abandoned wall at the back of Cougar

Canyon. After a few years of work (Gery Unterasinger bolting projects and Derek taking them off his hands) the area, Planet X, took off in terms of popularity. Routes like *Kurrgo* (5.14a), *The Illusionist* (5.14a), *Fudge Packer* (5.13d) and *Cosmos* (5.13c) defined the standard—only Acéphale had harder routes.

Between 2005 and 2010, a new group of players turned their attention to a giant box-shaped canyon sitting above the Alpine Club of Canada. Undaunted by the task of starting an immense new area from scratch, Simon Meis, Matt Pieterson and Ross Suchy slogged up into the canyon with their sights set on the Coliseum, a massive wall at the back of the drainage. Their efforts produced some of the longest routes in the Valley in a setting with amazing ambiance. *Sundog* (5.13a), *The Journey* (5.13c) and *The Shadow* (5.13d) were amongst their greatest prizes and highlighted an entirely new area. Below the Coliseum, Ian and Chris Perry set to work on the Hideaway and were soon joined by Greg Tos. When they finished, the wall was packed with many quality routes such as *Venturi* (5.11a), *Bass Ackwards* (5.12a) and *The Diamond* (5.12b), but it was really just a springboard to develop more impressive walls further up the canyon. The Perrys went on to develop some classic 5.12s on perfect stone up at the Notch, while Greg Tos turned his attention to the Lookout. This steep, blocky crag quickly filled in and featured a stack of excellent 5.12 and 5.13 climbs, some that required a 100-metre rope to descend! Standouts included *My Two Bits* (5.12b), *Spicy Elephant* (5.13b) and *Buffet Royal* (5.13c). With the development of these four Echo Canyon crags, any doubt that impressive finds can still be made close to home should have been finally put to rest.

The Future

Along with the progression of grades at popular areas and the discovery of new crags, recent years have also seen the addition of cutting-edge multi-pitch sport routes on Mt. Yamnuska. Will Gadd and friends were the first to strike with the completion of a multi-year project, *Yamabushi* (5.12d). Next was Sonnie Trotter, who joined Nick Rochacewich and friends to redpoint *The Mistress* (5.13a), and last but not least was the completion of *Blue Jeans* (5.13b), an eight-pitch route bolted by Nick Rochacewich and redpointed by Derek Galloway. This is, by far, the most sustained route in the Valley.

These multi-pitch routes may point toward a full circle evolution of climbing in the Bow Valley as young climbers, weaned in gyms and on sport routes, look to bigger challenges and adventures, setting standards along the way. Sport climbing has played a big part in this evolution, despite the early years of struggling and minimal acceptance, and will continue to help define standards in the future. When will the Bow Valley see it's first multi-pitch 5.14, or it's first single pitch 5.15? It probably won't be that long, as many kilometres of unexplored limestone cliffs still rest above the valley floor, waiting for motivated climbers to arrive. The discovery and development of these vast walls will require courage, love, and dedication, but will provide routes for another 100 years. When you're at the crags in this guide, choose your routes wisely, climb well, and when you're ready, make your own history.

HOW TO USE THIS BOOK

The climbing zones described in this book are generally ordered from east to west, the way in which they'd be encountered if approaching along the Trans-Canada Highway from Calgary. Each chapter (e.g., Grotto Canyon) includes an introduction with condition and approach information, along with overview maps that show the approach and the position of the various cliffs relative to one another. Along the top of the introduction page is a bar graph that shows the density of climbs as well as a hiking grade icon (1–downhill, flat, uphill or steep), a hiking time icon (2) and an elevation change icon (3–only if the approach warrants its inclusion).

Cliff Icons

Each cliff (e.g., Water Wall) contains a brief introduction and a number of icons that provide information about the character of the climbing at the crag (sun aspect, crag angle, etc.), along with written details of the approach, if necessary.

Cliff Footprints

The cliff maps in this book look straight down on the crag from above and show the distribution of the climbs along the base of the wall (a "footprint") along with key features to help with identification. See the sample map for specific features.

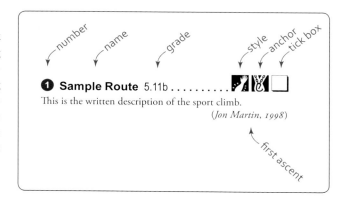

Cliff Photographs

Many cliffs in the book are also represented with a photograph. A red line shows the route's path and a white circle indicates the anchor. See the sample photo for more information.

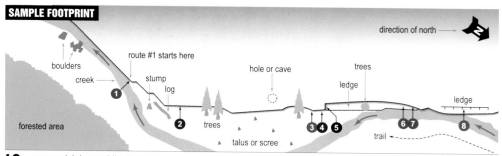

Route Descriptions

The routes in the book are coloured according to difficulty:

1 5.10d & below **1** 5.12a–5.12D **1** Project

1 5.11a–5.11d **1** 5.13a & above

This book uses the standard North American Tahquitz Decimal System, commonly referred to as the Yosemite Decimal System (YDS), to rate difficulty. Various icons describe problem style (see key on right), a "tick box" is provided for tracking your climbs and first ascent details come at the end of the paragraph.

Quality Ratings

This book does not included star ratings for climbs. This is intentional and is meant to help disperse climbers and thus reduce the impact (i.e., polishing) on the various limestone climbs. If you read the descriptions carefully, you'll find hints about quality, and the "Top 100" page will give you a good idea on where to focus your efforts if you are here on a short trip.

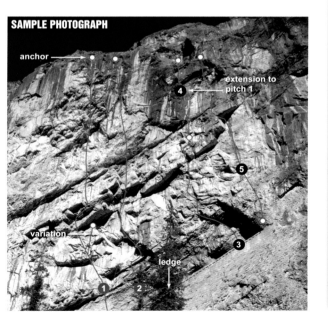

SAMPLE PHOTOGRAPH

anchor

extension to pitch 1

4

5

variation

ledge

3

1 2

Icons

Icon	Description
	Sun aspect (am/pm)
	Sun filtered by trees
	Sunny & No sun
	Crag dries fast
	Crag dry in rain
	Watch for falling rock
	Crag angle (4 options)
	Crag seeps
	Nice views from crag
	Stick clip advised
	Best done as multi-pitch
	Removable gear
	Runout or scary
	Reachy, best if tall
	Dynamic moves
	Pumpy or sustained
	Technical moves
	Powerful or bouldery
	Pockets and holes
	Small edges
	Slopey holds
	Tree anchor on top
	Fixed biners on top

WHERE DO YOU WANT TO CLIMB TODAY?

Best Rainy Day Crags
- ☐ Echo Canyon: Lookout & Notch
- ☐ Cougar Canyon: Planet X
- ☐ Grassi Lakes
- ☐ Lake Louise

Shortest Approaches
- ☐ Barrier Mountain: 15 min
- ☐ Heart Creek: 15 min & up
- ☐ Grotto Canyon: 8 min & up
- ☐ Cougar Canyon: 20 min & up
- ☐ Grassi Lakes: 5 min & up
- ☐ Tunnel Mountain: 15 min

Best Crags With Kids in Tow
- ☐ Heart Creek
- ☐ Cougar Canyon
- ☐ Grassi Lakes
- ☐ Lake Louise

Best Crags For Escaping the Heat
- ☐ Prairie Creek
- ☐ Acéphale
- ☐ Echo Canyon: The Notch
- ☐ Planet X at Cougar Canyon
- ☐ Carrot Creek
- ☐ Black Feather Canyon
- ☐ Raven's Crag
- ☐ Lake Louise

Best Crags For Escaping the Cold
- ☐ Barrier Mountain
- ☐ Bataan
- ☐ Echo Canyon: Hideaway & Lookout

Best Beginner Crags
- ☐ Barrier Mountain
- ☐ Heart Creek
- ☐ Cougar Canyon

- ☐ Grassi Lakes
- ☐ Tunnel Mountain

Best Crags for Cranking
- ☐ Prairie Creek
- ☐ Acéphale
- ☐ Bataan
- ☐ Echo Canyon: Lookout & Coliseum
- ☐ Planet X at Cougar Canyon

Crags with the Best Scenery
- ☐ Bataan
- ☐ Echo Canyon: Lookout & Coliseum
- ☐ Raven's Crag
- ☐ Lake Louise

Best Crags for Mixed Abilities
- ☐ Heart Creek
- ☐ Grotto Canyon
- ☐ Bataan
- ☐ Grassi Lakes
- ☐ Lake Louise

Best Crags for Finding a Partner
- ☐ Heart Creek
- ☐ Cougar Canyon
- ☐ Grassi Lakes
- ☐ Lake Louise

Best Crags for Strutting Your Stuff
- ☐ Acéphale
- ☐ Grassi Lakes
- ☐ Lake Louise

Crags with the Best Stone
- ☐ Acéphale
- ☐ Bataan
- ☐ Echo Canyon: Hideaway
- ☐ Carrot Creek
- ☐ Lake Louise

"DON'T THINK. JUST GO."

CLIMBING.
You have your reasons. We have your gear.

830 10th Avenue SW, Calgary | **mec.ca**

TOP 100 SPORT CLIMBS ʳ⁽⁺²⁾

5.8
- ☐ Neverland – Lake Louise
- ☐ Castle Anthrax – Lake Louise
- ☐ 10-69 – Lake Louise

5.9
- ☐ Imaginary Face – Lake Louise
- ☐ You Oughtta' Know – Heart Creek
- ☐ Callisto – Heart Creek
- ☐ Drill of a Lifetime – Barrier Mountain

5.10
- ☐ Cat's Paw (5.10a) – Cougar Canyon
- ☐ Xanadu (5.10a) – Grotto Canyon
- ☐ Flesh Gordon (5.10a) – Bataan
- ☐ Traffic (5.10a) – Lake Louise
- ☐ Public Enemy (5.10a) – Lake Louise
- ☑ Golden Horde (5.10a) – Grassi Lakes
- ☐ The Search (5.10b) – Lake Louise
- ☐ Merlin's Laugh Left (5.10b) – Carrot Creek
- ☐ Carom (5.10b) – Grassi Lakes
- ☐ Braveheart (5.10b) – Heart Creek
- ☐ Fagin's Fantasy (5.10b) – Prairie Creek
- ☐ Holiday in Cambodia (5.10b) – Black Feather Canyon
- ☐ Pin-toe Flakes (5.10c) – Cougar Canyon
- ☐ Critical Mass (5.10c) – Cougar Canyon
- ☐ Talamasca (5.10c) – Cougar Canyon
- ☐ Sister Ray (5.10c) – Black Feather Canyon
- ☐ Prime Cut (5.10d) – Cougar Canyon
- ☐ Far Corner of the Earth P2 (5.10d) – Bataan
- ☐ Memphis (5.10d) – Grassi Lakes

5.11
- ☐ Wicked Gravity (5.11a) – Lake Louise
- ☐ Farewell to Arms (5.11a) – Grotto Canyon
- ☐ Venturi (5.11a) – Echo Canyon
- ☐ Bold New Plan (5.11a) – Grassi Lakes
- ☐ Koyaanisqatsi (5.11a) – Barrier Mountain
- ☐ Some Like it Hot (5.11a) – Bataan

- ☐ Bloodline (5.11a) – Bataan
- ☐ Surface Tension (5.11a) – Cougar Canyon
- ☐ Canadian Pie (5.11a) – Echo Canyon
- ☐ Silk P2 (5.11a) – Grassi Lakes
- ☐ Meathooks (5.11a) – Grassi Lakes
- ☐ Mr. Rogers Smokes a Fat One (5.11b) – Lake Louise
- ☐ Sidewinder (5.11b) – Grotto Canyon
- ☐ Bloodsport (5.11b) – Lake Louise
- ☐ The Duck of Death (5.11b) – Lake Louise
- ☐ Beautiful Thing (5.11b) – Barrier Mountain
- ☐ Phantom Ledges (5.11c) – Echo Canyon
- ☐ DEW Line (5.11c) – Lake Louise
- ☐ Barchetta (5.11c) – Grotto Canyon
- ☐ Sisyphus Goes to Hollywood (5.11c) – Barrier Mountain
- ☐ Liquid Sky (5.11c) – Lake Louise
- ☐ Yoshimi Battles the Pink Robots (5.11c) – Echo Canyon
- ☐ Stone Age Romeos (5.11d) – Grotto Canyon
- ☐ Kinematic Wave (5.11d) – Bataan
- ☐ Grace Under Pressure (5.11d) – Grotto Canyon
- ☐ Crank Call (5.11d) – Bataan
- ☐ Mind Bender (5.11d) – Black Feather Canyon
- ☐ FFAntom Love (5.11d) – Echo Canyon
- ☐ Venom (5.11d) – Lake Louise
- ☐ Stage Fright (5.11d) – Lake Louise

5.12
- ☐ Nobody's Girl (5.12a) – Lake Louise
- ☐ The Warlock (5.12a) – Carrot Creek
- ☐ Voice of Fire (5.12a) – Grassi Lakes
- ☐ Dark Side of the Boom (5.12a) – Echo Canyon
- ☐ The Mighty Expectation of Relief (5.12a) – Prairie Creek
- ☐ Dance Me Outside (5.12a) – Grassi Lakes
- ☐ B60 OFO (5.12a) – Grassi Lakes
- ☐ Requiem (5.12a) – Barrier Mountain
- ☐ Tetris (5.12a) – Echo Canyon
- ☐ The Convincer (5.12b) – Heart Creek

- [ ] Bucking Horse (5.12b) – Acéphale
- [ ] Hickory Dickory Dock (5.12b) – Acéphale
- [ ] The Diamond (5.12b) – Echo Canyon
- [ ] The Gizzard (5.12b) – Carrot Creek
- [ ] Carnal Prayer Mat (5.12b)
     – Black Feather Canyon
- [ ] My Two Bits (5.12b) – Echo Canyon
- [ ] Fire in the Sky (5.12b) – Echo Canyon
- [ ] Deal With It (5.12c) – Acéphale
- [ ] Atlantis (5.12c) – Echo Canyon
- [ ] Smoky Eyes (5.12c) – Echo Canyon
- [ ] Dynomite (5.12c) – Lake Louise
- [ ] Swelltone Theatre (5.12c) – Acéphale
- [ ] Shooting Star (5.12d) – Cougar Canyon
- [ ] Rock Me Amadeus (5.12d) – Echo Canyon
- [ ] Nemo (5.12d) – Acéphale
- [ ] Jason Lives (5.12d) – Lake Louise
- [ ] Nirvana (5.12d) – Bataan

5.13

- [ ] Fresh Prince (5.13a) – Echo Canyon
- [ ] Telltale Heart (5.13a) – Raven's Crag
- [ ] Liar (5.13a) – Carrot Creek
- [ ] A67 (5.13a) – Prairie Creek
- [ ] Shooting Packer (5.13b) – Cougar Canyon
- [ ] Diamonds on the Inside (5.13b)
     – Echo Canyon
- [ ] Naissance de le Femme (5.13b) – Acéphale
- [ ] G Spot (5.13b) – Echo Canyon
- [ ] The Journey (5.13c) – Echo Canyon
- [ ] Buffet Royal (5.13c) – Echo Canyon
- [ ] Army Ants (5.13c) – Acéphale
- [ ] Whaleback (5.13c) – Acéphale
- [ ] Endless Summer (5.13d) – Acéphale
- [ ] Fudge Packer (5.13d) – Cougar Canyon
- [ ] Above the Clouds (5.13d) – Cougar Canyon

5.14

- [ ] Kurrgo (5.14a) – Cougar Canyon
- [ ] Leviathan (5.14a) – Acéphale
- [ ] Existence Mundane (5.14b) – Acéphale
- [ ] Bunda de Fora (5.14d) – Acéphale

○ GRZEGORZ FLOREK

Irene Tos on *Atlantis* (5.12c) at the Lookout.

Takeshi Abe on *Shooting Packer* at Planet X (5.13b). Photo by Gery Unterasinger.

CHAPTER 1

PRAIRIE CREEK

If you love steep, powerful pocket pulling on beautiful grey limestone, then Prairie Creek is as good as it gets. This pretty, north-facing cliff band sits in a peaceful forest west of Bragg Creek and features a great assortment of fun pitches. It's also the closest of all the Bow Valley sport climbing venues to Calgary, making it popular with the city crowd.

The climbs range from 7 to 18 metres in length and typically require short bursts of controlled power. Despite their diminutive stature, these lines can also build a surprising pump due to their continuity of tricky movement. If you want to hone your skills (and strengthen your tendons) for a trip to France, this is the place to do it. Prairie Creek is the only cliff in the region where virtually every route is climbed almost entirely on pockets.

BOSCO KWARK ON *BOTTOM FEEDER* (5.12B)

CONDITIONS

55 routes ←5.10 5.11 5.12 5.13→

The cliffs at Prairie Creek face northeast and are perpetually in the shade, so summer days are best for climbing. Don't leave your parka behind, though, even if it's warm. This area can be surprisingly cool, even in summer, and you'll have more fun if you're prepared. While the heavily-pocketed walls feature some amazing routes, they can also act like sieves early in the season, allowing snowmelt to trickle through the cliff causing major seepage problems. The same wet conditions may also be found after heavy rainstorms, so it's best to give the cliff a couple of days to dry out before attempting a visit.

APPROACH

From Canmore: Drive east on the Trans-Canada Highway toward Calgary and take Exit 161 A onto Highway 22. Set your trip metre to zero and head south toward Bragg Creek. At 7 km (4.3 miles), reach a round-about and continue south toward Bragg Creek. At 18 km (11.2 miles) reach a four-way intersection in the small town of Bragg Creek and turn left, continuing south on Highway 22. At 21.6 km (13.4 miles) reach a T-intersection and turn right onto Highway 66 heading west. At 41 km (25.5 miles) park in a pullout on the left side of the road.

From Calgary: Drive west on the Trans-Canada Highway toward Canmore and take Exit 161A onto Highway 22. Set your trip metre to zero and head south toward Bragg Creek. At 7 km (4.3 miles) reach a round-about and continue south toward Bragg Creek. At 18 km (11.2 miles) reach a four-way intersection in the small town of Bragg Creek and turn left, continuing south on Highway 22. At 21.6 km (13.4 miles) reach a T-intersection and turn right onto Highway 66 heading west. At 41 km (25.5 miles) park in a pullout on the left side of the road.

From South Calgary: Follow Highway 8 west toward Bragg Creek to an obvious round-about. Set your trip metre to zero and head south on Highway 22. At 11 km (6.8 miles) reach a four-way inter-

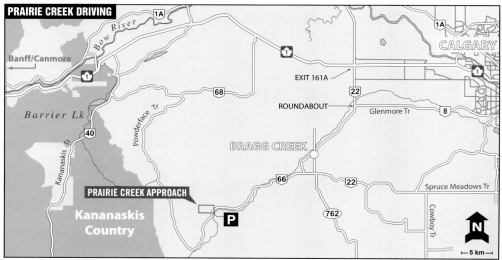

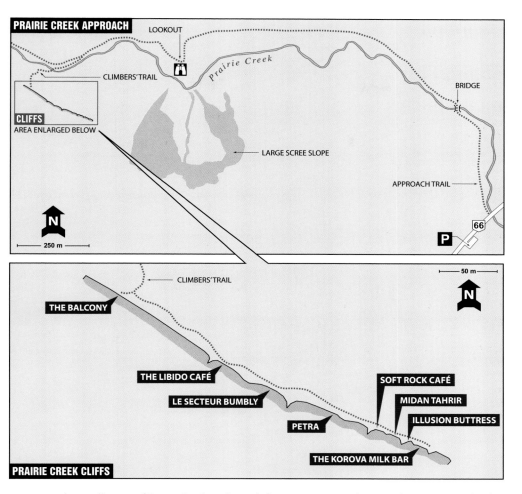

PRAIRIE CREEK APPROACH

LOOKOUT

Prairie Creek

CLIMBERS' TRAIL

BRIDGE

CLIFFS
AREA ENLARGED BELOW

LARGE SCREE SLOPE

APPROACH TRAIL

N

250 m

P

66

CLIMBERS' TRAIL

50 m

N

THE BALCONY

THE LIBIDO CAFÉ

LE SECTEUR BUMBLY

PETRA

SOFT ROCK CAFÉ

MIDAN TAHRIR

ILLUSION BUTTRESS

THE KOROVA MILK BAR

PRAIRIE CREEK CLIFFS

section in the small town of Bragg Creek and turn left, continuing south on Highway 22. At 14.6 km (9 miles) reach a T-intersection and turn right onto Highway 66 heading west. At 34 km (21.1 miles) park in a pullout on the left side of the road.

Hiking: From the parking lot, cross the road and follow a trail in the ditch that heads east toward a guardrail and Prairie Creek. From Prairie Creek, follow a well-worn trail upstream. After about 25 minutes of walking, a rocky lookout across from a large scree slope will appear. Look across the drainage—the wall of Prairie Creek is now visible as a sliver of a cliff that runs downhill to the right of the scree slope. From the base of the hill beyond the lookout, continue walking for about 320 metres to a faint fork in the trail (it occasionally has a cairn). Follow the climbers' trail left into the forest for 250 metres and cross Prairie Creek to reach the forest below the cliff band. A short, steep uphill grind leads to the base of the wall. The first crag encountered on the right is the Balcony and the Libido Café is a little further up the hill.

The Balcony

This wall is found immediately to the right of the point where the approach trail reaches the cliff. Climbs are listed from right to left, and all start off a ledge.

1 Limp Chimp 5.10d . . . .
5 bolts (7 m) A short-lived bulge gives way to slab climbing before the anchors. (*Tim Mang, 2008*)

2 Lemur Screamer 5.11b . . . .
5 bolts (7 m) Begin in a right-facing corner and finish out left. Awkward at the top. (*Tim Mang & Brad Cooke, 2008*)

3 Cheap Thrills & Monkey Skills 5.11c
5 bolts (9 m) Follow the grey streak past a bush to a fun roof encounter. (*Tim & Meahgan Mang, 2007*)

4 Ape Scrape 5.10b . . . .
4 bolts (8 m) A hard start leads to fun pod climbing. Finish above a chossy corner. (*Tim & Meahgan Mang, 2007*)

The Libido Café

This crag features short and incredibly bouldery routes that tackle a steep wall. The moves are explosive and the holds are smaller than anywhere elsewhere at Prairie Creek. Routes are listed from right to left.

5 Spro 5.12c . . . .
5 bolts (9 m) Start in front of a stump on the right end of

the wall. A boulder problem at ground level gives way to easier climbing above. (*JD LeBlanc, 1995*)

6 Ace Frehley 5.11c . . . .
4 bolts (10 m) Follow the right-trending weakness. A hard move at the first bolt leads to a tough finish over the lip. (*Daren Tremaine, 1995*)

7 Phat 5.12d . . . .
5 bolts (10 m) From the base of the right-trending weakness, climb directly through two boulder problems separated by a poor excuse for a rest. (*Daren Tremaine, 1995*)

8 Tool and Injection V5 . . . .
3 bolts (8 m) Tackles the steep bulge laced with thin seams. A stout boulder problem through the bulge will definitely make you grunt. (*Ryan Johnstone, 1995*)

9 Whip It V7 . . . .
3 bolts (7 m) A height-dependant boulder problem lurks above the second bolt. (*Ryan Johnstone, 2000*)

Le Secteur Bumbly

This vertical section of cliff features good moderate routes with the same amazing pockets and pods found on the steeper walls. It's a good place to drop your pack and warm up. Routes are listed from right to left.

10 Grimmia 5.10b . . . .
4 bolts (10 m) Start with big pods at two metres. Follow nice pockets to a short corner. (*Jon Jones, 1995*)

THE BALCONY

LIBIDO CAFÉ LEFT

LIBIDO CAFÉ RIGHT

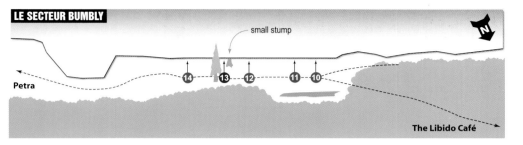

LE SECTEUR BUMBLY

small stump

Petra

⑭ ⑬ ⑫ ⑪ ⑩

The Libido Café

---

⑪ Pleb 5.9 . . . .

5 bolts (14 m) Start below a microwave-size hole at three metres. Cool and interesting climbing on generally good holds leads upward via some long pulls. *(Jon Jones, 1995)*

⑫ Sacagawea 5.10b . . . .

5 bolts (14 m) Start just right of a small, open book corner. Tricky moves link massive pods. Finish up and slightly left on the slab. *(Daren Tremaine, 2004)*

⑬ Bombus 5.11a . . . .

5 bolts (13 m) Start just right of a short, broken left-facing corner. Crimpy moves through the middle lead to easier climbing above. Share the same anchors as *Out on a Limb*. *(Jon Jones, 1995)*

⑭ Out on a Limb 5.10d . . . .

5 bolts (13 m) Start just left of the short, broken left-facing corner. Aim for the face to the right of the big right-facing corner above. *(Jon Jones, 1996)*

Petra

This cliff is the main attraction at Prairie Creek. It houses the longest and hardest routes and features overhanging pocket climbing at its best. Routes are listed from right to left.

⑮ Slot Jockeys 5.12b . . . . . .

4 bolts (11 m) Big, powerful moves link good holds. *(Daren Tremaine, 2000)*

⑯ The Blink's Powerful 5.12a . . . .

5 bolts (11 m) Start off the ledge and make some big spans between pods and pockets. *(Daren Tremaine, 2000)*

⑰ This Week in Bible Prophecy 5.12b . . . .

10 bolts (17 m) Prepare for pocket madness and a pump that hits just as you pull over the cruxy roof. Start just left of a short, left-facing corner. *(Daren Tremaine, 1995)*

LE SECTEUR BUMBLY 11

PETRA 19 17

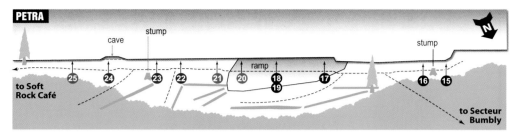

PETRA

stump

cave

ramp

stump

25 24 23 22 21 20 18 17 16 15
                        19

to Soft
Rock Café

to Secteur
Bumbly

⑱ The Mighty Expectation of Relief 5.12a

9 bolts (18 m) This fantastic route climbs *Booty Juice* to the fourth bolt before trending right on pockets. The seventh bolt is a glue-in.   (*Daren Tremaine, 1995*)

⑲ Booty Juice 5.12c

10 bolts (17 m) This is another great route. Climb out the right side of a large pod to big, dynamic moves on good holes. These lead through the overhang to a thin finish up a vertical wall.   (*Daren Tremaine, 1996*)

⑳ A67 5.13a

9 bolts (16 m) This classic moves out the left side of the pod. Pumpy pulls between good pockets drain you for the crimpy exit.   (*Ryan Johnstone & Daren Tremaine, 1997*)

㉑ Deep Shag 5.13a

7 bolts (14 m) Start at a low, microwave-size hole. Powerful climbing on pockets and small edges leads to a monster jug and a tough exit. Prepare for some tough clips!   (*PREP: Ryan Johnston; FA: Todd Guyn, 1997*)

㉒ Temple Recommend 5.11d

7 bolts (15 m) Start in front of a small tree that's holding up a log platform. After the initial stretch of fractured rock, big pockets lead to a two-part crux with a draining shake in between.   (*PREP: Ryan Johnston; FA: Knut Rokne, 2006*)

㉓ Robot Priests 5.11d

8 bolts (18 m) Start just right of a small cave at ground level. A few small, cruxy pockets above a little roof lead to a jug. Continue up great pockets to the anchors.   (*Jon Jones, 2002*)

㉔ Babe 5.11a

8 bolts (15 m) This amazing pocket climb starts on the left side of a small cave at ground level.   (*Jon Jones, 1996*)

㉕ Fagin's Fantasy 5.10b

6 bolts (17 m) This route is located five metres downhill of a tree that's growing next to the wall. Start under a big hole and negotiate around it on the left side. Great pocket climbing leads to the anchors.   (*Jon Jones, 1996*)

THE SOFT ROCK CAFÉ

MIDAN TAHRIR LEFT

MIDAN TAHRIR RIGHT

The Soft Rock Café

This crag features a collection of moderate, slabby routes and a couple steeper lines. Routes are listed from right to left.

26 Blind Faith 5.10b . . . . ☐

5 bolts (13 m) This is the first route left of the gully. It's slabbier than most on the wall, but has some excellent stone. *(Jon Jones, 1996)*

27 Seeing Red 5.9 . . . . ☐

5 bolts (9 m) Climb *Raisin Sex* to the first bolt, but head right following pockets to an anchor on the left side of the corner. *(Jon Jones, 1996)*

28 Raisin Sex 5.10c . . . . ☐

6 bolts (13 m) Start in front of a tree that supports a log platform. From the first bolt, trend left over the seam to slightly steeper terrain above. *(Jon Jones, 1996)*

29 Scat 5.10b . . . . ☐

5 bolts (14 m) This is the first route right of the steep overhang. Fun climbing between pockets and edges leads to anchors at the top of the wall. *(Jon Jones, 1996)*

30 A Pine in the Ass 5.11c . . . . ☐

5 bolts (14 m) Start between two low caves. Stepping right at the big roof is the crux. *(Jon Jones, 1996)*

31 Double Digit Inflation 5.11b . . . .

5 bolts (14 m) Start in the middle of a low cave. Climb directly through the steep terrain above. *(Jon Jones, 1996)*

32 Sidestep 5.9 . . . . ☐

3 bolts (9 m) This short, pocketed route follows the right side of the groove. *(Jon Jones, 1996)*

Midan Tahrir

This crag holds two of Prairie Creek's hardest routes as well as its sole, undone project. Routes are listed from right to left.

33 The Cryocooler 5.11b . . . . ☐

7 bolts (14 m) Start just left of the large groove. Amazing pocket climbing for the first five bolts gives way to small edge climbing near the anchors. *(Daren Tremaine, 1995)*

Popular Petra Link-ups

Saint Daren 5.12a . . . . ☐
Climb *This Week in Bible Prophecy*. Traverse left into *Mighty Expectation of Relief* at the 7th bolt.

Bible Juice 5.12c . . . . ☐
Climb *This Week in Bible Prophecy*. At the 7th bolt, traverse left all the way to *Booty Juice* and up.

Swimming to Cambodia 5.13a . . . . ☐
Begin on *This Week in Bible Prophecy*. At the 7th bolt, traverse left all the way to *A67* and up.

Saint Ryan 5.12a . . . . ☐
Climb *Mighty Expectations of Relief*. Traverse right into *This Week in Bible Prophecy* at the 7th bolt.

Booooties 5.12c . . . . ☐
Climb *A67* to the large pod. Exit out right into *Booty Juice* and finish up that route.

A1 5.13a . . . . ☐
Climb *A67* past the large pod to the 7th bolt. Move right and finish up *Booty Juice*.

Heavy Expectations 5.12d . . . . ☐
Climb *A67* to the 7th bolt. Move all the way right to *The Mighty Expectations of Relief* and up.

67 Shags 5.13a . . . . ☐
Climb *A67* to below the last bolt and traverse left into *Deep Shag* to finish.

57 Expectations 5.12b . . . . ☐
Climb *A67* to the large pod, move right and finish up *Mighty Expectations of Relief*.

34 Westland Dodge 5.12b . . . . ☐

6 bolts (15 m) From the fourth bolt of *The Silver Rocket*, traverse right into *The Cryocooler*. *(Daren Tremaine, 1995)*

35 The Silver Rocket 5.13a . . . . ☐

7 bolts (13 m) Sustained pocket pulling leads to a slopey, mid-height crux. Don't let your guard down—there's another hard move near the top. *(Daren Tremaine, 1995)*

36 Con Dila 5.13a . . . . ☐

8 bolts (15 m) Start in front of a stump. Relatively easy climbing leads to a heartbreaker crux in the upper bulge. *(Daren Tremaine, 1995)*

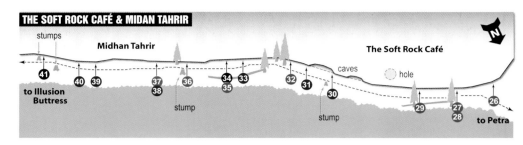

THE SOFT ROCK CAFÉ & MIDAN TAHRIR

37 Open Project . . . .

Climb *Escape Pod* to the base of the big overhang. The line climbs directly through the steepest part.

38 Escape Pod 5.11d . . . .

7 bolts (13 m) Climb through a streak of black, shattered rock to the base of the big overhang. Escape the difficulties by moving left around the corner to a set of anchors.
(Marcus Norman, 2000)

39 The Jester 5.11b . . . .

6 bolts (14 m) Pockets and pods lead to a cruxy bulge at the top of the wall. *(Marcus Norman, 2000)*

40 English Soccer Hooligans 5.11c . . . .

5 bolts (13 m) Scramble to a high first bolt next to a big hole. Great pods pepper the wall above, but a few small crimpers will keep you honest. *(Marcus Norman, 2000)*

41 Hot Pants Explosion 5.12c . . . .

5 bolts (11 m) This short, bouldery route links small pockets and edges together. It starts below a vegetated ledge. *(Marcus Norman, 1996)*

Illusion Buttress

This slightly overhanging cliff has technical climbs that utilize more edges than pockets. Routes are listed from right to left.

42 There Goes the Neighborhood 5.10b . . . .

6 bolts (14 m) This line is located just left of the gully and features sidepulls and edges. Don't forget to stem out to the gully behind you. *(Jon Jones, 2002)*

43 No Rest for the Wicked 5.12a . . .

5 bolts (13 m) This is a good route that requires more technical prowess than most at Prairie Creek. The sustained climbing requires good body position through a maze of sidepulls. Edges lead to the anchor at the top of the wall. *(Jon Jones, 1995)*

44 Bottom Feeder 5.12b . . . .

7 bolts (13 m) This is a harder, direct start to *Partners in Crime.* *(Daren Tremaine, 2002)*

45 Partners in Crime 5.12a . . . . .

6 bolts (13 m) This is a technical and sustained route that starts below a hole at three metres. From the third bolt, trend slightly to the right.
(PREP: Jon Jones & Roger Chayer; FA: Daren Tremaine, 2002)

46 Playing the Slots 5.11b . . . .

5 bolts (12 m) Start just right of the vegetated gully. Trend right onto the prow. *(Jon Jones, 1995)*

The Korova Milk Bar

This is the last section of the cliff band that has developed routes. It features slightly overhanging pocket climbing with hard starts followed by pumpy finishes. Routes are listed from right to left.

47 Droog 5.10b . . . .

4 bolts (14 m) Start in the small gully and negotiate good sidepulls en route the anchors. *(Jon Jones, 1995)*

48 Moloko Plus 5.11a . . . .

6 bolts (14 m) Start off the far right end of the low ledge. A powerful opening through a low bulge leads into sustained, pumpy pocket climbing. *(Jon Jones, 1995)*

49 Hermetically Sealed 5.12a . . .

6 bolts (11 m) Start off the low ledge just right of *Manic.* Don't let the bouldery start deter you, the climbing above is much less intense and very enjoyable. Finish at the *Manic* anchor. *(Daren Tremaine, 1995)*

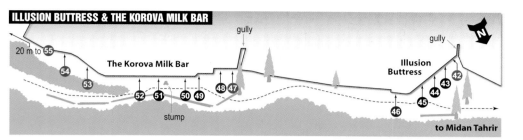

ILLUSION BUTTRESS & THE KOROVA MILK BAR

gully

20 m to 55

The Korova Milk Bar

54

53

52 51 50 49 48 47

stump

gully

Illusion
Buttress

42

43

44

45

46

to Midan Tahrir

50 Manic 5.12b . . . .

5 bolts (11 m) This is a great route with some fantastic moves between generally positive holds. Begin with hard moves off the low ledge's left end. (*Daren Tremaine, 1995*)

51 Roy Batty 5.12c . . . .

7 bolts (15 m) Start just left of the low ledge. Tricky clips with hard moves follow two positive pods at the first bolt—you'll wish that the sinker pod at the third bolt wasn't so far away. Easier above. (*Marcus Norman, 2000*)

52 Fuzzy Wobble 5.11c . . . .

6 bolts (14 m) This is the last route on the left before the wall angles uphill. Two cruxes on hard-to-locate pockets and edges are separated by a good rest. (*Jon Jones, 1995*)

53 Got Mersey Beat 5.8 . . . .

4 bolts (14 m) This route is located uphill, around the left end of the wall. Follow edges and pockets up a shallow groove before heading up the small, right-facing corner to the anchors. (*Greg Cornell, 2001*)

54 Alberta Bound 5.9 . . . .

4 bolts (14 m) Follow a right-trending corner for three bolts before pulling onto the slab above.
(*Greg Cornell, 2001*)

55 Chicklet Fangs 5.10c . . . .

6 bolts (16 m) The final climb is located about 20 metres uphill of *Alberta Bound*. Start by climbing up the steep bulge, then move left to an open book corner. Continue up the corner, with difficulty, to easier terrain above. A tricky onsight for the grade. (*John Pogson, 2010*)

ILLUSION BUTTRESS

THE KOROVA MILK BAR LEFT

THE KOROVA MILK BAR RIGHT

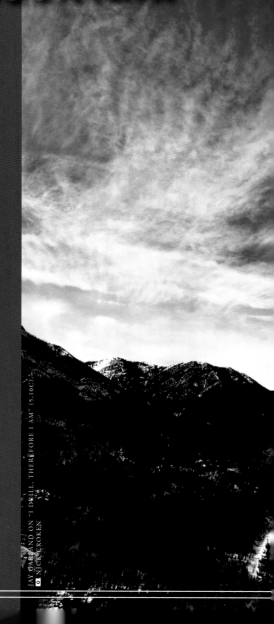

CHAPTER 2

BARRIER MOUNTAIN

After a long, cold winter of darkness, nothing lifts a climber's spirits like a bit of early-season scrambling on sun-kissed limestone, but in the Bow Valley the question is where to find it? The narrow canyons typical of the area are inhospitable when the sun is low and the days are short, so climbers itching to get out need to broaden their horizons. Enter Barrier Mountain, arguably one of the best early- and late-season venues in the Rockies. Its bright, wide-open aspect catches sun during the heat of the day, which makes it the perfect crag to shake off the winter rust and prepare for the upcoming climbing season.

The cliffs feature great views with a pleasantly short approach, and the nature of the climbing is predominantly vertical. Grades range from 5.7 to 5.12d, providing challenges for a good variety of ability levels, and technically-demanding cruxes are the name of the game. In fact, some of these vertical face climbs where once at the cutting edge of Rockies' difficulty and still challenge proficient climbers to this day, a testament to the technical prowess of the early sport climbing pioneers.

JAY GARLAND ON "I DRILL, THEREFORE I AM" (5.10C)
ⓞ NICK CROKEN

CONDITIONS

The climbing conditions at Barrier Mountain are usually perfect in the early spring and late fall. The sun hits the southwest-facing Barrier Wall late in the morning and heats it for most of the day, which creates comfortably warm rock when it's too cold elsewhere in the Rockies. During rainy spells, precipitation can be significantly less (or even non-existent) in this area if the storms are coming from the west, a nice feature of the mountain's easterly location. If it does get wet, however, the cliff dries very quickly and the seepage problems that plague some of the pocketed cliffs in the Bow Valley are of no real concern at this edgy crag. Enjoy the spring and fall, though. By the time summer rolls around, this crag gets too hot for most climbers, making it time to move on to cooler venues.

APPROACH

From Canmore: Drive east on the Trans-Canada Highway toward Calgary. Take Exit 118 (Kananaskis Country), set your trip meter to zero and head south on Highway 40. At 11.2 km (6.9 miles), pull into the left-hand ditch and park near an obvious road sign.

From Calgary: Drive west on the Trans-Canada Highway toward Canmore. Take Exit 118 (Kananaskis Country), set your trip meter to zero and head south on Highway 40. At 11.2 km (6.9 miles), pull into the left-hand ditch and park near an obvious road sign.

Hiking: The main trail heads into the forest near the road sign in the ditch. See each wall for specific approach directions.

BARRIER MOUNTAIN OVERVIEW

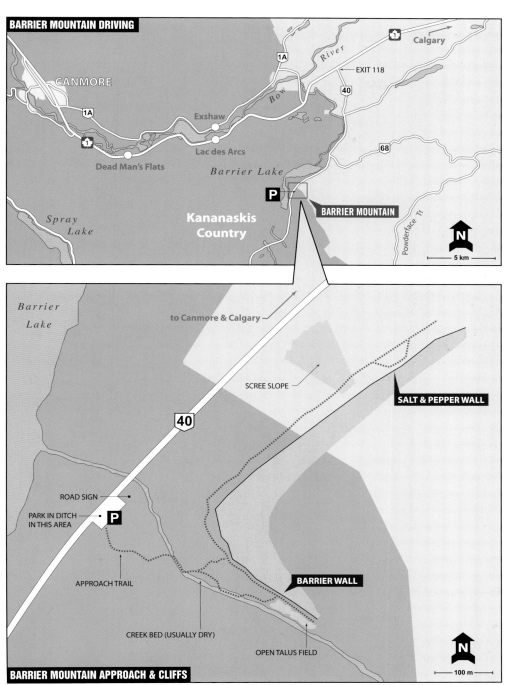

BARRIER MOUNTAIN DRIVING

CANMORE

Calgary

EXIT 118

Exshaw

Lac des Arcs

Dead Man's Flats

Barrier Lake

Spray Lake

Kananaskis Country

P

BARRIER MOUNTAIN

Powderface Tr

Bow River

N

5 km

BARRIER MOUNTAIN APPROACH & CLIFFS

Barrier Lake

to Canmore & Calgary

SCREE SLOPE

SALT & PEPPER WALL

40

ROAD SIGN

PARK IN DITCH IN THIS AREA

P

APPROACH TRAIL

BARRIER WALL

CREEK BED (USUALLY DRY)

OPEN TALUS FIELD

N

100 m

SALT AND PEPPER WALL

6 routes   ←5.10   5.11   5.12   5.13→

This small, rarely-visited wall is located on the east end of the Barrier Mountain cliff band. It sits above the highway and is shaded, making it a great escape from Barrier Wall if the sun becomes unbearable. The rock is bullet grey and black, and offers fine climbing on perfect edges of all sizes. It makes for a great combination with Barrier Wall, but is also worthy of an individual visit. The crag is dark and receives only a little sun in the evening—it needs a couple of days to dry out after moderate rainfall.

Approach: From the road, follow the main trail toward Barrier Wall. Shortly after the trail leaves the creek bed for the first time, watch carefully for a trail that branches left into the forest. Follow it uphill to the cliff base. Hang a left on another trail that traverses the cliff band and follow it downhill and east paralleling the highway. Shortly after passing over a large scree slope (across from the Barrier Lake picnic parking area), look for a faint trail that leads to the base of the wall at the top of a small hill.

Salt and Pepper Wall

Routes are listed from left to right.

1 Black Hole 5.10c . . . . ☐
8 bolts (18 m) This is the left-most route and is at the top of a small incline. Beautiful rock.   (*John Martin, 1999*)

2 Box Canyon 5.10b . . . . ☐
8 bolts (24 m) This route has fun climbing on predominately large holds with a couple of short, crimpy sections. From the first bolt, trend left into a corner feature before climbing straight up.   (*John Martin, 1999*)

3 Salt and Pepper 5.10a . . . . ☐
12 bolts (28 m) Climb straight up past two, short right-facing corners. Face climbing on positive edges and immaculate stone finish the pitch.   (*John Martin, 1999*)

4 Polka Dots 5.10d . . . . ☐
11 bolts (28 m) Climb broken rock to a small ledge and pull over a miniature roof. Tons of crimps on perfect rock lead to the *Salt and Pepper* anchors.   (*John Martin, 1999*)

5 Something Wicked This Way Comes 5.10c . . . . . . ☐
9 bolts (25 m) Climb the first four bolts of *Polka Dots*, veer right and follow the edge of the wall to an anchor at the base of a giant, left-facing corner.   (*John Martin, 2000*)

mossy ledge

dead tree

platform

to Barrier Wall & Parking

SALT AND PEPPER WALL

6 No Leaf Clover 5.10a . . . . ☐
14 bolts (35 m) Continue past the anchor of *Something Wicked This Way Comes* into the giant corner above. Fun climbing in a stunning position leads to anchors on the face. To reduce rope drag, backclean the first quickdraw and extend both the fourth and first anchor quickdraw. Unless you have a 70-m rope, lower twice.
    (*PREP: JD LeBlanc; FA: Scott Milton, 1998*)

Michelle Kollmuss on *I Drill, Therefor I Am* (5.10c).

SALT AND PEPPER WALL

mossy ledge

BARRIER WALL

50 routes ←5.10 5.11 5.12 5.13→

This expansive wall boasts many testpieces from the early days of Bow Valley sport climbing, and these lines haven't become any easier with time. The climbing is of a highly technical nature and the routes feature many small, yet positive crimps (and the odd sloper) littered across stippled grey and yellow faces. Many of the best routes are in the 5.11 grade and climb into a fine position at the very top of the wall, bypassing midway anchors along the way. Don't be discouraged, though, if you're not ready for 5.11 yet. The easier routes are also of fine quality, they just lack the exposure and positioning of their bigger brothers.

Approach: Follow the main trail from the parking area, starting to the right of the road sign in the ditch. The path follows the creek bed (which is usually dry) and occasionally loops into the forest before eventually heading left up to the base of the wall. Barrier Wall starts in the forest and curves up the hill, where it eventually becomes a scree slope scattered with large boulders.

Barrier Wall

This is a big stretch of wall with a lot of great routes. Most people concentrate on the right side, but don't be afraid to check out the routes further left as they are also quite good. Routes are listed from left to right.

① Koyaanisqatsi 5.11a . . . .

8 bolts (23 m) This is a great route with some fun climbing up a flakey crack. To start, traverse in from the left on yellow flakes. After clipping the second bolt, downclimb to the first bolt before climbing up the left side of the bolt line. *(Lawrence Ostrander, 1985)*

② Double Clutch 5.12a . . . .

6 bolts (23 m) This is a committing route that follows the right side of an arête. With only five bolts in 23 m, be prepared to run it out (the crux is well protected, though). Begin on the arête's left side where the first bolt is hidden above a small ledge. *(Lawrence Ostrander, 1987)*

③ Ideal for Living 5.11b . . . .

7 bolts + 1 piece of gear (28 m) Start below a small, left-facing corner on the left end of the wall. A couple of tough moves through the bottom of the corner lead to easier climbing above. The nut placement comes after the sixth bolt. If you're confident at the grade and have a good head, you may not need it. *(Lawrence Ostrander, 1985)*

④ The Great Outdoors 5.11a . . . .

8 bolts + 1 pin (25 m) Start below an oven-sized flake at two metres. Easy climbing to a high first bolt is followed

by excellent climbing up the yellow and grey groove above. Be prepared to lock it down for a few moves. *(Lawrence Ostrander, 1985)*

⑤ AKA 5.10c . . . .

6 bolts (18 m) This is a good, crimpy face climb up bullet rock. Finish on the *Channel Zero* anchors. *(Lawrence Ostrander, 1985)*

BARRIER WALL FAR LEFT

❻ Channel Zero 5.11b . . . .

6 bolts (16 m) Thin flakes with marginal footholds will test your skills right from the ground. Once at the base of the small yellow corner, attack it head-on finishing at anchors on the ledge above. (*David Dancer, 1989*)

❼ Bango 5.11a . . . .

6 bolts (16 m) This pitch climbs near the right edge of the wide, yellow streak above *Channel Zero*. It finishes with crimpy, leftward moves. (*Lawrence Ostrander, 1987*)

❽ Channel AKA 5.11b . . . .

11 bolts (29 m) Continue past the *Channel Zero* anchors to some fine climbing on super holds in the black rock. Quality. (*Lawrence Ostrander & David Dancer, 1985*)

❾ Winnebago Warrior 5.11b . . . . .

11 bolts (27 m) Those willing to make a small run-out above the *Channel Zero* anchors will be rewarded with another great extension. (*Lawrence Ostrander, 1987*)

❿ Through a Glass Darkly 5.11b . .

5 bolts + gear (25 m) Climb the right-trending crack using a mixture of gear and bolts for protection. Start just left of the forked tree. (*Lawrence Ostrander, 1985*)

⓫ The Roman Empire 5.10d . . . . .

4 bolts (16 m) Start just right of the forked tree next to the wall. Climb the wall trending to the right. A couple of tricky moves gain the slab. (*David Dancer, 1989*)

⓬ M.E.C. 5.10d . . . .

4 bolts (16 m) Climb directly into *The Roman Empire* at the third bolt. The start is located at the left end of a small ledge at one metre. (*David Dancer, 1989*)

⓭ Scribble Feet 5.11d . . . .

9 bolts (23 m) Climb *M.E.C.*, but launch into a couple of powerful moves through a small roof. Afterward, enjoy good edge climbing to the anchor. (*David Dancer, 1989*)

⓮ Fries and Gravy 5.12d . . . .

9 bolts (23 m) Climb *M.E.C.* and trend right, climbing through a white patch of rock. Tackle the small roof and weakness above on small crimps. (*Todd Guyn, 1995*)

⓯ Nuts of Steel 5.10a . . . .

3 bolts + gear (24 m) Follow a right-trending crack and ramp to the anchor of *Sensoria*. (*Kelly Tobey, 1984*)

BARRIER WALL LEFT

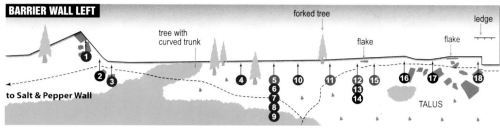

BARRIER WALL LEFT

to Salt & Pepper Wall

tree with curved trunk

forked tree

flake

flake

ledge

TALUS

⓰ Sensoria 5.12a . . . . 🎯 🤚 🪓 ☐

4 bolts (12 m) This beautiful route climbs up the left side of a large, yellow patch of rock. A tricky sequence on small edges will make you think. Although the crimps are small, they have bite. *(Lawrence Ostrander, 1989)*

⓱ Kiwi Fly 5.12c . . . . 🎯 ☐

7 bolts (17 m) The crux boils down to getting established over the roof. When in doubt, think left. *(F. Fisher, 1996)*

⓲ Cost of Living 5.11a . . . . ☐

4 bolts + 1 piton (19 m) This good route sees little traffic due to a mind-boggling runout to the first bolt. If you decide to go for it, climb onto a small ledge and make some easy but committing moves into a left-facing corner. Climb it to gain the bolt. *(Lawrence Ostrander, 1987)*

⓳ Age of Reason 5.11c . . . . ☐

4 bolts (19 m) This route is immediately left of the tree. A big runout to the first bolt is followed by a brief, but confusing crux. Easier above. *(Lawrence Ostrander, 1985)*

⓴ Where's Your Child? 5.12a . . . . ☐

8 bolts (18 m) This might be a decent route if it weren't for the rusty, ¼-inch bolts. *(Lawrence Ostrander, 1989)*

㉑ Requiem 5.12a . . . . 🪓 ☐

9 bolts (18 m) This pitch is one of the Rockies' forgotten gems and well worth the extra effort needed to set up a belay on the ledge. Use *Blank on the Map* to access the ledge. Enjoy the climbing. *(Andy Genereux, 1993)*

㉒ Blank on the Map 5.11a . . . 🤚 🪓 ☐

4 bolts (12 m) Begin just right of the tree. Good edge climbing on small flakes leads to a small ledge. The blank wall above puts an end to the good times. *(Jon Jones, 1993)*

㉓ Hollow Men 5.10b . . . . ☐

3 bolts (12 m) Easy climbing leads to a ledge and a very

small, flakey corner feature. A few hard moves lead leftward up the short, blank face. *(Lawrence Ostrander, 1985)*

㉔ I Drill, Therefore I Am 5.10c . . . . ☐

4 bolts (14 m) Hard-to-locate holds lead up bullet grey rock. Share the *Shadow Play* anchor. *(Jon Jones, 1993)*

㉕ Shadow Play 5.10a . . . . 🤚 ☐

4 bolts (13 m) Technical and fingery climbing unlocks a path through bullet grey rock. *(Lawrence Ostrander, 1985)*

㉖ A Taxing Affair 5.9 . . . . ☐

3 bolts (12 m) Climb up to a great hold at the base of the right-facing corner. Small, textured edges lead left to a series of perfect incut edges on the grey slab. *(Unknown)*

㉗ Regatta de Blank 5.12b . . . . . 🤚 🪓 ☐

11 bolts (38 m) Continue past the *Shadow Play* anchors to a very blank slab. Trend left to a crux on micro crimps, and continue left to better holds. A couple of well-spaced bolts lead to the anchors. This is a definite step up in difficulty from *Naked Teenage Girls*. *(Keith Haberl, 1988)*

㉘ One Way to Wangland 5.8 . . . . ☐

4 bolts (13 m) The right-facing corner. *(Kelly Tobey, 1985)*

㉙ Naked Teenage Girls 5.12a . . 🤚 ☐

13 bolts (38 m) Climb *One Way to Wangland* to the last bolt (use a long sling), step left and get ready. If you think you're proficient at highly-technical face climbing, consider this your final exam. Lower twice to descend. *(Todd Guyn & Keith Haberl, 1987)*

㉚ Current Account 5.10a . . . . ☐

7 bolts (16 m) Crimp through small bulges to the right of the hanging, right-facing corner. *(John Martin, 1993)*

㉛ Beautiful Rainbow 5.11a . . . . 🖐 🪓 ☐

14 bolts (40 m) This is one of the most enjoyable routes

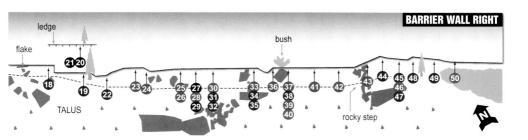

at Barrier Mountain—kind of a sport climber's version of the mixed classic, *Rainbow Bridge*. Climb directly above the *Current Account* anchor until you can move left to some amazing flake climbing. A medium-sized nut tames the runout to the anchor. To clean the pitch, belay up the second and make two rappels to the ground. (*Unknown*)

32 Beautiful Thing 5.11b . . . .

17 bolts (39 m) This brilliant route tackles the long, flake crack that rises above *Beautiful Rainbow*. It's a must-do and gains an excellent position. Lower twice to get down.
(*Andy Genereux, 2006*)

33 Front Row Center 5.7 . . . .

5 bolts (16 m) This pitch is located just right of a right-facing corner. Many positive flakes keep the difficulty at bay. (*Lawrence Ostrander, 1984*)

34 Sisyphus Goes to Hollywood 5.11c

11 bolts (33 m) This quality, exposed pitch continues past the *Front Row Center* anchors. Use small crimps to unlock the cruxes between positive holds. Dramatic lock-offs on jugs finish the pitch. If you're not sure you'll make it, lower twice to get down. (*David Dancer, 1987*)

35 In Us, Under Us 5.11b . . . .

11 bolts (36 m) Climb into the right facing-corner above *Front Row Center*. Spicy run-outs will keep you focused. Lower twice to get down. (*Lawrence Ostrander, 1985*)

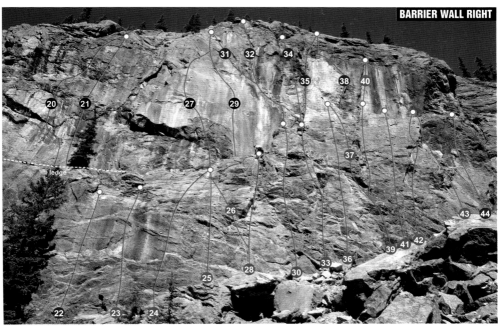

36 Serial Driller 5.9 . . . . ☐

7 bolts (18 m) Start left of an oven-sized block with a bush behind it. Trend slightly left before forging up the face left of the right-facing corner. *(John Martin, 1993)*

37 Raindance 5.9 . . . . ☐

6 bolts (18 m) Clip the first bolt of *There Goes the Neighbourhood*. Head left and move directly up the face just left of the right-facing corner. *(John Martin, 1993)*

38 The Flake 5.11a . . . . 🪓☐

13 bolts + gear (40 m) Continue up the huge, yellow flake above *Serial Driller*. Finish at the *In Us, Under Us* anchor. Lower twice to descend. *(Lawrence Ostrander, 1985)*

39 There Goes the Neighbourhood 5.9 . . . . ☐

8 bolts (18 m) Climb the right-facing corner to a small ledge. The anchor is at the break. *(Lawrence Ostrander, 1985)*

40 Closed Project . . . . ☐

41 Drill of a Lifetime 5.9 . . . . ☐

6 bolts (17 m) Climb the left side of a diagonal seam using positive holds of all sizes. A slight crux on less positive grips appears midway up. *(John Martin, 1993)*

42 Cadillac Jack 5.9 . . . . ☐

5 bolts (17 m) Start directly underneath the most prominent part of the diagonal seam. A couple of awkward moves gain a small ledge. Continue up and left toward the anchor on good holds. *(John Martin, 1985)*

43 Squeeze Play 5.10d . . . . ☐

6 bolts (15 m) Start off a cluster of boulders that form a ledge. A runout to the first bolt is followed by fun climbing up a flake to a small ledge. Continue up the right-facing corner to anchor above. *(Unknown)*

44 Feel Surreal 5.11c . . . . ☐

6 bolts (15 m) Climb through a large, yellow patch of rock to a flake. From here, fun climbing on good edges leads to an anchor on a ledge. *(Lawrence Ostrander, 1989)*

45 It's Not Over 'till the Fat Boy Sings 5.11b . . . . . . 🐾☐

14 bolts (29 m) Clip the first two bolts of *End Dance* before stepping left onto the face. After a crux that gains the midway break, trend lightly up the loose, right-facing

corner to a great exit. It climbs a lot steeper than it looks from the ground! *(Andy Genereux, 2006)*

46 End Dance 5.10c . . . . ☐

5 bolts (16 m) This fun route follows the obvious crack. *(David Dancer, 1985)*

47 Fat Bastard 5.11b . . . . ☐

14 bolts (29 m) Continue above the anchors of *End Dance*. *(Andy Genereux, 2006)*

48 Pull Fat Boy, Pull 5.11c . . . . 🎞☐

8 bolts (16 m) This pitch starts just right of the crack. A fingery crux on side-pulls is followed by bigger holds above. *(Andy Genereux, 2006)*

49 Why Won't She Sleep With Me? 5.11c . . . . . . 🎞☐

6 bolts (14 m) This fun route starts up a small, right-facing corner. A low crux is followed by a second that surmounts the bulge. *(Steve Birch & Andy Genereux, 2006)*

50 Open Project . . . . ☐

The last line on the right. The only hardware in place is an anchor.

BARRIER WALL FAR RIGHT

CHAPTER 3

ACÉPHALE

Acéphale, the Bow Valley's premier sport crag, sits nestled on the north end of Heart Mountain high above the Trans-Canada Highway. A visit to this cliff is mandatory for 5.12 to 5.14 climbers since the cliff band boast the highest concentration of difficult sport climbs in the Bow Valley and, quite possibly, Canada. The beautiful grey limestone walls are streaked in blues and yellows and littered with pockets, pods, pinches, crimps and the occasional tufa. The overhanging rock is excellent and sport climbers searching for athletic pitches in the heat of summer will find themselves in paradise. Climbers looking for quality pitches below 5.12 will probably be happier going elsewhere, though. The selection of moderate routes at this cliff is very limited.

JOSH MULLER ON "EXISTENCE MUNDANE" (5.13B)
◉ ZAK MCGURK

CONDITIONS

The predominantly north-facing walls of Acéphale see little sun and provide ideal conditions for summer cragging. However, the left side of the Lower Wall gets some morning sun, making it a good place to warm up before heading to the shaded Upper Wall. Down Under also receives sun until early afternoon, and is almost guaranteed to be crowd-free. The overhanging nature of many routes at Acéphale allow climbing in light or sporadic rainfall, but after moderate to heavy precipitation the walls can seep quite heavily and usually require a week of good weather to produce dry routes. The best bet after storms is the left end of the Lower Wall, which has few pockets and gets morning sun—it tends to dry faster than the heavily-pocketed (and shaded) Upper Wall.

APPROACH

From Canmore: Drive east on the Trans-Canada Highway toward Calgary and set the trip meter to zero after passing Exit 105 for Lac des Arcs. The highway soon passes over Heart Creek before paralleling two small ponds on the right protected by a guardrail. Just beyond the end of the guardrail is the Acéphale parking area in the ditch on the right, 2.2 km (1.4 miles) from the Lac des Arcs exit. To return to Canmore at day's end, it's necessary to drive an additional 6.4 km (3.8 miles) east toward Calgary before Exit 114 allows a turnaround for Canmore-bound traffic.

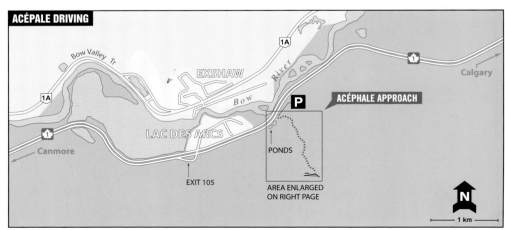

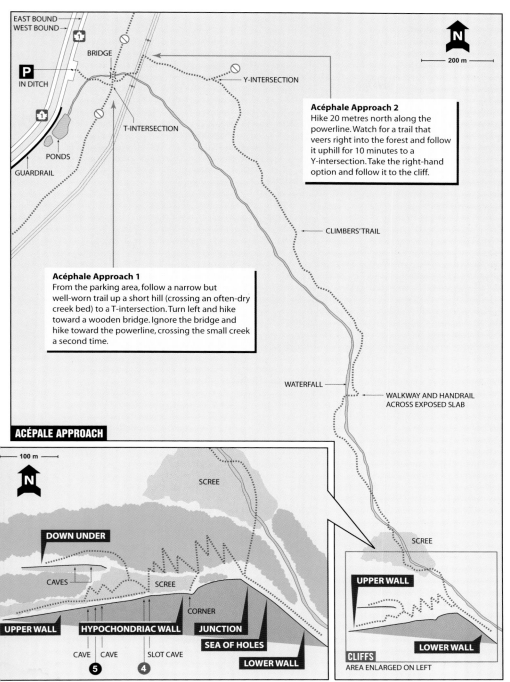

EAST BOUND
WEST BOUND

BRIDGE

P
IN DITCH

Y-INTERSECTION

PONDS

T-INTERSECTION

GUARDRAIL

Acéphale Approach 2
Hike 20 metres north along the powerline. Watch for a trail that veers right into the forest and follow it uphill for 10 minutes to a Y-intersection. Take the right-hand option and follow it to the cliff.

CLIMBERS' TRAIL

Acéphale Approach 1
From the parking area, follow a narrow but well-worn trail up a short hill (crossing an often-dry creek bed) to a T-intersection. Turn left and hike toward a wooden bridge. Ignore the bridge and hike toward the powerline, crossing the small creek a second time.

WATERFALL

WALKWAY AND HANDRAIL
ACROSS EXPOSED SLAB

ACÉPALE APPROACH

200 m

100 m

SCREE

DOWN UNDER

CAVES

SCREE

CORNER

SCREE

UPPER WALL

UPPER WALL   **HYPOCHONDRIAC WALL**   **JUNCTION**
                                        SEA OF HOLES
CAVE   CAVE   SLOT CAVE   **LOWER WALL**
❺   ❹

CLIFFS
AREA ENLARGED ON LEFT

LOWER WALL

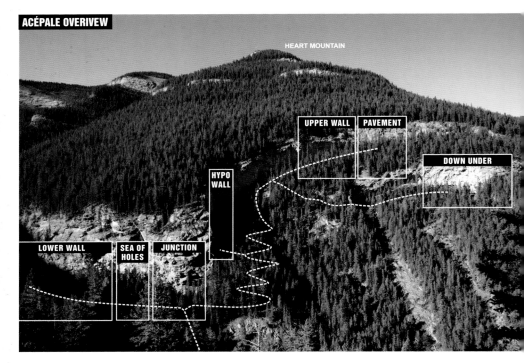

ACÉPALE OVERIVEW

HEART MOUNTAIN

UPPER WALL | PAVEMENT

HYPO WALL

DOWN UNDER

LOWER WALL | SEA OF HOLES | JUNCTION

From Calgary: Drive west on the Trans-Canada Highway toward Canmore. Take Exit 105 for Lac des Arc and re-enter the Trans-Canada Highway heading east. From here, follow the Canmore directions starting at Exit 105.

Hiking: From the parking area, follow a narrow but well-worn trail up a short hill to a T-intersection with another trail. Turn left and hike toward the power lines, crossing a small creek bed and ignoring a wooden bridge on the left. About 20 metres beyond the creek bed, the trail veers into the woods on the right. Follow it for 10 minutes to a Y-intersection and take the right-hand option. The trail then wanders up to a beautiful waterfall, perfect for a cool-down. From here, uphill switchbacks lead to a wooden walkway and chain handrail that protects a rightward traverse across a rock slab. Continue along the trail, crossing the stream occasionally, to the base of a large scree slope. Stay low and follow the trail through the streambed until it re-enters the forest on the right and heads uphill to the base of the Junction. Turn left for the Lower Wall and Sea of Holes, or right for more uphill switchbacks and the Upper Wall.

Interesting Fact: Acéphale was the name given to a secret and esoteric society founded by French writer George Bataille. Fascinated by human sacrifice, he used a decapitated man as the symbol for the group. According to legend, Bataille and the other members of Acéphale each agreed to be the sacrificial victim as an inauguration, but none of them would agree to be the executioner. An indemnity was offered for an executioner, but none was found before the dissolution of Acéphale shortly before World War 2.

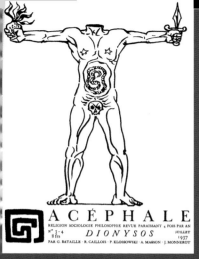

From the beginning it was a secret. Partly, because Grotto, then the only location for hard climbing near Canmore, was climbed-out and overrun, and a certain secretiveness, we thought, would stem the tide which reduced so many crags to 5.10. Then there was the problem of Tuzo, my rogue malamute, who needed a crag of his own to lord over, which was incidentally the original impetus for walking up the drainage on Heart mountain in the first place, and for that matter walking the isolated cliff lines that would later become Bataan. Beyond that, good weather was never a consideration in the first year or two of climbing at Acéphale. Fair weather climbers were just not interested, and I should add that none of us really cared to conceal the secret anyway, rather, we were all intent on revealing it which, of course, initiated the vicious circle where all true secrets are kept. In any case, at its origin, rain, seeping holds, a thermometer hovering around 9 or 10 degrees Celsius, and a winter wind hugging the cliffs was the norm. We felt ourselves to be the only people in the mountains on those hard days.

April and May of 1992 were the golden days of this suffering. The first activities that would be formative of the future took place in a blanket of cloud and under the most trying circumstances. Frozen fingers and body chills pointed to the true nature of the enterprise: not really modern sport climbing as we then believed, but something far more primitive, more a matter of haunting by, or ritual obeisance to the clearing in the moss and underbrush which slowly grew underneath the overhangs themselves. Apocryphal or not, Acéphale was the culmination of a string of developments (such a problematic word and so symptomatic) in the Bow Valley. The earliest and most influential of these areas was undoubtedly the Back of the Lake; the most short lived, but visionary, the Quarry at Exshaw; the most profane, the Water Wall in Grotto; the most spectacular and troglodytic, the Carrot Patch. All were shaped by a fairly porous brotherhood of souls in possession of the adept's technical knowledge and free time—for most, the window of a few months before the guiding season at the Cadet Camp began. And of course, this summertime military order and the primary organization of democratic society for which it stands, provides the crucial mirror of all that Acéphale in its original incarnation was/is against. A winter crag in the truest sense of the phrase, atomization only took hold of the key players when the cold could not forge the bonds of group belonging and communistic organization. That said, the betrayal of the secret society of Acéphale that happened the first summer, and every summer after that when the inclement weather finally cleared and the job seekers, junior development teams, and aspirants arrived, bears little resemblance to the unemployed negativity that coursed through the veins of what Georges Bataille and André Masson first dreamt up in 1937 as Acéphalic man…

THE LOWER WALL

30 routes ←5.10 5.11 5.12 5.13→

The excellent, compact grey limestone found on this cliff is of such high quality you could easily spend the entire season here, never once venturing to the Upper Wall (although that would be a grave mistake). The rock has a proliferation of crisp edges and fine-grained slopers, and the lines tend to be quite technical. The wall is vertical to slightly overhanging and gets sun from mid-morning to early afternoon. Included with the Lower Wall are the adjacent sectors Sea of Holes and the Junction.

Approach: Follow the hiking trail up from the highway. Near the end of the approach, the path will leave the creek bed and climb steeply toward the Lower Wall. The first sector encountered is the Junction. Follow the trail left to reach Sea of Holes and the Lower Wall.

The Lower Wall

Routes are listed from left to right.

1 **Keys in the Car** 5.10c . . . .

6 bolts (13 m) From the ledge, climb to a horizontal break. Follow a small, broken corner to an anchor in the scoop. Beware of loose rock out left. *(JD LeBlanc, 1994)*

2 **Nickel Bag** 5.10d . . . .

6 bolts (16 m) Start at the right end of the ledge and follow the seam to a bulge below the anchor. A 5.11c variation (7

THE LOWER WALL

bolts) moves right from the third bolt (clip one traversing bolt) to finish up *Girl Drink Drunk*. *(Daren Tremaine, 1993)*

3 **Girl Drink Drunk** 5.12a . . . . . .

8 bolts (18 m) Trend right from the ledge. Follow a corner to a bolt on the right side of a horizontal break. Sidepulls lead to small blue streaks and cauliflower rock. The crux comes near the top. *(Richard Jagger, 1992)*

4 **The Irradicator** 5.12a . . . .

6 bolts (18 m) Start where the small, left-trending ramp meets the ground. A hard boulder problem on perfect edges and incuts leads left to a rest. Finish by following a black streak through a steep headwall, being careful to keep the pump at bay. *(Richard Jagger, 1992)*

5 **Illy Down** 5.12c . . . .

8 bolts (19 m) Start with a good right-facing flake. Pull into a vicious boulder problem that trends up and right through the only weakness. After this rude awakening, enjoy mellower climbing up the thin blue streak to the anchor. *(JD LeBlanc, 1992)*

6 **Ice Cream head** 5.12d . . . .

5 bolts (15 m) This may no longer be climbable due to a broken hold left of the first bolt. If it's still possible, start on a big sidepull, trend right and follow the right side of a groove to some very small edges that are used to surmount a bulge. *(PREP: JD LeBlanc; FA: Todd Guyn 1993)*

7 **Ice Cream Head Direct** 5.13a

5 bolts (15 m) Nasty edges and miserable footholds provide a desperate path into *Ice Cream Head* at the first bolt. *(Derek Galloway, 2004)*

❽ Subbacultcha 5.12a . . . . . . ☐

6 bolts (10 m) Start to the left of a yellow streak and head for good holds in the flakes. A hard step left at the top spits off a fair number of potential successes. (*Daren Tremaine, 1992*)

❾ Justine 5.11d . . . . ☐

8 bolts (18 m) This route features great climbing on slopers and underclings. The crux involves pulling off a crimp that seems impossibly small, but massive footholds make it usable. To start, locate a small yellow streak and protruding first bolt. (*Richard Jagger, 1993*)

❿ La Part Maudite 5.12c 🧗🐾 ☐

6 bolts (20 m) To find this route, locate the narrow yellow streak above a ledge at four metres. Start by climbing over the left side of a roof. Some early difficulties give way to nice edging up a sporty 5.10 face. The anchor is over the ledge. (*Shep Steiner, 1993*)

⓫ Naissance de le Femme 5.13b . . . . . 🧗🐾 ☐

7 bolts (20 m) Head for the right side of the ledge at four metres. From here, climb through bulges and follow immaculate grey rock to a high crux that will likely spit you off a couple of times before you achieve redpoint success. (*PREP: JD LeBlanc; FA: Scott Milton, 1995*)

⓬ Deal With It 5.12c . . . 🧗🖐 ☐

8 bolts (22 m) This super popular line follows some amazing, compact grey rock. Several cruxes make you really earn your successful anchor clip. (*JD LeBlanc, 1993*)

⓭ Neoconstructionist 5.11b 🧗 ☐

5 bolts (14 m) Start to the left of the yellow streak. Awkward climbing leads to a ledge and a short overhanging section. Continue upward using hard-to-locate edges. The anchor clip is awkward. (*Tim Pochay, 1993*)

⓮ Wet Lust 5.13c . . 🧗👊🖐 ☐

10 bolts (25 m) The continuation of *Neoconstructionist* has a stopper crux off the midway anchor that might make you change your mind about adopting this route as a project. If you stick it, shake out and follow nice edges to another hard crux. Good luck. (*Todd Guyn, 1993*)

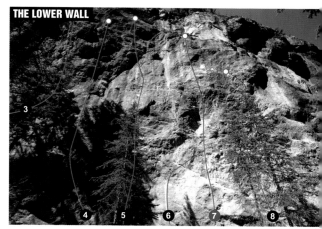

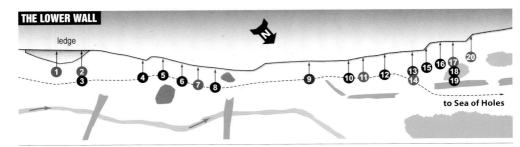

THE LOWER WALL

ledge

N

to Sea of Holes

⑮ Where's Mom? 5.12a . . . .

11 bolts (19 m) Awkward moves lead up a yellow streak to a cruxy stepped roof. Loop a little right, move back to the left and then enjoy great moves above. Named for a new mom that was slow to return to her project.

(PREP: Barb Clemes; FA: Bill Rennie, 1997)

⑯ Nemo 5.12d . . . .

11 bolts (22 m) Start in the small corner to the right of the yellow streak and follow it up and right around a small roof. A couple of crimpy moves in the first three metres give way to easier ground and a couple of excellent rests. Fire over the small roof and do your best to hang on until the anchors. *(Todd Guyn, 1993)*

⑰ The Dark Half 5.13a . . . . .

11 bolts (25 m) Climb awkwardly through the yellow ramp and corner to the base of a small roof on the left. Prepare to put your bouldering skills to work in the grey bulge, and then test your endurance up the beautiful, overhanging grey stone above. *(Helmut Neswabda, 1993)*

⑱ SR 16 5.12c . . . .

12 bolts (28 m) Climb *The Dark Half*, but continue up the corner to a short and burly grey headwall right of *The Last Dance*. The anchor consists of carabiners on the final two bolts. *(PREP: Shep Steiner; FA: Scott Milton, 2001)*

⑲ The Dark Dance 5.12c . . . .

11 bolts (27 m) Start up *The Dark Half* and finish on *The Last Dance*. An excellent route.

(Todd Guyn & Shep Steiner, 2000)

⑳ The Last Dance 5.13a . . . .

10 bolts (26 m) This is the last route on this section of wall. *(Helmut Neswabda, 1993)*

Sea of Holes

This is a short, steep wall found in the trees right of the Lower Wall. Unfortunately, the cliff rarely dries out and, as a result, the routes see little traffic and tend to be somewhat dirty. This is a shame, because the climbs are good.

㉑ Approach Route 5.11d . . . .

4 bolts (13 m) Follow a grey corner to a ledge. Head straight up the grey wall to the ledge anchor. Great climbing. *(Joe Buszowski, 1994)*

22

SEA OF HOLES   21   23   24

THE JUNCTION

30

28

26

27

29

㉒ Pandora 5.13c . . . .

16 bolts (31 m) From the top of *Approach Route*, continue to a higher anchor. Either belay up your partner or continue up the steep headwall to a rest before the crux at the last bolt. This route was first done at 5.13a with an artificial hold, which was later removed. To descend, lower to the second anchor, pull your rope and lower again.

(PREP: Joe Buszowski; FA: Scott Milton, 1998)

㉓ Pluvial Power 5.12a . . . .

5 bolts (12 m) Start below a yellow ledge. Follow dirty pockets to clean rock above. *(FA: Andy Genereux, 1995)*

㉔ Static Dynos 5.12a . . . .

6 bolts (12 m) Climb straight up and over a dirty hole at one metre. Continue on pockets to a shake at the break. You'll have a tough time dealing with the bulge above.

(PREP: Andy Genereux; FA: David Dornian, 1997)

㉕ Wouldn't You Like to Know 5.11d . . . .

4 bolts (11 m) Climb the white streak through a couple of holes starting just left of a large pack rat nest. *(Unknown)*

The Junction

This sector features long, sustained and slightly-overhanging routes that will keep you engaged all the way to the anchors. Loose starts aside, the rock is of high quality. Climbs are listed from left to right.

㉖ Bucking Horse 5.12b . . . .

13 bolts (33 m) Start left of a dirty flake. If you persist through the rotten bottom, you'll be rewarded with an endless stretch of great climbing above. *(Todd Guyn, 2004)*

㉗ Hickory Dickory Dock 5.12b . . . .

16 bolts (34 m) Using the dirty flake, head up and over the ledge to a no-hands rest. Punch past two fixed draws to a rest out left. Motor to the top. *(Todd Guyn, 2003)*

㉘ Duck Bill 5.12c . . . .

15 bolts (31 m) Climb the first four bolts of *Hickory Dickory Dock*. Trend left to more difficult climbing with a boulder crux that guards the anchor. *(JD LeBlanc, 2010)*

㉙ Go Ask Alice 5.12d . . . .

18 bolts (34 m) Start to the left of the yellow streak. Easy climbing to an excellent rest is followed by increasingly difficult moves (and clips) up to the blank wall. Surf around and finish with tricky mantles. *(JD LeBlanc, 2004)*

㉚ Lose Yourself 5.12b . . . .

14 bolts (30 m) Use the same start as *Go Ask Alice*. Head right at the grey headwall and follow the yellow streak to a powerful lip encounter. *(Dale Robotham, 2004)*

Dung Nguyen on Endless Summer (5.13d). Photo by Sonnie Trotter.

THE UPPER WALL

43 routes ←5.10 5.11 5.12 5.13→

The blue, grey and yellow streaks that colour the Upper Wall are littered with interesting features—a great selection of pockets, pods, pinches and edges make for fun and interesting climbing. This wall gets very little sun, which makes it a perfect crag for the hot months of summer. Bring a parka, even in July and August.

Approach: From the Junction at the Lower Wall, follow the trail rightward into the forest. After several switchbacks, there will be a short trail on the left that leads to the base of the Hypochondriac Wall. To reach the Upper Wall, continue up the trail until it emerges from the forest onto the base of a large scree slope. The first route (a project) is at the right end of a large slot cave. Continue uphill to locate all of the other climbs.

Hypochondriac Wall

This small sector features routes that might best be described as slightly overhanging slab climbing. Positive holds are a rare find on these lines and good technical skills will be of greater benefit than raw power. The routes are long and mentally exhausting; your mind certainly won't be wandering while you are climbing. Routes are listed from left to right.

❶ Quail 5.12c . . . .

13 bolts (33 m) Start on *Hypochondriac*. After moving past the fourth bolt above the ledge, climb up the corner's left side to the overhanging wall above. *(Todd Guyn, 2003)*

❷ Hypochondriac 5.12c . . . . . .

13 bolts (33 m) This is the best of the three routes. It suffers from a slightly bushy and dirty start, but don't let that deter you. Start off the small platform at the base of the big corner crack and continue up to a ledge. From the ledge, get ready for sustained climbing all the way to the anchors with very few positive holds. There is a bolt below the base of the corner crack that may be used to protect the poor climbing down low. Backclean it if you clip it.
(Helmut Neswabda, 1993)

❸ The Two Towers 5.12c . . . . . .

12 bolts (30 m) Start off the high platform below the obvious rotten tower. Climb through chossy rock, stemming between the wall and tower. From the top of the tower, try to figure out how to make upward progress without the benefit of handholds, an exercise that seems to go on forever. *(Todd Guyn, 2003)*

The Upper Wall

This is quite possibly the best wall in the Bow Valley and contains an amazing collection of difficult lines. Routes are listed from left to right.

❹ Open Project . . . . ☐
This line lies just beyond the right end of a large slot cave visible while hiking the trail to the Upper Wall.

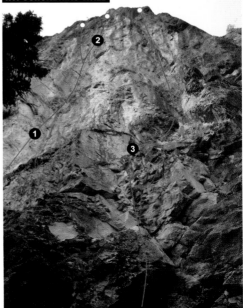

HYPOCHONDRIAC WALL

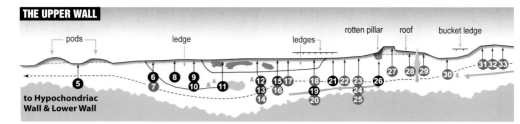

THE UPPER WALL

❺ Le Jeu Lugubre 5.12c . . . .

9 bolts (23 m) Climb between two prominent holes to a crux just before the third bolt. Traverse right on good holds to a couple of hard moves below the anchor, which is out of sight in a large scoop. This route is best cleaned on toprope. (*Shep Steiner, 1993*)

❻ Swelltone Theatre 5.12c . . . .

11 bolts (26 m) Start off the left end of the ledge. Traverse left, backcleaning some of the draws as you go to reduce rope drag. This climb is long and beautiful and features a rare body-length tufa. The crux comes up high, after the pump has settled in. (*Daren Tremaine, 1994*)

❼ Open Project . . . .

The line just to the right of *Swelltone Theatre*.

❽ Full Fathom Five 5.12b . . . .

8 bolts (21 m) Start near the left end of the ledge below a chossy roof. With the first bolt stick clipped, navigate through the choss to the blue rock above. This route is a bit sportier than the others. (*Shep Steiner, 1994*)

❾ Le Bleu du Ciel 5.12b . . . .

9 bolts (21 m) After climbing through an initial choss band, follow the left-hand bolt line past a hueco. The crux pulls a small roof below the anchors. (*JD LeBlanc, 1993*)

❿ Le Stade du Mirior 5.12b

10 bolts (22 m) Climb *Le Bleu du Ciel* to the third bolt before trending right on pockets and pods that lead over some small ledges. Watch the pump! (*Shep Steiner, 1994*)

THE UPPER WALL

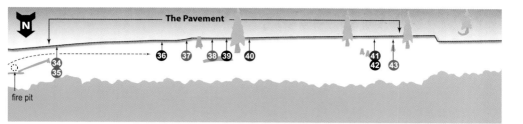

⓫ Project For a Materialist Sport Climber 5.12c . . . . ☐

7 bolts (22 m) A crimpy crux in the middle leads to easier climbing with a bit of a committing finish. Watch for some difficult-to-clip bolts in the lower half. Send the strongest group member up first! *(Shep Steiner, 1994)*

⓬ Bataille 5.11b . . . . ☐

5 bolts (10 m) Start between two boulders on the ledge using an undercling. Head up the grey and yellow steaks to a chain anchor. *(Dale Robotham, 1994)*

⓭ Dale's Extender 5.11b . . . . ☐

9 bolts (14 m) Climb *Bataille*, but instead of clipping the anchor, follow a pocketed line of bolts to the left and finish at a long chain anchor. *(JD LeBlanc, 2000)*

⓮ The Angry Inch 5.13b . . . . . . ☐

14 bolts (25 m) From the top of *Dale's Extender*, execute one really hard move off a mono. This route might be a very fast tick if you have tendons of steel! It might also end your climbing season... *(JD LeBlanc, 2000)*

⓯ The Warm-Up 5.11a . . . . ☐

4 bolts (10 m) Not a great warm-up, but it's all there is. Start at the bottom of the small, left-trending ramp and follow the blue streak to the anchor. *(Shep Steiner, 1996)*

⓰ Porthole to Hell 5.13c . . . . ☐

7 bolts (23 m) Climb *The Warm-Up* and follow a blue streak through a scoop on thin holds above. Gun for a big hole in the yellow rock and then run it out on easy terrain to the anchor. *(PREP: Shep Steiner. FA: Scott Milton, 2000)*

⑰ Sweet Thing 5.13b . . .

11 bolts (23 m) This popular line is a good introduction to the harder climbing at the crag. Start to the left of a shallow, right-facing corner and follow a blue streak to two cruxes separated by a bad shake. (*Todd Guyn, 1994*)

⑱ Whale Back 5.13c . . . .

9 bolts (23 m) Follow a small, blue streak to a roof. Beautiful climbing on pockets and pods leads to an amazing crux pulling onto the "whale back". Finish up the steep headwall.
(*PREP: Daren Tremaine; FA: Scott Milton, 2000*)

⑲ Jingus Americanus 5.12d . . .

7 bolts (14 m) From the ledge, climb over a choosy section and into a corner. The crux is at the top of the corner and involves a big slap to a sloper from a pocket. Part of the difficulty of this route is clipping the chains, so if you want the full tick, don't put long slings on the anchor!
(*Daren Tremaine & Ryan Johnstone, 1994*)

⑳ Fully Jingus 5.13d

10 bolts (26 m) Climb *Jingus Americanus* to the big slap move. Veer left on pods to hard moves on small holds slapping up the bulge.
(*PREP: Ryan Johnstone; FA: Scott Milton, 2002*)

㉑ Copacabana 5.12c . . . . . .

7 bolts (14 m) Start to the left of a yellow corner capped by a roof. From the ledge, pull the roof and head left into a scoop. Continue left to finish on *Jingus Americanus*. (*Daren Tremaine, 1994*)

㉒ The Hype 5.13b . . . .

10 bolts (23 m) Start to the right of a yellow corner capped by a roof. Follow the blue streak on edges and pockets to a high crux. (*JD LeBlanc, 1997*)

㉓ The Hood 5.13b . . . .

9 bolts (18 m) From the shattered ledge, head up to the horizontal break and veer left. Difficult moves in the overhang lead into a scoop. Finish with easier climbing on cool pockets. This route is probably the most tried 5.13 in the Rockies. (*PREP: JD LeBlanc; FA: Todd Guyn, 1993*)

㉔ Hairball 5.13c . . . .

7 bolts (17 m) Start on *The Hood*. Head right at the break

THE UPPER WALL

to thin moves that lead over the lip. Veer right and finish up *Altius*. (*PREP: JD LeBlanc; FA: Scott Milton, 1994*)

㉕ Open Project . . . .

The direct finish to *Hairball*.

㉖ Altius 5.12c . . . .

6 bolts (15 m) This ever-evolving route starts off the shattered ledge on the left side of a small cave. The climbing is continuously powerful all the way to the "bathtub" rail. Finish up a small corner. (*Daren Tremaine, 1993*)

㉗ Open Project . . . .

To the right of *Altius* is an abandoned project.

28 Leviathan 5.14a . . . .

9 bolts (29 m) Start at the back of the cave on a ledge using an undercling in the roof. This route is long, steep and beautiful—what more could you want? The overhanging business is down low, but don't expect a free ride to the anchors! (*PREP: Lev Pinter; FA: Scott Milton, 2001*)

29 Beam Me Up Scotty 5.13c . . . . . .

7 bolts (13 m) Start in the middle of the chossy ledge and crimp upward to the roof. Big moves and cryptic footwork end with a wild swing. A few tough moves close the deal. (*PREP: Scott Milton; FA: Lev Pinter, 2005*)

30 Open Project . . . .

An abandoned line right of *Beam Me Up Scotty.*

31 Bunda de Fora 5.14d . . . . . .

11 bolts (20 m) Start on the right side of the chossy ledge. A very powerful crux negotiates the roof. This route is a contender for the hardest in Canada. (*Lev Pinter, 2006*)

32 Endless Summer 5.13d . . . . .

11 bolts (19 m) Tricky edge climbing with an undercling rest leads to a redpoint crux at the lip. Stick the move, rest and hold on for the half-pad mono move that guards the anchor. (*PREP: Daren Tremaine; FA: Scott Milton, 2001*)

33 Existence Mundane 5.14b . . .

10 bolts (17 m) This athletic pitch features two very different and very hard cruxes separated by a poor rest. It was originally "prepared" with several key edges made of glue. All but one was removed to make the first free ascent. A couple of years later, Sonnie Trotter removed the final edge and luckily discovered a tiny crimp underneath that allowed him to send the route in a more natural state. (*PREP: Rick Conover; FA: Scott Milton, 1997*)

The Pavement

At the end of the wall, the cliff changes dramatically. Overhanging pocketed rock is abruptly replaced by dark grey, vertical stone with sparse, tiny edges. Routes are listed from left to right.

34 Army Ants 5.13c . . . .

8 bolts (14 m) Start to the left of a yellow streak. Burly slaps up a small corner lead to a poor rest and a powerful, crimpy section. If you're pumped, the moves under the anchor could be heartbreaking. (*Lev Pinter, 1995*)

THE UPPER WALL

㉟ The Unknown Stuntman 5.13d

11 bolts (25 m) Start up *Army Ants*, but make a vicious traverse right into a cool and cruxy dyno. If you fire it, don't get too exited—the real redpoint crux lurks above. (*PREP: Toni Lamprecht & Scott Milton; FA: Scott Milton, 2010*)

㊱ The 39 Steps 5.12d

6 bolts (13 m) Sustained crimping off the ground leads to a midway shake, a dynamic move and a well-deserved rest. If pumped, the top will prove to be more problematic than anticipated. (*Daren Tremaine, 1994*)

㊲ Jump You Prick, Jump 5.13a

7 bolts (16 m) Start with a unique jump move right off the ground. A V7 boulder problem utilizing pencil-sized sidepulls and edges is the crux and leads to nice 5.12a climbing above. (*Scott Milton, 2002*)

㊳ Ojas 5.14a

11 bolts (22 m) Difficult and technical edge climbing, punctuated by good rests, leads to an improbable-looking finish that utilizes some grisly footholds. Climb to the first bolt of *Icebox of Broken Dreams*, traverse left and backclean the draw to start. (*Lev Pinter, 2010*)

㊴ Icebox of Broken Dreams 5.12d .

8 bolts (18 m) Start this crimpy line left of a big tree growing two metres from the cliff. A tough start is followed by an interesting sequence on blankness. Mellow climbing follows before a final bulge crux. (*Matt Pieterson, 2006*)

㊵ La Pause Café 5.11c

5 bolts (10 m) Start to the right of the big tree. Boulder up to some hidden holds over a small roof before cruising baby-blue stone to the anchor. (*Daren Tremaine, 1994*)

㊶ Boner 5.11b

4 bolts (9 m) Climb the grey corner. (*Brett Wootton, 1994*)

㊷ Raging Boner 5.12d

6 bolts (12 m) From the *Boner* anchor, traverse right to some desperate undercling moves. (*Lev Pinter, 2009*)

㊸ Cochon Gronchon 5.13b

6 bolts (12 m) A viciously crimpy and technical crux at the second bolt stops most suitors in their tracks. If you survive this section, easier climbing with plenty of rests leads to a heartbreaking finish. (*Lev Pinter, 2009*)

THE PAVEMENT

DOWN UNDER

4 routes   ←5.10 5.11 5.12 5.13→

Down Under is an unjustly neglected crag located directly below the Upper Wall. It contains great pocket features in blue and grey streaks with routes of modest difficulty. This is a great place to find solitude and well worth the short approach hike.

Approach: From the right end of the big slot cave on the Upper Wall approach, head right into the forest. Follow a flagged trail that contours down and left to a short downclimb that gains the base of the wall. Traverse the base rightward past two large, rotten caves to another downclimb and the routes.

Down Under

Routes are listed from left to right.

❶ Pomme 5.10d . . . .

5 bolts (10 m) Scramble onto a ledge at two metres. Navigate good holds through a blue streak to some cool pockets before the anchor. Two partially-bolted, abandoned projects lie just above the anchor. (*Jon Jones, 1996*)

❷ Moving Target 5.12a . . . .

10 bolts (24 m) Start below a short, blue left-facing corner to the right of a ledge. White stone leads to blue-grey rock with some awesome pockets and pods. Just when the pump settles in, two cruxes appear. (*Jon Jones, 1996*)

❸ G'day 5.12a . . . .

7 bolts (19 m) Start one metre right of *Moving Target*. Two well-spaced bolts in white rock lead to solid stone in the blue streaks. Hard-to-locate holds may cause a pump to build very quickly. (*Jon Jones, 1996*)

❹ The Wizard of Oz 5.12a . . . . .

11 bolts (23 m) Start on the left side of a small ledge on the right end of the wall. Climb straight up on cool pods and pockets to a great finish through an overhang at the top. More traffic would make this classic. (*Jon Jones, 1996*)

DOWN UNDER

CHAPTER 4

HEART CREEK

With the exception of the difficult routes at the Bayon, Heart Creek contains the best concentration of moderate climbs in the Bow Valley. This small, picturesque canyon sees a constant flow of eager climbers throughout the summer and the well-maintained trail whisks visitors from parking lot to cliff in a mere 15 minutes, a real treat in the Bow Valley.

The canyon walls range from slabby to vertical and are generally comprised of high-quality, compact grey limestone, perfectly formed for friendly face climbing. This is a great area to sample Bow Valley sport climbing, try your first climb or even your first lead. The short hike and good concentration of routes also provides an ideal venue for climbers short on time, making this a very popular location with the after-work crowd.

CONDITIONS

Heart Creek is a perfect summer location, since the small valley is narrow and most of the walls are shaded from early afternoon onward, keeping the climbing relatively cool. In general, most of the crags dry very quickly after storms, but the Waterfall Wall and Bayon can seep well into the summer if the spring has been damp. Overall, the grey stone is very nicely textured, but because of the popularity of the area, some of the best climbs are starting to polish.

APPROACH

From Canmore: Drive east on the Trans-Canada Highway. Take Exit 105 for Lac des Arc and immediately turn right onto a gravel road that leads into the parking lot for Heart Creek.

From Calgary: Drive west on the Trans-Canada Highway and take Exit 105 for Lac des Arc. Turn left and take an overpass across the highway. Once on the other side, turn left onto a gravel road that leads into the parking lot for Heart Creek.

Hiking: The well-worn trail starts next to a wooden "Heart Creek Trail" sign in the parking lot. Follow the path, paralleling the highway, for about 10 minutes to a small grassy clearing on the right. From here, the trail curves to the right before crossing a bridge over Heart Creek. After the bridge, follow any of the small, braided trails to reach the wide, well-travelled Heart Creek canyon trail. From here, six minutes of hiking into the canyon on this excellent path leads to the first climbing area on the right, First Rock.

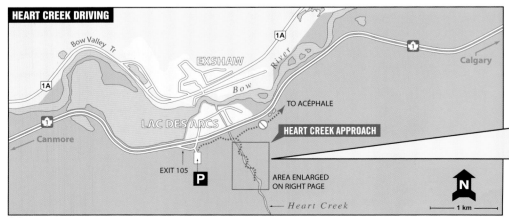

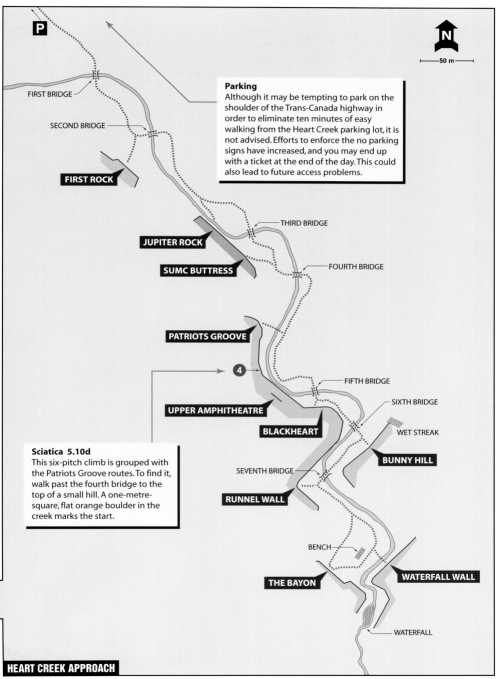

P

N

⊢—— 50 m ——⊣

FIRST BRIDGE

SECOND BRIDGE

FIRST ROCK

Parking
Although it may be tempting to park on the shoulder of the Trans-Canada highway in order to eliminate ten minutes of easy walking from the Heart Creek parking lot, it is not advised. Efforts to enforce the no parking signs have increased, and you may end up with a ticket at the end of the day. This could also lead to future access problems.

THIRD BRIDGE

JUPITER ROCK

SUMC BUTTRESS

FOURTH BRIDGE

PATRIOTS GROOVE

4

FIFTH BRIDGE

SIXTH BRIDGE

UPPER AMPHITHEATRE

WET STREAK

BLACKHEART

BUNNY HILL

SEVENTH BRIDGE

Sciatica 5.10d
This six-pitch climb is grouped with the Patriots Groove routes. To find it, walk past the fourth bridge to the top of a small hill. A one-metre-square, flat orange boulder in the creek marks the start.

RUNNEL WALL

BENCH

THE BAYON

WATERFALL WALL

WATERFALL

HEART CREEK APPROACH

FIRST ROCK

28 routes ←5.10 5.11 5.12 5.13→

This is an excellent wall with a fine assortment of great routes that's tucked away in the trees near the creek. The crag has an amazing collection of friendly holds—pockets, pods and positive edges—on bomber rock, but the popularity of the cliff is causing some of the best routes to polish. Expect to share First Rock with other parties on weekends and after work.

Approach: As the name implies, First Rock is the very first wall encountered upon entering the narrow valley. It's located on the right side of the canyon, shortly after crossing the first bridge. If you cross a second bridge, you just missed it.

First Rock

Routes are listed from left to right.

❶ Brownout 5.10c . . . .

8 bolts (21 m) Start off a small ledge accessed via a trail on the left end of the wall. A minimal selection of holds makes climbing past the yellow hole a real challenge. Once above the hole, continue up a fun slab to a series of small overlaps. Veer to the right and finish at the top of *Potentilla Pillar*. *(John Martin, 1995)*

❷ Potentilla Pillar 5.8 . . . .

10 bolts (29 m) Start in front of a tree on the left end of the wall. Climb through a bulge to gain a slab, continue past an anchor and follow a shallow groove to finish with a system of cracks. *(John Martin, 1995)*

❸ Heartfelt 5.10c . . . .

10 bolts (29 m) Easy climbing gains a high first bolt. A tough crux at the second bolt leads to nice 5.9 climbing through ledges (past an anchor on the right) to another tricky move over a small roof. *(John Martin, 2001)*

❹ Trio 5.6 . . . .

4 bolts (11 m) Great climbing on cool pods leads past a couple of ledges to the anchors. *(John Martin, 1993)*

❺ Heartline 5.7 . . . .

10 bolts (28 m) Continue above the anchors of *Trio*. Trend right across slabs to a fun roof. *(John Martin, 1995)*

❻ Less Than Zero 5.8 . . . .

4 bolts (12 m) Small pockets near the ground lead to great jugs and a big flake. Prepare for a tricky section leaving the big pod after the flake. *(John Martin, 1987)*

❼ Back to Zero 5.9 . . . .

5 bolts (13 m) Good edge climbing on the black face leads to a cruxy little roof at the top. *(Jon Jones, 1986)*

❽ A Dream of White Schnauzers 5.6 . .

10 bolts (? m) From the top of *Back to Zero*, continue upward on the face left of the loose corner. Because of the loose rock and debris, it's probably best to walk off the top instead of rappelling/lowering. *(John Martin, 1995)*

FIRST ROCK LEFT

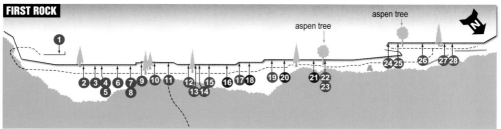

FIRST ROCK

aspen tree

aspen tree

9 Feel On 5.10b . . . .

5 bolts (13 m) Nice edge climbing leads to big holds in a flake. Above, a cool crux involving a long reach leads to easier climbing and the top. *(Andy Genereux, 1986)*

10 Feel On Baby 5.10b . . . .

5 bolts (14 m) Two crimpy sections are separated by big, blocky holds. *(Andy Genereux, 1987)*

11 Dynamic Dumpling 5.10d . . . .

4 bolts (15 m) Start two metres left of a short, left-facing corner. Good holds lead to a jug and a runout section on nice pods. *(Andy Genereux, 1986)*

12 Survival of the Fattest 5.10c . . . .

5 bolts (14 m) The stellar climbing on this pitch begins just right of a short, left-facing corner. Side-pulls lead to crimps, a perfect pod and the top. *(John Martin, 1993)*

13 Cavebird 5.9 . . . .

7 bolts (17 m) Follow a steeper-than-it-looks, juggy crack straight up to the highest anchor. *(Walter Lee, 1993)*

14 Pyramid Power 5.9 . . . .

4 bolts (12 m) Start on *Cavebird*, but follow the bolt line right of the flake. *(John Martin, 1993)*

15 Midnight Rambler 5.10c . . . .

4 bolts (12 m) Climb the light blue streak using great edges and the odd pod or pocket. *(Andy Genereux, 1986)*

16 Sweet Souvenir 5.11c . . . .

4 bolts (12 m) This tough, crimpy route is the first line right of the light blue streak. It requires some brute force to get to the ledge. *(E.J. Plimley & Michael Tessier, 2001)*

17 Honky Tonk Woman 5.10c . . . . . .

1 bolt + gear (10 m) Clip a high bolt on your way to the crack at five metres. Place a piece of gear (or two) in the crack then head for the anchors. *(Andy Genereux, 1986)*

18 Voodoo Lounge 5.11c . . . .

3 bolts (10 m) This great, bouldery route starts directly below the tallest tree growing on the right side of the high ledge. *(John Martin, 1995)*

19 Let It Bleed 5.10a . . . .

9 bolts (22 m) A vegetated start leads to nicer climbing above. Keep left of the corner/roof. *(John Martin, 1997)*

FIRST ROCK MIDDLE

20 Paint It Black 5.11a . . . .

10 bolts (21 m) This is the first route left of the big tree. Awkward climbing to underclings in the roof leads to great, airy climbing above. *(John Martin, 1996)*

21 Bitch 5.11b . . . .

3 bolts + gear (18 m) This ugly-looking route starts up a gear-protected corner before moving onto a face protected by rusty bolts. Finish up a dirty, gear-protected crack. Not recommended. *(Andy Genereux, 1986)*

22 Steel Wheels 5.10a . . . .

7 bolts (18 m) Start in front of an aspen tree. From the fourth bolt, trend left up a ramp and around a corner to a crack. Follow it back right to finish. *(John Martin, 2003)*

23 Sticky Fingers 5.10c . . . .

6 bolts (18 m) Climb *Steel Wheels* to the fourth bolt and continue above. Slopey holds on perfect rock lead to a hard-to-read crux. *(Andy Genereux & Bill Rennie, 1986)*

The next five routes are located on the far right-hand end of the wall at a small dirt ledge at the top of a small incline.

FIRST ROCK RIGHT

Bella Unterasinger on the Runnel Wall

24 Dandelions 5.8 . . . .

6 bolts (20 m) Start with unprotected climbing up an easy gully. After five metres, step right and finish up the slabby face. *(Jon Jones, 1986)*

25 Dead Flowers 5.10b . . . .

7 bolts (19 m) Start just right of the narrow, rocky gully. Nice pods lead to the first bolt and a stopper crux. Finish with miles of great slab. *(Andy Skuce, 1986)*

26 Brown Sugar 5.10a . . . .

3 bolts (10 m) Start off a small rock ledge. Tackle the bulge on pockets and edges and finish just over the roof above. *(John Martin, 1986)*

27 Heatburn 5.9. . . . .

3 bolts (10 m) Climb a slab to a no-hands stance before heading over a roof (a multitude of foot-holds ease the difficulty). Finish at the *Brown Sugar* anchor. A 5.10c variation (4 bolts, 12 m) continues directly above the no-hands stance to a tricky finish. *(John Martin, 1986)*

28 Wild Horses 5.9 . . . .

5 bolts (12 m) The right-most route features perfect grey rock with a couple of tricky sections. *(John Martin, 1986)*

JUPITER ROCK

26 routes   ←5.10 5.11 5.12 5.13→

Jupiter Rock features the same high-quality climbing and stone as its popular neighbor, First Rock, but boasts longer routes, less rock polish and fewer people. The slew of great 5.10s (with a handful of 5.11s) makes it well worth an extended visit, but the creek that runs along much of the base deters many passersby. In the early season, when the creek is high from melt water, getting on the wall is problematic at best, but by summer most of the routes become easily accessible and are well worth stopping for. The SUMC Wall, which is located in the trees just past Jupiter Rock, is also included in this zone.

Approach: Jupiter Rock is a couple of minutes upstream from First Rock on the right. If you reach the third bridge, you just missed it.

Jupiter Rock

Routes are listed from left to right.

① Limicoline 5.10c . . . .

Pitch 1 (5.10c, 8 bolts, 22 m) Start up a small slab that leads to some underclings. Work up tricky, right-trending sidepulls that lead to a small roof and the anchor. **Pitch 2** (5.10c, 4 bolts, 13 m) Four more bolts extend the pitch. *(John Martin (both), 1994)*

② Riparian 5.10a . . . .

Pitch 1 (5.9 8 bolts, 22 m) Follow a flake over a bulge to a roof. Surmount it on the left to gain a broken, left-facing corner. Climb directly to anchors below the treed ledge. **Pitch 2** (5.10a, 4 bolts, 13 m) Four more bolts extend the pitch. *(Andy Skuce (both), 1986)*

③ Aphrodite 5.10b . . . .

9 bolts (24 m) Brown hangers mark a line through multiple cruxes. The anchor is left of a big hueco. *(John Martin, 1993)*

④ Venus 5.10a . . . .

10 bolts (25 m) Use a thin seam to reach easier ground. Good holds in a flake lead to an anchor in the left side of a giant hueco at the top of the wall. *(Jon Jones, 1986)*

⑤ Ganymede 5.10c . . . .

9 bolts (25 m) Start two metres right of *Venus*. Climb straight up the broken, left-facing corner to an anchor in the back of the giant hueco. *(John Martin, 1993)*

⑥ Brontes 5.11a . . . .

8 bolts (23 m) Big moves between good holds will wear you down for the bouldery crux up high. A 5.10a variation (9 bolts, 23 m) climbs *Brontes* to the fourth bolt before heading right via one link-up bolt to finish on *Zippy the Pinhead*. *(Jon Jones, 1986; John Martin (var.), 1994)*

⑦ Zippy the Pinhead 5.11a . . . .

9 bolts (23 m) Some tough bulges down low lead to fun climbing above. Finish on *Brontes*. *(John Martin, 1994)*

⑧ Callisto 5.10a . . . .

12 bolts (28 m) This excellent, long route begins below a short corner. Fun climbing using great pockets leads into a left-facing corner near the top. Pull over the corner and finish up the vertical wall above. *(Chris Perry, 1983)*

⑨ For Your Eyes Only 5.10b . . . . . .

10 bolts (28 m) Start up *Callisto,* but branch right after the fourth bolt. Several 5.10 cruxes will keep you busy en route to the anchors. *(Andy Genereux, 1986)*

⑩ Puppet on a Chain 5.10c . . . .

8 bolts (26 m) Fun moves on mostly-positive holds equals a good route with several cruxes. *(Andy Genereux, 1986)*

⑪ Pacemaker 5.10c . . . .

9 bolts (26 m) A tricky start leads to easier terrain. Above, the angle and difficulties increase. *(John Martin, 1994)*

⑫ Heart of Darkness 5.11b . . . .

9 bolts (26 m) Begin below a grassy ledge. Above the ledge, enjoy nice face climbing on great rock. *(Jon Jones, 1987)*

⑬ Crimson Tide 5.11a . . . .

11 bolts (27 m) Begin just left of a small roof at three metres. Big moves between jugs lead through the initial bulge to a short, right-facing corner at the base of the yellow wall. From here, a couple of steeper, in-your-face cruxes guard the anchor. *(John Martin, 1996)*

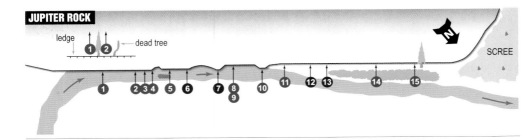

JUPITER ROCK

ledge — dead tree — SCREE

14 Heart of Gold 5.10c . . . .

10 bolts (26 m) A crux moving past the first bolt is followed by pleasant climbing to the base of the yellow wall. Continue up the yellow wall to another crux before the anchors. *(Andy Genereux, 1986)*

15 Last Call 5.10a . . . .

11 bolts (29 m) Start on the right end of the wall just left of a tree. A short slab leads to laybacking up a right-facing corner. Move onto the face right of the arête and over a big ledge en route to the anchor. *(John Martin, 1995)*

SUMC Buttress

This crag is part of the Jupiter Rock cliff band, but is located in the forest to the far left. To reach it, cross the third bridge on the main approach trail and watch for a trail leading into the trees on the right. Alternatively, hop the creek at the left end of Jupiter Rock and follow the cliff band into the trees (low water only). Routes are listed from left to right.

16 Glide 5.10b . . . .

6 bolts (15 m) Start between two trees growing next to the wall. Once through the initial, low bulge, enjoy easier climbing to the anchor. *(John Martin, 2000)*

17 Night and Day 5.10b . . . .

11 bolts (23 m) Climb *Glide* to the second bolt before trending right through slabby terrain to a short, vertical wall. Edges lead to another slab. Finish up a thin, vertical yellow streak *(Jason Rennie & Graig Langford, 2003)*

18 Original Route 5.10c . . . .

10 bolts (23 m) Climb direct on edges to a small tree on the slab at three-quarters height. Finish up the vertical, grey wall to the *Night and Day* anchor. *(Chris Perry, 1983)*

19 Fetish 5.10b . . . .

11 bolts (23 m) Climb just left of a moss streak and through a break in a small roof. Continue straight up, finishing up a short arête to the anchor. *(John Martin, 2004)*

JUPITER ROCK

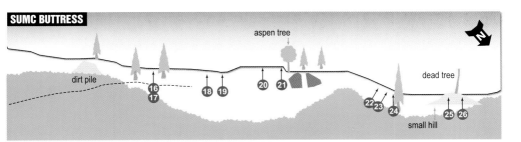

SUMC BUTTRESS

aspen tree

dirt pile

dead tree

small hill

---

⑳ Illusive Edge 5.10a . . . .

8 bolts (23 m) Start two metres left of the left-facing corner. A couple of low cruxes lead to a rest on a slabby ledge at mid-height. Continue straight up the arête above and finish with a short corner. *(John Martin, 2000)*

㉑ Hell's Bells 5.10a . . . .

10 bolts (25 m) Climb to a dirt ledge via a left-facing corner. Attack the bulge above head-on (the crux) or loop right for an easier, 5.8 solution. Continue up the juggy face right of the arête to the anchor. *(John Martin, 2010)*

㉒ Dancers at the End of Time 5.9 . .

6 bolts (15 m) Follow edges and sloping footholds up the left side of the bolt line. Layback up a crack and finish directly above to the anchor. *(John Martin, 2010)*

㉓ Avatar 5.10c . . . .

5 bolts (13 m) Start on *Dancers at the End of Time* and make a rightward traverse to reach the high, first bolt of

this climb. Balancey and technical moves tackle black rock and lead to a roof. Switch into layback mode for the small corner above. *(John Martin, 2010)*

㉔ Music of the Spheres 5.9 . . . .

5 bolts (13 m) This route is right of *Avatar*. Once at the base of the roof, make a big move before powering over the roof to clip the anchor. *(John Martin, 2010)*

㉕ Galileo 5.10a . . . .

9 bolts (21 m) Start left of a dead tree. Tricky moves lead past a roof to enjoyable, rambling climbing on jugs. Just when the climbing appears to get harder, a jug appears (and then it gets harder). *(John Martin, 2010)*

㉖ Sleeping Beauty 5.10a . . . .

11 bolts (26 m) This is the right-most route on the cliff. Fun face climbing ends with a right-facing corner. *(John Martin, 2010)*

SUMC BUTTRESS

AMPHITHEATRE SECTOR

27 routes   ←5.10 5.11 5.12 5.13→

This impossible-to-miss zone is comprised of the massive, blue-streaked wall on the right side of the valley and the shorter crags that sit on either end. It comes into view shortly after climbing a small hill just beyond the fourth bridge and features generally good stone and long routes. All four of the sectors (Patriots Groove, Sciatica, Upper Amphitheatre and Blackheart) get a varying amount of morning sun, but the shade arrives by early afternoon. The Upper Amphitheatre, which is high above the valley floor, is very secluded, but the other three zones offer crowd-free climbing as well, despite their trailside location.

Approach: The Amphitheatre Sector is located between the fourth and fifth Heart Creek bridges along the main trail. See each area for more detailed approach directions.

Patriot's Groove

To approach this small wall, hike over the fourth bridge and look for an area to cross the stream just before a small incline. Head into the trees to the base of the wall. Routes are listed from left to right.

❶ Data on Demand 5.11c . . . .

7 bolts (12 m) This is a good route up a yellow- and grey-streaked overhang. Climb past a short, left-facing corner before trending right up a diagonal crack.   (*Unknown*)

❷ Heartbeat 5.9 . . . .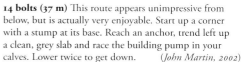

14 bolts (37 m) This route appears unimpressive from below, but is actually very enjoyable. Start up a corner with a stump at its base. Reach an anchor, trend left up a clean, grey slab and race the building pump in your calves. Lower twice to get down.   (*John Martin, 2002*)

❸ New Patriot 5.9 . . . .

14 bolts (37 m) Start on *Heartbeat*. At the first anchor, continue straight up the left side of the groove to a high anchor. Lower twice to get down.   (*John Martin, 2002*)

PATRIOT'S GROOVE

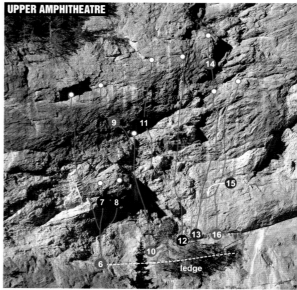

UPPER AMPHITHEATRE

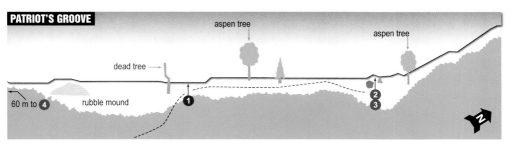

PATRIOT'S GROOVE

aspen tree

aspen tree

dead tree →

60 m to ④   rubble mound

---

④ Sciatica 5.10d . . . .

This is an easily-accessible six-pitch outing in the middle of Heart Creek. All you'll need is a 60-m rope, a fistful of draws and an itch to get up high. To find it, walk past the fourth bridge to the top of a small hill. A one-metre-square, flat orange boulder in the creek marks the start.

Pitch 1 (5.8, 3 bolts, 27 m) Climb an easy slab, staying right of the vegetated crack. Trend right to a small roof and an anchor.

Pitch 2 (5.8, 3 bolts, 23 m) Climb onto a vegetated ledge and up a black slab to a small roof. At the last bolt, trend left to an anchor below a big horizontal break.

Pitch 3 (5.10d, 8 bolts, 21 m) A well-textured black face leads to the base of a roof where the fun begins. Under cling leftward until you can reach a right-trending crack. Follow it past an overlap and up a left-facing corner to an anchor.

Pitch 4 (5.10d, 8 bolts, 23 m) Climb up and right to the base of a big roof. A few airy moves lead to slightly chossy rock and an anchor below a forked tree.

Pitch 5 (5.10b, 5 bolts, 20 m) Climb the blue streak left of the tree. Follow the corner and overhang to anchors on the slab above.

Pitch 6 (5.10d, 5 bolts, 14 m) Traverse left to the first bolt before continuing straight up on great water grooved crimps and pinches. Six rappels lead back to the ground. Hikers loiter near the creek below the route, so be extra careful not to dislodge loose rock.   (*Rob Owens, 2002*)

Upper Amphitheatre

The routes in this sector see little traffic and may be dusty, but the amazing array of holds and spectacular position should entice more climbers to venture up onto the ledge, To approach, contour rightward along the hillside from the right end of Blackheart Wall. Watch for a small platform below a huge yellow section of wall on the left and a clump of trees on the ledge on the right. Take care not to trundle rocks onto the trail below. Routes are listed from left to right.

⑤ Ground Floor, Going Up? 5.8 . . . . . .

5 bolts (25 m) This is the access pitch for the awesome routes above. Begin off a small platform below a huge yellow section of wall.   (*Marcus Norman, 2005*)

⑥ Open Project . . . .

This long, potential climb branches left off *Warmed By the Devils Fire* after a couple of bolts.

⑦ Warmed By the Devils Fire 5.12c . . . .

7 bolts (15 m) This short, bouldery route climbs straight out the middle of the steep overhang. Pull carefully past the chossy band at three-quarters height. A couple of bolts just left of the start might provide a direct start to the project mentioned above.   (*Knut Rokne, 2006*)

⑧ The Good Life 5.12d . . . .

7 bolts (15 m) Climb *Warmed By the Devils Fire* to the second bolt. Head right past a few desperate moves to better holds. (*PREP: Marcus Norman; FA: Knut Rokne, 2005*)

⑨ Open Project . . . .

This impressive-looking line continues up and left from the anchor of *Slackline King*.

⑩ Slackline King 5.10d . . . .

7 bolts (17 m) This pitch has some amazing holds. Start just left of a dead tree and follow blue stone into a corner. Finish on anchors above.   (*Marcus Norman, 2005*)

⑪ Arrival of the Fittest 5.12b . . .

14 bolts (30 m) Climb *Slackline Kings* to the fifth bolt. Branch right and follow a blue streak over two ledges to the base of a black wall. Excellent and pumpy climbing to the anchor will have your forearms burning. Only the fittest will arrive.   (*Marcus Norman, 2005*)

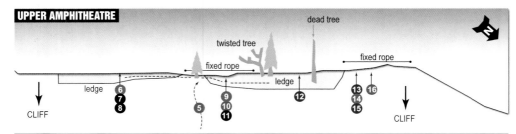

UPPER AMPHITHEATRE

dead tree

twisted tree

fixed rope

fixed rope

ledge

ledge

6
7
8

9
10
11

5

12

13 16
14
15

CLIFF

CLIFF

N

---

⑫ The Convincer 5.12b ....

11 bolts (31 m) Small boulder problems separated by buckets lead to an incredibly beautiful blue streak peppered with awesome holds. The quality of this pitch was meant to "convince" climbers that the ledge was worthy of more attention. *(Marcus Norman, 2004)*

⑬ Sling Thing 5.11b ....

8 bolts (26 m) Start at the right end of the tree ledge. Climb a small, left-facing corner before following a faint blue streak into the lightning bolt corner above. Make an airy traverse leftward, crank over the roof and forge up to the anchor. *(PREP: Randy Colman; FA: Knut Rokne, 2005)*

⑭ Open Project ....

Continue above the anchors of *Sling Thing*.

⑮ Skyscraper 5.11c ....

9 bolts (28 m) Climb *Sling Thing* to the third bolt. Branch right using hard-to-find holds to gain the security of the flakes. A tricky leftward move leads to the lightning bolt corner. Continue up and left via awesome but sporty terrain. *(PREP: Randy Colman; FA: Marcus Norman, 2005)*

⑯ Open Project ....

This direct start to *Skyscraper* needs another bolt.

Blackheart   to

This black wall is nestled in the trees on the left end of the massive Amphitheatre. The majority of the lines are long and start off a ledge on the right side. To approach, cut into the trees on the right shortly before the fifth bridge. Routes are listed from left to right.

⑰ Half a Heart 5.9 ....

5 bolts (19 m) Start to the left of a tree growing on the left end of the slab. After two bolts, trend right to the base of a roof. Pull the lip and finish above. *(John Martin, 1996)*

⑱ Kiss and Tell 5.10a ....

5 bolts (19 m) Start to the right of a tree growing on the left end of the slab. The initial steep section is the crux, followed by easy climbing above. *(John Martin, 2001)*

⑲ Have a Heart 5.10a ....

5 bolts (19 m) Start just left of two small trees growing on the slab. A cruxy opening gains the slab above. Pull a roof near the top before clipping the anchor. *(John Martin, 1996)*

⑳ Shoot from the Hip 5.10a ....

6 bolts (21 m) Start two metres right of two trees growing on the slab. A couple tricky slab moves lead to easier climbing above and a roof near the top. Finish at the *Have a Heart* anchor. *(John Martin, 2001)*

㉑ Heart Throb 5.10b ....

11 bolts (27 m) This is the right-most route, just left of a short, left-facing corner below the ledge. After some tedious slab climbing, climb up a vertical headwall on buckets with the occasional tricky move. *(John Martin, 1996)*

㉒ Bleeding Heart 5.11b ....

9 bolts (20 m) This is the left-most route and starts off a good ledge. Fun, well-textured stone leads to a bouldery sequence before the anchor. Finish on the anchors of *Heart Throb*. *(John Martin, 1996)*

The plant *Castilleja*, commonly known as Indian Paintbrush, is one of the many colourful wildflowers visible on the trail to Heart Creek. The flowers are edible and sweet, and were consumed in moderation by various Native American tribes as a condiment with other fresh greens.

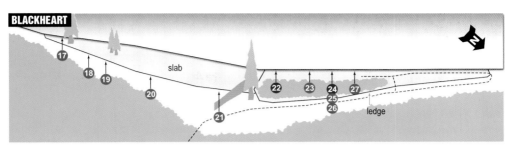

BLACKHEART

slab

ledge

23 Braveheart 5.10b . . . .

10 bolts (24 m) This fun route weaves through a series of small corner features just left of the big black corner.

(John Martin, 1996)

24 Blackheart Direct 5.11a . . . .

9 bolts (28 m) Start directly below the big, black corner. Easy climbing leads to a rightward crux and the base of a big corner. A small runout leads to good holds in the corner and a clear path to the top. *(John Martin, 1986)*

25 Blackheart 5.10b . . . .

9 bolts (28 m) Climb *Blackheart Direct* to the fourth bolt. Follow three bolts out right that avoid the crux of that climb and rejoin it to finish. *(John Martin, 1987)*

26 Heart of Stone 5.10c . . . .

10 bolts (28 m) Climb the first three bolts of *Blackheart Direct*. Head right through prickly rock and good holds toward a crack. After a few moves along the crack, a bouldery and balancey crux leads over a roof into tricky climbing that gains the anchor. *(John Martin, 1996)*

27 Heartbreaker 5.10b . . . .

9 bolts (26 m) Start two metres right of *Blackheart Direct*. Follow a right-trending line that links a corner into a crack. The crux is at the crack's top. *(John Martin, 1996)*

BLACKHEART

25 26

22 23 24 27 ledge

21

BUNNY HILL SECTOR

19 routes   ←5.10 5.11 5.12 5.13→

This zone consists of two slabby walls that sit on opposite sides of the creek. It's definitely the place to come to get your slab on and good footwork will get you much higher on these routes than brute strength alone. This is a popular area for beginners and groups.

Approach: Continue along the trail past the massive Amphitheatre wall to the sixth bridge. The *Bunny Hill* is immediately on the left after the sixth bridge and the *Runnel Wall* is in the trees on the right just after the seventh bridge.

Bunny Hill

This crag features long, well-protected slab routes. During spring run-off and after heavy rainfall, the base of the wall might be under water. Routes are listed from left to right.

1 Heartless 5.10b . . . .

6 bolts (15 m) This is the first route right of the large, permanently wet scoop. Good slab climbing leads to big holds over the roof. (*John Martin, 1995*)

2 Rat in a Cage 5.10a . . . .

4 bolts (11 m) Sparse holds make the low bulge more difficult than expected. Continue upward until it's possible to pull right around the corner. (*John Martin, 1997*)

3 Chip Butty 5.10a . . . .

4 bolts (11 m) This pitch starts just right of the left-facing corner. Climb through a series of overlaps. The hardest moves are near the bottom. (*John Martin, 1997*)

4 Simple 5.4 . . . .

4 bolts (11 m) The name is apt. Follow a juggy, diagonal seam leftward to the *Chip Butty* anchor. (*John Martin, 1997*)

5 You Oughtta' Know 5.9 . . . .

9 bolts (22 m) This is a nice, long slab route that gets progressively harder. (*John Martin, 1995*)

6 Come As You Are 5.9 . . . .

6 bolts (17 m) Climb past a diagonal crack to tricky moves by the third bolt. Easier above. (*John Martin, 1995*)

BUNNY HILL

1   2   3   4   5   6   7   8   9   10

7 **Until It Sleeps** 5.10d . . . .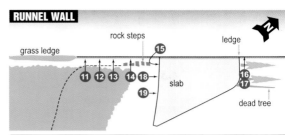

5 bolts (15 m) Easy climbing gains a high first bolt followed by two cruxes involving underclings and poor footholds. (*John Martin 1997*)

8 **Contemporary Cuisine** 5.10b

8 bolts (19 m) After a high first bolt, high-step through small yet positive flakes to some press moves and the roof crux. (*Chris Miller, 1994*)

9 **Rough, but Well Groomed** 5.9 . . . . .

7 bolts (19 m) Big holds aren't always positive. Good footwork will help. (*Chris Miller, 1994*)

10 **Carpe Diem** 5.10c . . . .

7 bolts (17 m) This route starts in a clump of trees on the right end of the wall. A never-ending series of underclings leads to the anchor. (*John Martin, 2000*)

Runnel Wall

From the seventh bridge, follow a trail rightward into the trees to approach. Routes are listed from left to right.

11 **The Tipsy Diaries** 5.10/5.11? . . . .

5 bolts (9 m) Begin at the right end of the small grass ledge growing against the base. Follow a left trending corner before pulling over onto the slab above. (*Unknown*)

12 **Scant Progress** 5.10/5.11? . . . .

4 bolts (9 m) Follow small edges through a vertical start to a slab finish just right of the white streak. (*Unknown*)

13 **Pressed to Act** 5.10/5.11? . . . .

3 bolts (8 m) A bulge off the ground leads to slab climbing all the way to the anchor. (*Unknown*)

14 **Piranha** 5.10/5.11? . . . .

2 bolts (8 m) Climb the grey slab to anchors. (*Unknown*)

15 **Runnel Vision** 5.4 . . . .

4 bolts (19 m) Start in the corner and follow water runnels to an anchor above a dirt slope. From the third bolt, a variation traverses right before finishing on the anchors of *Light at the End of the Runnel*. (*Unknown*)

16 **Departure** 5.10b . . . .

8 bolts (25 m) From the top of *Runnel Vision*, continue up the slab for two bolts before making a tricky transition onto

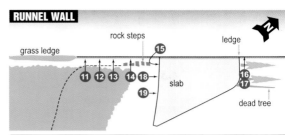

the face. A final, tricky bulge gains the anchor. (*Unknown*)

17 **Runnel You Want** 5.8 . . . .

7 bolts (28 m) Continue above the anchors of *Runnel Vision* following a fun, water-grooved slab. (*Unknown*)

18 **Light at the End of the Runnel** 5.4 . .

4 bolts (15 m) Start in the middle of the slab and follow one, long water runnel to a tree anchor. (*Unknown*)

19 **Runnel in the Jungle** 5.4 . . . .

3 bolts (15 m) This is the right-most route. Follow a low-angled slab with shallow water runnels. (*Unknown*)

RUNNEL WALL

THE BAYON SECTOR

30 routes ←5.10 5.11 5.12 5.13→

The Bayon is a short, steep swell of grey limestone hidden in the trees at the back of Heart Creek canyon. Like the other crags in this chapter, it's got a relatively easy approach and this makes it very popular with the after-work crowd. The cliff sees no sun, which makes it cooler than the other walls, and seeps heavily early in the season and after rainfall. The Bayon is home to the hardest routes at Heart Creek and the climbs are viciously short and powerful—come prepared. If this crag is on your hit list, pack a stick clip since most of the routes where designed with one in mind. The Waterfall Wall, which is also located at the far end of the canyon, is included in this section and has some quality, moderate pitches making it a great compliment to the Bayon.

Approach: From the Bunny Wall, continue along the trail for a couple minutes to the end of the canyon. Turn right and follow the cliff line into the forest to the base of the Bayon wall.

The Bayon

Routes are listed from left to right.

❶ Old Timer 5.13c . . . .

5 bolts (12 m) This short, powerful route sits by itself on a ledge on the far left end of the crag. A hard, crimpy start is followed by sustained climbing to a final crux before the anchor. *(PREP: JD LeBlanc; FA: Scott Milton, 2001)*

❷ Beat Farmer 5.12a . . . .

6 bolts (16 m) Scramble onto the blocky ledge to start. Head up a short, right-facing corner to another ledge and continue up the overhanging wall to a difficult finish. *(Marcus Norman, 2003)*

❸ Palm Sisters 5.12b . . . .

7 bolts (16 m) Scramble onto the blocky ledge to start. A tough opening gives way to multiple ledges. Rest up—the slopers near the anchor are brutal *(Dave Carley, 1997)*

❹ An Arm and a Leg 5.12b . . . .

8 bolts (18 m) Start on the right side of the blocky ledge. Difficult moves up a small, left-facing corner and flake lead to a hard slap to a small ledge. *(Randy Colman, 2001)*

❺ Mumblebunny 5.12c . . . .

9 bolts (19 m) Start on the far right side of the blocky ledge. Traverse right with difficulty into a left-facing corner. Sustained technical climbing for the next four bolts ends with a rest and short overhang. *(Randy Colman, 2001)*

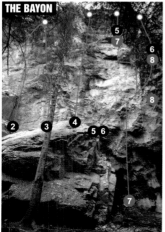

THE BAYON

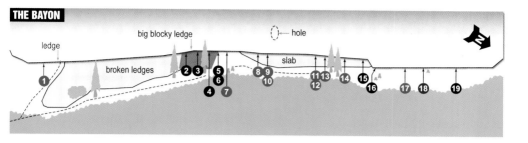

THE BAYON

ledge · big blocky ledge · hole · broken ledges · slab

6 Kung Pow 5.12b

10 bolts (19 m) Climb *Mumblebunny* to the base of the left-facing corner. Trend right around the corner before climbing straight up via nice edges. Finish with hard moves above the ledge. *(Marcus Norman, 2001)*

7 Mumblebunny Direct 5.13b

9 bolts (19 m) Start just right of the base of the blocky ledge. A vicious boulder problem connects into *Mumblebunney*. *(Scott Milton, 2001)*

8 Splash Down 5.13c

12 bolts (19 m) Start off the small slab at the base of the wall. Sustained, hard crimping leads left to finish on *Kung Pow*. *(PREP: Joel Labonte; FA: Derek Galloway, 2009)*

9 Tub Trauma 5.13a

5 bolts (9 m) Climb to the left of a large hole at five metres. Cool underclings and fun, slopey slaps lead to the anchor. *(PREP: Daren Tremaine; FA: Lev Pinter, 2001)*

10 Sonnie's Route 5.13a

6 bolts (12 m) Climb *Tub Trauma* to the second bolt before traversing right through the bottom of the hole. Continue straight up to anchors. *(Sonnie Trotter, 2004)*

11 Barb Wire 5.13a

5 bolts (12 m) Start below a left-facing stepped corner and roof system. Follow it to a few hard crimp moves and an easier finish. *(Derek Galloway, 2003)*

12 Intergalactic Planetary 5.13b

5 bolts (12 m) Climb *Barb Wire* to the second bolt. A hard boulder problem leads to a bolt out right. Easier climbing gains the anchor. *(Josh Muller, 2004)*

13 May the Funk Be with You 5.13b

5 bolts (13 m) Start just right of *Barb Wire*. Climb a short, left-facing corner before busting out your bag of tricks to get through the next two bolts. *(Daren Tremaine, 2000)*

14 Salty 5.13?

6 bolts (14 m) This quality route starts just right of two trees growing next to the wall. An opening boulder problem gains a jug over a small roof below the real business: a cool crux through powerful underclings and crimpers. The crux undercling has crumbled and the viability of the route is now in question. *(Daren Tremaine, 1999)*

15 The Throbbing Affirmation Of Love 5.12c

5 bolts (14 m) Climb the left side of a corner system to a great rest. The crux leads through the shallow corner above, finishing at the *Salty* anchor. *(Daren Tremaine, 1999)*

16 Dutch Boy Magic 5.12d

6 bolts (15 m) This route follows the corner and arête into a short face climbing section before finishing through ledges. This route will feel much harder than 5.12d until you unlock all of its subtleties. *(Nils Preshaw, 1999)*

17 Hecubus 5.13a

2 bolts (7 m) This routes is simply a boulder problem on a rope. *(Marcus Norman, 2000)*

18 Clump 5.11d

2 bolts (7 m) Navigate through vicious crimps en route to the anchor over the ledge. *(Marcus Norman, 1999)*

19 Short-lived Freedom 5.12c

1 bolt (7 m) This climb is characterized by a crimpy and balancey start followed by boulder moves and a mantle finish. *(Joel Labonte, 2010)*

Waterfall Wall

Routes are located from left to right.

20 Late Shift 5.10a . . . .

13 bolts (29 m) Start on the left-hand side of the wall where the trail dives into the woods. Head for the yellow rock scar before traversing right to gain a small corner and up over a roof. Long slings help with the drag. (*John Martin, 2004*)

21 Omnivore 5.10d . . . .

11 bolts (28 m) Start to the left of an often-wet hole. Climb through overlaps and angle right to a diagonal seam. More overlaps gain the anchor. (*John Martin, 1994*)

22 Big Chill 5.11a . . . .

7 bolts (17 m) Start just right of the often-wet hole. By-pass the angling roof on the left and continuing straight up. A small roof guards the anchor. (*John Martin, 2004*)

23 Trail's End 5.11a . . . .

8 bolts (15 m) Climb up and around the right side of the angling roof before veering slightly to the right. Follow overlaps to the anchor. (*John Martin, 1993*)

24 Masterbretter 5.11b . . . .

9 bolts (15 m) From the base of a diagonal fault, climb

up and left to yellow rock above an overlap. Finesse some bulges on the way to the anchor. (*Brett Mitchelson, 2000*)

25 Les Nuages 5.10d . . . .

6 bolts (16 m) Head up the yellow streak at the base of the diagonal fault. Move right after the fourth bolt then straight up to the anchor. (*John Martin, 1993*)

26 Fifty-two Pickup 5.10c . . . .

6 bolts (16 m) Head for a small roof, crank the lip on jugs and finish on nice rock. Devious! (*John Martin, 2004*)

27 Lazarus 5.11b . . . .

6 bolts (12 m) A boulder problem surmounts the roof. Great edge climbing leads upward. (*John Martin, 1993*)

28 Stretchmarks 5.10d . . . .

6 bolts (13 m) Start in a low corner and follow a faint break straight up on good rock. (*John Martin, 1993*)

29 Downdraft 5.10a . . . .

5 bolts (13 m) Start as for *Stretchmarks*. Head right to the first bolt and then directly upward. (*John Martin, 1993*)

30 Gridlock 5.10a . . . .

5 bolts (13 m) Bouldery moves off the ground lead to easier ground above. (*John Martin, 1993*)

WATERFALL WALL

Gery Unterasinger on The Convincer (5.12b) at the Upper Amphitheatre.

Some experiences come and go, but others have an impact so great, they change your life indefinitely. It was the winter of '94, and instead of buying me Christmas presents, my incredibly thoughtful parents took me on a ski trip to Alberta. Upon reflection, I'm now convinced that this voyage out west fundamentally changed me—my old life ended and my real life began on the first day of that family vacation.

I remember thinking how incredible the Rocky Mountains looked from the view of my window seat. They were lit by a late-morning sun, each peak glistening like a sharpened knife. The air in Calgary was summerlike from a rare Chinook wind, but my mind was fixed on getting out of the city ASAP and into those calling giants to the west.

There's an indescribable feeling when driving into the mouth of the Canadian Rockies for the first time. It's almost like a warm embrace, which is a paradox of sorts when you think about how cold they often are. I had never seen anything so powerful in my life and I recall jumping out of the car every two minutes to take pictures—it must have taken us hours to get to Canmore. And still, to this day, that stretch of beauty extending from Mount Yamnuska to Lake Louise is unparalleled in my eyes.

Shadows and light dance between the valleys provoking our imaginations, and each bend in the road offers a new perspective, a fresh adventure. Driving past the glorious and ancient Castle Mountain will remind you of Mother Nature's upper hand. Under this massive peak, in this crazy place, she is the boss. Anytime you leave the car and enter her world, you'll want to be prepared. Sun, wind, rain and hail can all occur in a matter of minutes, but it's always back to sun again. She will test your desire to be where you are, (which is where you want to be) and she will reward you for your visit with waterfalls, rainbows and lungs full of clean alpine air. It's a truly stimulating environment.

That week I surfed more powder than I had ever dreamed I could. I skated on a frozen Lake Louise and hiked around back to watch ice climbers work their magic on the famous

○ LAKE LOUISE BY SONNIE TROTTER

quartzite cliffs. I hadn't yet started climbing rocks myself, but the fire to be outside and play in this wild wonderland had definitely been ignited. I went home counting the days for when I could return.

As it turns out, it was three summers before the opportunity came again, and those years felt like

an eternity to a teenager stuck in south-
ern Ontario. After a number of seasons
climbing plastic, I got invited to com-
pete at the Junior National Championships in Nanaimo. My parents agreed to
take me back out west and turn it into
a "road trip" of sorts that would stretch
from Big Rock, Alberta to Horne Lake,
B.C. Our first stop was the Alpine Club
of Canada in Canmore, where I was
happily directed across the valley to the
pocketed cliffs of Grassi Lakes. After
shaking off the sparkling charm, it took
all of 10 seconds to meet some friendly
locals to climb with. It was here that I
ticked my first 5.12b, 5.12c and 5.12d,
each one steeper (and more fun) than
the last.

Then it was on to Lake Louise where I
climbed my first trad route, a 5.9 crack
system ending half way up the impressive Air Voyage wall. Next up was *Dew-
line* (5.11c), the tallest single pitch climb

ANDREW BURR

I had yet completed, and my hands shook from exposure when lowering from the chains.
In the Rockies, I met a network of passionate people who had moved to the area simply to
climb—they lived and breathed for it, the same way I did. There was an active community
in the Bow Valley that I admired, they knew what they had, and they valued every inch of it.

Since that first family vacation over a decade ago, I have become quite addicted to traveling
and climbing. I blame my folks. I've gone coast-to-coast and around the world in search of
quality lines, stunning backdrops and friendly communities. I've sampled some of the best
sport climbing around and even ticked a few gems here and there, but still, to me, no place
I've been to offers the same high-quality rock, paired with the extraordinary scenery and un-
limited possibilities, as the Bow Valley. There's more to do and see than anyone could hope
for in a lifetime. And it's steep. Which is why I keep going back, year after year. Which is
why we all keep going back, because we know what it has to offer, and it's enough to change
your world indefinitely.

CHAPTER 5
GROTTO CANYON

Grotto Canyon is a narrow gorge with a high concentration of routes in close proximity to one another. You can choose to climb in the creek bottom where you will enjoy a cool breeze and the scrutiny of interested weekend hikers, or you can head up into the forest to relax in shaded solitude. The canyon has a good selection of climbs, ranging from 5.7 to 5.13, that will keep all members of your party busy unlocking sequences on the highly technical slabs, vertical faces and gentle overhangs. Most routes start up compact, water-polished limestone, but give way to nicely textured rock above.

Grotto Canyon is home to some of the earliest sport climbs in the Canadian Rockies and hardware may date all the way back to 1982. Although many routes have been upgraded, expect to encounter the odd homemade hanger and tree anchor—it's good to come prepared. Like many early sport crags in North America, this area saw a brief period of hold manufacturing, which is evident on some of the Water Wall routes. Luckily, the practice was not replicated to the same extent anywhere else in the Bow Valley.

CONDITIONS

Except for the right end of the Water Wall and the Alley, the smooth, water-worn cliffs of Grotto Canyon see minimal seepage and make a great choice for post-rainfall climbing, especially if there's a slight breeze to speed drying. The canyon also provides a couple of great early- and late-season crags. The Water Wall and the Hemingway Wall both see sun for half the day and provide comfortable climbing in a variety of conditions. The remainder of the walls in the canyon also provide good multi-season climbing and compliment the Water and Hemingway walls nicely. Use daily conditions and crag aspect to make your selection. Likely the biggest issue in Grotto Canyon is seasonal creek meltwater, which can affect both the hiking *and* the climbing. High stream flows early in the season or after serious storms can make it difficult, but not impossible, to get into the canyon and to the base of many climbs.

APPROACH

From Canmore: Drive east on Highway 1A (Bow Valley Trail). After passing Gap Lake on your right, turn left at the "Baymag Plant #2" sign. Follow a dirt road for 30 metres before turning left onto a second, rougher dirt road, which terminates at the parking area. If the state of this second road concerns you, park opposite the turnoff being careful not to block access to the gravel pit. Walking from here adds about 10 minutes to the estimated approach times for the crags.

From Calgary: Drive west on the Trans-Canada Highway toward Canmore. Take Exit 114 for Exshaw and head north on Highway 1X/40. At the intersection with Highway 1A, set your trip metre to zero and turn left, heading west toward Exshaw. At 11.2 km (6.9 Miles) turn right at the "Baymag Plant #2" sign. From here, follow the post-sign driving/parking directions detailed in the paragraph above.

Hiking: From the parking area, hike up and over a small, grassy hill and follow a rocky trail that leads to the mouth of Grotto Canyon and a memorial bench. From the bench, either hike straight up the creek bed or follow a trail on the right across a polished slab and into the woods. The forested option is advisable when the creek is high or if you want to avoid multiple creek crossings.

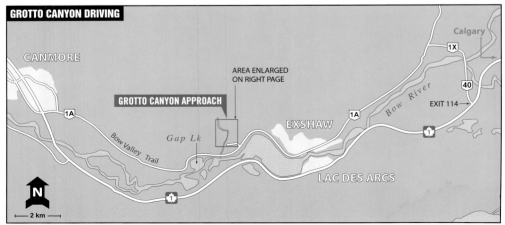

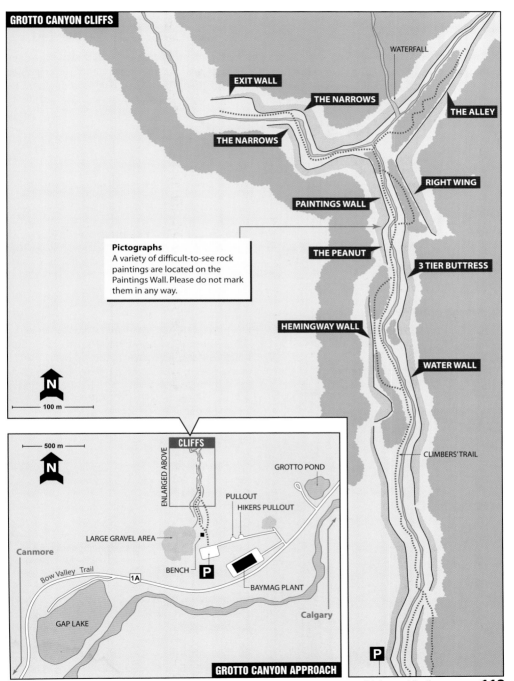

GROTTO CANYON CLIFFS

WATERFALL

EXIT WALL

THE NARROWS

THE ALLEY

THE NARROWS

RIGHT WING

PAINTINGS WALL

Pictographs
A variety of difficult-to-see rock paintings are located on the Paintings Wall. Please do not mark them in any way.

THE PEANUT

3 TIER BUTTRESS

HEMINGWAY WALL

WATER WALL

N

100 m

CLIMBERS' TRAIL

CLIFFS

ENLARGED ABOVE

500 m

N

GROTTO POND

PULLOUT

HIKERS PULLOUT

LARGE GRAVEL AREA

Canmore

Bow Valley Trail

1A

BENCH

P

BAYMAG PLANT

Calgary

GAP LAKE

P

GROTTO CANYON APPROACH

WATER WALL

40 routes

The routes at the Water Wall range from slabby, technical lines on the left to bold, featureless routes in the middle and overhanging power-endurance testpieces on the right. The left end of the crag dries quickly after rainfall, but the right side does not and is also affected by seasonal seepage. Included in this section is the Three Tier Buttress and Peanut, both located just upstream from the Water Wall.

Approach: When hiking into the canyon, this is the first wall on the right side.

Water Wall

Routes are listed from left to right.

1 Raindust 5.10c . . . . ☐
3 bolts (10 m) Start to the right of the corner and head up the slab. *(Sean Dougherty, 1985)*

2 Soft Option 5.10a . . . . ☐
3 bolts (10 m) Up the slab you go! *(John Martin, 1992)*

3 Kinesthesia 5.9 . . . . ☐
3 bolts (10 m) Climb straight up the grey slab passing a small roof on the left. *(John Martin, 1992)*

4 Breezin' 5.7 . . . . ☐
3 bolts (9 m) From the ground, follow a small ramp to the slab above. *(Dave Morgan, 1985)*

WATER WALL

5 Ill Wind 5.9 . . . . ☐
3 bolts (9 m) Start behind a small cluster of trees. Trend up and left through a steep section that eventually turns into a slab. *(Sean Dougherty, 1985)*

6 Canary in a Coal Mine 5.9 . . . . ☐
4 bolts (12 m) The slabby, restful start makes the roof feel easier than on the adjacent climbs. *(Sean Dougherty, 1985)*

7 Deviant Behaviour 5.10a . . . . ☐
4 bolts (12 m) Pull over the roof and follow a small corner to the top. *(Sean Dougherty, 1985)*

8 Loose Lips Sink Ships 5.10c . . . . . ☐
4 bolts (12 m) Start in a faint, right-facing corner. Pull through the roof on sidepulls. *(Andy Genereux, 1985)*

9 Lip Service 5.10d . . . . ☐
3 bolts (11 m) Climb to a large, flat jug at the lip of the roof. A few hard moves get you over the lip. Continue to anchors above the break. *(Sean Dougherty, 1985)*

10 Power Play 5.10c . . . . ☐
4 bolts (11 m) Start two metres left of the large, left-facing corner. Climb over the roof and follow a blocky corner to the top. *(Sean Dougherty, 1985)*

11 Spring Clean 5.10a . . . . ☐
4 bolts (10 m) Start in the big, left-facing corner. A few hard moves will deposit you over a roof and into another corner that leads to the anchors. *(Chas Yonge, 1985)*

12 Denkem 5.10a . . . . ☐
2 bolts (9 m) This route is located just right of the big, left-facing corner. *(Dennis Kemp, 1986)*

13 The Ablutor 5.10c . . . . ☐
3 bolts (9 m) This route is located three metres right of

the big, left-facing corner and follows a thin blue streak. It's tricky between the first two bolts. *(Chas Yonge, 1985)*

⑭ Scarface 5.11b .... ☐

3 bolts (12 m) This pitch starts up a very faint, open-book corner on the river-polished base of the wall. Climb straight up to anchors. *(Sean Dougherty, 1985)*

⑮ For Whom the Bell Tolls 5.11b .... ☐

4 bolts (10 m) Climb straight up to anchors. *(Sean Dougherty, 1985)*

⑯ Reflex Action 5.11d .. ☐

3 bolts (13 m) A slippery start gives way to edges and smears. Head slightly left after the first bolt before finishing on anchors to the right. *(Sean Dougherty, 1985)*

⑰ Cerebral Gore-tex 5.11c ☐

3 bolts (13 m) A river-polished start gives way to edges and smears. Trend right to anchors. Scary. *(Brian Balazs, 1985)*

⑱ Across the River and into a Tree 5.11c .... ☐

2 bolts (13 m) Start in a very small, right-facing corner and roof where the Water Wall changes character from climbable to seemingly impossible. A few difficult moves finesse around the first bolt. *(Dave Morgan, 1984)*

⑲ Cause and Effect 5.13a .... ☐

4 bolts (11 m) Start on *Across the River and Into the Trees,* but head right to a powerful crux on small crimps and lousy footholds. *(PREP: Shep Steiner; FA: Todd Guyn, 1991)*

⑳ Open Project .... ☐

㉑ Burn Hollywood Burn 5.13b .... ☐

5 bolts (12 m) Powerful pulls between crimps lead to a stance under the roof. A couple more hard moves seal the deal. *(PREP: Colin Zacharias; FA: Todd Guyn, 1991)*

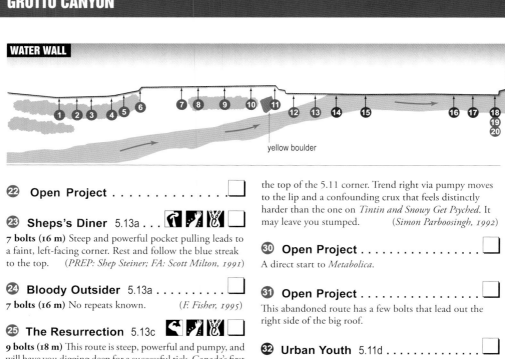

WATER WALL

yellow boulder

22 Open Project . . . .

23 Sheps's Diner 5.13a . . .

7 bolts (16 m) Steep and powerful pocket pulling leads to a faint, left-facing corner. Rest and follow the blue streak to the top.   (*PREP: Shep Steiner; FA: Scott Milton, 1991*)

24 Bloody Outsider 5.13a . . . .

7 bolts (16 m) No repeats known.   (*F. Fisher, 1995*)

25 The Resurrection 5.13c

9 bolts (18 m) This route is steep, powerful and pumpy, and will have you digging deep for a successful tick. Canada's first of the grade. (*PREP: Bruce Howatt; FA: Todd Guyn, 1991*)

26 Crimes of Passion 5.12d

7 bolts (14 m) This sustained climb features a full range of manufactured grips that lead to a big move near the top. It's fun if you can put the chipping debauchery in the back of your mind.   (*Marc Dube, 1990*)

27 Vapour Trails 5.13d . . . .

8 bolts (17 m) This difficult line has lost many holds over the years. The current status is unknown. (*Daren Tremaine, 1995*)

Traditionally, the next two climbs start by aiding to the first or second bolt, depending on how wet the slab is. The slab does go free, but doesn't increase the route's grade. It's just a chance to one-up your buddy.

**28 Tintin and Snowy
Get Psyched** 5.12d . . . .

8 bolts (16 m) Climb a 5.11 corner to a good shake at the top. Increasingly difficulty moves lead up and left to the lip, were you'll come face to come with the technical and powerful crux.   (*Simon Parboosingh, 1990*)

29 Metabolica 5.13a . . . .

10 bolts (16 m) Follow *Tintin and Snowy Get Psyched* to

the top of the 5.11 corner. Trend right via pumpy moves to the lip and a confounding crux that feels distinctly harder than the one on *Tintin and Snowy Get Psyched*. It may leave you stumped.   (*Simon Parboosingh, 1992*)

30 Open Project . . . .

A direct start to *Metabolica*.

31 Open Project . . . .

This abandoned route has a few bolts that lead out the right side of the big roof.

32 Urban Youth 5.11d . . . .

5 bolts (16 m) Begin off a vegetated ledge on the far right side of the Water Wall. Follow yellow rock through a small corner and roof to a horizontal break. From the break, head straight up to a chain anchor over the top.   (*Marcel Lehoux & Peter Charkiw, 1988*)

33 The Sting 5.10d . . . .

3 bolts (25 m) Start just left of the corner. A big runout between the first and second bolt, and funky tree anchor construction mars an otherwise decent climb.   (*Andy Genereux, 1985*)

Three Tier Buttress

This crag sits on the right-hand side of the creek just upstream from the left end of the Water Wall. The routes are steep and finish with tree anchors. The crag seeps throughout most of the year and consequently sees very little traffic. Routes are listed from left to right.

34 Stiff Upper Lip 5.10d . . . .

5 bolts (12 m) Climb up and over a series of small roofs on the way to out-of-sight anchors.   (*Geoff Powter, 1992*)

35 Short and Curly 5.10d . . . . . .

3 bolts (16 m) Climb *Stiff Upper Lip* to the horizontal

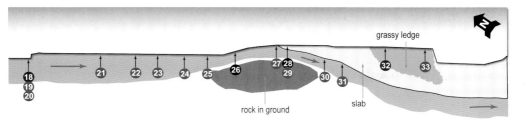

break before heading right. Follow an obvious weakness past two bolts to a tree anchor.

(Dave Morgan & Mark Zimmerman, 1985)

36 Too Low for Zero 5.11b . . . .

3 bolts (14 m) A featureless start leads to a bulge protected by two pitons. Trend right, following an obvious weakness to a tree anchor. *(Sean Dougherty, 1985)*

37 High Octane 5.11c . . . .

2 bolts (14 m) This pitch is located in the center of the wall and, with only two bolts, should keep you focused if you decide to step up to the plate. The tree anchor is over the top. *(Mark DeLeeuw, 1985)*

38 Dr. No 5.12b . . . .

5 bolts (14 m) Head up a shallow, open-book corner and surmount a couple of bulges on the way to a horizontal break. From here, three bolts protect fantastic climbing on pristine stone en route to the top. *(Joe Buszowski, 1988)*

39 Mr. Olympia 5.11d . . . .

4 bolts (13 m) This climb features a ridiculously high first bolt and committing moves above. Continue up and right to a tree anchor. *(Sean Dougherty, 1987)*

The Peanut

Directly across from the left end of the Tree Tier Buttress sits a lone route on a small wall.

40 KP Special 5.11a . . . .

2 bolts (6 m) This short route links two faint, left-trending seams together. It finishes on a tree anchor over the top. *(Sean Dougherty, 1985)*

THREE TIER BUTTRESS

35

34   36   37   38   39

Walk on the Wild Side (5.11c).

HEMINGWAY WALL

27 routes ←5.10 5.11 5.12 5.13→

The Hemingway Wall is sure to please climbers that prefer technical routes over those that favour brute strength. It features beautiful, compact grey stone with intricate climbs that utilize small edges. Good footwork along with a stiff shoe will go a long way toward success. This is a great venue on which to hone your technical climbing skills.

Approach: When hiking into the canyon, this is the first wall on the left side. It's directly across from the Water Wall.

Hemingway Wall

Routes are listed from left to right.

**❶ Death in
the Afternoon** 5.12a . . . .

5 bolts (17 m) Climb up the ramp on the left end of the wall to reach the first bolt. From here, nice face climbing leads to a big ledge and the anchor.
(*Geoff Powter & Brain Wyvill, 2001*)

**❷ The Importance
of Being Earnest** 5.12a . . . .

6 bolts (17 m) Crimpy face climbing leads to a crux gaining a big ledge. Another crux appears right before the anchor, just where you least want it. (*Sean Dougherty, 1985*)

❸ Cracked Rhythm 5.12c . .

4 bolts (13 m) This route features some wickedly small crimpers and footholds. Start off a small ledge and try not to split a tip on your way to the large break. A few more tricky moves gain the anchor. (*Joe Buszowski & JD Leblanc, 1988*)

❹ Chips Are for Kids 5.11b . . . . . .

5 bolts (15 m) The direct start to *Farewell to Arms* features large pulls on nice edges. Enjoy.
(*Keith Pike & Glen Zederayko, 1988*)

❺ Farewell to Arms 5.11a . . . .

5 bolts (15 m) A few slabby moves lead to a nice vertical section and a left-trending crack. Pull through a tricky bulge before strolling to the anchor. (*Dave Morgan, 1985*)

HEMINGWAY WALL LEFT

variation finish original finish

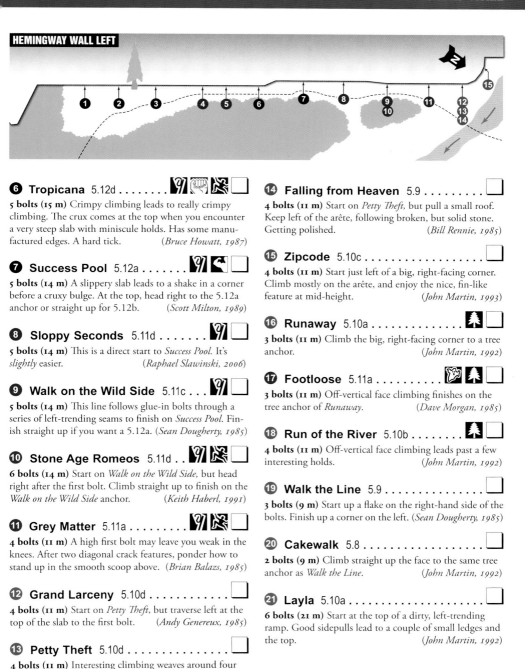

HEMINGWAY WALL LEFT

❻ Tropicana 5.12d . . . .

5 bolts (15 m) Crimpy climbing leads to really crimpy climbing. The crux comes at the top when you encounter a very steep slab with miniscule holds. Has some manufactured edges. A hard tick. *(Bruce Howatt, 1987)*

❼ Success Pool 5.12a . . . . . .

5 bolts (14 m) A slippery slab leads to a shake in a corner before a cruxy bulge. At the top, head right to the 5.12a anchor or straight up for 5.12b. *(Scott Milton, 1989)*

❽ Sloppy Seconds 5.11d . . . .

5 bolts (14 m) This is a direct start to *Success Pool.* It's *slightly* easier. *(Raphael Slawinski, 2006)*

❾ Walk on the Wild Side 5.11c . . .

5 bolts (14 m) This line follows glue-in bolts through a series of left-trending seams to finish on *Success Pool.* Finish straight up if you want a 5.12a. *(Sean Dougherty, 1985)*

❿ Stone Age Romeos 5.11d . .

6 bolts (14 m) Start on *Walk on the Wild Side,* but head right after the first bolt. Climb straight up to finish on the *Walk on the Wild Side* anchor. *(Keith Haberl, 1991)*

⓫ Grey Matter 5.11a . . . .

4 bolts (11 m) A high first bolt may leave you weak in the knees. After two diagonal crack features, ponder how to stand up in the smooth scoop above. *(Brian Balazs, 1985)*

⓬ Grand Larceny 5.10d . . . .

4 bolts (11 m) Start on *Petty Theft,* but traverse left at the top of the slab to the first bolt. *(Andy Genereux, 1985)*

⓭ Petty Theft 5.10d . . . .

4 bolts (11 m) Interesting climbing weaves around four bolts. *(John Martin, 1993)*

⓮ Falling from Heaven 5.9 . . . .

4 bolts (11 m) Start on *Petty Theft,* but pull a small roof. Keep left of the arête, following broken, but solid stone. Getting polished. *(Bill Rennie, 1985)*

⓯ Zipcode 5.10c . . . .

4 bolts (11 m) Start just left of a big, right-facing corner. Climb mostly on the arête, and enjoy the nice, fin-like feature at mid-height. *(John Martin, 1993)*

⓰ Runaway 5.10a . . . .

3 bolts (11 m) Climb the big, right-facing corner to a tree anchor. *(John Martin, 1992)*

⓱ Footloose 5.11a . . . .

3 bolts (11 m) Off-vertical face climbing finishes on the tree anchor of *Runaway.* *(Dave Morgan, 1985)*

⓲ Run of the River 5.10b . . . .

4 bolts (11 m) Off-vertical face climbing leads past a few interesting holds. *(John Martin, 1992)*

⓳ Walk the Line 5.9 . . . .

3 bolts (9 m) Start up a flake on the right-hand side of the bolts. Finish up a corner on the left. *(Sean Dougherty, 1985)*

⓴ Cakewalk 5.8 . . . .

2 bolts (9 m) Climb straight up the face to the same tree anchor as *Walk the Line.* *(John Martin, 1992)*

㉑ Layla 5.10a . . . .

6 bolts (21 m) Start at the top of a dirty, left-trending ramp. Good sidepulls lead to a couple of small ledges and the top. *(John Martin, 1992)*

HEMINGWAY WALL RIGHT

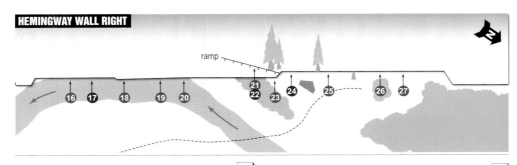

ramp

16 17 18 19 20 21 22 23 24 25 26 27

22 Delilah 5.11a . . . .

6 bolts (21 m) This is a challenging variation to *Layla*. At the first bolt, climb a bit right on small edges. Re-join *Layla* at the first of the small ledges. (*John Martin, 1992*)

23 Temptress 5.10c . . . .

2 bolts (13 m) Climb over a small overlap and into a shallow corner. A couple of tricky slab moves lead to good holds and the anchor. Another bolt leads to a tree anchor at the top, but this is not recommended. (*Andy Genereux, 1985*)

24 Siren Song 5.11a . . . .

5 bolts (13 m) Climb into the small roof from either side before pulling onto the slab above, where your technical skills will really be put to the test. (*John Martin, 1992*)

25 Nymphet 5.8 . . . .

6 bolts (21 m) Follow a zig-zag feature up a very enjoyable wall, passing a ledge and small overlaps en route to the anchor. (*Andy Genereux, 1985*)

26 Scheherazade 5.9 . . . .

6 bolts (21 m) Start in front of a cluster of trees. Climb up and left on nice holds to a small ledge. A seam leads left to the last bolt. (*John Martin, 1992*)

27 Lola 5.9 . . . .

5 bolts (21 m) Follow bolts right of the left-trending crack to a small ledge. Head straight up the slab to a small roof and the anchor. (*John Martin, 1993*)

HEMINGWAY WALL RIGHT

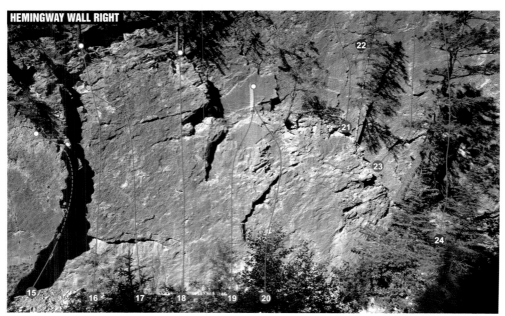

PAINTINGS WALL

27 routes ←—5.10 5.11 5.12 5.13→

This long cliff band starts just before the pictographs and extends all the way to the canyon's T-intersection. The climbing is mostly vertical, with some excellent 5.10 and 5.11 routes, and the narrowness of this section of canyon makes it one of the coldest areas in the Grotto drainage. This area holds snow and ice into early summer, which is great if it's hot but brutal if it's cold.

Approach: Continue upstream from the Water Wall area for two minutes to a point where the canyon narrows to just a few metres across. The first routes are located just before this point on the left-hand side of the creek.

Access Note

Take special care when climbing on routes 5 to 8. Please don't come into contact with the pictographs at the base of the wall.

Paintings Wall

Routes are listed from left to right.

1 Blaster 5.10a . . . . ☐

4 bolts (13 m) Follow polished jugs right of a dirt ledge at three metres. A yellow and white streak leads to the anchor on a small ledge. (*Chris Miller, 1992*)

2 Blindside 5.10c . . . . ☐

5 bolts (13 m) Climb *Blaster*, but continue up through grey rock to an anchor on a small ledge. (*John Martin, 1994*)

3 Scavenger 5.9 . . . . ☐

3 bolts (12 m) Start just right of *Blindside* and head for a monster jug at the first bolt. Continue up through a series of small corners and small ledges. (*John Martin, 1988*)

4 OK Corral 5.8 . . . . ☐

4 bolts (12 m) Climb the right-facing corner and join *Scavenger* at the last bolt. (*Chris Miller, 1990*)

5 Art of the Ancients 5.9 . . . . ☐

5 bolts (15 m) Start three metres left of the pictographs. Climb straight up to chain anchors. (*Chris Miller, 1990*)

6 Retrospective 5.10a . . . . ☐

6 bolts (15 m) Clip the first two bolts of *Art of the Ancients* before heading right through the scoop. Finish at the *Art of the Ancients* anchor. (*John Martin, 1994*)

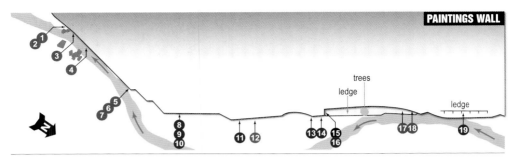

PAINTINGS WALL

trees
ledge
ledge

7 Left to Chance 5.10c . . . .

4 bolts (15 m) Climb to the third bolt of *Retrospective* before heading right into a yellow corner. After pulling over a small triangle-shaped roof, head back to the anchors of *Retrospective*. (*Dave Morgan, 1991*)

8 Cultural Imperative 5.11b . . . . .

6 bolts (16 m) Start in a shallow, water-polished corner which is easier than it first looks. Climb to a high first bolt under a roof and traverse left to a second bolt around the corner before heading up on good rock. (*John Martin, 1992*)

9 Peter Pan 5.11a . . . .

3 bolts (16 m) Climb *Cultural Imperative* to an aluminum hanger over a break before continuing to anchors in a left-facing corner. (*Albi Sole, 1987*)

10 Sidewinder 5.11b . . . .

6 bolts (16 m) Using the same start as *Cultural Imperative*, clip a high first bolt at the top of the corner and traverse right just above the break to a second bolt. Trend right on nice edges to a rest under the roof, crank it and continue up. (*Jon Jones, 1992*)

11 A New Dawn 5.12a . . . .

7 bolts (16 m) A water-polished start leads to nice climbing up a thin grey streak. From the top of the streak, trend right to anchors. (*Nigel Slater, 2009*)

12 Closed Project . . . .

13 Hellen Damnation 5.11d .

4 bolts (16 m) From the creek bed, negotiate a slick start to a high first bolt below a small roof. The crux is pulling through the overhang. (*Brian Wyvill, 1992*)

14 Tower of Pisa 5.11c . . . . .

5 bolts (16 m) Climb the bulgy, left side of the arête.

Finish on the *Hellen Damnation* tree anchor.
(*Sean Dougherty, 1985*)

15 Tour de Force 5.12a . . . .

7 bolts (14 m) From the ledge, chossy rock leads to an arête. The anchor is below a tree. (*Andy Genereux, 1992*)

16 Tour de Pump 5.11b . . . .

7 bolts (14 m) From the ledge, chossy rock leads to a clean face that's climbed using edges and a seam in the back of a corner. Pumpier than it looks! (*Andy Genereux, 1992*)

17 Jugthuggery 5.10a . . . .

4 bolts (13 m) From the ledge, face climb to a big, juggy, left-facing corner. (*Chris Miller, 1992*)

18 Pieces of Eight 5.10b . . . .

6 bolts (13 m) From the ledge, climb the big, left-facing corner for three bolts before trending right through jugs to anchors at the top of the wall. (*John Martin, 2008*)

PAINTINGS

WALL

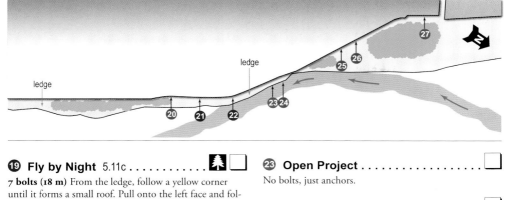

19 Fly by Night 5.11c . . . . 🌲⬜

7 bolts (18 m) From the ledge, follow a yellow corner until it forms a small roof. Pull onto the left face and follow a series of small bulges to the anchor. (*Jon Jones, 1992*)

20 Fast Forward 5.10c . . . . ⬜

2 bolts (9 m) From the ledge, climb through a blue patch and skirt the small roof on the left. (*John Martin, 1992*)

21 Walk, Don't Run 5.11b . . . . ⬜

3 bolts (10 m) From the ledge, follow a streak over a small roof on the way to the anchor. (*John Martin, 1992*)

22 Rush 5.11b . . . . ⬜

3 bolts (10 m) From the ledge, follow a thin blue streak to a small roof. Crank it and follow a short corner to the anchor. (*John Martin, 1992*)

23 Open Project . . . . ⬜

No bolts, just anchors.

24 Layaway Plan 5.10c . . . . ⬜

5 bolts (15 m) Start on the far right end of the ledge. Follow a grey streak to the face left of the corner on the upper half of the route. (*Chris Miller, 1992*)

25 Watusi Wedding 5.10a . . . . ⬜

4 bolts (11 m) Climb straight up on smooth but positive holds. (*Chris Miller, 1992*)

26 Jesus Drives a Cadillac 5.10b . . . . ⬜

4 bolts (11 m) The arête. (*Chris Miller, 1992*)

27 Open Project . . . . ⬜

PAINTINGS WALL

THE RIGHT WING

21 routes ← 5.10 5.11 5.12 5.13 →

This crag is nestled in the trees across from the Paintings Wall and hosts a nice collection of short and long routes, which range from 5.9 to 5.11. Due to the out-of-the-way nature of this cliff, solitude is almost guaranteed. Please take care not to knock rocks down the hill as they will most certainly fall into the narrow canyon below, which is often busy with hikers.

Approach: This crag sits on the right-hand side of the canyon and may be approached from two directions. From the pictographs, cut across a small rock slab and into the trees on the right side of the creek. Alternatively, from the canyon's T-intersection follow a trail over rock slabs on the right into the forested hillside.

The Right Wing

Routes are listed from left to right.

❶ Knight Shift 5.10a . . . . ☐
3 bolts (8 m) Start left of a large block. Climb grey and yellow rock to an anchor over the top. (*Dave Dornian, 1988*)

❷ Cameo 5.9 . . . . ☐
4 bolts (12 m) Start off the top of the large block. Follow big holds for three bolts before heading right up a ramp to an anchor over the top. (*John Martin, 1992*)

❸ Diamond Sky 5.10b . . . . ☐
5 bolts (12 m) Start on the right-hand side of the large block. A low-angle start leads to a steeper section near the top of a small corner. (*Dave Dornian, 1988*)

❹ Charm 5.10b . . . . ☐
5 bolts (12 m) Start just to the left of a ledge at two metres. Climb up and right heading for a small, right-facing corner. (*John Martin, 1993*)

❺ Blind Faith 5.10a . . . . ☐
4 bolts (12 m) Start to the right of a narrow pillar and climb up through a corner. (*John Martin, 1993*)

❻ Silhouette 5.10b . . . . ☐
4 bolts (12 m) Climb through shattered rock down low to better rock above. (*John Martin, 1993*)

❼ Tapdance 5.10a . . . . ☐
4 bolts (13 m) Climb the face to the right of the large crack. (*John Martin, 1992*)

❽ Yellow Wedge 5.9 . . . . ☐
3 bolts (14 m) Follow good holds to a ledge at the halfway point. Continue up corners above. (*John Martin, 1985*)

❾ Lemon Pie 5.10b . . . . ☐
5 bolts (14 m) Climb a short ramp and bypass a small roof. Continue straight up. (*John Martin, 1985*)

❿ Lime Street 5.9 . . . . ☐
4 bolts (14 m) Start to the right of *Lemon Pie*. After two bolts, join *Lemon Pie* to finish. (*John Martin, 1993*)

⓫ Pink Cadillac 5.10a . . . . ☐
4 bolts (12 m) Start to the left of a tree growing against the wall. Follow aluminum hangers up a groove to anchors over the top. (*John Martin, 1992*)

THE RIGHT WING

ledge

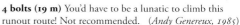

⑫ Caught in the Crossfire 5.10b . . . . ☐

4 bolts (11 m) Start just right of a short corner. Climb up and over a roof at the top. *(Chris Miller, 1990)*

⑬ Supplication 5.10b . . . . ☐

3 bolts (11 m) Follow aluminum hangers through low-angle terrain until it's possible to pull around a small corner. *(John Martin, 1987)*

⑭ Soma 5.11c . . . . ☐

4 bolts (9 m) Climb through a narrow yellow streak to a small overlap and up. *(John Martin, 1992)*

⑮ Hush 5.11c . . . . ☐

3 bolts (9 m) Start in a shallow corner. The tough crux is low down. *(John Martin, 1992)*

⑯ Subliminal Seduction 5.11c . . . . . . ☐

8 bolts (19 m) Head for the lone, large glue-in bolt. Climb through a break and head for a shallow corner and up. *(John Martin & Mark Whalen, 1992)*

⑰ Lunatic Madness 5.11a . . . . 🐾 ☐

4 bolts (19 m) You'd have to be a lunatic to climb this runout route! Not recommended. *(Andy Genereux, 1985)*

⑱ Lithium 5.10d . . . . ☐

6 bolts (15 m) Start right of the main weakness in the middle of the wall. Tricky down low. *(John Martin, 1992)*

⑲ Joyride 5.8 . . . . ☐

2 bolts (6 m) Start behind two trees and follow good holds through the groove. *(John Martin, 1992)*

⑳ Aggressive Treatment 5.10c . . . . . . ☐

6 bolts (14 m) Start off a dirt ledge to the left of a tree. Fun climbing on nice holds ends when the rock changes color and the holds disappear. *(Andy Genereux, 1985)*

㉑ Night Life 5.11a . . . . ☐

5 bolts (14 m) This is the last line on the right side of the wall. Start off a block using crimps. Climb gingerly past the hollow-sounding flake. *(Andy Genereux, 1992)*

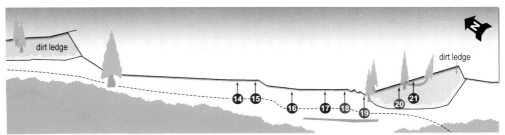

THE NARROWS

33 routes ←5.10 5.11 5.12 5.13→

If you hang a left at the canyon's T-intersection, the smooth, riverside walls slowly snake upstream, eventually forming a tight canyon called the Narrows. With plenty of shade, this zone is often cooler than the rest of the canyon making it a great place to escape summer's heat. A few of the routes are best done as two pitches to avoid rope drag, and this will necessitate two rappels to get back down. The Exit Wall, close to the Narrows, is also included in this section.

Approach: At the canyon's T-intersection, turn left. The Narrows begin where the canyon walls constrict and extend until they re-open upstream.

The Narrows

Routes are listed from left to right.

① Bogus 5.10d . . . .
1 bolt (6 m) The name says it all. Avoid. (*Tom Fayle, 1987*)

② Mighty Mark 5.12b . . . .
2 bolts (8 m) Climb an open-book corner to gain a face on the right. (*Janet Brygger & Anthony Neilson, 2001*)

③ Mighty Mite 5.12a . . . .
2 bolts (8 m) Climb the face just left of the prow. There is ground-fall potential between the first and second bolt so beware. This was one of the Bow Valley's first 5.12 testpieces. (*Mark DeLeeuw, 1987*)

④ The Midden 5.9 . . . .
3 bolts (12 m) Work up a smooth groove to a wide slot and the anchor. (*Chas Yonge, 1982*)

⑤ Kubla Kahn 5.6 . . . .
3 bolts (14 m) From the bolt above the break, head right to jugs in the flakes and up. (*Unknown*)

⑥ Xanadu 5.10a . . . .
8 bolts (21 m) This fine route features a crux at the bottom and a crux at the top with beautiful, clean gray stone in between. (*John Martin, 1992*)

⑦ Mendocino 5.11a . . . .
5 bolts (16 m) Struggle up a short corner to a slab that connects with the left side of a groove. (*John Martin, 1992*)

THE NARROWS

THE NARROWS

treed scree slope

Exit Wall

T-Intersection,
Right Wing &
Alley

N

8 Malibu 5.10c

5 bolts (16 m) Start below the groove. Difficulties give way to easier, low-angle terrain above. *(John Martin, 1992)*

9 Monterey 5.10a

4 bolts (16 m) A tough start gives way to easier slab climbing. Stay right of the groove. *(John Martin, 1992)*

10 Baker Street 5.10d

1 bolt (9 m) A low first bolt is followed by a long runout to a one-bolt anchor. *(Sean Dougherty, 1987)*

11 Dr. Watson 5.9

1 bolt (9 m) A high first bolt right of a broken patch of rock leads to another one-bolt anchor. *(Sean Dougherty, 1987)*

12 Lost World 5.10a

2 bolts (12 m) Climb a weakness through a smooth slab. It's a long way from the second bolt to the tree anchor on the right. *(Bruce Keller, 1985)*

13 Hollow Earth 5.9

3 bolts (12 m) Start to the left of the sloping ledge. Climb straight up to a tree anchor. *(John Martin, 1992)*

14 Moriarty 5.9

2 bolts (12 m) Climb onto a sloping ledge before continuing up to a tree anchor. *(John Martin, 1987)*

15 Harder than It Looks 5.10c

1 bolts (11 m) This is the left-most route. Scramble up a left-facing corner to a high first bolt. From here, climb the arête to a tree anchor. *(Andy Genereux, 1985)*

16 Monkey in a Rage 5.11a

2 bolts (11 m) A high first bolt leads to a scoop. The crux comes pulling onto the small slab. *(Sean Dougherty, 1985)*

17 Guitarzan 5.10b

2 bolts (11 m) Climb slightly left of the arête to a ridiculously high first bolt above a large, square roof. Pull around to the right side of the arête and continue to an anchor directly left of a scraggly tree. *(Frank Campbell, 1989)*

18 George of the Jungle 5.10c

2 fixed pins (11 m) Climb a thin seam that becomes a shallow corner protected by two fixed pins. *(Brian Balazs, 1985)*

19 Impending Impact 5.10a

2 fixed pins (12 m) A very high first bolt and rock polish scares most climbers away. *(Andy Genereux, 1985)*

⑳ Smooth Move 5.10b . . . . 🌲⬜

3 bolts (12 m) The route features slab climbing up compact, grey stone. Hard to read from the ground. It's much easier if you use the crack to the right. (*Jay Kae, 1995*)

㉑ Tiny Tim 5.9 . . . . 🌲⬜

This toprope route is accessed via a tree anchor at the top of the wall.

㉒ Narrow Escape 5.8 . . . . ⬜

3 bolts (9 m) Start to the left of the corner. A thin seem leads to a series of small ledges. (*Unknown*)

㉓ Break Up 5.8 . . . . ⬜

3 bolts (9 m) From the corner, work up to a ledge and straight up to the anchor. (*Unknown*)

㉔ Trading Places 5.10c . . . . . . 🪨🧗⬜

6 bolts + gear (42 m) Climb a ramp that heads left to a dirty crack and seam. Follow the seam to a bolted slab. (*Chas Yonge, 1985*)

㉕ Undertow 5.10c . . . . 🧗⬜

13 bolts + gear (42 m) Climb a ramp that heads left to a seam. Place a few pieces of gear before angling right to a bolt on the slab. Good luck above—the holds on the slab all seem to face the wrong way. (*John Martin, 1992*)

㉖ Neorevisionist 5.11d . . . . ⬜

9 bolts (18 m) Climb a ramp for three bolts before traversing right around a series of corners to a set of anchors on the slab. (*John Martin, 1993*)

㉗ Tabernaquered 5.10d . . . . . . 🪨🧗⬜

7 bolts (25 m) From the anchor of *Neorevisionist*, climb a yellow, right-facing corner before trending right onto a slabby, grey face. At the ramp, trend back left and exit out the top of the right-facing corner. Best done as a multi-pitch to reduce rope drag. (*Chas Yonge, 1985*)

㉘ Magical Mystery Tour 5.11b . 🪨🧗⬜

9 bolts (25 m) From the anchor of *Neorevisionist*, head well right into the land of steep slab. Eventually head for a weakness below a yellow streak and the anchors. Best done as a multi-pitch to reduce drag. (*John Martin, 1993*)

㉙ Open Project . . . . ⬜

㉚ An Acquired Taste 5.13b . . . 🧗🪨⬜

7 bolts (17 m) Follow the left-trending weakness through a wall that's as smooth as a baby's bum. Two cruxes will try to spit you off. You'll love it or hate it. (*Derek Galloway, 2008*)

㉛ Mirage 5.11d . . . . 🐾🌲⬜

5 bolts (20 m) Rappel in or climb *An Acquired Taste* to reach the belay stance. From here, a big runout guards the

THE NARROWS

first bolt and might make you think twice about committing. A couple of cruxes past more closely-spaced bolts lead to a tree anchor. (*Mark DeLeeuw, 1988*)

Exit Wall

This wall is located just past the Narrows on the right-hand side of the creek. Routes listed from left to right.

32 Open Project . . . .

Start left of a cluster of trees. Climb a right-facing corner to a jug and pull over a small overlap and up.

33 Blackend 5.11c . . . .

6 bolts (15 m) Start right of a cluster of trees. Climb through a series of small overhanging corners with a crux at the fourth bolt. (*Daren Tremaine, 1992*)

Interesting Fact: In the early '90s, Todd Guyn was one of the Bow Valley's strongest climbers and to train, he would run laps on Grotto's routes. On his best day, he climbed *A Farewell to Arms* (11b), *Walk on the Wild Side* (11c), *The Importance of Being Earnest* (12a), *Cracked Rhythm* (12c), *Tropicana* (12d), *Tintin and Snowy Get Psyched* (12d), *Crimes of Passion* (12d), *Shep's Diner* (13a), *Burn Hollywood Burn* (13b) and *The Resurrection* (13c), all with no falls.

Ryan Johnstone on Barchetta (5.11c).

THE NARROWS

EXIT WALL

THE ALLEY

18 routes   ←—5.10 5.11 5.12 5.13—→

This quality cliff sits high above the creek up the right fork of Grotto Canyon's T-intersection. The cliff hosts a fine collection of excellent 5.11s and low 5.12s that have more texture than the majority of routes in the canyon, making a visit well worth the extra hike. Take special care when hiking near this cliff as any rocks dislodged may tumble down and seriously hurt unsuspecting hikers below.

Approach: Head right at the canyon's T-intersection and follow slabs until it's possible to scramble through a break on the right side, which gains the steep, forested hill above. Follow a steep trail for five minutes to the very top of the hill where the routes begin. If it rains, the scramble that accesses the forest will get extremely slippery. Be careful.

The Alley

Routes are listed from left to right.

❶ Hee Haw 5.12c . . . .

3 bolts (7 m) Start at the top of the hill just down from the grey slab. Follow orange and grey streaks to anchors in a small corner.   (*Ryan Johnstone, 1994*)

❷ Scream Saver 5.12a . . . .

6 bolts (15 m) Climb a crack and pull onto the wall via some tough moves to gain a higher crux. (*Dean Tremaine, 1996*)

**❸ The Unwholesome
One Is After Your Seed** 5.11a . . . .

4 bolts (13 m) Start to the right of the crack. Climb through a corner to finish up a yellow streak.
(*Mike Orr & Ian Cox, 2006*)

❹ White Noise 5.12c . . . .

4 bolts (12 m) Start in front of a small tree. Navigate through overhanging rock with many sidepulls.
(*Daren Tremaine, 1994*)

**❺ A Fetching
Bell Shape, Small
but Perfectly Formed** 5.12d . .

5 bolts (12 m) A brutal crux off the ground leads to another crux near the top. (*Daren Tremaine, 1995*)

❻ Knight Moves 5.11a . . . .

6 bolts (15 m) Start to the right of a large cube jutting out of the wall at two metres. Fun climbing leads to a ledge halfway up. Enjoy the view behind you before continuing to the anchor at the top of the corner. (*Jon Jones, 1987*)

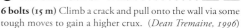

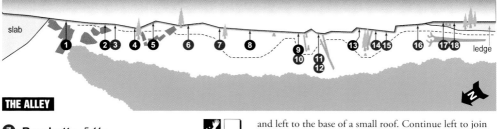

THE ALLEY

7 **Barchetta** 5.11c . . . .

7 bolts (15 m) Climb through blue rock to a small roof before skirting hanging slabs on their right. Veer back left to the anchor. One of the Alley's best. (*Joe Buszowski, 1987*)

8 **Path of the Moose** 5.12a . . . .

6 bolts (15 m) Follow a yellow corner to a face. The crux is at the last bolt. (*Glen Zederayko, 1989*)

9 **Get Your Ducks in a Row** 5.12b . . . . .

5 bolts (14 m) From the small platform, fight your way through a series of small overlaps to the top. (*Daren Tremaine, 1994*)

10 **Submission Direct** 5.11b . . . .

6 bolts (14 m) Start just below the small platform. Climb past a corner to a yellow streak, and follow it to the top. (*Andy Genereux, 1990*)

11 **Submission** 5.11d . . . .

7 bolts (15 m) From the top of a yellow pillar, climb up

and left to the base of a small roof. Continue left to join *Submission Direct*. (*Joe Buszowski, 1987*)

12 **Crossroad** 5.11d . . . .

5 bolts (15 m) From the top of the yellow pillar, head for a roof and follow a corner that finishes with some great moves near the anchor. (*Mark Dube, 1987*)

13 **Snakes and Ladders** 5.12a . . . .

7 bolts (15 m) Start on a platform supported by two large trees. Climb through a series of small overlaps that have few downward-pulling holds. (*Dave Thomson, 1991*)

14 **Fear No Art** 5.11b . . . .

5 bolts (15 m) Start off the left side of the ledge at three metres. Good face climbing leads through a couple of tough roofs. (*Keith Haberl, 1988*)

15 **Big-breasted Girls Go to the Beach and Take Their Tops Off** 5.11b . . . .

6 bolts (15 m) Stat off the right side of the *Fear No Art* ledge and head up the slab to a cruxy roof. Enjoy the terrain above. (*Scott Milton, 1988*)

16 **Grace Under Pressure** 5.11d . . . .

6 bolts (15 m) Start between two ledges at three metres. A somewhat scary opening gives way to tough moves pulling over the bulge. Excellent climbing leads to the top. One of the best routes on the wall. (*Jim Sandford, 1987*)

17 **Tears of the Dinosaur** 5.11b . . . . . .

5 bolts (15 m) Scramble onto the ledge at three metres and start just left of two small stumps. A lot of courage is required to gain the first bolt, but good climbing lurks above. (*Keith Haberl, 1988*)

18 **Engines Burning** 5.11b . . . .

5 bolts (15 m) Start to the right of *Tears of the Dinosaur*. The climbing is so enjoyable, you'll wish the route was twice as long. (*Chris Miller, 1990*)

NICK ROCHACEWICH ON VISHNU (5.13c) © SIMON MEIS

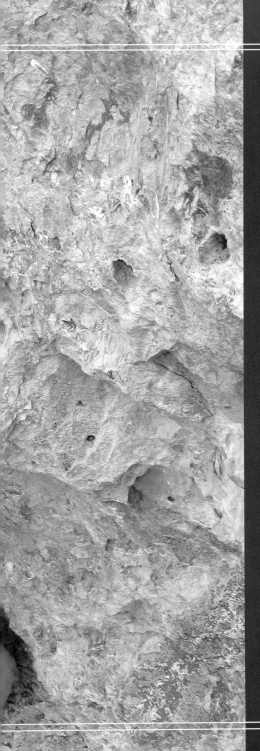

CHAPTER 6

BATAAN

If it weren't for the grueling uphill approach, Bataan would certainly be a contender for the most popular crag in the Bow Valley. The quality of the limestone is unparalleled and the position high above the scenic valley is magnificent. Bataan's vertical and slightly-overhanging walls feature many long and sustained routes that are littered with pockets, jugs and edges—endurance is the name of the game! The majority of the climbs are in the 5.11 to 5.13 range, and the routes are predominantly of the highest quality. Despite the burly hike, Bataan is consistently increasing in popularity as climbers slowly begin to realize that the rewards of climbing on the pristine blue, grey and yellow streaks far outweigh the effort required to reach them.

CONDITIONS

Being generally south facing, Bataan has one of the longest climbing seasons in the Bow Valley, and is the closest thing in the corridor to a year-round area. The season stretches from early spring to late fall, with winter days being climbable provided the skies are clear and the daytime high is between 0° and 5°C. The cliff is best avoided during the heat of summer, though, when temperatures at the sun-baked crag can easily be 10° to 15°C warmer than on the valley floor. After significant rainfall, the lower walls dry quickly, but the Eyes of Bataan and the Pacific Theatre sectors may seep for days.

APPROACH

From Canmore: Drive east on Bow Valley Trail, which becomes Highway 1A on the outskirts of town. Set your trip metre to zero at Elk Run Boulevard. At 1.8 km (1.1 miles), watch for a pullout on the left. Park here.

From Calgary: Drive west toward Canmore and take Exit 91. Turn east (left) onto Highway 1A and set your trip metre to zero at Elk Run Boulevard. At 1.8 km (1.1 miles), park in the pullout.

Hiking: Pick up a trail that starts at the right (south) side of the parking lot. Once on top of the slope, the trail intersects a well-worn horse path just beyond the power lines. Turn left and follow this path past a trail sign and into the trees (ignore the trail that goes left at the sign). Continue hiking.

After exiting the trees, reach the base of a large bench where the approach trail intersects a couple of popular biking and hiking trails. At this intersection, look for a forked tree on the right. From here, follow a trail that heads uphill toward the now-visible cliffs of Bataan (if the trail is not heading toward the cliffs, it's the wrong one). Eventually skirt the left edge of a large mining scar. A large rock cairn in the back, left corner of the mining scar marks the entrance to the forest and the beginning of the uphill difficulties. Follow relentless, steep switchbacks though the trees to the base of the First Cave. Continue uphill along the trail to reach the remaining walls.

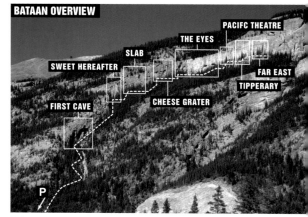

BATAAN OVERVIEW — PACIFC THEATRE, THE EYES, SLAB, SWEET HEREAFTER, FAR EAST, TIPPERARY, FIRST CAVE, CHEESE GRATER, P

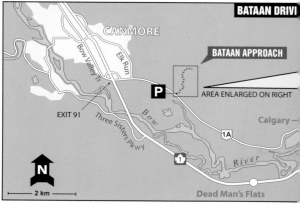

BATAAN DRIVI — BATAAN APPROACH — AREA ENLARGED ON RIGHT — CANMORE — Bow Valley Tr — Elk Run — P — EXIT 91 — Three Sisters Pkwy — Bow — Calgary — 1A — River — N — 2 km — Dead Man's Flats

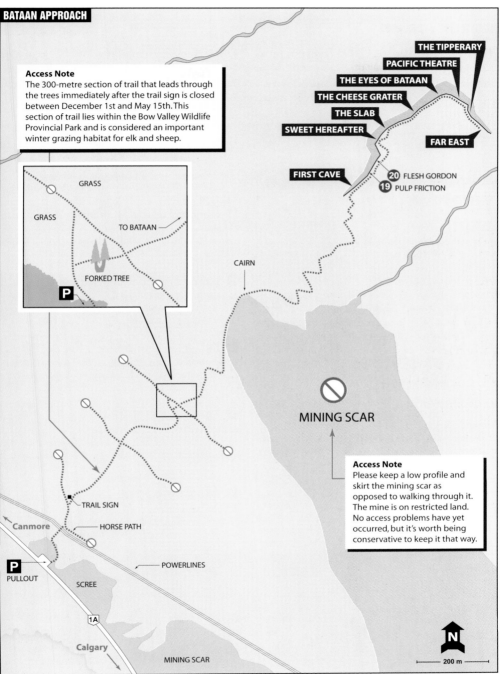

BATAAN APPROACH

Access Note
The 300-metre section of trail that leads through the trees immediately after the trail sign is closed between December 1st and May 15th. This section of trail lies within the Bow Valley Wildlife Provincial Park and is considered an important winter grazing habitat for elk and sheep.

THE TIPPERARY
PACIFIC THEATRE
THE EYES OF BATAAN
THE CHEESE GRATER
THE SLAB
SWEET HEREAFTER
FIRST CAVE
FAR EAST

20 FLESH GORDON
19 PULP FRICTION

GRASS
GRASS
TO BATAAN
FORKED TREE
P

CAIRN

MINING SCAR

Access Note
Please keep a low profile and skirt the mining scar as opposed to walking through it. The mine is on restricted land. No access problems have yet occurred, but it's worth being conservative to keep it that way.

TRAIL SIGN
Canmore
HORSE PATH
P
PULLOUT
POWERLINES
SCREE
1A
Calgary
MINING SCAR

N
200 m

FIRST CAVE

20 routes   ←5.10 5.11 5.12 5.13→

The First Cave has some excellent climbing on mostly-vertical stone. Although the lower band of rock is a bit chossy, it only accounts for a small portion of the climbing and is well worth enduring to reach the bullet-hard stone above. The routes are long, sustained and consistently interesting. This crag could easily occupy an entire day, and is good in winter or on cold days due its sheltered location.

Approach: This is the first wall encountered when the approach trail intersects the cliff band. Look for a big cave.

First Cave

Routes are listed from left to right.

1 Near Miss 5.10a . . . .

11 bolts (23 m) This is the first route encountered when approaching Bataan from the parking lot. Start off a small platform and climb up a corner to reach excellent climbing on textured, grey rock.   *(Ian & Chris Perry, 2003)*

2 Solar Power 5.12b . . . .

13 bolts (22 m) This quality line tackles a very blunt arête. Climb *Free Energy* to the sixth bolt (use a long sling) and trend left to the base of the arête. Good grips with poor footholds characterize the difficulties. *(Ian & Chris Perry, 2004)*

3 Free Energy 5.11c . . . .

12 bolts (24 m) From the platform, climb a chossy-looking groove with good holds to a roof. Crank the lip to reach solid stone. Great moves above! A 5.11c variation (15 bolts, 26 m) traverses right past a black hanger at the second-to-last bolt to *Photo Finish*.   *(Ian & Chris Perry, 2003)*

4 Photo Finish 5.11b . . . .

11 bolts (27 m) Climb *Free Energy* to the third bolt before angling right, under the roof. Initially, swim through buckets, but get prepared to think up above. A 5.11b variation (15 bolts, 30 m) traverses right at the third-to-last

bolt just above a small roof. Clip one bolt before finishing on *Hanging by the Moment*.   *(Ian & Chris Perry, 2003)*

5 Hanging by the Moment 5.11d . . . .

13 bolts (30 m) This long route climbs directly above the rebar rungs and has two tricky cruxes separated by a good rest in a hueco. Look for the chain draw.   *(Roger Chayer, 2002)*

6 Borrowing from the Beggar 5.11d

12 bolts (30 m) Climb *Hanging by the Moment* to the seventh bolt before following edges right, into a left-facing corner with great climbing.   *(Roger Chayer, 2002)*

7 Fill 'er Up with Jesus 5.11d . . . .

11 bolts (29 m) Climb *Hanging by the Moment* to the sixth bolt and traverse right to some tricky (and tiring) layback moves. Save some juice for the crux.   *(Roger Chayer, 2002)*

8 The Divide 5.12a . . . .

14 bolts (30 m) Tread lightly just left of a rotten, left-facing corner. Persist, because the climbing above is excellent on bullet-hard, grey stone. The stout crux pulls over a small roof.   *(Ian & Chris Perry, 2007)*

9 Shear Stress 5.11b . . . .

11 bolts (29 m) If you can digest the chossy start, you'll be amply rewarded with great climbing all the way up the long, grey wall above.   *(Ian & Chris Perry, 2001)*

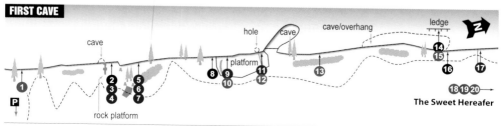

⑩ GRIP Profile 5.11d . . . . ☐

12 bolts (27 m) Climb *Shear Stress* to a horizontal break above the third bolt. Move right and follow corner features up excellent rock. (*Ian & Chris Perry, 2001*)

⑪ The Kinematic Wave 5.11d . . . . ☐

13 bolts (27 m) Steep climbing on jugs leads to sustained moves on positive edges. A must do!
(*Ian & Chris Perry, 2003*)

⑫ Open Project . . . . ☐

Needs a few more bolts and a scrub. This could be a great line!

⑬ Open Project . . . . ☐

⑭ Bob's Humble Heart 5.12a . . . . ☐

13 bolts (19 m) Begin at a small stance above the lip of the cave. To reach it, either climb *Blue Blood* and traverse left along the ledge (7 bolts) or climb *Blood Line* to the ledge and traverse left behind a small tree (6 bolts). Belay up your partner and then enjoy sustained climbing on small edges and pockets. Rap from the belay stance to reach the ground. (*Brian Wyvill, 2004*)

⑮ Open Project . . . . ☐

With a few more bolts, this could be good.

⑯ Blue Blood 5.12a . . . . . . ☐

16 bolts (35 m) Tackle the grey streak that rises from the base of the wall to the very top. Start with a chossy face on the right side of the cave. Better rock above. (*Ian & Chris Perry, 2009*)

⑰ Blood Line 5.11a . . . . ☐

15 bolts (33 m) Start off a narrow platform and climb carefully to a ledge. From here, enjoy a parade of buckets to the anchors. Classic.
(*Ian & Chris Perry, 2009*)

⑱ Open Project . . . . ☐

Needs a lot of work.

⑲ Pulp Friction 5.10c . . . . ☐

14 bolts (30 m) Hike three minutes up the trail from *Blood Line* to find this isolated climb.

Start off a small platform to the right of a large hole and head up a small, left-trending ramp to reach the first bolt. Climb the right side of a blank shield of grey, prickly rock. No excuses for foot slips! (*Ian & Chris Perry, 2003*)

⑳ Flesh Gordon 5.10a . . . . ☐

14 bolts (41 m) Hike another three minutes up the trail from *Pulp Friction* to find this exceptional route. Follow a left-leaning corner and slab all the way to the top of the cliff. Enjoy perfect holds in water-sculpted, pocketed rock. Bring up your second and make two rappels to get back to the ground. (*Greg Golovach, 2001*)

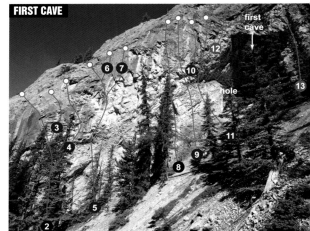

THE SWEET HEREAFTER

14 routes ←5.10 5.11 5.12 5.13→

This crag features long, vertical routes with cruxes that tend to come high on the wall. Keep the pump at bay, or risk some heart-breaking finales.

Approach: This sector is located 15 minutes up the approach trail from First Cave.

The Sweet Hereafter

Routes are listed from left to right.

1 Fingers in a Blender 5.10a . . . . ☐
10 bolts (26 m) This fun route rambles up solid grey stone to an anchor in vertical rock. (*Roger Chayer, 1998*)

2 Jaws 5.10b . . . . ☐
11 bolts (28 m) Follow nice edges and an occasional pocket. Good fun! (*Jon Jones & Jacquie Puscus, 1998*)

3 Fresco 5.11c . . . . ☐
10 bolts (28 m) Begin just left of a detached pillar. Tricky climbing leads to a bouldery crux pulling past a small bulge at mid-height. Easier above. (*JD LeBlanc, 1998*)

4 Too Little Too Late 5.12a . . . . ☐
10 bolts (26 m) Scramble up the left side of a chossy

crack to a high first bolt. Follow a grey streak above. Lots of tricky climbing leads to a bouldery crux right before the anchor. Aptly named. (*Jon Jones, 1998*)

5 Culture of Fear 5.12a . . . . ☐
13 bolts (28 m) Climb *Too Little Too Late* to the fifth bolt before following glue-ins to a slab below a grey overhang. Powerful climbing leads to the anchor. Backclean the bolt at the top of the crack to reduce drag. (*Roger Chayer, 1998*)

6 Fear of the Hereafter 5.11c . . . . . ☐
13 bolts (31 m) Climb *Culture of Fear* to just below the grey overhang. From here, traverse right to finish on *The Sweet Hereafter*. (*Roger Chayer & Jon Jones, 2000*)

7 The Sweet Hereafter 5.12a . . ☐
13 bolts (30 m) From the top of the crack, follow a right-trending grey streak. Although the crux comes down low, don't expect a free ride to the top! (*Roger Chayer, 1998*)

THE SWEET HEREAFTER

pillar

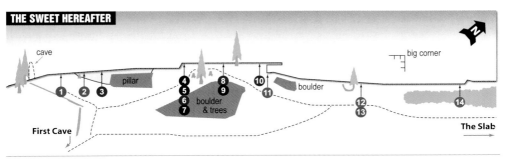

THE SWEET HEREAFTER

cave

pillar

① ② ③

④
⑤
⑥ boulder
⑦ & trees

⑧
⑨

⑩
⑪

boulder

⑫
⑬

big corner

⑭

First Cave

The Slab

---

⑧ Faraway So Close 5.11d . . . . .

15 bolts (30 m) From the no-hands rest on *With or Without You,* move left up a corner system via hard moves. Rejoin *With or Without You* at the last bolt.   (*Jon Jones, 2000*)

⑨ With or Without You 5.12b . . . .

16 bolts (30 m) Follow pockets just left of a grimy flake to a no-hands rest at mid-height. A cruxy blank section leads to plenty of mid-5.11 climbing en route to the anchor.   (PREP: *Roger Chayer; FA: Todd Guyn, 2001*)

⑩ The Filth and the Fury 5.11d . . .

12 bolts (30 m) Start just right of the grimy flake. Climb some less-than-perfect rock through a groove to a short, right-facing corner. A couple of hard moves guard passage to the anchor.   (*Jon Jones, 2000*)

⑪ Open Project . . . .

Needs some cleaning.

⑫ Open Project . . . .

⑬ Dirty Book 5.10a . . . .

12 bolts (32 m) Climb an approach pitch to the base of a left-facing corner. Fun laybacking leads to a face-climbing bypass on the right to avoid less-than-desirable rock in the crack. A 70-metre rope makes it up and down. Otherwise, lower twice. This good climb is unfortunately marred by rat shit near the top of the corner.   (*Jon Jones, 2000*)

⑭ Open Project . . . .

Not completely bolted.

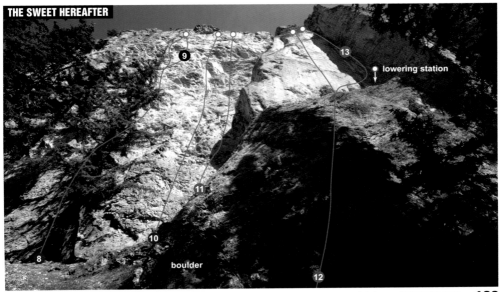

THE SWEET HEREAFTER

9

13

lowering station

11

10

8   boulder   12

THE SLAB

19 routes ←5.10 5.11 5.12 5.13→

This is a heavily-pocketed section of cliff that offers technical, vertical climbing on the left and steep pocket pulling on the right. It's one of very few walls in the Bow Valley where you can climb an entire route on pockets and nothing else.

Approach: Continue up the approach trail from the Sweet Hereafter for five minutes.

The Slab

Routes are listed from left to right.

❶ Open Project . . . . ☐
Shares the same start as *Give the People What They Want.*

❷ Give the People What They Want 5.12b . . . . ☐
6 bolts (15 m) Start on the first platform uphill from the large corner. Scramble onto a small ledge to gain the first bolt and follow a yellow streak through a sea of pockets to a crux at the very end. *(Jon Jones, 2001)*

❸ The Candy Man 5.11a . . . . ☐
5 bolts (10 m) Start on the second platform uphill from the large corner. Climb straight up on edges and pockets to anchors in the scoop. *(Jon Jones, 1999)*

❹ Beat the Clock 5.11d . . . . . . ☐
7 bolts (15 m) Start on the third platform uphill from the larger corner. Negotiate two tricky scoops on the way to the anchor. The second scoop is reachy. *(Jon Jones, 2000)*

❺ Scruples 5.11c . . . . ☐
7 bolts (16 m) Climbs the yellow streak. A bouldery move lurks below the last bolt. *(Jim Gott, 1998)*

❻ Crushed Velvet P1 5.12a . . . . . ☐
6 bolts (17 m) Start off the fourth platform uphill from the large corner. Follow a grey streak on pockets to a boulder problem gaining a ledge and the anchor.
(Roger Chayer; FA: Todd Guyn, 1998)

❼ Crushed Velvet P2 5.12d . . . . . ☐
14 bolts (30 m) Continue climbing above the anchor to a crux on sloping edges that gains a right-facing, layback corner. Pull over the bulge to positive holds. An excellent line! *(PREP: Roger Chayer; FA: Todd Guyn, 1998)*

❽ Exit Planet Dust P1 5.11b . . . . . ☐
7 bolts (17 m) Shares the same start as *Crushed Velvet* (pitch 1), but veers right at the third bolt. Nice pockets.
(Roger Chayer, 2001)

❾ Exit Planet Dust P2 5.12c ☐
15 bolts (28 m) Continue straight up above the anchor. Climb a small, right-facing corner to a thin and reachy crux on grey stone. *(PREP: Roger Chayer; FA: Todd Guyn, 2001)*

❿ The Arch 5.12d . . . . ☐
15 bolts (30 m) From the anchors of *Exit Planet Dust P1*, follow pockets up a right-facing corner to an arch. Cranking over the top of the arch is tough. *(Todd Guyn, 2002)*

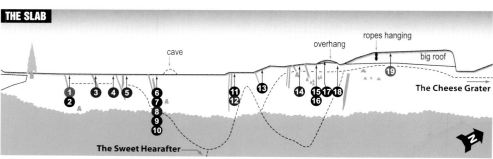

THE SLAB

cave

ropes hanging

overhang

big roof

The Cheese Grater

The Sweet Hearafter

⓫ Heavy Breathing 5.12b . . . . . . 🔲

11 bolts (23 m) From the platform, scramble up a ramp to reach a high first bolt. Great climbing up a small, left-facing corner leads to a roof. Crank to a hueco before launching into a series of moves on cruxy, small pockets.
(PREP: Jon Jones; FA: Todd Guyn, 2001)

⓬ Crank Call 5.11d . . . . 🔲

12 bolts (28 m) From the *Heavy Breathing* hueco, climb rightward into a small, right-facing corner. Finish with some classic Velcro climbing. A fantastic route! *(Jon Jones, 2000)*

⓭ September Eleven 5.12c . . . . . 🔲

13 bolts (30 m) From the platform, follow a blue streak through pockets to a seam. A desperate crux leads over the bulge to a difficult Velcro finish to gain the anchor.
(PREP: Ryan Johnstone, 2001; FA: Todd Guyn, 2001)

⓮ Buena Vista Social Club 5.11c 🔲

7 bolts (14 m) Start off a small platform and follow the yellow streak through a shallow, right-facing corner on pockets and edges. Look left! *(Roger Chayer, 1999)*

⓯ The Way of All Flesh 5.12b . . . . . . 🔲

14 bolts (28 m) This two-faced route is a journey. Powerful pulling on pockets leads over a small roof and is followed by engaging and technical climbing with a shocking lack of holds. *(Daren Tremaine, 1999)*

⓰ Post-apocalyptic Wasteland 5.12a . . . . . . 🔲

7 bolts (15 m) This is a fun pocket route. Climb *The Way of All Flesh* to a small roof and traverse right on pockets to finish on *Jive Turkey*. *(Daren Tremaine, 2000)*

⓱ Jive Turkey 5.12c . . . 🔲

6 bolts (14 m) This fun gymnastic route starts up a shallow groove above a small cave. Big moves between positive holds lead through the roof. Veer right to a crux on small pockets. *(Greg Dickie, 2000)*

⓲ Jive Turkey Direct 5.12c . . . . 🔲

6 bolts (14 m) Start directly right of *Jive Turkey* (two fixed draws). Steep, powerful pocket pulling leads through several bulges. *(JD LeBlanc, 2002)*

⓳ Open Project . . . . 🔲

THE SLAB

hanging gear ⟶

small cave

THE CHEESE GRATER

15 routes ←5.10 5.11 5.12 5.13→

Despite the name, the rock on this cliff is actually not that sharp or unpleasant. The crag hosts a few outstanding routes and is definitely worth a stop to warm up before heading on to The Eyes of Bataan.

Approach: Continue uphill from the Slab sector for five minutes.

The Cheese Grater

Routes are listed from left to right.

❶ Only the Lonely 5.10a . . . . ☐
10 bolts (26 m) Start directly left of a large, right-facing corner. Follow positive edges through a small corner system to anchors at the top of the wall. A great warm-up.
(Ian & Chris Perry 2007)

❷ Vicious 5.11c . . . . ☐
10 bolts (28 m) Tackle the grey-blue wall just right of the large, right-facing corner. Climb the corner for three bolts, step right and wave goodbye to the jugs. *(Jon Jones, 2000)*

❸ Chalk 5.10c . . . . ☐
7 bolts (19 m) Start on the left edge of a small cave. Fun climbing up a corner crack leads to a great slab finish up the scoop. *(Jon Jones, 2001)*

❹ Cheese 5.11d . . . . ☐
11 bolts (27 m) Continue, with difficulty, past the anchors of *Chalk*. *(Jon Jones, 2001)*

❺ Significant Digits 5.11b . . . . ☐
14 bolts (30 m) From a large platform, climb a left-facing corner and step right onto the face. Excellent climbing up a flake and overhanging wall above leads to a sporty finish! *(Ian & Chris Perry, 2001)*

❻ Goldfinger 5.11c . . . . ☐
12 bolts (30 m) From the platform, scramble onto a ledge with a small tree. Follow a gold streak to a roof. Sustained to the anchor. Excellent! *(Ian & Chris Perry, 2003)*

❼ Pick Pocket 5.12c . . . . . ☐ ☐ ☐ ☐
8 bolts (17 m) From the platform, scramble onto the tree ledge. Follow pockets up a yellow streak and skirt a roof

THE CHEESE GRATER

ledge

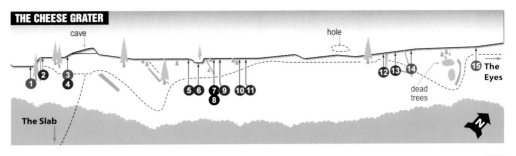

on the right. A hard pocket pull to small edges stands between you and the anchor. *(Ian & Chris Perry, 2004)*

8 Picked Pocket 5.12c

12 bolts (28 m) The extension. *(Derek Galloway, 2009)*

9 Critical Path 5.11c

7 bolts (16 m) Scramble onto a ledge just left of some low-cut tree stumps. Climb over a small, chossy band to great rock above. A few powerful moves off edges are required to get past the last bulge. *(Ian & Chris Perry, 2004)*

10 Monkey Business 5.11a

7 bolts (17 m) Scramble onto a ledge. Follow good holds up a yellow streak to a crux at its end. *(Jon Jones, 2004)*

11 Some Like It Hot 5.11a

12 bolts (28 m) Start in a small, right-facing corner two metres right of some stumps. Follow a grey streak to a hanging pillar and the start of the fun. Backclean the bolt at the top of the crack to reduce drag. *(Jon Jones, 2001)*

12 Broken English 5.11a

11 bolts (29 m) Start immediately left of the first platform. Tricky climbing in the lower half leads to a much easier, but sporty finish up a flake. *(Jon Jones, 2001)*

13 Dangling Modifier 5.11a

11 bolts (29 m) Start off the first platform and enjoy good climbing to a fun exit over a small roof. A 5.10b variation (10 bolts, 30 m) traverses left at the sixth bolt to finish on *Broken English*. *(Jon Jones, 2001)*

14 Ghosts of Thousands 5.10c

8 bolts (19 m) From the second platform, climb to a ledge at the base of a large corner. Continue up the right side to anchors above. *(Roger Chayer, 2001)*

15 Open Project

Interesting Fact: Bataan is named after the infamous, 96-km World War II "Bataan Death March" that took place in the Philippines in 1942. Thousands of American and Filipino soldiers died during this week-long prisoner of war transfer. It occurred after the three-month Battle of Bataan, one of the last stands of American and Filipino soldiers against the Japanese.

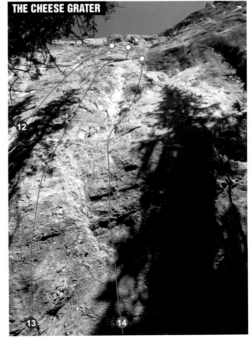

THE EYES OF BATAAN

41 routes ←5.10 5.11 5.12 5.13→

This large, sweeping section of light blue rock offers many inspiring lines in the 5.12 to 5.13 range, and holds the majority of the hard routes at Bataan. It's worth making the walk up from the lower walls just to check this crag out and enjoy the amazing views. When it's dry, it's hard to beat the climbing at this cliff. The Pacific Theatre, Tipperary, and Far East sectors are also included in this zone.

Conditions: This cliff is a serious, south-facing sun trap and is one of the best early- and late-season walls in the Bow Valley. Spring and fall are the prime seasons, but winter days can also be very doable, provided the high temperatures range from 0° to 5°C and the skies are clear. The only downside to this amazing sector is seepage. Early spring is often very dry because the ground is still frozen, but by late spring and early summer, the ground starts to thaw and the pockets begin to seep. Late summer and fall offer dry conditions once again.

Approach: The Eyes of Bataan sector is five minutes up the approach trail from the Cheese Grater wall.

The Eyes of Bataan

Routes are listed from left to right.

❶ Pushing Forty 5.11b . . . . □

15 bolts (33 m) Start on the left-hand side of the steep, pocketed overhang. A crack leads to a pocketed slab were you'll ponder each move. Use a 70-metre rope or lower twice to get down. Good quality. *(Greg Golovach, 2001)*

❷ Forever Young 5.13c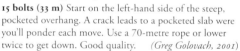

11 bolts (22 m) This route takes a direct line up the steep, pocketed overhanging wall. Start just right of *Pushing Forty* to gain a ledge and the base of the route. A sea of

steep pockets leads to a vicious boulder problem at the lip. *(PREP: Gery Unterasinger; FA: Derek Galloway, 2006)*

❸ PHD Support Group 5.12d . . . . .

13 bolts (24 m) Start in a corner, climb onto a slab and trend left on good pockets up an overhanging ramp to a rest. A hard crux is followed by sustained climbing. Don't wobble off the monos at the top. *(Simon Meis, 2009)*

❹ Welcome to the Fabulous Sky Lounge 5.12b . . . .

12 bolts (29 m) Climb a pocketed corner to a chain draw. Undercling left and head up a beautiful blue streak. Back-clean the first draw to reduce drag. *(Roger Chayer, 2003)*

THE EYES OF BATAAN

anchor for 11 & 13

rope ladder

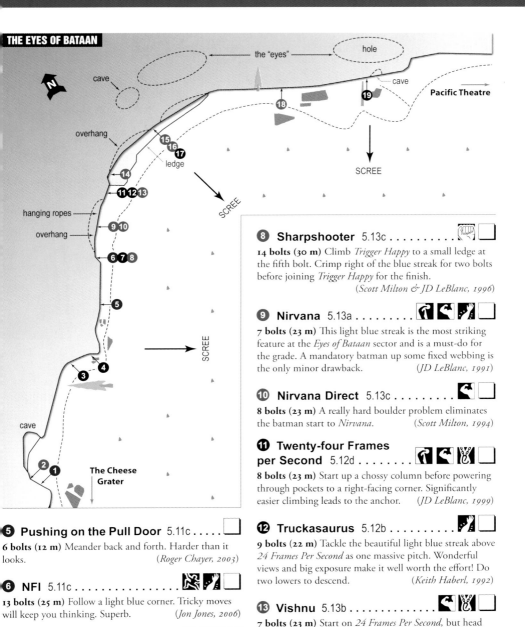

8 Sharpshooter 5.13c . . . .

14 bolts (30 m) Climb *Trigger Happy* to a small ledge at the fifth bolt. Crimp right of the blue streak for two bolts before joining *Trigger Happy* for the finish.
(Scott Milton & JD LeBlanc, 1996)

9 Nirvana 5.13a . . . .

7 bolts (23 m) This light blue streak is the most striking feature at the *Eyes of Bataan* sector and is a must-do for the grade. A mandatory batman up some fixed webbing is the only minor drawback.   *(JD LeBlanc, 1991)*

10 Nirvana Direct 5.13c . . . .

8 bolts (23 m) A really hard boulder problem eliminates the batman start to *Nirvana*.   *(Scott Milton, 1994)*

11 Twenty-four Frames per Second 5.12d . . . .

8 bolts (23 m) Start up a chossy column before powering through pockets to a right-facing corner. Significantly easier climbing leads to the anchor.   *(JD LeBlanc, 1999)*

12 Truckasaurus 5.12b . . . .

9 bolts (22 m) Tackle the beautiful light blue streak above *24 Frames Per Second* as one massive pitch. Wonderful views and big exposure make it well worth the effort! Do two lowers to descend.   *(Keith Haberl, 1992)*

13 Vishnu 5.13b . . . .

7 bolts (23 m) Start on *24 Frames Per Second*, but head right gunning for the blue streak. Serious fingerboard training will come in handy at the crux.
(PREP: JD LeBlanc; FA: Ross Suchy, 2004)

14 Closed Project . . . .

5 Pushing on the Pull Door 5.11c . . . . .

6 bolts (12 m) Meander back and forth. Harder than it looks.   *(Roger Chayer, 2003)*

6 NFI 5.11c . . . .

13 bolts (25 m) Follow a light blue corner. Tricky moves will keep you thinking. Superb.   *(Jon Jones, 2006)*

7 Trigger Happy 5.12a . . . .

16 bolts (30 m) This long, fun route starts on *NFI*, but cuts right at the first bolt. Crazy pocket pulling ends with a cruxy traverse and steep, juggy climbing to the anchor.
(PREP: Roger Chayer; FA: Ryan Greenberg, 2005)

THE PACIFIC THEATRE

⑮ Ride 5.13b . . . .

7 bolts (16 m) Start on a ledge using a high, right under-cling. Branch left above the first bolt and climb over a bulge. Head straight up to a heartbreaking crux before the anchor. (*PREP: Daren Tremaine; FA: Chris Weldon, 2007*)

⑯ Jacob's Ladder 5.13a

8 bolts (16 m) Start on *Ride*, but power straight up to a hard boulder problem. Finish with slightly easier, enjoy-able climbing. (*JD LeBlanc, 1992*)

⑰ Extension Ladder 5.12c . . . . . .

9 bolts (33 m) This great extension to *Jacob's Ladder* on steep, black rock doesn't add much difficulty due to an excellent rest. You can *just* get down with a 60-metre rope. Tie a knot at the end of your rope! (*Simon Meis, 2007*)

⑱ Open Project . . . .

Start off the ledges to the right of the tree growing against the cliff.

⑲ Eyes Wide Shut 5.12a . . . .

18 bolts (33 m) This long, pumpy and exposed classic follows a blue streak that skirts the left edge of the right "eye". The seemingly-useless first bolt is simply meant to keep the rope out of the way at the start. The fourth bolt is doubled due to poor rock quality. Clip the right one, traverse left and then move the draw to the left bolt. The climbing above is superb. Enjoy! (*Ian & Chris Perry, 2005*)

The Pacific Theatre

The Pacific Theatre is the beautifully streaked, slightly-overhanging face right of the Eyes of Bataan. The routes are long and sustained and have some powerful cruxes. Snowmelt from above can be a problem in the morning, but the streaks usually dry by late afternoon. Routes are listed from left to right.

⑳ Open Project . . . .

Start in the cave to the left of the tree.

㉑ Open Project . . . .

Start right of the tree. A nice looking line.

㉒ Freedom in Chains 5.13c . . . .

10 bolts (25 m) Start on a detached block. Technical and pumpy moves weave up the light blue streak. This is one of the best routes of its grade in the Bow Valley.

(*PREP: Roger Chayer; FA: Scott Milton, 2004*)

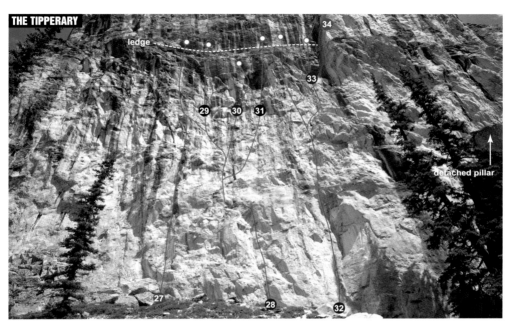

THE TIPPERARY

34

33

29 30 31

27 28 32

ledge

detached pillar

㉓ Above the Clouds 5.13d

10 bolts (25 m) This line was originally bolted during a very wet season. It was only a patch of dry rock! Two difficult and intricate cruxes are separated by a thank-God jug. (*PREP: Scott Milton; FA: Derek Galloway, 2006*)

㉔ Leaning in the Wind 5.12c ...

12 bolts (25 m) Start on *Above the Clouds*, but follow the corner up a yellow streak, which gets progressively harder up high. The final sting-in-the-tail is the anchor clip!
(*PREP: Sandra Studer; FA: Todd Guyn, 2003*)

㉕ Cartoon 5.12d ...

9 bolts (23 m) Start off a ledge to the right of the large chimney-corner. A crimpy crux leads to sustained climbing. (*PREP: Roger Chayer; FA: Greg Dickie, 1999*)

㉖ Dressed Up in Pearls 5.12a ...

7 bolts (23 m) Start off a ledge to the right of the large chimney-corner. Prepare for crimpy and balancey climbing. (*Roger Chayer, 1999*)

The Tipperary

This sector is located just one minute around the corner from The Pacific Theatre. It features some great routes that offer technical challenges on slopers and edges on a slightly overhanging wall. Late afternoon sun. Routes are listed from left to right.

㉗ Open Project ...

This is a direct start to *Saving Grace*. The bolting is not finished.

㉘ Saving Grace 5.11c ...

10 bolts (22 m) Start up a short corner on the right side of the small pillar. Difficult climbing on edges and slopers gains the fourth bolt. Climb left with difficulty to great finger buckets near the top. (*Roger Chayer, 2001*)

㉙ It's a Long, Long Way 5.12a ..

10 bolts (23 m) Climb *Saving Grace* to the fifth bolt before launching straight up a shallow groove. Great crimpers in the overhang! (*PREP: Roger Chayer; FA: Todd Guyn, 2001*)

㉚ Thief 5.11c ...

9 bolts (23 m) Climb *Saving Grace* to the fourth bolt before climbing straight up a thin grey streak into a high, right-facing corner. A tricky move exiting the corner is followed by jugs. (*Jon Jones, 2000*)

③ Burning Desire 5.12c . . .

11 bolts (23 m) Climb *Saving Grace* to the top of the short pillar. A big move to the right is followed by a long, hard move straight up (the crux). Sustained, mid-5.11 to the top. (*PREP: Jon Jones, 2001; FA: Todd Guyn, 2002*)

③ Tipperary 5.11d . . . .

12 bolts (23 m) Start in a shallow corner four metres left of a fully-detached pillar. A crux at the fourth bolt gives way to fun jugs and a pre-anchor crux. (*Jon Jones, 2001*)

③ Far Corner of the Earth 5.11d . . . . .

12 bolts (23 m) Start on *Tipperary*. From the midway rest, traverse right before continuing straight up to a hard move that guards the anchor. Backclean the bolt before the rest to reduce rope drag. (*Jon Jones, 1998*)

③ Far Corner of the Earth P2 5.10d . . . .

10 bolts (19 m) From the last bolt of the first pitch, continue up a corner using a thin crack on the right. Great exposure! Lower twice to get down. Extending draws at the transition will eliminate rope drag. (*Jon Jones, 1998*)

The Far East

The last sector on the cliff band is a rarely-visited wall with couple of good routes on the left side worth checking out. The sun doesn't hit this crag until late afternoon. Routes are listed from left to right.

③ Mutton Chops 5.11a . . . .

11 bolts (28 m) Start three metres left of a tree. Angle right through prickly edges, buckets and slopers to a technical finish left of the corner. (*Jon Jones, 2001*)

③ Mutton Chops Variation 5.10c . . . . . .

11 bolts (28 m) Climb *Mutton Chops* to the base of the high, right-facing corner before heading right on good holds to a crack. (*Jon Jones, 2001*)

③ Jagged Edge 5.10d . . . .

11 bolts (28 m) After a short crack, think like Velcro to help get to the positive flake above. (*Jon Jones, 2001*)

③ Jagged Edge Alternate Start 5.10b . .

11 bolts (30 m) Using a tree, chimney upward until you can step onto the wall. Trend left, joining *Jagged Edge* below the flake. (*Jon Jones, 2001*)

③ Death by a Thousand Cuts 5.11c . . . .

13 bolts (29 m) Start just right of the tree. A long prickly face ends with a crux right at the top. (*Jon Jones, 2002*)

④ Walking on Broken Glass 5.11c . . . .

8 bolts (16 m) Climbing on broken glass. (*Jon Jones, 2004*)

④ Open Project . . . .

Needs bolts and cleaning. Another sharp line!

THE FAR EAST

Zak McGurk on PHD Support Group (5.12d). Photo by Gery Unterasinger.

CHAPTER 7
ECHO CANYON

E cho Canyon is located on the west end of Grotto Mountain and encompasses the entire box canyon perched above the Alpine Club of Canada. The potential is staggering, and has already produced four worthy areas: the Hideaway, the Lookout, the Coliseum and the Notch. Each of these sectors has a full selection of routes with a distinct style and ambiance. The lines range in difficulty from 5.8 to 5.13+, and run the gamut from vertical crimpfests to overhanging endurance marathons, all with breathtaking views to remind you why climbing in the Bow Valley is like nowhere else.

There is no doubt that the future of Bow Valley sport climbing lies within the towering walls of Echo Canyon. Herein lies a seemingly endless supply of new routes awaiting the motivated few, as well as testpieces that will challenge future generations for years to come. Make the slog up and be part of it!

CONDITIONS

The majority of Echo Canyon receives morning sun that stretches into mid- or late afternoon, with the exception of the right-hand cliff line, which stays in the shade until late afternoon or early evening. The best time to visit is in the spring and fall, but if you are willing to chase the shade and accept less-than-perfect redpoint conditions in certain sectors, the summer months are definitely workable. See each area for more detailed information.

APPROACH

From Banff: Drive east on the Trans-Canada Highway toward Canmore. Take Exit 91 and turn left on Bow Valley Trail, which soon becomes Highway 1A. Take the second left onto Indian Flats Road, follow it to the Alpine Club of Canada clubhouse and park.

From Calgary: Drive west on the Trans-Canada Highway toward Canmore. Take Exit 91 and turn left on Bow Valley Trail, which soon becomes Highway 1A. Take the second left onto Indian Flats Road, follow it to the Alpine Club of Canada clubhouse and park.

From Canmore: Drive east on Bow Valley Trail, which becomes Highway 1A. Turn left onto Indian Flats Road, follow it to the Alpine Club of Canada clubhouse and park.

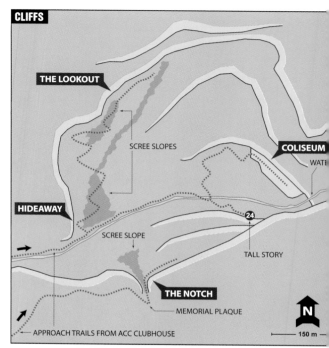

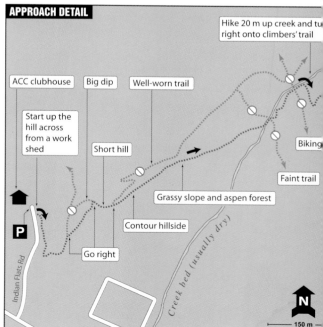

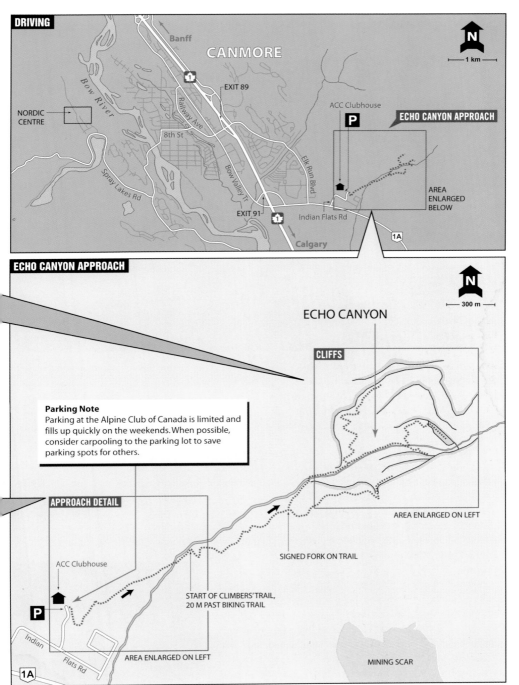

DRIVING

Banff

CANMORE

N
1 km

NORDIC CENTRE

EXIT 89

ACC Clubhouse

P

ECHO CANYON APPROACH

AREA ENLARGED BELOW

EXIT 91

Indian Flats Rd

Calgary

1A

ECHO CANYON APPROACH

N
300 m

ECHO CANYON

CLIFFS

AREA ENLARGED ON LEFT

Parking Note
Parking at the Alpine Club of Canada is limited and fills up quickly on the weekends. When possible, consider carpooling to the parking lot to save parking spots for others.

APPROACH DETAIL

ACC Clubhouse

P

SIGNED FORK ON TRAIL

START OF CLIMBERS' TRAIL, 20 M PAST BIKING TRAIL

Indian Flats Rd

AREA ENLARGED ON LEFT

MINING SCAR

1A

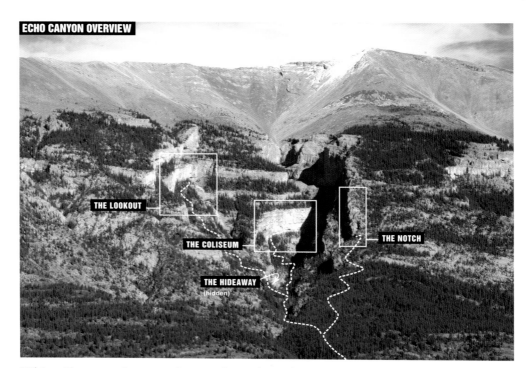

ECHO CANYON OVERVIEW

THE LOOKOUT

THE COLISEUM

THE NOTCH

THE HIDEAWAY
(hidden)

Hiking: The approach is somewhat complex, and your first attempt may be a little frustrating as there are a lot of trail options to reach the climbers' trail at the mouth of the canyon. If you have trouble, simply make sure you always take the right-hand trail options, which eventually lead into the creek bed. Once in the creek bed, follow it upstream to the mouth of the canyon and the climbers' trail, which is just beyond the biking trail. Below are the directions for the trail link-up most climbers use.

From the clubhouse parking lot, locate a well-worn trail that leads up the hillside across from a work shed. At the first opportunity, go right and contour along the hillside. This trail soon spits you out onto a well-worn trail at the bottom of a big dip. Take a right and follow the well-worn trail up a short hill to a small loop and an intersection with a less-travelled trail. Don't go left and follow the well-worn trail up the ridge. Instead, turn right and follow the less-travelled trail, which contours along the hillside and leads across a grassy slope and aspen forest before dropping into the creek bed. Pick up the trail on the right side of creek bed and follow it upstream past a faint trail and then a well-worn biking trail that both cross the creek. The climbers' trail leading into Echo Canyon is located about 20 metres past the biking trail on the right-hand side of the creek, and is about 10 minutes from the parking lot (if you pass twin slabs in the creek bed and encounter small canyon walls on either side of the creek, you've gone too far). Follow the switchbacking climbers' trail for about 25 minutes to a signed fork. See the specific area descriptions for the remaining approach directions from this landmark.

THE HIDEAWAY

26 routes   ←—5.10 5.11 5.12 5.13—→

The highly-technical and cryptic nature of the climbing at this cliff might catch you off guard until you get used to the hard-to-read sequences. The rock is never overhanging, except for the occasional small roof, and the routes favour those with strong fingers and a good sense of body position. The Hideaway has the shortest and easiest approach of all the climbing areas in Echo Canyon, and makes a good springboard for those looking to venture further uphill.

Conditions: This cliff gets sun from morning until early afternoon and makes a good early- and late-season venue. During the heat of summer the wall gets pretty hot, so wait until mid-afternoon to visit. In rainstorms, this vertical wall gets wet quickly, but dries fast after the rain has stopped.

Approach: From the signed fork in the trail, go left and contour down to the creek bed negotiating a couple of small rock steps along the way. Follow the creek upstream for about 10 minutes until the Hideaway comes into view on the left side of the creek. Follow a short trail to the base of the wall.

The Hideaway

Routes are listed from left to right.

① Hidden Pleasures 5.10c . . . .

11 bolts (24 m) Start off a log platform and climb immaculate grey stone on perfectly sculpted holds to anchors in some cool chert knobs.   *(Unknown)*

② Mantle Delight 5.10c . . . .

11 bolts (21 m) From the log platform, climb through broken terrain to the top of a groove. Trend right on great rock to a small mantle before the anchor. *(Greg Tos, 2005)*

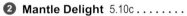

THE HIDEAWAY

③ Welcome Mat 5.11b . . . .

8 bolts (17 m) This is the first route encountered upon reaching the wall from the approach trail. Funky climbing on sidepulls leads up a yellow corner to bigger holds and a small crux before the anchors.   *(Greg Tos, 2005)*

④ The Wedge 5.11c . . . .

7 bolts (15 m) A tough crux gains a wedge-shaped hold. Tricky sidepulls above.   *(Ian Perry, 2004)*

⑤ Frosty Flakes 5.11b . . . .

5 bolts (11 m) Two crimpy cruxes are separated by a monster jug.   *(Ian Perry, 2004)*

⑥ Hidden 5.11a . . . .

11 bolts (30 m) Head up a grey slab left of a big, yellow corner until it's possible to step right onto the flawless, water-sculpted grey face. It's a bit sporty climbing from the last bolt to the anchor.   *(Greg & Irene Tos, 2005)*

⑦ Bass Ackwards 5.12a . . . .

11 bolts (30 m) This fantastic route opens with a small crux that gains the grey streak above. From the streak's top, another crux stands between you and a beautiful finish.   *(Zac Robinson, Aaron Pellerin & Greg Tos, 2004)*

⑧ Waiting for the Sun 5.12a . . . .

10 bolts (24 m) Hard and insecure entry moves lead to great laybacking up a right-facing corner capped by a small roof. A tricky lip encounter leads to an easy stroll up sculpted holds.   *(Chris & Ian Perry, 2004)*

THE HIDEAWAY

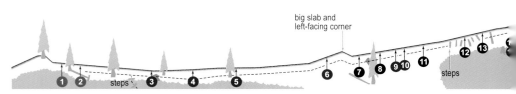

big slab and
left-facing corner

**❾ Waiting for
the Sun Alternate Start** 5.11c . . . .

10 bolts (24 m) Trend left through grey rock and join the original line at the base of the corner. Nice. (*Greg Tos, 2006*)

❿ Venturi 5.11a . . . .

14 bolts (30 m) The is the must-do 5.11 on the wall. Spectacular climbing follows a thin seam up a grey wall to a rest in a large scoop. Exit out left to slightly easier climbing and anchors very high on the wall. (*Chris & Ian Perry, 2004*)

⓫ Spinal Reach 5.12b . . . .

12 bolts (23 m) Be prepared to get your crimp on. Start up a small, right-facing corner and trend right onto a grey, crimpy wall. Once at the break, the climbing gets a bit easier and much less crimpy. (*Greg Tos, 2004*)

⓬ Thumb Wars 5.12c . . . .

9 bolts (15 m) Start halfway up the steps. A thuggish crux pulls past the low roof and leads to a tough micro-crimp crux below the anchor. (*Greg Tos, 2004*)

⓭ Last Call 5.12c . . . .

10 bolts (23 m) Begin at the top of the steps. Technical and sustained face climbing weaves up the beautiful grey streak. (*Greg Tos, 2004*)

⓮ Undercover Brother 5.12a . . . . . .

11 bolts (23 m) This route begins in front of a small tree with technical sidepulls, underclings and crimps. Sustained to the anchor. (*Greg Tos, 2004*)

⓯ Undercover Brothers 5.11c . . . .

18 bolts (38 m) From the anchors of *Undercover Brother*, trend left onto a tough slab. Jug thuggery leads up the overhang above. Lower twice to descend. (*Greg Tos, 2006*)

⓰ The Diamond 5.12b . . . .

7 bolts (14 m) This pitch is a must-do for the grade. Amazing holds lead to a baffling traverse right past a yellow corner. Great climbing above. At the last bolt, climb left in order to reach the anchor. (*Greg Tos, 2004*)

**⓱ Pinchy
Sidepull Undercling** 5.12d . . . . . .

3 bolts (13 m) An improbable boulder problem guards passage at the first bolt. (*Simon Robins & Greg Tos, 2004*)

⓲ Spring Fever 5.11d . . . .

11 bolts (20 m) Climb the right side of a corner to a very tricky bulge. Easy, but still-tricky climbing gains the anchor above. (*Greg Tos, 2005*)

⓳ The Hermit 5.12b . . . .

11 bolts (31 m) Start in front of a two-pronged tree. Slopey edges lead to a short corner. Pull around to the right and prepare for difficulty in the upper corner and roof. Better than it looks. (*Greg & Irene Tos, 2004*)

⓴ Phantom Ledges 5.11c . . . .

13 bolts (32 m) This is a great route with some spooky (but safe) moves over the multiple hanging slabs up high. Start off a platform between two sets of trees below a large roof. (*Zac Robinson, Greg & Irene Tos, 2004*)

㉑ Willy Wonka 5.12a . . . .

11 bolts (24 m) Climb *Willie Nelson* to the fifth bolt, and continue up the corner to a stout move heading back right over a bulge. Finish on *Willie Nelson*. (*Greg Tos, 2005*)

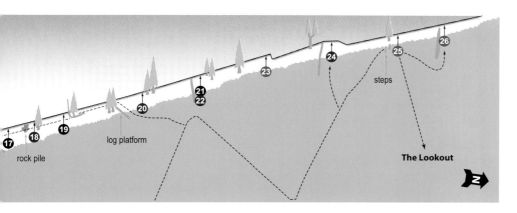

rock pile

log platform

steps

The Lookout

22 Willie Nelson 5.11a . . . . ☐

10 bolts (24 m) Good climbing leads up a left-facing corner to a horn-shaped jug. Move right onto the face and finish straight up. *(Zac Robinson, 2004)*

23 Closed Project . . . . ☐

24 Yoshimi
Battles the Pink Robots 5.11c . . . . ☐

10 bolts (19 m) This superb route is well worth the walk to the end of the wall. Perfect edges lead to a cool roof encounter before the anchors. *(Marc Andre Cousineau, 2009)*

25 Closed Project . . . . ☐

26 Buffy Against the Vampires 5.10a . . ☐

12 bolts (27 m) The last route climbs a lot better than it looks. Head up a small, left-facing corner and work through overlaps to anchors at the top of the wall.
(Marc Andre Cousineau &Andrew Henman, 2009)

THE HIDEAWAY

THE LOOKOUT

53 routes ←5.10 5.11 5.12 5.13→

 70 min. 530m to 660m

The Lookout is comprised of the long cliff band on the west side of Echo Canyon. It's a great area, and some of the longest and steepest routes in the region are found here, with a few requiring a 100-metre rope to descend! The cliff band is home to climbs from 5.8 to 5.13+, so just about anyone can enjoy a fun day soaking up the sun and taking in the spectacular views, provided they can handle the one-hour-plus uphill approach. For those so motivated, a significant reward will be found at journey's end.

Conditions: The best windows for this zone are spring and fall, when morning sun is welcome and afternoon shade provides perfect sending temperatures. Summer is workable, but you'll want to sleep in and head up midday to avoid hot rock. Because the cliff is such a good sun trap, it can also provide good conditions on sunny, mid-winter days, even when the temperature is close to zero. Seepage can be an issue in the spring, but once the routes dry out, wet holds usually aren't a problem thereafter. The overhanging Atlantis Wall remains dry during rainfall, and is a good choice for stormy, unsettled days.

Approach: From the Alpine Club of Canada, hike for 35 minutes to the signed fork in the trail, take the left option and contour down to the creek bed. Follow it upstream until you are below a large scree slope on the left. From here, follow a trail up the slope past the Hideaway. The trail then makes large switchbacks up the scree slope and through trees to the base the Lookout cliff band. The first wall you encounter is Echo Cave, reached by a short side trail. The other walls are 10 minutes farther uphill.

Echo Cave

This small cave is located at the base of the long, ascending cliff band that makes up the entire Lookout. The routes at this sector don't actually scale the cave, but instead tackle the wall just to the right. The rock is solid grey and compact, and the crag receives morning sun only partially shielded by some large trees. Seepage

is a major issue at this crag, so if you find it dry, take full advantage. Routes are listed from left to right.

❶ **Morpheus** 5.12b . . . .
9 bolts (22 m) This line tackles an overhanging path of jugs up the right edge of the cave. If you find it dry, give it a try since it doesn't stay dry for long! *(Greg Tos, 2006)*

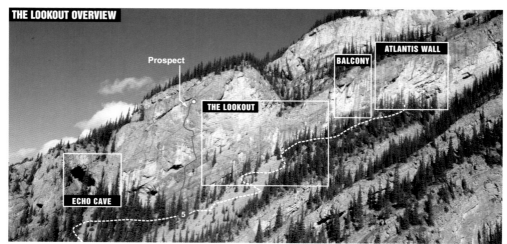

THE LOOKOUT OVERVIEW — Prospect, THE LOOKOUT, BALCONY, ATLANTIS WALL, ECHO CAVE

② Echo 5.13a . . . .

9 bolts (22 m) Technical climbing leads to a thought-provoking crux at mid-height and a pumpy finish.
(*Aaron Pellerin & Greg Tos, 2006*)

③ Closed Project . . . . ☐

④ Destination Unknown 5.12d . . . .

8 bolts (16 m) The right-most line is very good and has bouldery sections of climbing involving long reaches between cool pockets and crimps. Milk the good rest! (*Mike Cummings & Greg Tos, 2007*)

⑤ Prospect 5.10b . . . .

This route is located about 60 metres uphill from Echo Cave. It's a fun, four-pitch climb on good rock. All pitches are 5.10 and you'll only need 11 draws and a 60-metre rope.

Pitch 1 (5.10b, 10 bolts, 30 m) Climb an obvious corner to gain a small ramp. Above, tackle steep rock on nice, positive features, which eventually morph into smaller holds. A series of rightward moves over a small bulge follows, and is the crux, but the difficulties are softened if you find the hidden holds. Finish by cranking onto a large ramp with a spacious belay stance. Nice stone.

Pitch 2 (5.10a, 5 bolts, 15 m) Climb a short, steep orange and yellow face on decent, but slightly crumbling holds. A tricky move leftward gains a ramp. Follow it up and right, bypassing a rappel station used on the descent, to a two-bolt anchor on a good ledge just above.

Pitch 3 (5.10c, 10 bolts, 30 m) Climb over a small bulge and up steep, grey rock above. Negotiate a small roof near the top by moving slightly left and then back to the right. Good holds lead to the belay. This pitch is arguably the best of the grade in the entire Echo Canyon. Excellent features abound, but the most memorable are the perfectly formed underclings and fabulous pockets at two-thirds height.

Pitch 4 (5.10a, 10 bolts, 25 m) Traverse left on a textured slab before heading up a steep and featured yellow wall. On the right, watch for a large rock scar where some refrigerator-sized blocks were removed after the pitch was bolted. (If you are wondering why the line doesn't go right, this should answer your question). Continue up a short corner and over another tricky bulge just below the anchor. The finish may be a little loose, but is easy. Rappel the route to descend.
(*Ian & Chris Perry, 2009*)

ECHO CAVE

PROSPECT

5.10a

5.10c

5.10a

rap anchor

5.10b

The Lookout

This section of cliff band extends uphill past the end of the scree slope. It's a nice stretch of vertical, grey limestone that's been tortured over the millennia by rain, which has resulted in perfectly sculpted handholds. The vertical routes climb like technical puzzles that challenge both mind and muscle. Although the wall is very exposed to rainfall, it dries quickly and rarely seeps. The cliff sees full sun until mid-afternoon, making it a great choice on cold, clear days. Routes are listed from left to right.

❻ November Rain 5.9 . . . .

6 bolts (15 m) This is the slabby and technical face left of the large, right-facing corner. Nice chert knobs and a featureless finish make it worthwhile. *(Jeff MacPherson, 2008)*

❼ Texas Hold'em 5.11a . . .

9 bolts (23 m) Weave a path up immaculate grey rock to the anchor. The first big roof isn't as hard as it looks. *(Jeff MacPherson, 2009)*

❽ Crying Roof 5.11a . . . .

8 bolts (19 m) This fun route tackles excellent grey and yellow rock just right of a right-facing corner. From the jug rail at the top of the yellow streak, crank straight up and over the roof. *(Marc Andrés Cousineau & Greg Tos, 2008)*

❾ Sheep Metal 5.8 . . . .

8 bolts (19 m) Climb the blunt prow to a jug rail before making a rightward traverse on amazing chert bands. Finish up the slab. Shares anchors with *Crying Roof*. *(Marc Andrés Cousineau, Greg Tos & Allen Buchard, 2008)*

❿ Remembrance Day 5.9 . . . .

12 bolts (29 m) Start at the base of a cluster of trees. Climb a nice crack up a shallow corner before pulling onto a clean, grey face. Trend right across technical, stippled rock toward the anchor. *(Greg Tos, 2008)*

⓫ Pale Ale 5.10d . . . .

11 bolts (27 m) This great route is tucked away at the top of a cluster of trees. The hardest climbing

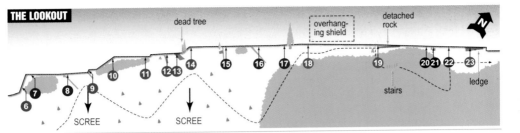

comes in the bottom third, and is followed by easier but sustained climbing to the anchor. *(Jeff MacPherson, 2008)*

⑫ Graduation 5.10d . . . . ☐

8 bolts (27 m) Big holds and a steep start give way to slabby and technical territory above. *(Simon Robins, 2009)*

⑬ Sandbox 5.10d . . . . ☐

6 bolts (28 m) Climb a mungy and loose corner. Likely the worse route at the cliff. *(Simon Robins, 2008)*

⑭ Caramel Macchiato 5.10a . . . . ☐

12 bolts (28 m) Interesting moves in the right-facing corner lead to a no-hands rest at the end. Finish with excellent climbing up the prickly undulating face above. *(Greg Tos, 2007)*

⑮ No Love 5.11b . . . . ▨ ☐

11 bolts (26 m) This pitch features great, thought-provoking climbing up perfect grey rock. Starts off a platform below a short, left-facing corner. *(Jeff MacPherson, 2008)*

⑯ Watchman 5.11c . . . . ▨ ☐

9 bolts (27 m) Expect some intricate puzzle solving on prickly grey rock. At the fourth bolt, trend rightward into a corner and up a yellow streak. Finish with a committing balancing act near the anchor. *(Greg Tos, 2007)*

⑰ Aragon 5.11d . . . . ☐

12 bolts (27 m) Multiple cruxes will keep you perplexed all the way to the anchor. Starts just left of a big tree with a dead top. *(Aaron Pelleron & Greg Tos, 2007)*

⑱ Closed Project . . . . ☐

⑲ Closed Project . . . . ☐

⑳ Wasted on the Way 5.12b . . . . . . ▨ ☐

8 bolts (18 m) This pitch has sustained, technical climb-ing with few rests on nice grey rock. Share the same anchor as *Tetris*. *(Gery Unterasinger, 2010)*

㉑ Tetris 5.12a . . . . ▨ ☐

8 bolts (18 m) This fantastic route starts in front of a few tree stumps. It's tricky enough to keep you on your toes until the crux at the very last bolt. *(Greg Tos, 2010)*

㉒ Tickornot 5.11b . . . . ▨ ☐

12 bolts (22 m) An easy start and finish bookend a sus-tained middle section. *(Greg Tos, 2009)*

㉓ Start Line 5.10d . . . . ▨ ☐

8 bolts (23 m) This is a good warm-up on nice rock with some great stipple climbing. From a small ledge, climb up to a bigger ledge and a no-hands rest. A great crux moves over the small roof and is followed by sustained, technical climbing to the top. *(Greg & Irene Tos 2007)*

The Balcony ▨ ▨

This small zone is located between the Lookout and Atlantis walls. It's a beautiful, blue-streaked face perched above a steep, blank slab. Use the fixed line to access the spacious ledge at its base. Routes are listed from left to right.

**㉔ Eleven
Months of Summer** 5.12b . . . . . ▨ ▨ ☐

14 bolts (29 m) This technical masterpiece weaves a path up a fat blue streak on handholds so small they would be considered crappy footholds on any other route. The lower half is where the business is, but the bulge before the anchor also packs a punch. *(Greg Tos, 2010)*

㉕ Stedler and Walldorff 5.10d . . . . . ▨ ☐

17 bolts (34 m) Start below a yellow, left-facing corner. Technical and balancey climbing leads to a great roof crux. Fancy footwork on water-pocked stone leads to the upper roof and a final crux sequence. *(Simon Robins, 2010)*

Atlantis Wall

Just past the Balcony, the trail leads to the Atlantis Wall, a tall overhanging face with a large slab at its right end that blocks further hiking. Upon first inspection, the wall looks a tad chossy, but after a few burns the routes prove to be solid and steep with great flow. If you like long endurance routes, you won't be disappointed—some lines require a 100-metre rope for an up-and-down lower! The crag stays dry in the rain, making it a good choice for suspect forecasts, but does seep from above after big storms (it requires a few days to dry out). Routes are located from left to right.

26 Rozgrzewka (AKA Warm-up) 5.11c

19 bolts (43 m) This long route has two distinctly different flavors (you'll see). Start up the arête on the pillar on the far left end of the wall. (*Greg Toss, 2010*)

27 Pump Up the Jam 5.11a

11 bolts (25 m) Start just right of a large, right-facing corner. The difficulties come in the first half of the route pulling past a small roof and onto a small slab above. (*Marc Andre Cousineau, 2010*)

28 Closed Project

29 Funky Bunch 5.10b

7 bolts (13 m) This is the easiest route on the wall. After four bolts of nice "up" climbing, angle left onto a slab to reach the anchor. A 5.10b variation trends left from the sixth bolt and finishes on *Pump Up the Jam*. (*Marc Andre Cousineau & Katherine Stack, 2009*)

30 Fresh Prince 5.13a

17 bolts (30 m) Climb *Funky Bunch* to the fourth bolt and climb straight up a thin, grey streak. After a tough sequence at the top, head left to a no-hands rest in the big hole. Beautiful climbing lies above, with a sequential and crimpy crux before the anchor. (*Aaron Pellerin, 2010*)

31 Closed Project

32 Bug's Life 5.12b

10 bolts (23 m) Start below an angular roof at three metres. After a mellow start, a series of cruxes lead up a small corner system to the last bolt where you'll have to dig deep and charge for the anchor. (*Aaron Pellerin, 2010*)

33 My Two Bits 5.12b

11 bolts (25 m) This outstanding pitch has multiple cruxes that will test you throughout. Start on top of the two-metre-high pillar. (*Aaron Pellerin & Greg Tos, 2009*)

ATLANTIS WALL

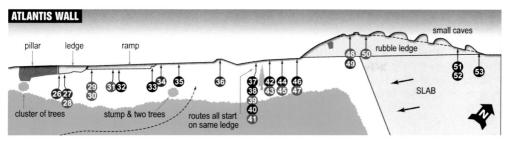

ATLANTIS WALL

34 FFAntom Love 5.11d ......

12 bolts (21 m) This fantastic route has sustained 5.11+ climbing and several mini cruxes. Watch out! (*Greg Tos, 2009*)

35 Respected Silence 5.12c .

8 bolts (16 m) This pitch has a tough start and features fantastic slapping up dueling vertical rails. It's not as easy as you might expect to get to the anchor. (*Greg Tos, 2010*)

36 The Midget 5.11b ......

4 bolts (12 m) Climb a small corner system with interesting holds throughout. Short but sweet. (*Greg Tos, 2009*)

37 Burn to Shine 5.12d ......

16 bolts (37 m) This long, overhanging pumpfest has a powerful crux near the end. Start on *Atlantis*, and traverse

left along the ledge to the route's base. You can *barely* get down with a 70-metre rope. (*Gery Unterasinger, 2010*)

38 All You Can Eat P1 5.12c ......

11 bolts (25 m) After a thin and technical crux, enjoy a fun finish that requires jumping between jugs.
(*PREP: Gery Unterasinger; FA: Derek Galloway, 2010*)

39 Closed Project ......

The extension to *All You Can Eat*.

40 Atlantis 5.12c ......

11 bolts (23 m) This is the route that convinced people the Lookout was worthy of attention. Climb onto a ledge via a weakness and step right before tackling the flake feature and slick face. Things get hard fast at the small roof. Claw your way to the anchor. (*Greg Tos & Jay Audenart, 2008*)

ATLANTIS WALL

41 Closed Project . . . . ☐

The extension to *Atlantis*.

42 Bone Thief 5.12c . . . . ☐

12 bolts (23 m) Climb onto a ledge and up a tricky, right-facing corner. Trend right up a thin blue streak and past a powerful crux and clip. Steady now.   (*Greg Tos, 2010*)

43 Closed Project . . . . ☐

The extension to *Bone Thief*.

44 Buffet Royal P1 5.12a . . . . ☐

9 bolts (20 m) Funky moves through the leaning, left-facing corner down low are followed by a pumpy finish, which ends under a roof.   (*Aaron Pellerin, 2008*)

45 Buffet Royal P2 5.13c . . . ☐

23 bolts (40 m) The extension to *Buffet Royale* is one of the best of its grade in the Bow Valley. It becomes hard and sustained immediately after the midway anchor, but mellows at an okay rest under a small roof. Another powerful section leads over the roof to a good shake and a beautiful black streak with a heart-breaking crux at the end.   (*PREP: Aaron Pellerin; FA: Derek Galloway, 2009*)

46 Spicy Elephant P1 5.12c . . . . ☐

14 bolts (27 m) This great line works up edges to a committing move passing the slab. Fun jugs lead to a rightward traverse and a crux followed by a surprisingly easy roof encounter. A couple of tricky moves guard the chains.   (*Greg Tos, 2008*)

47 Spicy Elephant P2 5.13b . . . . ☐

22 bolts (40 m) From the midway anchor, trend right to a blue streak and prepare for an onslaught of cruxes separated by rests. An amazing route!   (*Greg Tos, 2008*)

48 Diamonds on the Inside 5.13b . . . . ☐

22 bolts (42 m) This route is for endurance affectionados. Technical climbing leads past a cool tufa to a powerful and pumpy sequence out a big roof. A technical crux leads to a very hard redpoint crux up high.   (*Greg Tos, 2010*)

49 Runaway Lane 5.11d . . . . ☐

7 bolts (13 m) This short route branches right from *Diamonds on the Inside*. Grab the tufa!.   (*Greg Tos, 2009*)

50 Closed Project . . . . ☐

51 Burn One Down P1 5.12c . . . ☐

10 bolts (19 m) Begin near the top of a ledge on a rotten pillar. Pull over a big roof and work up big underclings and sidepulls to the base of a small, left-facing corner. Hard and committing moves lead up the corner to a much needed rest. Another tough crux guards the anchor. (*Greg Tos, 2009*)

52 Burn One Down P2 5.12d . . . . . . ☐

17 bolts (35 m) Rest and continue up great rock with no really hard moves, but with a building pump. It may not end well.   (*PREP: Greg Tos; FA: Gery Unterasinger, 2010*)

53 Back and Beyond 5.12a . . . . ☐

17 bolts (30 m) If one of the three cruxes doesn't get you, the exposure just might! The rock at the start is a bit suspect, but the rest holds a lot of charm. To lower, tie a knot in your rope and tram back down the line, or you might end up dangling in space.   (*Greg Tos, 2009*)

ATLANTIS WALL

THE COLISEUM

23 routes ← 5.10 5.11 5.12 5.13 →

The three crags that comprise the Coliseum are found near the top of Echo Canyon. The landmark cliff—the Saddle Up Wall—is an obvious tall, white band of limestone that's perched above a scree ledge. This crag has caught the eye of many a daydreaming climber over the years, but remained undeveloped until recently. It now offers long, exposed routes on an overhanging sheet of stone dripping with blue and grey streaks. For those who prefer a little less air under their feet, there is great climbing down the slope on the steep Pie Wagon Wall or on the slightly overhanging Little Wall.

Conditions: Because the crags at the Coliseum offer two different aspects, it's possible to climb at this area throughout the summer provided you start early and follow the shade. But if you want prime conditions for the mostly south-facing Saddle Up Wall, you'll be happier if you target early- and late-season days. Seepage can be a problem in the spring, but it usually doesn't last for long. However, the drainage used for the approach will go from pleasant boulder hopping in the morning to a raging torrent by late afternoon. It can be difficult and downright dangerous to cross. Use extreme caution.

Approach: From the Alpine Club of Canada, hike for 35 minutes to the signed fork in the trail, take the left-hand option and contour down to the creek bed. Follow it upstream, past the Hideaway on the left, to a long slab on the right side of the creek (about 50 minutes to here). From the top of the slab, continue up the creek for a few more minutes to water-polished slabs. Follow the slabs to a sometimes cairned trail that leads up the hillside on the left toward the cliff band. The first wall encountered is the Pie Wagon Wall. Continue up the trail for 10 minutes to the Little Wall and the Saddle Up Wall.

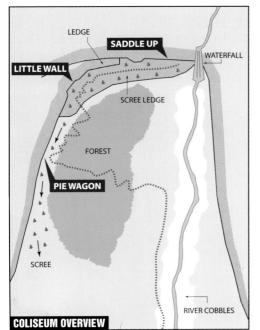

LEDGE

SADDLE UP

WATERFALL

LITTLE WALL

SCREE LEDGE

FOREST

PIE WAGON

SCREE

RIVER COBBLES

COLISEUM OVERVIEW

Pie Wagon Wall

This is a steep wall with a fine collection of long, pumpy routes. There is enough here for a full day, but you may want to only sample a couple of routes to let your legs rest before continuing the slog to the upper walls. Routes are listed from left to right.

❶ Pie Wagon 5.12c . . . .

11 bolts (27 m) From the two platforms at the base of the wall, tricky climbing through right-trending blue streaks leads to a no-hands rest before a roof. Continue up and right to a hard lip encounter. (*Matt Pieterson & Simon Meis, 2004*)

❷ Cake Parade 5.12b . . . .

9 bolts (27 m) Start right of a slot cave. Sustained climbing through a series of small, broken corner features leads to a hard sequence moving right over a small corner and roof. Relentless. (*Matt Pieterson & Josh Lavigne, 2005*)

❸ Dim Sum 5.12b . . . .

7 bolts (18 m) Follow a grey streak to a powerful crux that will leave you hanging on by the skin of your teeth. Finish below the chossy bulge. (*Ross Suchy, 2009*)

PIE WAGON WALL

hole rock platform

N

---

❹ Canadian Pie 5.11a . . . .

11 bolts (32 m) This nice warm-up pitch tackles a large, right-facing corner. *(Ross Suchy & Simon Meis, 2005)*

❺ G Spot 5.13b . . . .

12 bolts (30 m) Start just right of *Canadian Pie*. Climb a shallow groove to a good shake before launching into power-endurance climbing through the two big roofs. Really nice! *(Ross Suchy & Simon Meis, 2007)*

❻ Closed Project . . . .

❼ Hot for Teacher 5.11c . . . .

5 bolts (12 m) Start off the highest platform and follow a blue streak. *(Ross Suchy & Josh Zuber, 2006)*

Little Wall

This boxy-roofed crag houses some of the most powerful routes at the Coliseum and can easily keep you busy for the entire day. It can also be used as a staging area for

occasional forays over to the Saddle Up Wall. It does get some shade in the early morning and again in the late afternoon. Routes are listed from left to right.

❽ The Mud, the Blood and the Beer 5.12b . . . . .

7 bolts (20 m) Start on the far left end of the slot cave, below a blue, right-facing corner. A powerful start leads to great, pumpy climbing up the steep wall above. *(Ross Suchy & Matt Pieterson, 2004)*

❾ Smokey Eyes 5.12c . . . . .

7 bolts (23 m) Start two metres right of *The Mud, the Blood and the Beer*. Navigate through blocky corners and a roof with a real slap in the face at the third bolt! Very good. *(Ross Suchy & Matt Pieterson, 2005)*

❿ Strike Like a Cobra 5.13d . . . . . .

8 bolts (19 m) This powerful testpiece involves fairly technical climbing up a very small, right-facing corner. Start out the middle of the slot cave. *(Matt Pieterson, 2005)*

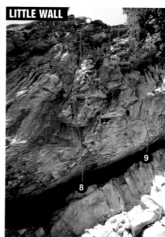

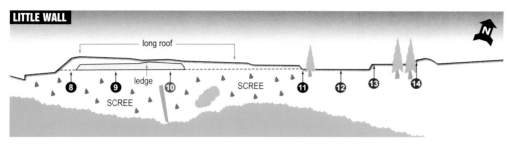

LITTLE WALL

long roof

ledge

SCREE

SCREE

8   9   10   11   12   13   14

⓫ Fat Bastard 5.12b . . . .

6 bolts (16 m) Start off the far right end of the slot cave (pre-clip the first two bolts). Hard-as-nails climbing right off the ground, leads to easier and interesting climbing up to the anchor.   (*Ross Suchy & Mike Donnelly, 2005*)

⓬ If You Drill It, She Will Come 5.11b . . . .

6 bolts (17 m) Start just right of a tree growing at the right end of the slot cave. Fun climbing on cool flowstone leads up a shallow corner. Enjoy good sidepulling on the slab above.   (*Matt Pieterson & Ross Suchy, 2005*)

⓭ Animal Burger 5.11d . . . .

5 bolts (15 m) Big pulls between positive holds finish abruptly with a balancey slab. (*Matt Pieterson & Ross Suchy, 2006*)

⓮ Teenage Feeling 5.11c . . . . . .

5 bolts (13 m) Start in front of two trees growing close to the wall. Follow a grey streak above the small, chossy cave.   (*Matt Pieterson, 2006*)

Saddle Up Wall

This cliff is the crown jewel of the Coliseum and features unparalleled ambiance. The routes are long and pumpy, and offer exposure that's sure to give even the most jaded climber a few butterflies. And the spring snowmelt creates a seasonal waterfall that provides a stunning backdrop. Seepage can be a problem in the early season and after heavy rainfall, but most routes remain climbable. Routes are listed from left to right.

⓯ Closed Project . . . .

⓰ Thaczucked 5.11c . . . .

7 bolts (16 m) Start just left of a short, right-facing blocky corner. Trend left on sidepulls to anchors at a horizontal break.   (*Ross Suchy, 2008*)

⓱ Zoophycus P1 5.12c . . . .

16 bolts (35 m) Start left of a large, blocky ledge. Sustained climbing up a shallow corner leads to a crux at the end. Amazing! (*Ross Suchy, Matt Pieterson & Simon Meis, 2005*)

⓲ The Fullphycus 5.13a . . .

21 bolts from ground (45 m) The extension moves slightly right past the midway anchor to a big move that gains the bottom of a small, right-facing corner. Technical and sustained climbing leads to the anchors. Lower twice to get down. (*Ross Suchy, Matt Pieterson & Simon Meis, 2005*)

⓳ Dungeon Dweller 5.12c . .

13 bolts (25 m) Start four metres right of *Zoophycus*. Juggy sidepulls in a crack lead to a funky crux getting into and over a blocky roof. A no-hands rest will give you a chance to turn around and take in the amazing view before continuing. Don't bother climbing the extra three bolts to the cordalette anchor.   (*Ross Suchy & Simon Meis, 2006*)

⓴ Closed Project . . . .

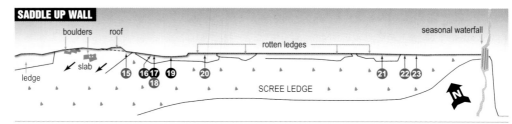

SADDLE UP WALL

boulders roof — rotten ledges — seasonal waterfall

slab — ledge — SCREE LEDGE

15 16 17 18 19 20 21 22 23

㉑ Sundog 5.13a . . . . . .

17 bolts (45 m) Climb a right facing-corner off a large block and pull leftward onto the face after the second bolt (backclean the first two bolts). Layback to a horizontal break and traversing right to a tough crux and a big move that requires determination. Shake well by the midway anchor and prepare for a big move, a tricky clip and pumpy climbing to the top. Use long slings on and around the midway anchor to reduce potentially brutal rope drag. Lower twice to descend. (*Ross Suchy & Matt Pieterson, 2004*)

㉒ The Shadow 5.13d . . . .

17 bolts (45 m) Tricky climbing up an overhanging wall gains a hanging corner. Stem and press your way up the corner, and save lots of energy for the difficult exit. Shake out before making the final push to the anchor, fighting hard through a final endurance crux. Lower twice to get down. (*Matt Pieterson, 2005*)

㉓ The Journey 5.13c . . . .

18 bolts (38 m) This beautiful-looking line scales a clean, overhanging face and moves into a faint, left-facing corner at mid-height. A constant barrage of cruxes will keep the outcome in doubt until the bitter end! Lower twice to get down. (*Ross Suchy & Simon Meis, 2009*)

Tall Storey Wall

Follow the Coliseum approach until it leaves the creek and starts up a steep hill on the left. From here, continue upstream, trending right toward a ledge at the base of the wall. A small amount of scrambling is required to reach the ledge and the base of the route.

㉔ The Tall Storey 5.11c . . . .

This is an excellent multi-pitch sport climb and easily one

SADDLE UP WALL

of the best of its grade in the Bow Valley. With outstanding stone, interesting climbing and no straightforward pitches, you'll feel like you've really earned a cold beer by day's end.

Pitch 1 (5.11c, 12 bolts, 30 m) Climb bullet-hard rock directly into a technical crux. From here, the climbing eases, but stays interesting. Finish on a fractured ledge system.

Pitch 2 (5.11c, 12 bolts, 30 m) This stellar pitch never lets up. After an initial crux over a roof, a testy corner leads to excellent rock and a final crux before a leftward traverse to the belay.

Pitch 3 (5.10c, 8 bolts, 25 m) Climb a small corner and bulging wall to a shattered ledge. Follow the ledge left to the belay.

Pitch 4 (5.11b, 9 bolts, 20 m) Technical climbing leads up a groove and past the left side of a small roof. Trend left on good holds to the belay below an overhanging corner.

Pitch 5 (5.10d, 8 bolts, 20 m) Good holds lead up steep rock to the base of an obvious roof. Move right around the roof before heading up a short corner and easier ground to reach the belay on a big ledge.

Pitch 6 (5.10c, 16 bolts, 35 m) Awkward moves lead leftward from the ledge to a small roof. Above it, follow a corner and ramp on great holds to the base of a large roof and a mid-pitch anchor. If you want to stretch it out and speed up your day, continue leftward past two more protection bolts to reach a higher belay anchor.

Pitch 7 (5.11a, 10 bolts, 25 m) Technical climbing up a groove leads to beautiful chert knobs. Regroup before tackling the final crux: a steep and very exposed move below the final ledge. This is an outstanding finish to a memorable climb. *(Ian & Chris Perry, 2009)*

Descent: It's possible to rappel the route, but keep in mind that some of the pitches are 30 meters long, so be extra cautious—tie knots!—if using a 60-metre rope. Note that reaching the first pitch's anchor requires either back-clipping or a tricky swing. An alternative to rappelling involves hiking down the ledge system to the Notch and on from there. If you choose this option, note that the ledge is steep, loose and exposed at times; some might not be very comfortable descending in this manner. Rocks dislodged during this descent will end up falling down to the Notch, so great care should be used to protect climbers below.

THE TALL STOREY

5.11a

5.10c

combine

ledge

chain on tree

5.10d

5.11b

5.10c

back-clip or swing in to reach next anchor

5.11c

5.11c

24

approach

I'm half way up *The Journey*, a freshly bolted project at the Coliseum, a sport climbing venue above Canmore. It's a monster pitch of overhanging limestone—a spider's web of blue-grey water streaks weave up the wall above me. The moves are hard, at my limit, and I just barely stick the improbable "Windmill Move", an arcing, dynamic reach to a two-finger pocket. Copping a quick shake, I try and calm my racing mind before heading into the crux above.

The geometry of the amphitheater in which I'm climbing seems to magnify the exposure. I'm surrounded by huge sweeping walls of stone, and my belayer is out of sight perched on a sloping scree ledge above a 100-metre cliff. Resting isn't really working out—my forearms are reaching an advanced state of lactic acid engorgement. I eyeball the crux and a distant quickdraw. Why didn't we put more bolts up here? I clamp down on my fear and launch up-ward. I stuff four of my fat fingers into a shallow pod. My left hand milks a small, somewhat illusionary pinch. I'm overextended and struggle to find a key right foothold. My forearms have reached critical melt down and I imagine warning lights and sirens going off in some internal muscular control room. I stab for a good hold, but all I grab is a palm full of rough blank stone. I pitch off, briefly weightless before the rope and failure catch up to me.

Dangling now, I relax and take in my surroundings. We are high in Echo Canyon on the south face of Grotto Mountain. As if focused through a giant lens, the April sun shines straight into the amphitheater and warms the wall. It is early spring, and although the tem-peratures at this cliff are perfect for sending, Canmore can be seen far below, blanketed in fresh snow. The canyon is eerily quiet today, muffled by the new powder, as if the world is holding its breath. On the approach, we post-holed like elk though 30 cm drifts, a gift from the fierce, spring storm. The forest below is heavy with snow; it looks like Christmas.

Everything about the route I'm attempting is intimidating. It climbs off the farthest end of the approach ledge in the back of a huge amphitheater of stone. With a 70-metre rope, you can *just* lower to the ground, provided you jump from the anchor without clipping! As with much of the rock in the Bow Valley, the limestone is roughly textured and intricately featured. On-sighting is difficult here; hidden holds abound, and since no one has sent this route yet, there is precious little chalk to show the way. (Note to self: make more tick marks!) Micro-scopic stone "bubbles" sporadically cover the face and provide excellent friction, but often crumble underfoot, adding to the feelings of insecurity. And as if to make matters worse, the route's length and difficulty required a certain sparseness of bolts. The so-called benefit to this is the gaps make for soft falls, especially when dropping from the top of the 35-metre pitch!

In addition to the overbearing breadth of the rock face, a waterfall cascades over the route, add-ing additional "atmosphere". Still hanging in my harness, I watch as updrafts blow the water up into fanciful spirals, making rainbows and sun dogs in the strong spring sunlight above me. Strangely, the geometry of the wall is such that the route rarely gets wet, but the belayer is not so lucky—it basically rains intermittently between updrafts on the belay ledge far below. Elaborate tarp systems and Gortex suits (as well as bribes and begging) are employed to retain reluctant belayers and today I have recruited Nick, a friend from Canmore, along with his buddy Danny and Nick's black husky, Loki. I convinced them that the sunny day would make for perfect climbing temperatures at the cliff—conveniently, I forgot to mention the belay conditions.

Once, when asked who would like to climb at the Coliseum I replied, "It helps to climb hard, 5.12 will do, and you should like to climb on Yamnuska, or something similarly scary to help you deal with the exposed nature of the routes". Afterward, it occurred to me that these prerequisites might leave a rather small group of potential local climbers interested, but then again since we were building routes mostly for ourselves, it didn't really matter. We began jokingly referring to the Coliseum as "Canmore's Premiere Adventure Sport Crag".

Simon Meis on The Journey (5.13c).

○ ROSS SUCHY

Back to the task at hand. Nick is yelling something from below, but I can't hear him over a building thunder from above. I look up to see a river of snow exploding over the top of the cliff! The sun has just reached the back of the large hanging bowl above, and the sudden warming has caused an avalanche over the climb! In awe, I watch the white stream, as thick as an industrial smoke stack, arc through the air, easily clearing the belay ledge and crashing into the void below. It is a spectacular and briefly terrifying display, but is essentially harmless to us where we are. I am struck by the surreal nature of my position: I am under the avalanche, watching the stream of snow rush by, the sun backlighting it brilliant white. Bracing my feet against the wall and leaning out on the rope, I try to put my hand in the flow. I can touch the water, but can't quite reach the snow. Below Nick is staring in awe and Danny is madly taking photos. Loki takes it all in stride.

Eventually the avalanche tapers off, although it continues in fits and spurts throughout the afternoon. I half-heartedly work on the upper moves of the route, but my mind is both numb and over-stimulated from the excitement. Later, as we are descending out the mouth of the amphitheater, we encounter an oozing mass of snow. The avalanche debris and water have built up to a critical mass of slush, and this slurry is flowing and oozing down the canyon. We are forced to run to stay in front of the flow, until we can escape from the canyon to the sunny slopes far below. Back in town, friends ask about our day. I reply, "Just another day at Canmore's Premiere Adventure Sport Crag".

THE NOTCH

34 routes ←5.10 5.11 5.12 5.13→

The gorgeous, blue-streaked walls of the Notch sit on the east side of Echo Canyon, high above the Alpine Club of Canada. This is a newly developed area, but it already features some of the best overhanging 5.11 and 5.12 climbing in the Bow Valley—there are over 30 outstanding routes to keep you busy. The climbs are steep and physically demanding on rock that is perfectly formed. An array of pockets, mini jugs and sculpted edges define some amazing and intricate lines that forge up steep faces usually reserved for the lofty grade of 5.13. Combine this with the incredible mountain scenery and a day at the Notch certainly won't disappoint.

Conditions: The crags at the Notch have a northwest aspect and remain in the shade until late in the afternoon. This makes the area a great choice on hot days, but in cooler weather you'll really want to bundle up—the base can hold snow until May. Early-season and post-downpour seepage can be a problem (that's where those cool pockets and streaks originated), but many of the steep routes on the main crag remain climbable during light and moderate rain storms.

Approach: From the Alpine Club of Canada, hike for 35 minutes to the signed fork in the trail and take the right-hand option. Another 30 minutes of steep switchbacks through the trees followed by steep scree and rock bands lead to a memorial plaque overlooking Echo Canyon. From here, follow the scree slope downhill to the base of the main crag. The first routes encountered on the right are *The Atrocity*, and *Rock Me Amadeus*. To reach the Upper Notch (5 minutes), follow a trail next to the wall that heads uphill from *Blue Flame*. Cross rock slabs to a large switchback and then hike back toward the wall.

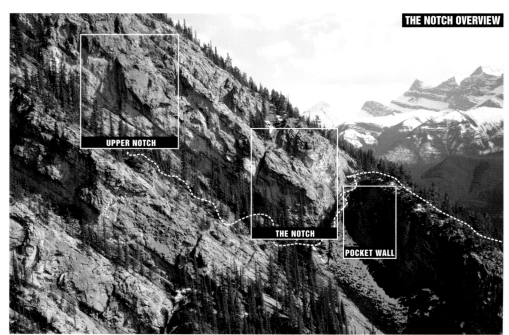

THE NOTCH OVERVIEW

UPPER NOTCH

THE NOTCH

POCKET WALL

The Notch

The main crag. Routes are listed from left to right.

❶ Blue Flame 5.11c . . . .
9 bolts (21 m) This route begins 10 metres left of a slot cave. Tread lightly through a loose, yellow band to better rock and a crux up the prominent blue arête. Finish on bullet stone. *(Ian Perry, 2007)*

❷ The Eternal Flame 5.12c . . .
11 bolts (22 m) Begin on the far left side of the slot cave. A short section of loose climbing gains the crack above and better rock. Excellent, sustained moves on pockets and edges lead to the anchor above. *(Ian Perry, 2008)*

❸ Closed Project . . . .

❹ Burning Down the House 5.11d . . .
12 bolts (26 m) Climb *The Roof Is On Fire* to the seventh bolt before branching left over a break. Great climbing leads to anchors below the large roof. *(Ian Perry, 2009)*

❺ The Roof is on Fire 5.11d . . . .
8 bolts (18 m) Start just right of the slot cave. Trend right out the steep overhang on slightly friable rock to a tricky lip encounter. From here, the rock gets very solid and presents another crux before the anchor. *(Ian Perry, 2007)*

❻ Fire in the Sky 5.12b . . . . . .
10 bolts (16 m) If you like big throws, this route will be right up your alley. Climb easily onto a small stance at the base of a friable weakness before heading straight out the overhang. The rock over the lip is bullet and features small pockets and edges. A monster throw to a bucket is the key to the final roof. *(Ian Perry, 2005)*

❼ Silver Tip 5.11c . . . .
7 bolts (17 m) This is a nice route that follows a left-trending silvery-blue streak to anchors at the base of an overhanging pillar feature. The huge jugs peter out halfway up. *(Ian Perry, 2007)*

❽ Tipped Off 5.12c . . . .
10 bolts (25 m) Continue above the anchor of *Silver Tip* to a burly roof encounter. Mantel onto the slab above. *(PREP: Ian Perry; FA: Derek Galloway, 2009)*

❾ Fuzzy Logic 5.11a . . . .
7 bolts (20 m) Start below a blunt prow and trend left on buckets to a tricky section. Head straight up to anchors. *(Ian Perry, 2007)*

❿ The Next Logical Step 5.12c . . .
12 bolts (27 m) Continue above the anchors of *Fuzzy Logic*. Climb a steep corner to a crux moving left and a pumpy finish. *(PREP: Ian Perry; FA: Derek Galloway, 2009)*

⓫ Standard Deviation 5.11b . . . .
12 bolts (26 m) Climb *Fuzzy Logic* for four bolts before branching right up the corner feature. It's steep near the top, but monster jugs keep it reasonable. *(Ian Perry, 2010)*

THE NOTCH

14
15
16
17

18
19
20
21
22
23

⑫ Peyto Power 5.12a . . . . 🖐️📋

10 bolts (24 m) This great route climbs the right side of a blunt, yellow prow. Steep and pumpy moves lead to a slight crux gaining the Cyclops hole. Good holds lead to the anchor. Named after Ian Perry's faithful dog who kept him company during many long days spent cleaning and bolting the routes at the Notch. *(Ian Perry, 2009)*

⑬ Silver Bullet 5.12a . . . . 🖐️📋

11 bolts (25 m) It doesn't get much better than this. Climb to the grey streak and the base of a very overhanging wall. Brilliant moves on perfect holds lead out the overhang to monster jugs at the lip. Enjoy! *(Ian Perry, 2007)*

⑭ The Dark Side of the Boom 5.12a . . . 📋

9 bolts (26 m) Start below a hole and work your way up the prickly face to a crux gaining jugs in a large hole. Jugs lead to anchors above. *(Gery Unterasinger, 2005)*

⑮ One Hit Wonder 5.11c . . . . 📋

10 bolts (25 m) This is the second route left of the arête. Fun, moderate climbing leads to a one-move-wonder crux on some very crappy crimpers that lead over the bulge at the top. *(Ian Perry, 2005)*

⑯ Melting Wax 5.10d . . . . 📋

7 bolts (21 m) This good climb is just left of the arête. Interesting holds on water-worn rock lead to a crux pulling over the top. A variation cuts right at the fifth bolt. Clip one bolt and finish on *Swerve Driver*. *(Ian Perry, 2005)*

⑰ Swerve Driver 5.10a . . . . 📋

6 bolts (19 m) Start on the right of the arête. Easy climbing leads to a high first bolt. Trend to the left side of the arête and continue to anchors. *(Ian Perry & Chris Perry, 2005)*

⑱ Edge Grinder 5.11a . . . . 📋

6 bolts (20 m) Start right of the arête. *(Ian Perry, 2010)*

⑲ Mithril 5.11b . . . . 📋

6 bolts (14 m) Traverse left on underclings to the first bolt and continue straight up on nice holds to anchors over the top. *(Ian Perry, 2005)*

⑳ Micro Climb-it 5.12a . . . . 🪂📋

5 bolts (14 m) Power through an incredibly steep and fun start to smooth sailing above. *(Ian Perry, 2005)*

㉑ Acid Wash 5.11c . . . . 📋

7 bolts (15 m) Climb the bluish-yellow groove to a short, left-facing corner. A tricky section of climbing leads to easier ground. *(Ian Perry, 2005)*

㉒ The Columbian Milkman 5.10a . . . . . 📋

5 bolts (12 m) Start just right of a short, left-facing corner. Climb straight up, all the while groping for holds in the prickly grey rock. *(Ian Perry, 2010)*

㉓ Three's a Crowd 5.10c . . . . 📋

4 bolts (12 m) More hold groping leads to the third bolt. Trend left to the last bolt of *The Columbian Milkman* and finish straight up. *(Ian Perry, 2010)*

㉔ The Atrocity 5.12a . . . .

10 bolts (25 m) Scramble up a slab to an open-book corner and the start of the route. Trend left on blocky buckets and edges that pack a surprising pump. Climbs better than the name suggests. *(Ian Perry, 2007)*

㉕ Rock Me Amadeus 5.12d . .

10 bolts (25 m) Start two metres up the slab. Sustained technical climbing features two cruxes separated by a decent rest. *(Gery Unterasinger, 2005)*

Pocket Wall

This crag is located on the left side of the scree slope when looking downhill. It features a small collection of vertical, pocketed climbs starting off a rock platform. Routes are listed from left to right.

㉖ Romeo et Juliet 5.11b . . . .

4 bolts (14 m) Start two metres uphill from the rock platform. Trend slightly left to a bouldery crux at the second bolt. Easier but sporty climbing leads to the anchor. *(Jasmine Caufield, 2005)*

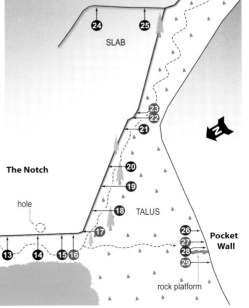

㉗ Monte Cristo #4 5.10d . . . . ☐

4 bolts (14 m) From the rock platform, climb the yellow streak to the top of a right-facing corner. Cool pocket moves are followed by fun jugs. One of the better warm-ups in the area. *(Ian Perry, 2005)*

㉘ Cohiba 5.11a . . . . ☐

6 bolts (15 m) From the rock platform, strenuous two finger pocket moves lead to small edges at mid-height and jugs to the top. *(Ian Perry, 2005)*

㉙ Have a Cigar 5.10a . . . . ☐

7 bolts (17 m) Stat below a rock platform. A small yellow slab leads to a couple of tough moves scraping over a roof. Fun jug climbing to the anchors. *(Ian Perry, 2007)*

Upper Notch

These climbs are not as steep as the ones below, but feature smaller holds and more technical moves. Although there are only a few routes, they are of high quality. The base is a steep slab, which makes hanging out a tad awkward—this is not a great place for a dog. A rock slide in 2009 left a lot of loose rock on the approach slab, and random rockfall is still a real concern—beware. Routes are listed from left to right.

㉚ Vanilla Sky 5.12a . . . . ☐

10 bolts (24 m) This is the second route left of the big corner. Climb up a faint grey streak to some cool pocket moves. Finish up a blunt arête with a tricky barn-door move before the finish. *(Ian Perry, 2006)*

㉛ Frozen Ocean 5.12b . . . ☐

12 bolts (26 m) Easy climbing leads up the wall one metre left of the big corner. A sparsely-pocketed face moves into a long cruxy section that follows a zigzag feature to the anchor. *(PREP: Ian Perry; FA: Gery Unterasinger, 2007)*

㉜ Closed Project . . . . ☐

㉝ Closed Project . . . . ☐

㉞ To the Edge and Beyond 5.11c . . . ☐

12 bolts (29 m) Begin just right of the big corner. A short pocketed section leads to good climbing up the arête. Finish with some cool dish features on the slab before the anchor. *(Ian Perry, 2009)*

㉟ Closed Project . . . . ☐

UPPER NOTCH

CHAPTER 8

COUGAR CANYON

Sandwiched between Mount Lady MacDonald and Grotto Mountain lies Cougar Canyon, Canmore's back-yard crag. This long and beautiful gorge is peppered with 18 cliffs that boast over 260 routes, and is by far the Bow Valley's largest and most popular climbing area. The routes range from 5.5 to 5.14 and feature all styles, including two-bolt power sprints and 24-bolt endurance marathons. From slabby to overhanging and everything in between, there is great climbing for everyone in Cougar Canyon.

MARC BOURDON ON MEGOMIANA 5.12A AT PLANET X

CONDITIONS

Cougar Canyon's walls tend to dry early in the season and stay relatively seepage free throughout the summer and fall. However, the slabby to vertical nature of many of the crags leaves the rock exposed to the mercy of the weather and the cliffs get wet quickly during rainstorms. (The only exception to this is Planet X, which is climbable in light to moderate rain.) Luckily, most of the walls dry quickly once the clouds have parted and the storms have moved on, making this canyon a good post-rain venue.

APPROACH

From Canmore: Follow Benchlands Trail to the top of the hill and turn right on Elk Run Boulevard. Immediately turn left into the parking lot for Cougar Canyon.

From Calgary: Drive west on the Trans-Canada Highway toward Canmore. Take Exit 91 for Canmore and turn left onto Bow Valley Trail. Follow it eastward and turn left onto Elk Run Boulevard. Follow this road to the top of the hill, cross Cougar Creek and immediately turn right into the parking lot.

From Banff: Drive east on the Trans-Canada Highway toward Canmore. Take Exit 89 for Canmore and turn left onto Benchlands Trail. From this point, follow the Canmore directions outlined above.

Hiking: From the parking lot, easily follow the trail upstream along the creek for 10 minutes to an old, broken earth dam. Enter the creek drainage and continue hiking upstream. After another 10 minutes, the House of Cards wall will be visible on the left.

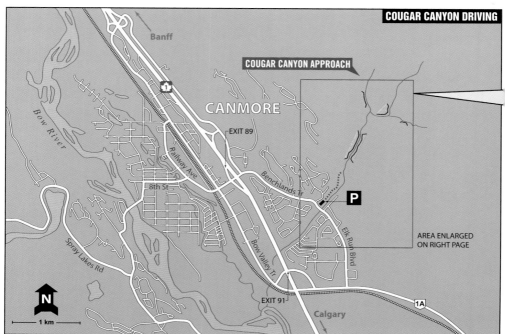

COUGAR CANYON DRIVING

COUGAR CANYON APPROACH

Banff

CANMORE

EXIT 89

Bow River

Railway Ave

8th St

Benchlands Tr

Elk Run Blvd

P

AREA ENLARGED ON RIGHT PAGE

Spray Lakes Rd

Bow Valley Tr

EXIT 91

Calgary

1A

N

1 km

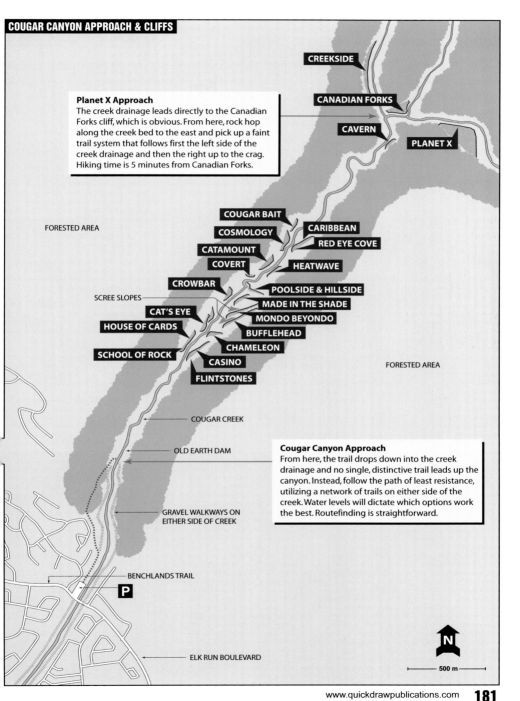

COUGAR CANYON APPROACH & CLIFFS

CREEKSIDE

CANADIAN FORKS

Planet X Approach
The creek drainage leads directly to the Canadian Forks cliff, which is obvious. From here, rock hop along the creek bed to the east and pick up a faint trail system that follows first the left side of the creek drainage and then the right up to the crag. Hiking time is 5 minutes from Canadian Forks.

CAVERN

PLANET X

FORESTED AREA

COUGAR BAIT

COSMOLOGY

CARIBBEAN

RED EYE COVE

CATAMOUNT

COVERT

HEATWAVE

CROWBAR

SCREE SLOPES

POOLSIDE & HILLSIDE

MADE IN THE SHADE

CAT'S EYE

MONDO BEYONDO

HOUSE OF CARDS

BUFFLEHEAD

CHAMELEON

FORESTED AREA

SCHOOL OF ROCK

CASINO

FLINTSTONES

COUGAR CREEK

OLD EARTH DAM

Cougar Canyon Approach
From here, the trail drops down into the creek drainage and no single, distinctive trail leads up the canyon. Instead, follow the path of least resistance, utilizing a network of trails on either side of the creek. Water levels will dictate which options work the best. Routefinding is straightforward.

GRAVEL WALKWAYS ON
EITHER SIDE OF CREEK

BENCHLANDS TRAIL

P

N

500 m

ELK RUN BOULEVARD

HOUSE OF CARDS SECTOR

142 routes ←5.10 5.11 5.12 5.13→

This is the first group of crags encountered while walking up the Cougar Creek drainage, and features six major cliffs and a few minor ones, all within minutes of each other. The walls are predominately vertical, with varied routes ranging from 5 to 43 m in length and 5.7 to 5.11 in difficulty. The stone has many flavours: grippy and grey, smooth and yellow, blocky and angular, technical and edgy or slabby and balancey. Take your pick.

Conditions: The beauty of the canyon is that you can always find sun or shade, depending on which side of the creek you choose. The left side of the creek catches plenty of sun in the morning, while the right side stays is the shade until the evening. If it rains, the walls get wet very quickly, but tend to dry quickly once the rain stops. Note that some of the crags may be inaccessible when the creek is high.

Approach: This is the first group of walls encountered while hiking upstream. They're hard to miss.

School of Rock

This is a downstream, satellite wall of House of Cards. Routes are listed from left to right.

❶ Rock 201 5.8 . . . .

2 bolts (7 m) Climb past a slanted ledge. (*John Martin, 1992*)

❷ Empty Nest 5.9 . . . .

2 bolts (7 m) Start off a boulder next to the wall and climb polished rock on good holds. (*John Martin, 1989*)

❸ Rock 301 5.10b . . . .

2 bolts (6 m) Climb the smooth face. (*John Martin, 1992*)

❹ Rock 401 5.10c . . . .

1 bolt (6 m) With only one bolt at the start, this is a committing lead. A better toprope than lead, perhaps?
(*John Martin, 1992*)

❺ Five Minutes in Hell 5.11c . . . . . .

2 bolts (5 m) A boulder start leads to an easy finish.
(*Unknown*)

❻ School of Rock 5.11c . . . .

2 bolts (5 m) This route starts off the right end of a ramp. After a boulder problem, the difficulty subsides. Trend left to the anchor of *Five Minutes of Hell*. (*Unknown*)

SCHOOL OF ROCK

HOUSE OF CARDS

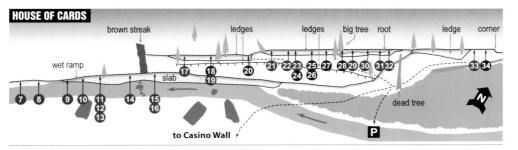

House of Cards diagram showing routes from left to right: wet ramp, brown streak, slab, ledges, big tree, root, ledge, corner, dead tree, to Casino Wall, P (parking), N (north arrow)

House of Cards

This is the impressive cliff that rises from the left side of the creek. It hosts some excellent and long 5.10 to 5.11 routes. The rubbly ledges pose a rockfall hazard at this crag. Be careful. Routes are listed from left to right.

❼ Dreamcatcher in a Rusted Malibu 5.8 . . . .

5 bolts (9 m) Climb through a yellow patch of rock and trend right to the base of a short and loose, right-facing corner. Follow it up and right. *(Greg Cornell, 2001)*

❽ Kim and Murray 5.8 . . . .

5 bolts (9 m) Start about four metres right of *Dreamcatcher in a Rusted Malibu*. Weave a path through smooth, grey rock to a shared anchor. *(Greg Cornell, 2001)*

❾ Innuendo 5.10a . . . .

3 bolts (9 m) Climb past a small, left-trending ramp at three metres. Pick your way between yellow patches of rock. *(John Martin, 1992)*

❿ Fly by Wire 5.10d . . . .

4 bolts (9 m) Start off of an often-wet ramp. Tough moves lead to a faint open-book corner at the second bolt. Battle over a bulge and trend left to the same anchor as *Innuendo*. *(John Martin, 1992)*

⓫ SPF P1 5.9 . . . .

6 bolts (26 m) Belay from the left end of a slab above the creek. Climb to the left of a small tree. Good holds lead to an anchor on a small ledge. *(John Martin, 1999)*

⓬ SPF P2 5.10a . . . .

6 bolts (13 m) Continue up the arête above the anchor to a crux over a small roof. A tough move on the crimpy yellow face guards the anchor. Lower twice to get back to the ground. *(John Martin, 1999)*

⓭ Solarium 5.10a . . . .

12 bolts (41 m) Climb *SPF* to just below the small ledge. Trend right to a tricky section up a steep, slabby face. Beautiful climbing on chert knobs and edges follows. Lower twice using the *SPF* anchor to descend. *(Steve Stahl, 1989)*

⓮ Aqualung 5.9 . . . .

11 bolts (42 m) From the slab, follow good rock to the left of the big brown streak and the base of a large corner. Follow the slab left to the same anchor as *Solarium*. The easiest way to clean the route is to belay up the second. Make two rappels using the *SPF* anchor (pitch 1) to descend. *(John Martin, 1990)*

⓯ Slowpoke 5.8 . . . .

13 bolts (30 m) Climb right of the big brown streak to a ledge. Continue up a right-facing corner to a high anchor. *(John Martin, 1998)*

⓰ Fidget 5.10c . . . .

19 bolts (43 m) Continue above the *Slowpoke* anchor for a massive pitch of intricate climbing on good stone. Lower twice to get down. *(John Martin, 1998)*

⓱ Cold Case 5.10c . . . .

12 bolts (28 m) Start on the far left of a ledge next to a small tree. Climb through yellow rock, passing a tree on the right. Pull onto a black slab (the crux), using a cool, crimpy rail. Finish with fun climbing to an anchor just right of a large tree on the top. *(John Martin, 2004)*

⓲ Going Under 5.11a . . . .

13 bolts (29 m) Start to the left of two trees on a ledge. Work up a yellow streak on edges and sidepulls to a ramp right of a tree growing out of the wall. (A long sling above the ramp will reduce rope drag.) A cool sequence leads over the roof to nice edge pulling. *(John Martin, 2004)*

HOUSE OF CARDS

19 Frozen Assets 5.10b . . . . 🔲

13 bolts (29 m) Climb *Going Under* to the fourth bolt. Break right and follow edges straight up the wall. Traverse left at the last bolt and finish on the anchors of *Going Under*. *(John Martin, 2004)*

20 Boulevard of Broken Dreams 5.11b . . . . . . 🔲

12 bolts (23 m) Start three metres right of two trees growing on a ledge. Trend slightly left on crimpers to a ledge. A nasty, micro-crimp crux with poor footholds leads off the ledge. Easier climbing follows. *(John Martin, 2004)*

21 Talamasca 5.10c . . . . 🔲

18 bolts (43 m) This outstanding, long pitch starts off the left end of a ledge, just right of a tree growing straight out from the wall. A long stretch of beautiful edge climbing leads to fun laybacking up a right-facing corner and a midway anchor. Continue up to an amazing finish way off the deck. Lower twice to get down. *(John Martin, 1995)*

22 Sun Dogs 5.10c . . . . 🔲

10 bolts (24 m) The crux involves getting to and past the first bolt. After that it's smooth sailing on perfect rock with great grips. *(John Martin, 1998)*

23 New Ashtaroth 5.10c . . . . 🔲

10 bolts (24 m) Follow a small, right-facing corner to good edges and side-pulls that end at a midway anchor. *(John Martin, 2002)*

24 Asharoth 5.11a . . . . 🔲

18 bolts (44 m) Continue past *New Ashtaroth* to a small ledge. Trend left up a flake to a cruxy roof encounter on cool holds. *(John Martin, 2002)*

25 Painted Smile 5.11b . . . . 🔲

11 bolts (25 m) Crimp up the black face to a cruxy yellow bulge before the anchor. *(John Martin, 2002)*

26 Shangri-La 5.11b . . . . 🔲

19 bolts (44 m) Great crimps lead above *Painted Smile* to a roof. Crank the lip to a couple of balancey moves that guard the anchor. *(John Martin, 2002)*

27 Is That Your Dog? 5.11b . . . . . 🔲

9 bolts (25 m) This is the furthest right route on the ledge and starts up a small, right-facing corner. Two hard cruxes are separated by a stance. The first is technical and involves micro crimpers that would be considered poor foot holds, and the second is powerful. *(Geoff Powter, 1992)*

28 Heliopolis 5.11b . . . . 🔲

15 bolts (29 m) Start in front of a large tree that has a prominent root growing against the wall. Cruise up the wall to a high crux on perfect sidepulls and edges. *(John Martin, 1994)*

CASINO WALL & FLINTSTONES WALL

29 Byzantium 5.10b . . . .

14 bolts (29 m) Start two metres right of a large tree with a prominent root growing along the wall. Climb a great wall peppered with nice edges, mini-flakes and cruxes throughout its entire length. Classic. *(John Martin, 1989)*

30 Redline 5.10b . . . .

13 bolts (28 m) Red hangers mark the way up another brilliant route. Technical edging will keep you on your toes all the way to the anchor. *(John Martin, 2002)*

31 Londinium 5.10c . . . .

15 bolts (30 m) Fun, sustained climbing on good edges leads to a high and tricky crux trending right.
(John Martin, 1997)

32 Sarantium 5.10d . . . .

13 bolts (30 m) Start at the right end of a large root growing along the wall. Fun, positive jugs lead to technical moves on small edges. *(John Martin, 1998)*

33 I Heard a Ga-Zump 5.10d . . . .

7 bolts (19 m) Start four metres left of a rotten, yellow left-facing corner. Nice climbing on jugs and edges leads to a crux pulling through a bulge on underclings and slopey footholds (a deadly mix). Finish up a prickly slab.
(Brian Spear, 1995)

34 Revenge of the Luddite 5.11a . . . .

5 bolts (18 m) Start immediately left of the rotten, yellow left-facing corner. The first bolt is high, but the climbing to it is easy. Nice moves lead over many small overlaps on good rock. *(Brian Spear, 1995)*

Casino Wall

This wall used to be quite chossy, but it has cleaned up and become one of the busiest crags along Cougar Creek. The routes are long, fun and the best of their grade in the canyon. They are listed from left to right.

35 Straw Dogs 5.10c . . . . . .

10 bolts (11 m) Great technical climbing leads up a clean, grey face on perfect crimpers. Belay on a ledge below the route. *(Chris Perry & Ian Perry, 2004)*

36 Wild Card 5.10a . . . .

4 bolts (9 m) Start in front of a tree growing next to the wall. Enjoy great climbing on sidepulls of all sizes.
(John Martin, 2006)

37 Long Shot 5.10c . . . .

4 bolts (9 m) Start one metre right of a tree growing next to the wall. Climb straight up on smooth edges and join *Wild Card* at the third bolt. *(Ian Perry, 2004)*

38 Black Jack 5.10a . . . .

3 bolts (9 m) Climb straight up through small ledges. Finish up the left side of an open-book corner. *(John Martin, 2005)*

39 Luxor 5.10a . . . .

14 bolts (33 m) This recent addition starts to the right of a large tree. It's good, but still has a bit of loose rock that will clean up over time. From a high ledge, traverse left before finishing straight up. *(John Martin, 2009)*

40 King of Clubs 5.10a . . . .

10 bolts (31 m) Enjoy great climbing on positive holds all the way to the anchor. *(Chris Perry, 2004)*

41 Ace of Spades 5.11a . . . .

14 bolts (31 m) Fun, but thought-provoking moves lead to an overhang under the anchor.
(Ian Perry, Chris Perry & John Martin, 2004)

42 Aces High 5.10d . . . .

13 bolts (32 m) This is the first route right of a large tree. Trend left over a series of ledges to a diagonal seam and a groove. A cruxy leftward traverse is followed by a bouldery exit over a roof. *(John Martin, 2002)*

Interesting Fact: Every climbing area has a few workhorses that establish the majority of the new climbs, but in the Bow Valley, John Martin takes this passion to an entirely new level. In Cougar Canyon alone, he is responsible for an astonishing 64% of the routes (170 out of the 262 bolted climbs). With a rough price of $4 per bolt and approximately 1,490 bolts placed, that puts his total cost at around $6,000.00!

And then there's the labour. The rock in the canyon is not always super solid, and John estimates that he has easily spent 10 to 20 hours cleaning each pitch. (If you doubt these figures, check out the debris piles at the base of Casino Wall some day). Based on his estimate, the total labour works out to roughly 2,550 hours, or 319 eight-hour work days. So, if you run into John at the crag, offer to buy him a beer at day's end. His efforts have been truly mind blowing!

43 **Full House** 5.10b . . . . ☐

13 bolts (32 m) Climb *Ace High* to the top of the groove. Continue straight up, avoiding the roof on the right. Use a shared anchor. *(Chris Perry & John Martin, 2002)*

44 **Loaded Dice** 5.10c . . . . ☐

13 bolts (30 m) Climb *Snake Eyes* to mid-height before making a cruxy, leftward traverse to red hangers. Sustained climbing leads to anchors over the ledge. *(John Martin, 2009)*

45 **Snake Eyes** 5.10c . . . . ☐

11 bolts (28 m) Climb to a high first bolt on the slab. Sustained climbing on grey rock leads to a couple of tricky moves getting through the high overlaps. *(John Martin, 2002)*

46 **Poker Face** 5.10a . . . . ☐

12 bolts (30 m) A right-facing corner leads to the base of a left-trending ramp. Follow a grey streak past a hidden bolt before finishing up a right-facing corner. *(Chris Perry, 2002)*

47 **Conspiracy Theory** 5.10c . . . . ☐

9 bolts (23 m) This lone route lies about 17 metres right of *Poker Face*. From the mossy, left-trending ramp above the second bolt, trend right through good rock to a couple of tricky moves on smooth stone. *(John Martin, 2006)*

48 **Black Slabbath** 5.11a . . . . . . ☐

6 bolts (15 m) Start just right of a large tree growing next to the wall. Hard, balancey moves gain the slab. Small crimps lead to a final roof before the anchor. *(Patrick Delaney, 2005)*

49 **Click Click Boom** 5.10b . . . . ☐

6 bolts (14 m) Start just right of a large tree growing against the wall. Climb to the right-trending corner and onto the slab at its end. Finish above the roof. The hardest part is getting to the first bolt. *(John Martin, 2008)*

CASINO WALL

FLINTSTONES WALL

50 Straight Flush 5.10b . . . .

5 bolts (13 m) This plumb line tackles the middle of the slab. Finish over roofs near the top. *(John Martin, 2006)*

51 Flush 5.9 . . . .

5 bolts (13 m) This is the right-most route. Trend left, using the corner to your right when possible. Finish on *Straight Flush*. *(John Martin, 2006)*

The Flintstones Wall

This cliff is a downstream satellite crag of Casino Wall. Routes are listed from left to right.

52 Wilma 5.10a . . . .

5 bolts (14 m) Start just right of a tree against the wall. A bulge leads to small chert crimps. *(John Martin, 2007)*

53 Bam Bam Got His Funk 5.9 . . . . . .

6 bolts (11 m) From the first bolt, trend left to midway overlaps. Finish up chert crimps. *(Brandon Pullman, 2006)*

54 Fred 5.9 . . . .

4 bolts (11 m) Climb to the first bolt on *Bam Bam Got His Funk*, but continue straight up. *(John Martin, 2007)*

55 Pebbles Has Her Groove 5.7 . . . . .

3 bolts (11 m) From a high first bolt, climb over a small roof to a right-trending corner. Continue straight up to anchors. *(Brandon Pullman, 2006)*

CASINO WALL

Pete Thurlow on Aces High (5.10d)

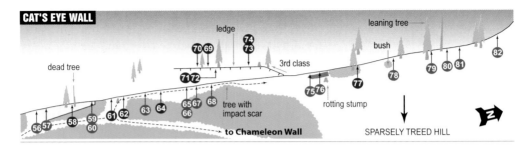

CAT'S EYE WALL

Cat's Eye Wall

This is a great place to soak up some sun and climb long routes on tacky, grey rock. Continue upstream from House of Cards to the next big wall on the left. Routes are listed from left to right.

56 Cat's Paw 5.10a . . . .

5 bolts (20 m) Climb a slab left of a crack, with a tricky initial bulge. Continue straight up on great holds to the anchor. A slightly easier variation loops right at the fourth bolt. (*John Martin, 1989*)

57 Cat's Eye 5.10b . . . .

6 bolts (21 m) Follow a crack until it's possible to pull onto the face. A few tricky moves lead to a stance under a stepped roof. Crank it and head for the top. (*John Martin, 1989*)

58 Doctor Tongue's 3-D House of Slave Chicks 5.11c . . . .

7 bolts (23 m) Start between two trees growing on a ledge. The crux is down low, so power up and get it done. If you can get past the overlaps, the ascent should be in the bag. (*Sean Dougherty, 1989*)

59 Double Play 5.10d . . . .

6 bolts (24 m) Start in a yellow corner at the top of a ledge. Climb a crack in the back of a roof to the second bolt and cut left onto the face. Figure out how to surmount the overlaps and enjoy the climbing above. (*John Martin, 1994*)

60 Double Header 5.10a . . . .

7 bolts (24 m) Climb *Double Play*, but continue straight up past the second bolt using a cool pocket to connect the cracks. Rejoin *Double Play* at the top of the crack and head for the anchor. (*John Martin, Sean Dougherty, 1989*)

61 Coconut Joe 5.11a . . . .

9 bolts (26 m) Start just right of a cluster of small trees.

Climb onto a ledge, passing one tricky move. A perplexing boulder problem over the roof leads to some amazing climbing through chert bands above. (*John Martin, 1998*)

62 Ephemera 5.11b . . . .

9 bolts (25 m) Smooth slopers lead to a high first bolt. Continue over a bulge and into the business: a tough crux through a yellow patch of stone with horrible footholds. Easier above. (*John Martin, 1999*)

63 Iguana Moon Trek 5.10a . . . .

6 bolts (18 m) Start below a tree growing on a high ledge. Climb to the tree and then around it on the left side. Follow the steep arête above on good sidepulls. (*John Martin, 1994*)

CAT'S EYE WALL

CAT'S EYE WALL

Labels on photo: 70 72, 66 69 71 73 74, ledge, 60, 58 59, 57, 56, ramp, scramble, 61 62 63 64, 65 67 68

64 Rough Trade 5.11b . . . .

7 bolts (20 m) Low angle climbing leads to a huge roof with surprisingly good holds. *(John Martin, 1991)*

65 Virtual Light 5.10a . . . .

2 bolts (9 m) This short route ends at a ledge. Stretch between holds on the smooth wall. *(John Martin, 1994)*

66 Swan Lake 5.10a . . . .

7 bolts (21 m) Continue above the anchors of *Virtual Light*. Fun climbing on big holds leads out the right side of the huge roof. *(John Martin, 1992)*

67 Lapidarist 5.10c . . . .

3 bolts (10 m) This route is just right of *Virtual Light*. It ends with a balancey move by the last bolt. The anchors are on the wall above the ledge. *(Sean Dougherty, 1989)*

68 Impulse 5.10a . . . .

3 bolts (10 m) Start just left of a rock-scarred tree. Connect delicate moves between good holds. *(John Martin, 1990)*

69 Dressed to Kill 5.11b . . . .

12 bolts (32 m) From the ledge, head up a corner and trend left over a line of red line hangers. Brilliant face climbing leads directly to anchors at the top of the wall. This can be done in one big pitch from the ground via *Lapidarist* or *Impulse*. This is a very good route.

(John Martin, 1989)

70 Incantation 5.11c . . .

11 bolts (32 m) From the ledge, follow red hangers up great stone. Alternatively, climb it in one pitch from the ground via *Lapidarist*. This is an excellent climb and comes highly recommended. *(John Martin, 2000)*

71 Wilt 5.11c . . . .

9 bolts (26 m) Start just left of a big tree growing on a ledge. A long reach over a yellow roof leads to jugs and sustained climbing on bullet stone. A sporty runout gains the anchor. *(Sean Dougherty, 1989)*

72 Moon Over Miami 5.11c . . . .

10 bolts (26 m) From the first bolt of *Wilt*, head right to a monster jug. Move left into a corner system with a couple of nice pocket moves. *(Sean Dougherty, 1989)*

73 Altered States 5.11b . . . .

9 bolts (20 m) Start off the right end of a ledge. Trend left over a difficult roof to a jug, and continue up to a ramp. Pull the roof to a chert knob finish. *(John Martin, 1990)*

74 Ancient Life 5.11d . . . .

5 bolts (13 m) Climb to the first bolt on *Altered States* and move right, with difficulty, to gain a jug. Another hard section leads to good holds. *(Dave Thomson, 1990)*

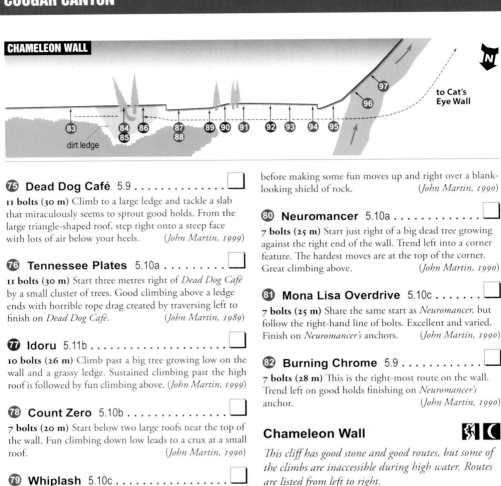

CHAMELEON WALL

83 84 85 86 87 88 89 90 91 92 93 94 95 96 97

dirt ledge

to Cat's Eye Wall

N

75 Dead Dog Café 5.9 . . . . ☐

11 bolts (30 m) Climb to a large ledge and tackle a slab that miraculously seems to sprout good holds. From the large triangle-shaped roof, step right onto a steep face with lots of air below your heels. *(John Martin, 1999)*

76 Tennessee Plates 5.10a . . . . ☐

11 bolts (30 m) Start three metres right of *Dead Dog Café* by a small cluster of trees. Good climbing above a ledge ends with horrible rope drag created by traversing left to finish on *Dead Dog Café*. *(John Martin, 1989)*

77 Idoru 5.11b . . . . ☐

10 bolts (26 m) Climb past a big tree growing low on the wall and a grassy ledge. Sustained climbing past the high roof is followed by fun climbing above. *(John Martin, 1999)*

78 Count Zero 5.10b . . . . ☐

7 bolts (20 m) Start below two large roofs near the top of the wall. Fun climbing down low leads to a crux at a small roof. *(John Martin, 1990)*

79 Whiplash 5.10c . . . . ☐

4 bolts (18 m) Start to the left of a dead tree growing against the right end of the wall. Follow a corner leftward

CHAMELEON WALL

83 84 85 86 87 88 89 90 91 92 93 94 95 96 97

before making some fun moves up and right over a blank-looking shield of rock. *(John Martin, 1990)*

80 Neuromancer 5.10a . . . . ☐

7 bolts (25 m) Start just right of a big dead tree growing against the right end of the wall. Trend left into a corner feature. The hardest moves are at the top of the corner. Great climbing above. *(John Martin, 1990)*

81 Mona Lisa Overdrive 5.10c . . . . . . ☐

7 bolts (25 m) Share the same start as *Neuromancer*, but follow the right-hand line of bolts. Excellent and varied. Finish on *Neuromancer's* anchors. *(John Martin, 1990)*

82 Burning Chrome 5.9 . . . . ☐

7 bolts (28 m) This is the right-most route on the wall. Trend left on good holds finishing on *Neuromancer's* anchor. *(John Martin, 1990)*

Chameleon Wall

This cliff has good stone and good routes, but some of the climbs are inaccessible during high water. Routes are listed from left to right.

83 Ten Years After 5.10a . . . . ☐

6 bolts (19 m) Begin at the base of a vegetated, right-trending ramp. Climb through sidepulls down low and finish up the ramp left of the arête. *(John Martin, 1998)*

84 Faux Pas 5.11b . . . . ☐

6 bolts (19 m) Start just left of two trees growing close to the wall. From a ledge above the second bolt, trend left into a grey corner. Climb it, pull past a roof and continue up a small corner above. *(John Martin, Sean Dougherty, 1989)*

85 Zona Rosa 5.10d . . . . ☐

6 bolts (18 m) Climb *Faux Pas* to the ledge. Continue straight up into white rock and trend right to anchors below the big roof. *(John Martin, 1998)*

CROWBAR WALL

grassy ledge

---

86 Long Time No See 5.11a . . . . . .

8 bolts (18 m) Climb onto a ledge above a right-facing corner. Continue over a small roof and into some technical moves on small edges over another roof. Finish on *Zona Rosa's* anchors. *(John Martin, 2003)*

87 Orange Crush 5.10b . . . .

6 bolts (17 m) This fun and interesting route moves through a couple of roofs before finishing with slab moves that gain the anchor under a big roof. *(John Martin, 1998)*

88 Open Project . . . .

The continuation to *Orange Crush*.

89 Cold Shoulder 5.11a . . . .

4 bolts (12 m) Scramble to a high first bolt. Use just the right blend of power and balance to finesse the roof. Finish straight up. *(John Martin, 1989)*

90 A Colder Shoulder 5.11a . . . . . .

5 bolts (12 m) Scramble onto a small ledge below a big, blocky spine. Powerful slaps up the spine lead to tricky climbing that gains the anchor. *(John Martin, 2003)*

91 Chameleon 5.10c . . . .

5 bolts (21 m) This route follows a large corner. Although the bolts are sparsely placed, there always seems to be one just when you really need it. *(Sean Dougherty, 1989)*

92 Lounge Lizard 5.11b . . . .

8 bolts (21 m) Start just right of a large corner. Big moves on good holds lead to a tricky arête up high. No lounging around. *(John Martin, 1994)*

93 Thrushold 5.10d . . . .

7 bolts (21 m) This is the second route right of the large corner. Good holds through a smooth, water-polished start lead to technical and balancey climbing above. The crux is at the last bolt. *(John Martin, 1989)*

94 Dry Heat 5.10a . . . .

6 bolts (18 m) Lots of cruxes. *(John Martin, 1998)*

95 Call of the Wild 5.10a . . . .

6 bolts (18 m) Climb to an interesting pod at the first bolt and continue straight up over a bulge. Finish on the same anchor as *Dry Heat*. *(John Martin, 1998)*

96 Back to the Future 5.9 . . . .

4 bolts (12 m) Prepare for a crux off the ground and one at the anchor. Easier climbing in between. *(John Martin, 1998)*

97 The Truth is Out There 5.9 . . . .

4 bolts (11 m) A pretty steep start leads to slabby climbing. *(John Martin, 1999)*

Crowbar Wall

This is the orange wall that rises out of the creek upstream from Cat's Eye wall. The angular features make for some technical and strenuous climbing. Inaccessible during high water. Routes are listed from left to right.

98 Lougheed the Great 5.7 . . . .

3 bolts (8 m) A path of jugs. *(Greg Cornell, 2001)*

99 Depth Charge 5.11b . . . .

3 bolts (8 m) Pull through a slick bottom with sparse footholds to a textured upper half. *(Sean Dougherty, 1989)*

100 Diphtheria 5.10b . . . .

2 bolts (8 m) A slick start leads to a corner and a chain anchor. *(Chas Yonge, 1989)*

101 Terminal Velocity 5.11a . . . .

5 bolts (13 m) Start off a large boulder at the base of the wall. Climb over a difficult roof to a jug and veer right onto a clean, yellow face. The technical crux comes at the last bolt. *(John Martin, 1994)*

102 Blockhead 5.9 . . . . ☐

3 bolts (11 m) Start just right of *Terminal Velocity*. Climb to a grey ramp and follow it to a chain anchor.

(Sean Dougherty, 1989)

103 Blockbuster 5.11a . . . . ☐

7 bolts (15 m) Start in the same place as *Blockhead*, but climb right around two small corners and up at the second bolt. Follow the line of least resistance through the corners and roofs. *(John Martin, 1989)*

104 Doppler Affect 5.11c . . . . ☐

5 bolts (15 m) Fight your way through the lower overhang and onto the face above. Climb straight up and join *Blockbuster* near the top. *(John Martin, 1996)*

105 Shockwave 5.10d . . . . ☐

7 bolts (18 m) Struggle over the first roof and into a series of unidirectional holds. At the fourth bolt, angle left around a nose feature. Head right into a corner and up to the anchor. *(John Martin, 1989)*

106 Surface Tension 5.11a . . . . ☐

8 bolts (21 m) Climb *Shockwave* to the fourth bolt and veer right. A crux gains the hanging slab, which leads to a second crux. *(Marcel Lehoux & Peter Charkiw, 1989)*

107 Critical Mass 5.10c . . . . ☐

7 bolts (22 m) This is the must-do route on the wall and is identified by a chain draw on the second bolt. Four, rapid-fire 5.10 cruxes will keep you busy on the way to the anchor. *(John Martin, 1990)*

108 Fresh Start 5.11d . . . . 🧗 ☐

8 bolts (23 m) Start right of the chain draw. Slowly work your way through an endless sea of technical climbing to a no-hands rest and the top. *(Unknown)*

109 Suzie Q 5.11c . . . . 🧗 📷 ☐

5 bolts (13 m) This short route packs quite a few punches en route to the chain anchor. *(John Martin, 1997)*

110 Island Experience 5.11a . . . . ☐

8 bolts (25 m) This is a difficult start to *Islands in the Stream*. Start up impossible-looking, water-polished stone. *(John Martin, 1990)*

CROWBAR WALL

CROWBAR WALL

BUFFLEHEAD WALL

anchor (don't clip it). Climb to the right, past a small, spindly-looking tree and onto a grey face. Follow the left-hand bolt line through excellent edges. (*John Martin, 1989*)

113 Mean Street 5.11a . . . .

10 bolts (33 m) Climb *Islands in the Stream* to the big, grassy ledge. Powerful climbing through steep, yellow rock leads to a white jug. Great moves lead over a small roof. Finish on the *Face Value* anchor. (*John Martin, 1990*)

114 Argon 5.10a . . . .

12 bolts (33 m) Climb *Face Value* to the first bolt on the upper face. Make a rising traverse rightward past a hole to a small, left-trending corner system. Follow it to a white jug bellow a small roof. Cut right around the corner to low angle terrain and up. (*John Martin, 1989*)

115 Supernatural 5.11b . . . .

10 bolts (27 m) Climb straight up through a series of small, left-facing corners to a ledge. Tricky moves gain a big corner. Trend left to some hard undercling moves over a roof. (*John Martin, 2008*)

116 Supernatural Direct 5.10b . . . .

10 bolts (30 m) Climb *Supernatural* to the big corner and continuing up it instead of trending left. (*Steve Stahl, 1989*)

117 Jack of Clubs 5.10b . . . .

8 bolts (21 m) Technical climbing down low leads to a midway break. Tricky moves lead into a short, left-facing corner capped by an orange roof. Continue straight up to anchors over the roof. (*Steve Stahl, 1989*)

118 Sleeping Dog 5.10a . . . .

6 bolts (27 m) A technical start leads to a ledge. Follow a groove right of a yellow patch to a midway break and a big move. Continue straight up to a bolt just right of the *Jack of Clubs* anchor and a runout to the top. (*John Martin, 1989*)

119 Slow Turning 5.10a . . . .

5 bolts (27 m) Start just left of a small, left-facing corner. A crimpy start leads to easy, but sporty climbing and a midway break. Continue up a tricky, left-facing corner to a sporty anchor run. (*John Martin, 1989*)

120 The Devil You Know 5.10a . . . .

8 bolts (25 m) Scramble onto a small ledge just left of a tree growing beside the wall. From the second bolt, climb *Slow Turning* to the midway break. Traverse right along the break and head upward via a tough move. (*John Martin, 2008*)

111 Islands in the Stream 5.9 . . . . .

7 bolts (27 m) This line is a journey along a series of left-leaning ramp features. It ends at the apex of the cliff.
(*John Martin, 1989*)

112 Face Value 5.10b . . . .

12 bolts (33 m) Climb *Islands in the Stream* to the midway

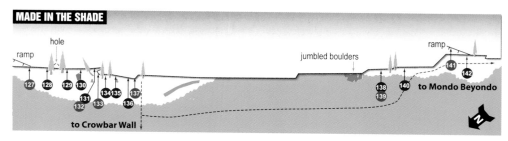

MADE IN THE SHADE

ramp / hole / jumbled boulders / ramp / to Mondo Beyondo / to Crowbar Wall

Bufflehead Wall

This small wall is above a large scree slope in the trees right of the creek. Routes are listed from left to right.

121 Bufflehead 5.10a . . . .

3 bolts (9 m) This is the left-most route and climbs straight up on edges. The Bufflehead is a small, American sea duck. *(John Martin, 1998)*

122 Bafflegab 5.10b . . . .

4 bolts (9 m) Work up sidepulls and underclings to a short, right-facing corner. Watch the tricky move before the anchor. Bafflegab is a slang term that refers to confusing or generally unintelligible jargon. *(John Martin, 1998)*

123 Baby Steps 5.10c . . . .

5 bolts (9 m) This is the right-most route. Trend right up sidepulls and underclings to the top of the wall. Traverse left to the anchors of *Bafflegab*. *(John Martin, 1999)*

Mondo Beyondo Wall

This small wall is located in the trees on the right side of the creek. Routes are listed from left to right.

124 Mondo Beyond 5.11a . . . .

6 bolts (16 m) The left-most route starts just right of a left-trending dirt ramp. The quality is high, with sustained climbing down low that leads to a crux pulling over the upper roof. *(John Martin, 1998)*

125 Little Feat 5.11a . . . .

6 bolts (15 m) Start in the yellow rock and power through underclings to easier climbing. One tricky move guards the anchor. *(John Martin, 1999)*

126 Short Haul 5.10d . . . .

3 bolts (10 m) Start just right of a tree. Climb through blocky underclings and sidepulls. *(John Martin, 1999)*

Made In the Shade Wall

This wall has a split personality. On the left, the routes are highly technical on clean grey rock, and on the right they tackle a white and orange wall with a more physical flavour. Routes are listed from left to right.

127 Penumbra 5.10b . . . .

11 bolts (29 m) Start off a dirty, left-trending ramp. Climb up and right into *Umbra*. *(John Martin, 2003)*

128 Umbra 5.11c . . . .

11 bolts (29 m) Begin left of two large trees growing next to the wall. A technical corner down low leads to fun jug climbing and a second technical section up the final slab. *(John Martin, 2003)*

MADE IN THE SHADE

129 Tender Mercies 5.11a . . . .

13 bolts (30 m) Start just right of the two large trees. Tricky moves end at a shake in a short corner. Continue through very slabby and technical overlaps to anchors above. *(John Martin, 1990)*

130 Shady Lady 5.11b . . . .

11 bolts (33 m) This is the direct start to *Made in the Shade*. *(John Martin, 1995)*

131 Made in the Shade 5.10c . . .

11 bolts (33 m) Stem up the corner until it's possible to pull onto the face at the first bolt. Sustained and thought provoking in its entirety. *(John Martin, 1989)*

132 The Gloaming 5.10c . . . .

9 bolts (22 m) Start on *Made in the Shade*, but continue up the corner until it's possible to pull onto the face just above the second bolt. Straightforward climbing ends just below the anchor. *(John Martin, 2003)*

133 Crash Course 5.10b . . . .

1 bolt (10 m) Start just right of the large corner. Slap up a large fin to the first and only bolt. Keep your head together and you'll do fine on the slab. *(John Martin, 1994)*

134 Clip Joint 5.11c . . . .

3 bolts (10 m) Start in front of two trees growing next to the wall. Powerful slaps up a blunt prow lead to underclings. Continue upward until its possible to pull around onto the slab. *(John Martin, 1994)*

135 French Connection 5.11d . . . .

2 bolts (9 m) This is the first route right of the two trees. Slim pickings for handholds and footholds lead to a couple of good grips at the first bolt. Still-difficult climbing leads to the anchors above. *(Justin Ralph, 1990)*

136 Tree Men 5.11a . . . .

3 bolts (9 m) Poor handholds and footholds lead to better grips, but the footwork stays desperate. *(Peter Charkiw, 1990)*

137 Crybaby 5.10a . . . .

3 bolts (10 m) Follow a small, right-trending corner through a series of sidepulls. *(John Martin, 1990)*

138 Skyjack 5.11b . . . .

9 bolts (22 m) A great finger crack leads up a corner to a

MADE IN THE SHADE

ledge and the base of a large roof. Switch gears and power through the roof on edges. *(Geoff Powter, 1993)*

139 Shadow of Turning 5.9 . . . .

7 bolts (22 m) Climb *Skyjack* to the base of the large roof. Head right to the *High Wire* anchor. *(John Martin, 1990)*

140 High Wire 5.11b . . . .

9 bolts (22 m) Start just right of two skinny trees growing next to the wall. Difficult underclings lead to a no-hands rest. Continue through a fractured corner until its possible to pull onto the face above. *(Justin Ralph, 1990)*

141 Pin-toe Flakes 5.10c . . . .

6 bolts (19 m) This super fun route links a series of flakes. Scramble up a left-trending ramp to reach the first bolt. The flakes may sound hollow, but you'll be having so much fun, it won't bother you. *(Kim Heidel, 2000)*

142 Kokopelli 5.11a . . . .

5 bolts (11 m) Start four metres left of a rotten corner. Grunt to the top of a large flake and execute a few tricky face moves. *(Nathan Cando, 2003)*

POOLSIDE SECTOR

33 routes ←5.10 5.11 5.12 5.13→

A short walk past the House of Cards sector is a cluster of five crags, the first of which is Poolside Wall. This sector starts at the big bend in the creek and extends upstream to Catamount Wall on the left. While this area has a good collection of nice moderates, it also contains a small collection of steep, powerful lines, perfect for those looking to test their mettle.

Conditions: The walls on the left side of the creek receive lots of sun, while the walls located on the right side receive shade for most of the day. Rain will quickly put an end to an outing, but the walls dry quickly once the rain has stopped.

Approach: From the House of Cards sector, hike upstream for a few minutes. The trail takes a shortcut into the trees on the right side of the drainage before emerging at a big bend in the creek and a cliff on the right that extends into the creek, the Poolside Wall.

Poolside Wall

This steep wall is comprised of smooth, rounded rock. A good dose of power is required to succeed on the various climbs. Routes are listed from left to right.

❶ Stygian Ayre 5.12d . . . .

4 bolts (9 m) A steep start leads directly into the first of two hard boulder problems on slick holds. Once you hit the black rock, the ascent should be in the bag. Ignore the two homemade hangers. (*Mark DeLeeuw, 1989*)

❷ Chandelle 5.12a . . . .

3 bolts (10 m) Climb under a slanting corner. Work over a small roof to better holds. (*Mark DeLeeuw, 1989*)

❸ Dark Star 5.11d . . . .

7 bolts (16 m) Slick start to easy finish. (*John Martin, 1990*)

❹ Bob's Yer Uncle 5.11b . . . .

5 bolts (14 m) Start in a small corner feature. A very polished start leads to a fun crux pulling over a small roof. Afterward, the black rock provides plenty of textured holds on the way to the anchor. (*John Martin, 1990*)

❺ Party Line 5.10d . . . .

5 bolts (13 m) Climb blue streaks and veer right onto the black rock. (*John Martin, 1990*)

❻ Poolside Pleasures 5.10d . . . .

4 bolts (13 m) Start just left of a large roof at four metres. Pleasant. (*John Martin, 1988*)

POOLSIDE WALL

❼ The Diving Board 5.10d . . . .

3 bolts (11 m) A fall before the first bolt would be a bad idea. Follow a crack until your standing on the diving board. Moving off it is the crux. (*John Martin, 1990*)

Hillside Wall

This cliff is just uphill from Poolside Wall and features thin and technical routes with the occasional powerful move. Routes are listed from left to right.

❽ Bronco 5.10d . . . .

4 bolts (11 m) Start off the big rock platform and follow a crack over a roof to small chert edges. (*Ian Perry, 2008*)

❾ Strength in Numbers 5.11d . . . .

6 bolts (11 m) Start on the right side of the rock platform. Very small crimpers make you earn the easier face climbing above. (*Ian Perry, 2008*)

10 Plastic Surgery 5.11b . . . . 〼

6 bolts (12 m) Climb through a series of overlapping roofs to a crux up the arête. *(Ian Perry, 2008)*

11 Pearl 5.11a . . . . 〼

6 bolts (15 m) Climb the steep corner with a white streak running down it. Fun but cruxy moves up the corner lead to easier climbing above. *(Ian Perry, 2008)*

12 Slimper 5.10b . . . . 〼

6 bolts (15 m) Start just right of a rock jutting out of the ground. Climb the face on mostly good holds to anchors at the top of the wall. *(Ian Perry, 2008)*

Covert Wall

This is a sunny wall with nice vertical edge climbing on grey and orange rock. Routes are listed from left to right.

13 Cloak and Dagger 5.10c . . . . 〼

5 bolts (18 m) Start to the right of the loose-looking blocks. Climb to a small ledge before tiptoeing up the orange slab and over small overhangs to the anchor. *(Unknown)*

14 Under Cover 5.10b . . . . 〼

6 bolts (18 m) Finesse the grey slab. *(Steve Stahl, 1989)*

15 Covert Action 5.10b . . . . 〼

6 bolts (19 m) After climbing onto a ledge at two metres, follow a crack to its end. Head for a grey roof on the way to the anchor. *(Chas Yonge, 1989)*

16 Cover-up 5.10d . . . . 〼

7 bolts (20 m) Climb the face to the left of the zigzag corner. Finish up the slab. *(John Martin, 1989)*

17 Deep Cover 5.10b . . . . 〼

7 bolts (20 m) Start to the right of a zigzag corner. An ugly opening leads to a nice, grey slab. *(John Martin, 1991)*

Catamount Wall

This nice wall has both steep, powerful routes and moderate, vertical routes. To find it, continue upstream from Poolside Wall for a few minutes to the next big wall on the left side of the creek. Routes are listed from left to right.

18 Rising Collateral 5.12b . . . . 〼

4 bolts (6 m) This short and bouldery route tackles the overhanging corner. *(Unknown)*

19 Catatonic 5.12c . . . . 〼

6 bolts (10 m) Start off a boulder at the base. A hard power problem between the second and third bolt is followed by still-difficult climbing to the anchor. *(Jeff Relph, 2003)*

20 Vagotonic 5.12d . . . . 〼

9 bolts (17 m) This steep and sustained route has some big pulls between holds that you'll wish were better. Start just left of the base of the right-trending ramp. *(Jeff Relph, 2003)*

21 Open Project . . . . 〼

22 Law and Order 5.10b . . . . 〼

4 bolts (21 m) Start by scrambling up a right-trending ramp to a right-trending corner. Fun moves leading into the corner are followed by an intermittent crack and a crux pulling past the upper roof. *(John Martin, 1991)*

㉓ Rainy Day 5.9 . . . . ☐

6 bolts (15 m) Start off the left end of a low ledge. Climb carefully over some dirty ledges. Nice face climbing above. *(Patrick Delaney, 2009)*

㉔ Open Season 5.9 . . . . ☐

4 bolts (15 m) Big holds through yellow rock lead past a ledge to a crimpy, shallow scoop. *(John Martin, 1992)*

㉕ Abilene 5.9 . . . . ☐

5 bolts (17 m) Fantastic climbing on perfect edges and sinker buckets snakes up a faint yellow streak. *(John Martin, 1991)*

㉖ Cabin Fever 5.10b . . . . ☐

5 bolts (18 m) Start in front of a tree growing on a ledge. Hard-to-read moves lead straight up. *(John Martin, 1991)*

㉗ Catamount 5.10a . . . . ☐

5 bolts (15 m) Start just right of a tree growing off a ledge. A low crux with a perfect edge is followed by easier climbing to a roof and an exciting finish. *(John Martin, 1996)*

㉘ Chisum Trail 5.9 . . . . ☐

5 bolts (25 m) Begin around the corner from *Catamount*. Climb straight up before making a rightward move onto a slab peppered with chert knobs. *(John Martin, 1991)*

Heatwave Wall

This crag is not super inspiring, but it does have a few decent routes on it. It's located directly across from Catamount Wall. Routes are listed from left to right.

㉙ Heatwave 5.10c . . . . ☐

5 bolts (14 m) Begin left of a small tree and right-facing corner. Work up sidepulls and edges. *(John Martin, 1990)*

㉚ Global Warming 5.10a . . . . ☐

4 bolts (14 m) Fun climbing up a right-facing corner leads to anchors above a small roof. *(John Martin, 2005)*

㉛ Cold Snap 5.10b . . . . ☐

4 bolts (11 m) Start two metres right of a right-facing corner. Negotiate interesting stone down low before trending right to anchors above a small corner. *(John Martin, 2005)*

㉜ Hot to Trot 5.10c . . . . ☐

4 bolts (11 m) A tough start leads to easier climbing above. Share the anchor with *Cold Snap*. *(John Martin, 2005)*

㉝ Enthalpy 5.10a . . . . ☐

4 bolts (11 m) This is an easier, one-bolt start to *Hot to Trot*. Begin just left of a small pillar feature and trend left to the second bolt of *Hot to Trot*. *(Chas Yonge, 2005)*

COVERT WALL

CATAMOUNT WALL

HEATWAVE WALL

COSMOLOGY SECTOR

28 routes ←5.10 5.11 5.12 5.13→

Located about halfway up Cougar Creek, this sector sees far less traffic than the others and is a good bet if you're looking for some piece and quiet. The main attraction, Cosmology Wall, is packed full of fun and challenging routes that require solid fitness and good puzzle-solving skills to conquer. This area is definitely worth a little bit of extra walking. Check it out.

Conditions: Like the rest of Cougar Canyon, the walls on the left of the drainage receive lots of sun, while those on the right are shaded for most of the day. Once the rain has stopped, the crags dry quickly, and creek levels don't play much of a role at this sector—climbing is possible during high water.

Approach: Hike upstream past Poolside Sector for a few minutes. Cosmology Wall is on the left.

Cosmology Wall

This is the main attraction if you decide to venture further upstream. Routes are listed from left to right.

1 Navigator 5.9 . . . .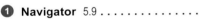
3 bolts (14 m) Scramble up a small chimney on the left end of the wall to a high first bolt. Positive footholds make the slopers workable. (*John Martin, 1990*)

2 Nine to Five 5.10b . . . .
4 bolts (14 m) This pitch is not as juggy as it looks from the ground. Start one metre right of a small chimney and pick carefully through the slopers. (*John Martin, 1990*)

3 Cat and Mouse 5.10c . . . .
4 bolts (14 m) Start just left of a tree growing next to the wall. More slopers. (*John Martin, 1990*)

4 Archaos 5.10d . . . .
8 bolts (21 m) Climb the slab to a tricky crux gaining the corner. Good holds lead up the left side. (*John Martin, 1991*)

5 Honeymoon Suite 5.10c . . . . . .
10 bolts (22 m) From the right side of a small cave, follow a left-trending flake to cruxy underclings at the end. Continue up the right side of the corner to a fun roof encounter before the anchor. (*John Martin, 1998*)

COSMOLOGY WALL

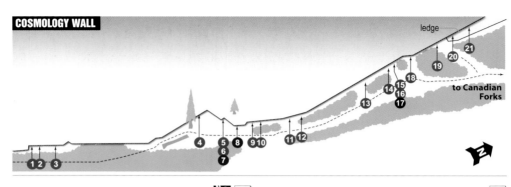

COSMOLOGY WALL

ledge
to Canadian Forks

 Big Bang Theory 5.10b

9 bolts (23 m) Start just right of *Honeymoon Suite*. Where the grey and yellow rock meet, trend left to a technical crux at a small bulge. *(John Martin, 1998)*

 Event Horizon 5.11a

9 bolts (23 m) Start on *Big Bang Theory*, but climb straight up into a yellow shield of rock. A hard move left is followed by sustained and crimpy climbing to a slab below the anchor. *(PREP: Larry Ostrander; FA: John Martin, 1998)*

8 Neutronium 5.11a

11 bolts (23 m) Start below a small tree growing on the wall. Climb around it on the left, and follow great incuts to a roof encounter. *(John Martin, 1998)*

9 Indigo 5.10d

10 bolts (22 m) Constant cruxes will keep you busy from bottom to top. Start at the base of a right-trending roof at ground level. *(John Martin, 1989)*

10 Lucille 5.10d

9 bolts (23 m) Start under a right-trending roof using incut edges. You'll encounter most everything during your ascent: a steep and powerful start, balancey crimps, jugs, chert edges, and sidepulls through a bulge. *(John Martin, 1998)*

11 History of Time 5.10c

8 bolts (23 m) A tricky start and a few hard moves up the crack are followed by pleasant 5.9 climbing to hidden anchors up and left of the last bolt. *(John Martin, 1989)*

12 Doctor Gage's Meat Inspection 5.10d

4 bolts (15 m) Start up the left side of an arête. The climbing is difficult until it's possible to pull around the right side of the arête. Finish up the slab. *(Scott Withers, 1999)*

13 Timescape 5.9

5 bolts (15 m) Start between two clumps of trees. Climb up and left on good holds and finish under a roof. *(John Martin, 1998)*

 Milk Run 5.5

4 bolts (14 m) Buckets lead up slabby terrain to the anchors. *(John Martin, 1998)*

 Cosmic String 5.8

10 bolts (32 m) Climb the slabby corner past chain anchors on the right all the way to the top of the wall. Can be done in two pitches. If you don't have a 70-metre rope, you'll need to lower twice. *(John Martin, 1989)*

16 Prime Cut 5.10d

13 bolts (35 m) Follow the slab to chain anchors at mid-height. Sidepull onto the wall and follow a crack feature to the anchors. The brilliant stone is getting a tad polished. *(John Martin, 1990)*

 Outer Limits 5.12a

9 bolts (25 m) Ramble up a slab to the base of the wall on the right. Head for the arête using crimps, and follow it until it's possible to use a crack feature on the left. Stout for the grade with great exposure. *(Tom Fayle, 1991)*

18 Dead Heat 5.10b

4 bolts (13 m) Start in a clump of trees to the right of the slab. Climb the small corner and make a couple of hard moves to the right. Easier above. *(John Martin, 1990)*

19 Octavius and His Magic Trumpet 5.10a

9 bolts (16 m) Climb through edges to the right of the chossy flake. *(Jeff Relph, 2002)*

20 Gaia 5.9 . . . . 🏃 ☐

9 bolts (27 m) Head straight up and pull a little roof to gain a break. Continue to anchors. *(John Martin, 1994)*

21 Entropy 5.10a . . . . 🏃 ☐

8 bolts (27 m) This is the right-most line of bolts. Find a path through all the edges. *(John Martin, 1992)*

Cougar Bait 🏃 ▨

This short, steep yellow wall is located just upstream of Cosmology Wall. Routes are listed from left to right.

22 Cougar Attack 5.10c . . . . ☐

5 bolts (11 m) Climb the face to the left of the dirty corner before crossing over to the right wall. Finish up a blank slab. *(Unknown)*

23 Cougar Bait 5.12b . . . . ☐

5 bolts (11 m) Start in front of a dead, uprooted tree. From the break, move left using a corner and a right-hand sidepull to gain a good hold above. *(Blake Horbay, 2005)*

24 Open Project . . . . ☐

Red-eye Cove Wall 🏃 ☾

This is a shattered-looking wall behind a cluster of large boulders by the creek. Routes are listed from left to right.

25 Red-eye Jedi 5.10b . . . . ☐

4 bolts (9 m) The left line. Work your way up shattered and angular rock. *(Jeff Relph, 2002)*

26 Block Party 5.10b . . . . ☐

5 bolts (9 m) The right line. Work your way up more shattered and angular rock. *(Jeff Relph, 2002)*

The Caribbean Wall 🏃 ☾

This crag is located on the same cliff line as Red-eye Cove Wall, but is further up the forested hillside. Routes are listed from left to right. No topo.

27 Trinidad 5.11b . . . . ☐

12 bolts (28 m) This pitch is located near the left end of the wall, just right of a big, blocky roof. The climbing up high is good, but a high first bolt combined with a chossy lower wall discourages most climbers. *(John Martin, 1991)*

28 Gin and Juice 5.11a . . . . ☐

11 bolts (28 m) Start off a small, mossy ledge. Follow edges through black rock to a diagonal break. Blue streaks lead to anchors at the top of the wall. *(Jeff Relph, 2002)*

COSMOLOGY WALL

RED-EYE COVE WALL

COUGAR BAIT

CANADIAN FORKS SECTOR

59 routes ←5.10 5.11 5.12 5.13→

Despite having a few walls that are worth the walk, this sector has the longest approach in the canyon and consequently sees very little traffic. This is a great place to escape the crowds and enjoy climbing in solitude (most of the time). The Canadian Forks cliffs are the warmest in the canyon and are climbable during early and late season, while Planet X sees no sun and is best suited for warm summer days.

Conditions: Creekside and Canadian Forks walls are the sunniest in the entire canyon, and make for excellent early- and late-season outings. These crags also dry very quickly after rain. Planet X sees no sun, but stays dry during moderate rainstorms. It seeps in the early season, though.

Approach: Hike 25 minutes upstream from Cosmology Sector to where the creek forks. The left fork contains Creekside, while the right fork contains Canadian Forks and Planet X.

Cavern Wall

This is the big overhanging wall on the right side of the creek about five minutes downstream from Canadian Forks. Routes are listed from left to right.

❶ Gery's Route 5.12d . . . .

8 bolts (22 m) From the top of the chossy slab, pull onto the wall and follow a crumbly flake until it's possible to pull onto a crimpy overhanging face. (*Gery Unterasinger, 2007*)

❷ Natural Selection 5.11c . . . .

6 bolts (12 m) Start just right of a large slab. Good luck unlocking the moves on the blank lower section. Follow a grey, right-trending ramp above. (*John Martin, 1991*)

❸ Evolution 5.10b . . . .

5 bolts (13 m) Follow a shallow, white, open-book corner before angling up right on good holds. (*John Martin, 1991*)

Creekside Wall

This decent wall is overshadowed by the more attractive Canadian Forks wall. If you want some variety, check it out. Routes are listed from left to right.

❹ Hockey Night in Canada 5.8 . . . . . .

2 bolts (13 m) Start just left of a hole in the horizontal break. Climb direct to chain anchors. (*John Martin, 1991*)

❺ Strandline 5.10b . . . .

3 bolts (13 m) Start right of a hole in a horizontal break. Runout at the second and third bolt. (*John Martin, 1991*)

CAVERN WALL

❻ Dynosoar 5.11a . . . .

3 bolts (14 m) Head through a low scoop to a cruxy roof encounter. (*John Martin, 1991*)

❼ Stone Cold 5.10c . . . .

5 bolts (14 m) Start two metres right of *Dynosoar*. Head for a roof and an easier lip encounter. (*John Martin, 1991*)

❽ Some Like It Hot 5.11a . . . .

5 bolts (13 m) Follow the thin, yellow streak to a sloping ledge and a big roof. (*John Martin, 1992*)

❾ Tilt 5.11b . . . .

6 bolts (15 m) Start on the left end of a permanently wet patch of rock. A glassy start leads to a yellow and blue streak with a tricky lip encounter. (*John Martin, 1991*)

❿ Withering Heights 5.11b . . . . . .

6 bolts (15 m) Start below a yellow corner. Step over permanently wet rock and head up the corner. Exit the roof through the obvious weakness. (*John Martin, 1991*)

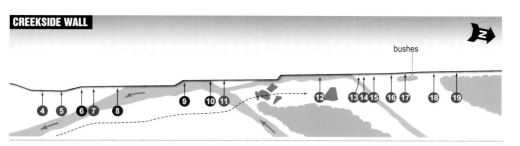

CREEKSIDE WALL

bushes

⑪ Arcana 5.10d . . . . ☐

4 bolts (12 m) Use cheater stones to step over the permanently wet start. Head up a yellow streak and traverse right, under a roof, before pulling the lip.   (*John Martin, 1991*)

⑫ Open Project . . . . ☐
Abandoned. Some bolts may be missing.

⑬ Lunch Rambo Style 5.10b . . . . ☐

3 bolts (12 m) White rock on the right end of the permanently wet patch leads to a bolt below a roof. Traverse left to a left-facing corner (try to keep your feet dry). Finish straight up.   (*John Martin, 1992*)

CREEKSIDE WALL

always wet

always wet

⑭ Café Rambo 5.10b . . . . ☐

4 bolts (15 m) Begin two metres right of *Lunch Rambo Style* and climb to a jagged pod in a bulge. A couple of hard moves surmount the bulge and lead to a bolt out left. The anchors are over the top.   (*John Martin, 1992*)

⑮ Lysdexia 5.10c . . . . ☐

3 bolts (15 m) Great climbing up positive edges of all sizes leads to some cool undercling moves. The finish is easier, but runout.   (*John Martin, 1991*)

⑯ When Worlds Collide 5.10c . . . ☐

4 bolts (14 m) This route climbs a left-facing corner system just right of a powder blue streak below a grassy ledge. Climb to a small roof and around it on the left side. At the grassy ledge, traverse right on edges to reach the anchor.   (*John Martin, 1991*)

⑰ Gondwanaland 5.10b . . . . ☐

4 bolts (14 m) Start in front of bushes. The crux is low and pulls over a small roof. After a rest, continue up nice edges to the top.   (*John Martin, 1991*)

⑱ Continental Drift 5.10b . . . . ☐

4 bolts (14 m) Fun climbing on cool holds leads to a crux pulling over a bulge at mid-height. From the last bolt, trend left on chert bands to the anchor.   (*John Martin, 1991*)

⑲ Burmese 5.10a . . . . ☐

3 bolts (14 m) Climb straight up into a yellow scoop and a no-hands rest. A couple of big moves on big holds will have you on the slab in no time flat. Traverse left on cool chert edges to the anchor.   (*John Martin, 1991*)

Canadian Forks 🧗 🔨 ☀

This is a very warm and sunny wall that features some excellent climbs and glorious solitude most of the time. Routes are listed from left to right.

20 The Nomadic Struggle 5.10d . . . . . ☐

4 bolts (10 m) This pitch is located about 70 metres left of Canadian Forks. It's the left-hand line. (*Greg Cornell, 2001*)

21 Prisoners of the Sun 5.10a . . . . ☐

4 bolts (10 m) The right-hand route. (*Greg Cornell, 2001*)

22 Prima Donna 5.10c . . . . ☐

4 bolts (11 m) This is the first route on the Canadian Forks crag. Start to the left of a small tree and climb through prickly yellow rock. Exit the corner to reach the anchor. (*John Martin, 1994*)

23 Diva 5.10c . . . . 🧗 ☐

4 bolts (12 m) Start to the right of a small tree. Stem easily up a corner to a crux near the top. (*John Martin, 1994*)

24 Broken Chord 5.9 . . . . ☐

4 bolts (15 m) From an orange ledge, follow a line of bolts up textured, protruding holds. (*John Martin, 1994*)

25 Stepping Razor 5.10b . . . . ☐

8 bolts (18 m) Start just left of a corner. Scale a steep slab to a corner and a beach ball-sized-sized hole. Head up and over the hole to anchors on the right. Steeper than it looks! (*John Martin, 1994*)

26 Paper Cup 5.11c . . . . ☐

4 bolts (8 m) Follow a faint corner to anchors above a ledge. (*Patrick Delaney, 2008*)

27 Dance Macabre 5.11a . . . . ☐

3 bolts (8 m) Slopers and pockets lead to edges and anchors above the ledge. (*John Martin, 1991*)

28 Spite 5.11a . . . . ☐

9 bolts (23 m) This route follows glue-in bolts. Start below a small corner and roof at two metres. Fight your way through slick, pocketed rock to a pod. Fun climbing on black rock leads to the anchors. (*Serge Angelluci, 1991*)

29 Elixir Left 5.11d . . . . ☐

5 bolts (13 m) A serious effort is required to reach a pair of jugs in the grey rock. After you've recovered, follow the left-hand line of bolts to an anchor below the ledge. (*John Martin, 1994*)

30 Elixir Right 5.11d . . . . ☐

6 bolts (13 m) From the pair of jugs on the previous climb, follow the right-hand line of bolts. (*John Martin, 1994*)

31 Phlogiston 5.11c . . . . ☐

7 bolts (13 m) Find two pockets in the break and follow a faint, white groove. Finish up the corner. (*John Martin, 1991*)

32 Lean Cuisine 5.11b . . . . ☐

6 bolts (16 m) A more difficult start to *Free Lunch* boulders past two bolts before joining that route. (*John Martin, 1994*)

Creekside & Cavern Wall

60 m to 20 & 21

ramp

CANADIAN FORKS

ramp

to Planet X

33 Free Lunch 5.10c . . . .

5 bolts (16 m) A crux right off the ground is followed by nice climbing up the grey, orange and white rock to anchors over the ledge. (*John Martin, 1991*)

34 Some Can Whistle 5.10c . . . .

8 bolts (24 m) Struggle up a slick start to reach the security of a corner. (*John Martin, 1993*)

35 Whistlestop 5.10a . . . .

7 bolts (24 m) Big pulls off smooth holds gain a break. Join *Some Can Whistle* to finish. (*John Martin, 1994*)

36 Some Can Dance 5.10d . . . .

5 bolts (16 m) Hard moves surmount the roof. Climb through the corner to anchors out right. (*John Martin, 1994*)

37 Carioca 5.10a . . . .

5 bolts (16 m) Pull over a small roof to slabby terrain and a second roof. (*John Martin, 1994*)

38 Hidden Agenda 5.10a . . . .

7 bolts (20 m) Scramble up broken ledges to a right-facing corner. Follow orange rock up a shallow corner to a high hole. Straight up to anchors. (*John Martin, 1994*)

39 Ricochet 5.9 . . . .

9 bolts (22 m) From the second bolt of *Hidden Agenda*, head right on great holds. Pull a roof on the left side and head up right to anchors over the ledge. (*John Martin, 1994*)

Planet X

This is a huge, impressive wall that seems to come out of nowhere during the approach. It's one of the newer additions to the Bow Valley's crag collection, and is producing some of the hardest routes around (there are three open 5.14 projects). From Canadian Forks, turn 180 degrees and follow a small drainage for five minutes. Routes are listed from left to right.

40 Open Project . . . .

This pitch is waiting for a power beast and a climbing technician all rolled into one. When completed, it will certainly be one of the hardest pitches in the Bow Valley.

41 Closed Project . . . .

CANADIAN FORKS

42 John Doe 5.12b . . . .

6 bolts (14 m) This is a difficult route to read. Start in front of a hole and try to keep the pump at bay while unlocking the tricky sequence. *(Unknown)*

43 Open Project . . . .

Unlocking the sequence of moves above *John Doe* will yield another 5.14.

44 Closed Project . . . .

45 Kurrgo 5.14a . . . .

16 bolts (34 m) This stunning line tackles the steepest part of the wall. From the midway break, a grey streak leads to an incredible crux. From here, it's hard all the way to the anchor. *(PREP: Scott Milton; FA: Derek Galloway, 2006)*

46 Fudge Packer 5.13d . . . .

18 bolts (32 m) This power-endurance testpiece gives most a real run for their money. A 5.12b start gains the midway break. Two cruxes separated by a poor excuse for a rest is followed by a race to the chains. *(PREP: Gery Unterasinger & Derek Galloway; FA: Scott Milton, 2005)*

47 Shooting Packer 5.13b . . . . . .

18 bolts (35 m) This must-do link-up combines the pumpy start of *Shooting Star* with the amazing bulge on *Fudge Packer*. Very popular. *(Matt Pieterson, 2005)*

48 Shooting Star 5.12d . . . .

17 bolts (32 m) The most sought after route on the wall has no stopper moves, but is continually hard and will test your endurance. Climb a right-facing corner to the midway break. Launch up the overhanging wall above with no hesitation. *(PREP: Keith Haberl; FA: Unknown)*

49 Cosmos 5.13c . . . .

15 bolts (30 m) Tricky face climbing leads to the midway break. A tough crux gains the overhanging wall above, and another tough crux at the stepped upper roof. *(PREP: Gery Unterasinger; FA: Derek Galloway, 2007)*

50 Sticky Buns 5.13a . . . .

15 bolts (26 m) This great route might be a fast tick for boulderers. From the midway break, a crimpy crux gains the corner and good holds. Powerful slaps lead over the bulge to a still-difficult finish. To the midway break, it's a good 5.11c. *(Derek Galloway, 2003)*

51 Moon Boots 5.11c . . . .

6 bolts (14 m) Climb grey streaks. Trend right over a small roof to anchors at the midway break. *(Paul McSorley, 2003)*

CANADIAN FORKS

52 The Illusionist 5.14a . . . . .

13 bolts (27 m) Start just left of a skinny, knee-high tree stump. The business hits above the midway break. Sustained climbing leads to a powerful sequence that surmounts the massive roof on holds you'll wish were better. Climb the first half of *The Illusionist* to the midway break and finish on *Moon Boots* for a technical 5.11c.
(*PREP: Gery Unterasinger; FA: Sonnie Trotter, 2007*)

53 Open Project . . . .

This line features one super hard boulder problem.

54 First Light 5.12b . . . . . .

11 bolts (20 m) Climb carefully to a no-hands rest on a ledge. Trend left via sustained moves on cool holds to a bouldery crux. (*Gery Unterasinger, 2007*)

55 Before Dark 5.11c . . . .

11 bolts (21 m) Climb *First Light* to the ledge. Continue straight up via steep jugs and a very long move to a more technical finish. When dry, this route makes a great warm-up. (*PREP: Sam Lighter & Simon Meis; FA: Simon Meis 2006*)

56 After Dark 5.12c . . . .

24 bolts (43 m) Continue above the anchors of *Before Dark*. Follow the blue streak to a cruxy bulge on sloping and hard-to-locate edges. Great climbing gains the anchors. Lower twice. Rope drag can be a major issue on this excellent pitch. Manage it very carefully for a trouble-free ascent. (*PREP: Sam lighter & Simon Meis; FA: Simon Meis 2006*)

57 The Hot Gates 5.13a . . . . . .

16 bolts (35 m) Start up a short, left-facing corner next to a tree. From a dirty ledge, battle through small edges to a much-deserved rest. Take the left line to a huge bucket, a boulder problem and some tough climbing to gain the anchor. (*PREP: Todd Guyn; FA: Derek Galloway, 2007*)

58 Timber 5.13a . . . .

17 bolts (35 m) Climb *The Hot Gates* to the rest and continue straight up. The pump builds continuously until the anchors are clipped.
(*PREP: Simon Meis; FA: Derek Galloway, 2007*)

59 Meconium 5.12a . . . .

16 bolts (35 m) This excellent, long route has a bit of everything. Technical climbing down low leads to a break, which is followed by steep climbing up the blue streak above. (*PREP: Louis-Julien Roy; FA: Derek Galloway, 2005*)

PLANET X

Turn back the clock about 25 years. Sport climbing was just becoming established in the Bow Valley, but at that time the bolt holes had to be drilled by hand—a very tiring procedure. The first bolt would take about 15 minutes to drill, the next a little longer, and so on until soon you were so exhausted that drilling a hole seemed to take forever. Placing ten or so bolts in a day would feel like a pretty good day's work. A few years later, the first hammer drills showed up in the Bow Valley and things were never the same again—holes could be drilled in seconds rather than minutes. Suddenly, it became practical to establish bolted routes on quartzite crags like those at Lake Louise (hand drilling a bolt hole in quartzite reportedly took well over an hour), and it became much easier to drill on overhanging rock because you could drill one handed and at arms length. The production rate of new routes increased dramatically, but so did the number of new climbers. It soon became clear that a lot more new routes were going to be required and that they would have to be equipped with better quality bolt hangers and top anchors. The days of homemade hangers and funky top anchors, often of unknown strength and reliability, were over.

Belay platform construction at Grassi Lakes

The question was, who was going to pay for all the hardware? From 1987 to 1992, 75% of the new rock climbs in the Bow Valley were established by just three individuals, and 85% by just five or six individuals. At that time, an average 25-metre sport climb cost about $35 to equip using bolts and stainless steel hangers. Occasionally, a friend would donate a few dollars to help offset costs, but the bulk of the expense of building the routes that were being enjoyed by so many was being borne by just a few individuals. In 1993, I met with a few of the local route builders to discuss the possibility of setting up a gear fund to help pay for fixed hardware on climbs. I took our draft plan to Peter Tucker at the Mountain Equipment Co-op (MEC) who was immediately sold on the idea and arranged a start-up grant of $1,500. Further donations from the Alpine Club of Canada and several individuals quickly followed and The Association of Bow Valley Rock Climbers (TABVAR) was on its way.

Since that time, TABVAR has raised and disbursed over $80,000, almost $30,000 of which has come from donations from MEC. It is important to note here that not all Bow Valley route builders seek funds from TABVAR, and sometimes TABVAR is unable to fully fund those that do because of budget limitations. About 85% of TABVAR's expenditures have been on hardware, split approximately 80:20 between new routes and retrofits of existing routes, comprising some 2,000 pitches in all. The remainder has been used to purchase construction materials for trail work and climbing platforms.

By far, the biggest single project undertaken by TABVAR has been the Grassi Lakes Erosion Reduction Project (2003 to 2006). This project was conceived and managed by Chris Miller and resulted in

Andy Genereux making bolt hangers, circa 1987

the construction of all the climbing platforms, stairs and trails leading from the Upper Lake to the dam. Approximately $10,000 was spent on materials and another $8,000 worth of materials were donated. Even more remarkable is the amount of time and effort expended by all the volunteers who gave up valuable climbing time to ferry building materials down from the road and to assist with the construction work, some 700 worker hours in all. And this doesn't include the countless hours put in by Mike Radik and Chris Miller, who could be found working there at all hours of the day. Mike's contribution was immeasurable, from providing tools and design expertise to putting in seemingly limitless hours of dedicated work.

In 2010, TABVAR embarked on another ambitious project—The Anchor and Protection Bolt Replacement Project—to address the problem of substandard protection bolts and top anchors on local climbs. Unfortunately, until about 2002, many route builders in the Bow Valley were still using the cheaper non-stainless steel bolts combined with stainless steel hangers. This mixing of metal types leads to chemical reactions that greatly accelerate the corrosion of the bolts. In addition to this, repeated lowering through top anchors eventually cuts deep grooves in them and they need to be replaced. This is likely to be a never-ending project.

Early bolt on Abracadabra, Carrot Creek

TABVAR has been a great success both in terms of numbers and quality of projects supported. Through the route building standards voluntarily undertaken by those wishing to be compensated by TABVAR, we now enjoy a world-class standard of sport climbs. It is hoped that local climbers, climbing organizations and users of this guidebook will continue to support TABVAR through donations, both of cash and time.

—www.tabvar.org

JON JONES (ALL)

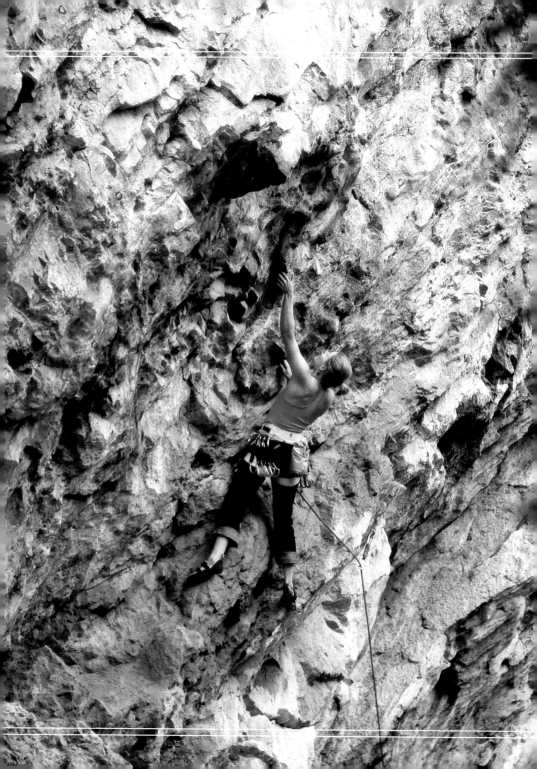

CHAPTER 9

GRASSI LAKES

Perched above two beautiful, emerald green lakes and overlooking the townsite of Canmore sits one of the Bow Valley's most popular crags, Grassi Lakes. The area's heavily-pocketed walls contain a varied selection of fun, gymnastic routes, which provide great challenges for both the beginner and seasoned veteran alike. The crags range in angle from less than vertical to steeply overhanging and offer an abundance of pitches from 5.5 to 5.13c, with the majority of climbs in the lower half of that range. Because of the crag's convenience and friendly grades, many choose to hone their skills here before venturing up to some of the more remote (and difficult) crags, like Bataan and Acéphale. Finally, because of Grassi's almost roadside location, this area makes a perfect place for an after work climbing fix or simply a chill day at the cliff.

EVA HUPIN-FLELE ON 'COOL SENSATIONS' (5.12A) ◯ ZAC MCGURK

CONDITIONS

Although the unique, pocketed stone in this area is not as compact as elsewhere in the Bow Valley, the routes at Grassi Lakes have cleaned up very well over time and the climbing is now clean, secure and enjoyable. However, helmets are still strongly advised when climbing or belaying at the base of the walls. Pockets of loose rock may still be found on certain climbs and grazing big horn sheep (and careless tourists) on the road above may trundle debris down the hillside onto unsuspecting climbers below (the Rectory, Ghetto, White Imperialist, Golf Course, and Graceland are the most heavily-affected zones.) Grassi Lakes is also home to a few important walls that remain climbable in the rain. These include the Rectory, the right end of White Imperialist and Meathooks. After a wet spell, however, the heavily-pocketed walls will seep, but many of the routes will return to a climbable state within a week of dry weather.

APPROACH

Grassi Lakes offers two different options for parking and approaching: the upper parking lot, which is popular due to its short, easy walk, and the lower parking lot, which is more commonly used by day hikers looking to access Grassi Lakes. The walk from the lower parking area is the longest, but can still be quite useful if the upper approach road happens to be closed for roadwork.

From Calgary: Drive west on the Trans-Canada Highway. Take Exit 93 and immediately turn left

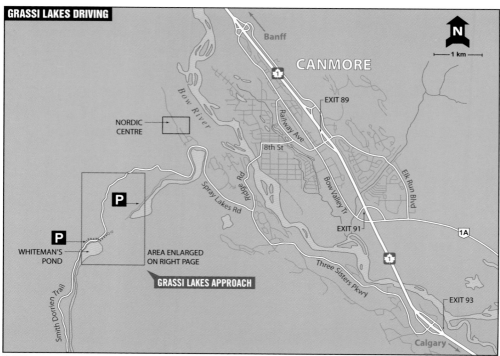

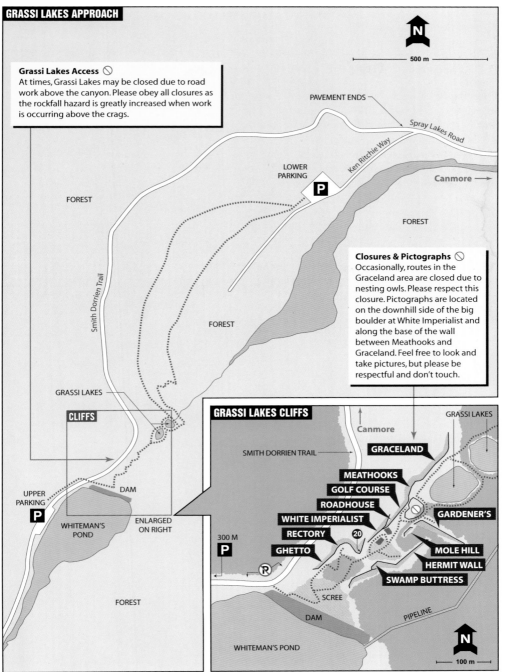

GRASSI LAKES APPROACH

N

500 m

Grassi Lakes Access ⊘
At times, Grassi Lakes may be closed due to road work above the canyon. Please obey all closures as the rockfall hazard is greatly increased when work is occurring above the crags.

PAVEMENT ENDS

Spray Lakes Road

Ken Ritchie Way

LOWER PARKING

P

Canmore →

FOREST

FOREST

FOREST

Smith Dorrien Trail

Closures & Pictographs ⊘
Occasionally, routes in the Graceland area are closed due to nesting owls. Please respect this closure. Pictographs are located on the downhill side of the big boulder at White Imperialist and along the base of the wall between Meathooks and Graceland. Feel free to look and take pictures, but please be respectful and don't touch.

GRASSI LAKES

CLIFFS

UPPER PARKING

P

DAM

WHITEMAN'S POND

ENLARGED ON RIGHT

FOREST

GRASSI LAKES CLIFFS

Canmore ↑

GRASSI LAKES

SMITH DORRIEN TRAIL

GRACELAND

MEATHOOKS

GOLF COURSE

ROADHOUSE

GARDENER'S

WHITE IMPERIALIST

RECTORY

20

MOLE HILL

GHETTO

HERMIT WALL

SWAMP BUTTRESS

300 M

P

Ⓡ

SCREE

DAM

PIPELINE

N

100 m

WHITEMAN'S POND

onto Three Sisters Parkway. Follow this winding road until it's possible to turn left onto Spray Lakes Road. Follow this road to the lower or upper parking areas (see Canmore directions).

From Banff: Drive east on the Trans-Canada Highway and take Exit 89 (Canmore Town Center). Turn right onto Railway Avenue and, at the second set of lights, turn left onto 8th Street. Drive west to the third intersection and turn left onto 8th Avenue, which eventually becomes Ridge Road. At Spray Lakes Road turn right and follow it to the lower or upper parking areas (see Canmore directions).

From Canmore: Drive west on 8th Street to the third intersection and turn left onto 8th Avenue. Follow 8th Avenue, which eventually becomes Ridge Road, and turn right onto Spray Lakes Road. Drive past the Nordic Center until the paved road becomes gravel (the Smith Dorrien Trail).

To reach the upper parking lot, follow the gravel road to the top of the hill and park in the lot at the edge of Whiteman's Pond, which is situated between Ha Ling peak and the east end of Mt. Rundle (obey all "No Parking" signs). Walk along the gravel road and pick up a trail that descends into the canyon below the earth dam. The first wall encountered on the left is the Ghetto.

To reach the lower parking lot, take a left onto a dirt road (Ken Ritchie Way) just before the pavement ends on Spray Lakes Road. Follow this dirt road to a parking lot. From here, locate the Grassi Lakes trialhead sign and follow the trail (the left option is steeper) up to two, small, beautiful lakes (the Grassi Lakes). The first area on the right above the second lake is Graceland.

Bonnie de Bruijn on Yellow Peril (5.10b).

UPPER GRASSI

 60 routes ←5.10 5.11 5.12 5.13→

This sector is home to some of the hardest routes at Grassi Lakes as well as some of the best stone, and will have you craning your neck as you make your way down the trail. Lots of cool pockets and pods litter the face, and provide great features upon which to scale the vertical and overhanging walls. This sector encompasses four of the main cliffs of the crag, the Ghetto, the Rectory, the White Imperialist and the Hermit wall.

Approach: This is the first area encountered on the left when descending into the canyon. It begins at the first set of stairs and continues to the top of the steep hill just beyond White Imperialist.

The Ghetto

This is the very first wall encountered on your left, with steep stairs running down its entire length. It's home to some excellent, long 5.11s and 5.12s. Routes are listed from left to right.

❶ Raw 5.12a . . . .

7 bolts (15 m) This is the first route you'll encounter while descending the stairs. Start below a pod and climb over a small roof before tackling a steep prow head-on with all you've got.   (*Roger Chayer & Bruce Keller, 1996*)

❷ Lush 5.12a . . . .

9 bolts (21 m) This pitch is just downhill from *Raw*. Fun climbing on pockets and pods leads through a steep bulge. Head straight up to anchors at the top of the wall.
    (*Roger Chayer & Richard Jagger, 1997*)

❸ Touch 5.11b . . . .

9 bolts (22 m) Another fun line takes an easier path through a steep bulge. The large heuco at mid-height isn't as "sweet" as is looks from below.   (*Roger Chayer, 1997*)

❹ Coming Through Slaughter 5.11c . . . .

11 bolts (23 m) Start on *Touch*, but head right at the fourth bolt. Backcleaning the eighth bolt below the small roof will help minimize rope drag.   (*Roger Chayer, 1996*)

❺ Radio Flyer 5.12a . . . .

11 bolts (23 m) Climb *Voice of Fire* to the third bolt before angling left to a rest at the top of a small ramp. Difficult moves through a right-leaning corner are followed by fun climbing to the anchor.   (*Roger Chayer, 1996*)

THE GHETTO

❻ Voice of Fire 5.12a . . . .

11 bolts (23 m) Nice 5.10 climbing leads to a midway anchor on the left side of a triangle-shaped roof feature. Bouldery moves out the left side of a bulge lead to a rest in a scoop before the anchor.   (*Roger Chayer, 1995*)

❼ Le Nettoyeur 5.12a . . . .

10 bolts (23 m) Climb through two rotten pods down low to better rock and a midway anchor on the right side of the triangle-shaped roof feature (5.10). Bouldery moves lead out the right side of a bulge to a rest in a scoop. Gun for the anchor above.   (*Roger Chayer, 1995*)

The Rectory

This is the second wall encountered on the left, and is at the bottom of all the steep stairs. The steep rock and fun, gymnastic climbing is very gym-like. This is a great wall to tick your first 5.12. Enjoy. Routes are listed from left to right.

❽ Two Different Worlds 5.12b . . .

5 bolts (11 m) This is a blank-looking line at the left end of the wall and is landmarked by a white streak. Traverse rightward into a large pod before attacking the face on minimal holds. Easier above. *(Stefan Butler & Greg Dickie, 1999)*

❾ Blood of Eden 5.12a . . . . . .

6 bolts (13 m) Climb a right-trending ramp until it's possible to step left and begin a battle on sidepulls and gastons. *(Roger Chayer, 1997)*

❿ Soft Machine 5.11c . . . .

7 bolts (14 m) From the top of the ramp, sustained climbing on edges leads to a slightly frightening anchor clip. Don't worry, it's a safe fall! *(Roger Chayer, 1997)*

⓫ Cool Sensations 5.12a . . . .

10 bolts (16 m) A few big holds and cool pockets get you off the ground before a thin and slightly desperate crux gains some pods. Shake out well before taking on the rest of the pumpy route. *(Roger Chayer, 1997)*

⓬ Blunt 5.12a . . . .

8 bolts (15 m) Climb *Cool Sensations* to the third bolt and traverse right to good pockets. Tackle the roof via one of two options before gaining a good shake and a mad dash for the anchors. *(Roger Chayer, 1996)*

⓭ Blunt Direct 5.12b . . . .

9 bolts (16 m) A short boulder problem leads into *Blunt*. Wet most of the year. *(Peter Arbic, 1996)*

⓮ The Gimp 5.12c . . . .

8 bolts (18 m) A short-lived but thin crux leads to easier climbing above. *(Simon Parsons, 1999)*

⓯ Resilience 5.13c . . . .

7 bolts (11 m) Start off a large, flat boulder at the base of the wall. There is a very stout crux in the middle of the route. The area testpiece. *(Frank Bergeron, 2008)*

⓰ Full Tilt 5.12c . . . .

9 bolts (11 m) Take on the big roof in a roundabout way. Most people finish at the midway anchor, but five more

THE RECTORY

bolts of fun 5.11+ climbing leads to another set of anchors at the top. (*PREP: Sean Elliott; FA: Jake King, 1997*)

⑰ Nice Try 5.12d . . . .

9 bolts (18 m) A great crux sequence makes this route worth a try. Start off a jumble of boulders on the right end of the wall. (*Simon Parsons, 1999*)

⑱ Massive Attack 5.12c . . . . .

7 bolts (14 m) A bouldery start leads to a very crimpy finish. (*Sean Elliott, 1997*)

⑲ Fuel 5.12c . . . .

6 bolts (14 m) A bouldery start leads to a tough roof encounter on a flake that somehow manages to stay put despite years of tugging. Finish on the *Massive Attack* anchor. This route is a fun and bouldery 5.11c if you stop at the anchor under the big roof. (*Roger Chayer, 1997*)

Swamp Buttress

This crag is located on the right side of the canyon, just before the large jumble of boulders that lead to the White Imperialist wall. These are not the best climbs, but easy access to the top makes them popular nonetheless. Routes are listed from left to right.

⑳ Deviant 5.11c . . . .

4 bolts (12 m) This short and steep route has two powerful cruxes separated by a good rest. It's found directly opposite the three Swamp Buttress climbs. (*Houston Peschl, 1995*)

㉑ Swamp Buttress Left 5.10d . .

4 bolts (9 m) Big reaches near the ground lead to a couple of "thank god" pods over the roof. (*Rob Stanton, 1995*)

㉒ Swamp Buttress Center 5.10c . .

4 bolts (9 m) This pitch shares a few holds with its neighbor on the right, but takes an independent line starting at the base of the small roof. (*Rob Stanton, 1995*)

㉓ Swamp Buttress Right 5.10d . . . .

4 bolts (9 m) This is the best line of the three and features big, powerful moves throughout. Thankfully, the holds are all positive. (*Unknown*)

㉔ Oh! That Thing 5.12a . . . . . .

5 bolts (9 m) Scramble up ramps just right of *Swamp Buttress* to a belay station. The climbing is very cruxy leaving the hole halfway up the route. (*Roger Chayer, 1997*)

White Imperialist

This is, by far, the most popular wall at Grassi. It features vertical moderates on the left and overhanging testpieces on the right. A very social atmosphere makes for a fun day, but don't expect peace and solitude if you stop here to climb. Routes listed are from left to right.

㉕ Carom 5.10b . . . .

7 bolts (18 m) This is an unlikely gem tucked behind a lone tree. After an initial, awkward move, undercling along a series of small roofs to superb climbing that leads up a flawless grey slab. (*John Martin, 1997*)

㉖ Spin 5.10b . . . .

6 bolts (14 m) This is another fun, off-the-radar route. Climb big, bubbly pockets to a large move over a roof. Finish up perfect, prickly edges. (*John Martin, 1997*)

SWAMP BUTTRESS

㉗ Pink Flamingos 5.10c . . . . ☐

8 bolts (16 m) This pitch is located just right of a large, right-facing corner. Fun climbing on pockets and jugs leads to an anchor on a ledge (5.9). Continue up to a big roof were the 5.10 business begins. *(John Martin, 1997)*

㉘ White Imperialist 5.10d 🖐️🪜🏃 ☐

6 bolts (15 m) Begin with thin pockets and marginal foot-holds. Follow slopers through a yellow rock patch to a juggy roof and the top. *(Joe Buszowski, 1986; Jon Martin, 1994)*

㉙ Yellow Peril 5.10b . . . . 🖐️↙️

7 bolts (14 m) Begin just left of the "eyes". Tricky pocket climbing leads to a fun roof. *(John Martin, 1994)*

㉚ Golden Horde 5.10a . . . . . 🎒🖐️↙️

6 bolts (15 m) Begin just right of the "eyes". Good pockets down low morph into big moves between large holds higher up. *(John Martin, 1994)*

㉛ Red Menace 5.10c . . . . 🎒🖐️☐

5 bolts (15 m) Fun climbing on pockets leads to a no-hands rest on a ledge. Climb a grey streak on shrinking holds to the anchor. *(Joe Buszowski, 1986)*

㉜ Dark Design 5.10b . . . . ☐
6 bolts (15 m) Follow a bolt line left of a right-facing corner

halfway up the wall. From the ledge, continue up solid stone to a sinker mono (or a sinker two-finger pocket for the ladies), which is the crux. *(John Martin, 1995)*

㉝ Gizmo 5.8 . . . . ☐

5 bolts (12 m) Climb onto a small ledge at the top of a flake before scrambling straight up on good holds to an anchor above a large pod. *(John Martin, 1995)*

㉞ Johnny Mnemonic 5.10a . . . . . 🖐️↙️

7 bolts (19 m) Start just right of a flake. Enjoy good climbing on cool pockets. NG *(John Martin, 1995)*

㉟ Lawyers, Guns and Money 5.9 . . . ☐

6 bolts (15 m) Start in a short, right-facing corner at ground level. Big holds lead to a crux near the top on small pockets. *(Chris Miller, 1999)*

㊱ Rhymes with Orange 5.10c . . . . . . ☐

5 bolts (14 m) Prepare for a cruxy section that climbs a lot steeper than it looks. *(John Martin, 1995)*

㊲ Bubble Theory 5.10c . . . . . 🎒🐟☐

4 bolts (11 m) Power through a bouldery start and pocketed overhang to easier ground above. *(John Martin, 1995)*

㊳ Open Project . . . . ☐
Branch left from *A Bold New Plan* at the midway point.

WHITE IMPERIALIST

39 A Bold New Plan 5.11a . . . . . .

8 bolts (16 m) Start on *Bubble Theory* and make a tricky traverse right at the first bolt. Do all you can to keep the pump at bay on some of the biggest holds imaginable. Backclean the first bolt after clipping the second to reduce rope drag. *(Sean Elliott, 1997)*

40 A Bold New Plan Direct 5.12a . . .

7 bolts (16 m) One tough boulder problem leads into *A Bold New Plan*. *(Sean Elliott, 1997)*

41 No Tickee No Laundry 5.12b . . . . .

9 bolts (15 m) This pitch features a long, fingery boulder problem with draining clips. It climbs out a steep overhang to a rest on a vertical stance. The finish is no cakewalk. Clean it on a toprope. *(Peter Arbic, 1997)*

42 Chinatown Left 5.12a . . . . .

7 bolts (14 m) Start off the top of a boulder. Climb left around a corner onto the face before heading straight up through the overhang on big, pumpy pods to anchors above. Clean it on a toprope. *(Peter, Arbic, 1997)*

43 Chinatown Right 5.12b . . . . . .

8 bolts (14 m) Start on *Chinatown Left*, but follow the right-hand line of bolts to a tough boulder problem below the anchor. *(Peter Arbic, 1997)*

44 Dance Me Outside 5.12a . . . . . .

10 bolts (14 m) This is the 5.12 of choice at White Imperialist. Follow fixed draws up the lower rail to a crux

WHITE IMPERIALIST

gaining the higher rail. The slopey-pod finish feels desperate with a pump. *(Peter Arbic, 1997)*

Hermit Wall

This is a big cliff on the right-hand side of the canyon with a baseball diamond-shaped feature clearly visible in the middle. It's shady and cool with great pocket routes that become increasingly appealing as the lineups grow at White Imperialist. This crag used to be a popular mixed climbing venue, which explains the stray bolts and scratch marks on the rock. Routes are listed from left to right.

45 Open Project . . . .

Don't be tempted. The bolts go nowhere.

46 Cold Fusion 5.10d . . . .

8 bolts (19 m) This fun route links pockets and pods up light grey rock. Begin left of a ramp. *(John Martin, 1995)*

47 Dakar 5.11c . . . .

10 bolts (22 m) A fun route with a distinct crux leaving a right-facing corner. Start below a hole. *(Roger Chayer, 1995)*

48 Silk P1 5.10d . . . .

7 bolts (15 m) This fun route links cool pockets to a midway anchor. *(John Martin, 1995)*

49 Silk P2 5.11a . . . .

12 bolts (22 m) Continue to steep buckets and a short crux below the upper anchors. *(John Martin, 1995)*

50 Ain't it Hell? P1 5.10d . . . .

6 bolts (15 m) Start off a small ledge at ground level. Climb to anchors at mid-height. *(John Martin, 1995)*

51 Ain't it Hell? P2 5.11b . . . .

10 bolts (21 m) Continue into a short, steep corner before struggling onto the ramp above. *(John Martin, 1995)*

52 The Eyes Have It 5.10b . . . .

4 bolts (10 m) Start off a boulder. Climb through two eye-like pods to small pockets and edges. *(John Martin, 1995)*

53 Say It Ain't So 5.10c . . . .

3 bolts (8 m) Climb a grey streak that's bordered on both sides by yellow rock. *(John Martin, 1995)*

HERMIT WALL

49 51 55 57 45 46 47 48 50 52 53 54 56

54 Mr. Manners 5.11a . . . .

8 bolts (20 m) This route has near-perfect holds and ascends the baseball diamond-shaped feature at the top of the wall. (*John Martin, 1995*)

55 Strike Out 5.11c . . . .

8 bolts (20 m) This weird route utilized many holds on the neighbouring lines. It becomes independent near the top. (*Unknown*)

56 Green Room 5.11a . . . . .

8 bolts (19 m) Start just left of a rotten, left-facing corner. Climb onto a ledge and launch straight up through the baseball diamond-shaped feature, using big moves to link big holds. (*Paul Stoliker, 1995*)

57 Cry Wolf 5.10c . . . .

5 bolts (11 m) This short route is located at the wall's right end at the top of a slab. Follow a trail up the backside of Swamp Buttress to the base of the route. (*John Martin, 1996*)

Roadhouse

This small crag is located on the opposite side of a large boulder at the right end of White Imperialist. Routes are listed from left to right.

58 Real Good Time 5.10a . . . .

6 bolts (12 m) The buckets run out near the end. Small holds guard the anchor. (*Unknown*)

59 Roadhouse Grill 5.9 . . . .

5 bolts (13 m) Giant pockets all the way baby. (*Unknown*)

Molehill

This small crag is located directly opposite of Roadhouse, just before the trail heads down the scree slope.

60 Lemming 5.11b . . . .

4 bolts (10 m) Trend left on good pods. A couple of really tough moves on bad edges lead up to a jug. Finish on easier terrain above. (*Knut Rokne, 1999*)

ROADHOUSE

58 59

LOWER GRASSI

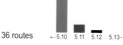

36 routes   ←5.10   5.11   5.12   5.13→

This sector boasts the highest concentration of easy to moderate climbing in the entire canyon, which makes it extremely popular, especially on the weekends and after work. The walls are highly pocketed and contain some really fun routes. The beautiful emerald lakes at the center of this sector give it a very pleasant ambiance, much nicer than the barren, dusty terrain surrounding some of the crags in the Upper Grassi sector. This zone gets congested with hikers, so take care when above not to knock rocks off the walls. The hikers below likely won't appreciate the hazard. The entire left side of this sector has regular rock fall from above, so a helmet (and great vigilance) is highly recommended at all times.

Approach: Hike downhill past the Upper Grassi sector to a steep hill. The climbing in the Lower Grassi sector starts partway down the steep hill and continues all the way down to a small lake at the bottom of the canyon. Please keep on the main tail and avoid taking shortcuts down the steep slope as erosion is becoming a problem.

The Golf Course

This crag is located on the left, about halfway down the scree slope above some platforms. It's the go-to wall for climbers new to the sport and is always busy. Be sure to wear a helmet here, as there is frequent rock fall from above and nowhere to hide. Routes are listed from left to right.

❶ Tiger 5.5 . . . .

6 bolts (14 m) This pitch is located near the top of the platforms. Enjoy lots of great pods.
(Chris Miller, 1999)

❷ Elk Don't Golf 5.5 . . . .

6 bolts (15 m) This is a longer version of the route on the left. *(Chris Miller, 1999)*

❸ I'd Rather Be Golfing 5.5 . . . .

6 bolts (17 m) This route begins off a platform on a right-trending seam. The crux is trying to figure out which is the best jug to use. *(Paul Stoliker, 1991)*

❹ Hole in One 5.7 . . . . . .

9 bolts (22 m) Begin off the platform on the second, right-trending seam. One slightly steep section down low is all that separates you from easier climbing all the way to the anchors. *(Jon Jones, 1995)*

❺ Birdie 5.6 . . . .

8 bolts (23 m) Start off the lowest platform and follow a line of glue-in bolts on the right side of the scoop. *(Unknown)*

❻ Chip Shot 5.6 . . . .

8 bolts (23 m) From the bottom of the platforms, trend right up a diagonal break to a high first bolt. Finish straight up kinda' dirty pockets and pods. *(Unknown)*

THE GOLF COURSE

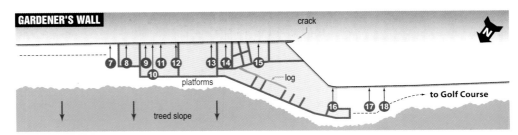

GARDENER'S WALL

crack

platforms   log

treed slope

to Golf Course

Gardener's Wall  to

This crag is located in the trees on the right side of the canyon, halfway down the steep hill—follow a trail along the cliff on the right into the trees. This heavily-pocketed wall features many easy routes that are perfect for beginners, especially routes 8 to 11 which have closely-spaced bolts. Routes are listed from left to right.

7 Rock Garden 5.9 . . . .

4 bolts (12 m) This is the left-most route. Big sandy pods lead to a chain anchor. *(Unknown)*

8 Holes to Heaven 5.10a . . . .

9 bolts (12 m) Climb straight up on good pockets. *(Roger Chayer 2003)*

9 Lumpy Lane 5.9 . . . .

9 bolts (12 m) Big pockets lead to the same anchor as *Holes to Heaven*. *(Sara Rainford, 2001)*

10 Pothole Alley 5.9 . . . .

10 bolts (12 m) This pitch climbs like the name suggests. A variation trends right to the *Rocky Road* anchor. *(PREP: Roger Chayer & Sara Rainford; FA: Kern Hendricks, 2000)*

11 Rocky Road 5.9 . . . .

10 bolts (12 m) Positive pockets lead straight up. *(PREP: Roger Chayer & Sara Rainford; FA: Kern Hendricks, 2000)*

12 Gardener's Question Time 5.9

6 bolts (16 m) Climb straight up on good pockets to a shallow scoop. Continue to hidden anchors above (avoid the anchors to the right). *(Dave Morgan, 1986)*

13 Pocket Full of Worms 5.9 . . . . .

5 bolts (11 m) Too many pockets make hold-finding tricky. *(Paul Stoliker, 1992)*

14 Horrorculture 5.8 . . . .

7 bolts (13 m) Follow pockets past a diagonal break to anchors over a slight bulge. *(Chris Miller, 1999)*

GARDENER'S WALL

7   8   9 10 11   12

16

15

14

13

⓯ I Must Mention Gentians 5.10a . . . . . .

9 bolts (19 m) This route is located left of a large corner crack. As you climb, the pump sneaks up until the final overhang, where it catches you. *(Kern Hendricks 1995)*

⓰ Weed 'em and Reap 5.10b . . .

9 bolts (21 m) This route tackles the overhanging, bulging wall right of a large corner crack. Start way down at the bottom of the wall and climb to increasingly steep pockets that will suck out your energy as you search for a path over the bulges. *(Sara Rainford & Annie Yu, 1999)*

⓱ Bucket City 5.10b . . . .

6 bolts (14 m) Start off of a couple of flat boulders. Steep and in-your-face right from the get-go. *(Jon Jones, 1995)*

⓲ Fiberglass Undies 5.10c . . . .

8 bolts (11 m) Small pockets make the start tricky. Don't worry, because buckets will appear. *(David Dancer, 1988)*

Meathooks

The wildly steep and featured Meathooks wall is located on the left side of the canyon at the bottom of a scree slope. There aren't many crags that allow you

to climb on such an absurd angle at such a moderate grade, but you'll still need lots of endurance. This is a good training crag. Routes are listed from left to right.

⓳ Buckets from Hell (AKA Choss Toss) 5.10d . . . .

6 bolts (12 m) This pitch is short and steep, but still packs a punch. *(Eric Dumerac, 1997)*

⓴ Meathooks 5.11a . . . . . .

7 bolts (14 m) Start off the right side of the third platform (counting from the bottom). By the time you reach the last-bolt crux, you'll likely be out of juice. *(Daren Tremaine, 1994)*

㉑ Stormtroopers in Drag 5.11b . . . .

7 bolts (15 m) This line is similar to *Meathooks*, but with a slightly harder crux gaining the last bolt. Start off the left side of the bottom platform. *(Chris Robertson & Roger Chayer, 1997)*

㉒ Holey Shit 5.11c . . . .

9 bolts (19 m) This climb has no really hard moves, but the pump will probably catch up with you by the end. Start off the right side of the bottom platform. *(Jon Jones, 2000)*

MEATHOOKS

㉓ The Harlot 5.11d . . . . . .
9 bolts (20 m) Although there are a couple of cruxes, the pump will decide how far you go. (*Jon Jones, 2000*)

㉔ Open Project . . . .
Nothing but some random hardware.

㉕ B60 OFO (AKA Thirty Something) 5.12a . . . . . .
12 bolts (29 m) This is the longest and pumpiest route on the wall. Just when you think you have it the bag, the jugs will disappear. Solo up easy terrain to a big hole to start and backclean the first draw to reduce rope drag.
(*Mark Whalen & Eric Hoogstraten, 2001*)

㉖ Born from the Mountains 5.10c . . . . . .
8 bolts (15 m) It's hard to believe this short and crazy-steep route, is only 5.10. Start in the back of the cave on the right end of the wall. (*Eric Hoogstraten, 2001*)

Graceland

A sea of pockets extends up a tall, vertical wall above a beautiful lake. These are some of Grassi Lake's longest routes and a good pump is guaranteed. Routes are listed from left to right.

㉗ Open Project . . . .
This line is about five metres left of a prominent dugout on the left side of the wall.

㉘ You Ain't Nothing but a Hangdog 5.10d . . . .
4 bolts (10 m) A quick crux right off of the ground is followed by nice climbing to the anchor. (*Jon Jones, 1998*)

㉙ It's Now or Never 5.11a . .
14 bolts (29 m) Climb *Memphis* to a midway anchor and branch left through pockets to a hollow-sounding flake. Make one big move off the flake before continuing straight up on pockets to the anchor.
(*Nigel & Rosie Slater, 2007*)

㉚ Memphis 5.10d . . .
13 bolts (29 m) This brilliant, long pitch of pocket climbing is a must do.
(*David Dancer & Jon Jones, 1999*)

㉛ Graceland 5.10d . . . .
6 bolts (13 m) Interesting bubbly rock leads to a crux just where you'd most expect it—the roof. (*David Dancer, 1988*)

㉜ Elvis Lives 5.10c . . . .
7 bolts (13 m) Big pockets all the way. Fun. (*Unknown*)

㉝ Heartbreak Hotel 5.10d . . .
9 bolts (21 m) Good pockets end at the roof, and are replaced by crimps. (*Chris Miller, 1999*)

㉞ Sunglasses and Sideburns 5.10c . . . .
8 bolts (17 m) Sustained climbing on great pockets all the way to the anchors. (*Chris Miller, 1999*)

㉟ Honeymoon in Vegas 5.10d . . .
8 bolts (17 m) A crux with few good holds makes getting above a ledge tricky. Interesting pocket moves above. Begin at the base of a right-trending ramp. (*Roger Chayer, 1999*)

㊱ Moody Blue 5.11b . . . .
7 bolts (17 m) After a short crux on flat edges, buckets take you to the anchor. Begins halfway up a right-trending ramp. (*Nigel & Rosie Slater, 2007*)

GRACELAND

behind every
GREAT SEND
there is a
GREAT BELAYER

GRIGRI 2

- Compatible with all UIAA single ropes from 8.9 to 11mm
- New progressive descent control system
- 25% smaller and 20% lighter

To become a great belayer, go to
www.petzl.com/GRIGRI2

CHAPTER 10

CARROT CREEK

The narrow Carrot Creek canyon is located just inside the boundary of Banff National Park and features spectacular climbing on impressive walls that loom over the frigid waters below. The canyon features two climbing zones that are unique in the Bow Valley, and distinctly different from one another. The first, the Raven's Nest Buttress, features smooth, open-handed holds on bubbly water-worn limestone that is mostly vertical or slightly-overhanging. The routes tend to be fairly long and intricate, and create a burning forearm pump that doesn't dissipate quickly. The second zone, the Cave, features exceedingly steep and powerful climbing out one of the largest and most impressive caverns in the entire area. Even if you don't plan to climb, it's worth the walk up just to have a look. Regardless of which venue you choose, the majority of the best pitches are between 5.11 and 5.12, and within this grade spread exists a very healthy selection of climbs. Good routes exist on either end of this spectrum, but the selection is much more limited.

DEREK GALLOWAY ON "THE HUMMINGBIRD ARÊTE" (5.12A). GERY UNTERASINGER

CONDITIONS

When it comes to climbing conditions, Carrot Creek offers the best of both worlds. The Cave is a south-facing sun trap where it's possible to climb in the winter on mild, sunny days, the Raven's Nest Buttress is predominately shaded, making it the perfect place to climb during the hottest days of summer, and the remaining crags provide good conditions during spring and fall. The creek's level changes throughout the year, and spring run-off can make accessing the canyon more difficult than in times of low water. Finally, bear encounters aren't that uncommon here. Leave your dog at home, carry bear spray and make lots of noise (or use a bear bell) during the approach to avoid any unwanted surprises.

APPROACH

From Canmore: Drive west on the Trans-Canada Highway. At the park gates, set your trip meter to zero. Drive for 1.5 km and turn right onto an unmarked paved road that leads into the parking lot for Carrot Creek. To return to Canmore, zero your trip meter and drive west. At 1.2 km, use a paved turn-around between the east- and west-bound lanes to re-enter the highway heading east toward Canmore.

From Banff: Drive east on the Trans-Canada Highway toward Canmore. At the Banff National Park entrance/exit gates, turn around and head west, back toward Banff. Set your trip meter to zero, drive 1.5 km and turn right onto a short, unmarked paved road that leads to the Carrot Creek parking lot.

Hiking: From the parking lot, head through a gate (please close it behind you) and follow an overgrown road through the center of a grassy field. Hike through a small, wooded area before entering a large, deforested clearing. The road follows the left-hand side of the clearing to its end (about 20 minutes to here) before connecting with a trail that leads left to a small hill, down to the creek and on to a creek crossing. Cross to the creek's west side and hike upstream to a second creek crossing that leads back to the creek's east side just prior to the canyon's entrance (about 45 minutes to here). The first walls encountered are Westside Buttress on the left and Entrance Wall on the right.

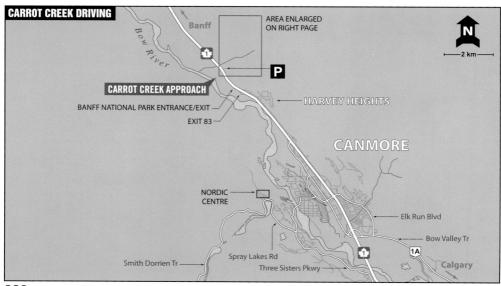

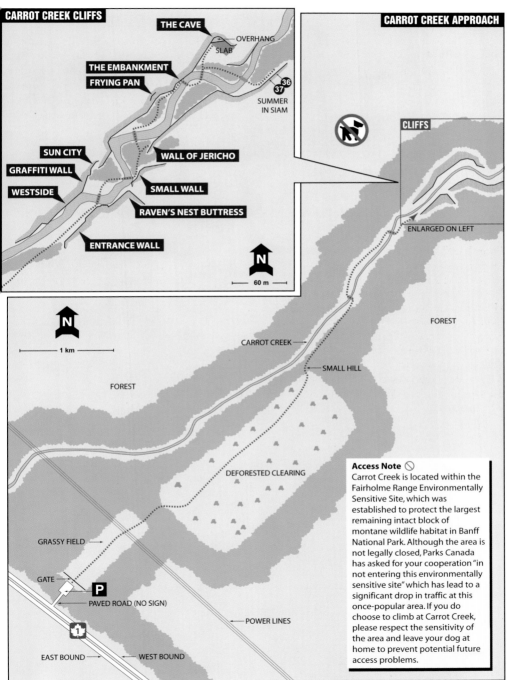

CARROT CREEK CLIFFS

THE CAVE

OVERHANG

SLAB

THE EMBANKMENT

FRYING PAN

36
37

SUMMER
IN SIAM

SUN CITY

GRAFFITI WALL

WESTSIDE

WALL OF JERICHO

SMALL WALL

RAVEN'S NEST BUTTRESS

ENTRANCE WALL

N

60 m

CARROT CREEK APPROACH

CLIFFS

ENLARGED ON LEFT

FOREST

N

1 km

CARROT CREEK

SMALL HILL

FOREST

DEFORESTED CLEARING

GRASSY FIELD

GATE

P

PAVED ROAD (NO SIGN)

POWER LINES

1

EAST BOUND

WEST BOUND

Access Note ⊘
Carrot Creek is located within the
Fairholme Range Environmentally
Sensitive Site, which was
established to protect the largest
remaining intact block of
montane wildlife habitat in Banff
National Park. Although the area is
not legally closed, Parks Canada
has asked for your cooperation "in
not entering this environmentally
sensitive site" which has lead to a
significant drop in traffic at this
once-popular area. If you do
choose to climb at Carrot Creek,
please respect the sensitivity of
the area and leave your dog at
home to prevent potential future
access problems.

Dung Nguyen on Carnivore (5.12d). Photo by Matt Mueller.

RAVEN'S NEST BUTTRESS

89 routes   ←5.10 5.11 5.12 5.13→

The bulk of the climbing in Carrot Creek is located within this narrow section of canyon. All the walls are good, but the main attraction is definitely the towering Raven's Nest Buttress, home of the Carrot Creek "death pump".

Conditions: The narrow width of this canyon combined with its high walls and icy creek waters keep the crags chilly, perfect for hot days in the summer. Keep in mind that during spring run-off, accessing some of the routes can become quite difficult.

Approach: These are the first crags encountered upon entering the canyon.

Westside Buttress

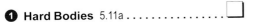

Flooding in the spring of 2005 redirected the creek to the base of this wall leaving the majority of the routes at this crag inaccessible. Those without specific descriptions are inaccessible at this time. Routes are listed from left to right.

❶ Hard Bodies 5.11a . . . .

4 bolts (9 m) A short stint of face climbing is capped by a dirty and loose overhang.   (*Andy Genereux, 1992*)

❷ The Venice Strut 5.12b . . . .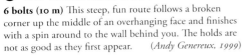

6 bolts (10 m) This steep, fun route follows a broken corner up the middle of an overhanging face and finishes with a spin around to the wall behind you. The holds are not as good as they first appear.   (*Andy Genereux, 1999*)

❸ Muscle Beach 5.11d . . . .

5 bolts (9 m) This steep line follows an arête that leans over the creek. Watch the third clip. (*Andy Genereux, 1992*)

❹ Beach Balls 5.11c . . . .

3 bolts + gear (11 m) Start around a corner and climb above the creek. The corner requires a couple of pieces of gear.   (*Andy Genereux, 1992*)

❺ Wetback 5.10b . . . .

5 bolts (16 m) Climb a left-facing corner to a right-trending ramp that leads to chain anchors.   (*Jon Jones, 1992*)

❻ Gringo 5.10c . . . .

5 bolts (14 m) Start just right of a left-facing corner. Pull past a low roof before continuing straight up to anchors.
                                (*Jon Jones, 1992*)

WESTSIDE BUTTRESS

WESTSIDE BUTTRESS AND GRAFFITI WALL

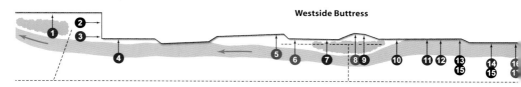

Westside Buttress

7 Salsa Inglesa 5.11a . . . .

3 bolts (10 m) A slippery start leads to a diagonal seam and a small, hard roof. Easier above. *(Jon Jones, 1992)*

8 April Fool 5.10b . . . .

3 bolts (8 m) This short route starts in a faint, open-book corner. *(Jon Jones, 1992)*

9 Self Abuse 5.11a . . . .

2 bolts (8 m) Start just right of *April Fool*. Tackle a crux in the middle of the wall before finishing at a shared anchor. *(Jon Jones, 1992)*

Routes 10 through 20 are currently inaccessible due to the creek's direction of flow.

10 Stink Finger 5.11b . . . .

3 bolts (9 m) *(Jon Jones, 1992)*

11 The New Painted Lady 5.11a . . . .

4 bolts (10 m) *(Jon Jones, 1992)*

12 Just Another John 5.11b . .

4 bolts (9 m) *(Jon Jones, 1992)*

13 The Fine Print 5.12a . . . . .

3 bolts (14 m) *(Jon Jones, 1992)*

14 Comfortably Numb 5.11b .

4 bolts (15 m) *(Jon Jones, 1992)*

15 Silver Surfer 5.12a . . .

4 bolts (20 m) *(JD LeBlanc, 1993)*

16 Summertime Blues 5.10b

5 bolts (15 m) *(Jon Jones, 1992)*

17 Summertime Blues P2 5.10d . . . .

9 bolts (25 m) *(Jon Jones, 1992)*

18 Bite the Rainbow 5.10c . . . .

5 bolts (15 m) *(Jon Jones, 1992)*

19 Mistral 5.11c . . . .

6 bolts (15 m) *(Jon Jones, 1992)*

20 Scirocco 5.10c . . . .

4 bolts (15 m) *(Jon Jones, 1992)*

Graffiti Wall

This crag is located directly across from the Raven's Nest Buttress and features a collection of short, crimpy routes that ascend a slightly-overhanging, black face. Routes are listed from left to right.

WESTSIDE BUTTRESS

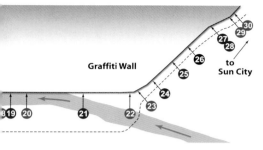

Graffiti Wall

to
Sun City

㉑ The Hardest
5.8 in the Rockies 5.11c . . . . ☐

4 bolts (14 m) A slippery start leads to a boulder problem that tackles the left end of a roof. *(Jon Jones, 1992)*

㉒ Aquacide 5.10d . . . . 🔳☐

2 bolts (10 m) This is the first route right of a left-facing corner (on the right-hand end of a big roof). Slippery climbing leads to anchors above the roof. *(Jon Jones, 1991)*

㉓ Monkey Puzzle 5.10d . . . . 🔳☐

4 bolts (10 m) This pitch is just right of *Aquacide*. Edges lead to a stance under a small roof where you can ponder the moves over the lip. Finish at a shared anchor. *(Jon Jones, 1991)*

㉔ Dayglo Rage 5.11c . . . . ☐

4 bolts (12 m) Climb grey rock just right of a thin, yellow streak. Angle rightward before pulling over the top to the anchor. *(Jon Jones, 1991)*

㉕ Physical Graffiti 5.11d . . . . ☐

4 bolts (11 m) Ascend a beautiful streak on edges and slopers while battling through a series of small breaks. *(Jon Jones, 1991)*

㉖ No More Mr. Nice Guy 5.12a . . . . ☐

4 bolts (11 m) Located in the center of the wall, this line runs just right of a yellow streak. Prepare for a one-two punch at the end. *(Jon Jones, 1991)*

㉗ Young Guns 5.11b . . . . ☐

5 bolts (12 m) This quality route starts in a yellow corner and climbs over a roof on its left side. Follow edges to an anchor above a small ledge. *(Andy Genereux, 1991)*

㉘ Suspended Sentence 5.11c . . . . ☐

6 bolts (15 m) Climb *Young Guns* to the second bolt before heading right to a small overlap. Fight your way through the overlap and continue to anchors above the ledge. Another worthy pitch. *(Andy Genereux, 1991)*

㉙ The Last Word 5.10d . . . . ☐

5 bolts (15 m) Start to the left of a tree. Climb a slab to a small corner and finish on the same anchor as *Suspended Sentence*. *(Andy Genereux, 1992)*

㉚ American Graffiti 5.10a . . . . ☐

9 bolts (20 m) Follow buckets up a right-trending ramp to a manageable crux that gains the anchors. Lots of Fun. *(Andy Genereux, 1991)*

GRAFFITI WALL

SUN CITY

Sun City

This is the only truly sunny wall in this sector, and the long routes that ascend the prickly grey face offer a bit more friction than the surrounding walls. From Graffiti Wall, follow the cliff base up a small hill to reach the start of the three routes. Routes are listed from left to right.

31 Third Degree Burn 5.12b . . . . . .

13 bolts (33 m) Start to the right of the first cave above the slab. A couple of cruxes lead into *Sun City*. This route tends to seep a lot. *(Andy Genereux, 1992)*

32 Sun City 5.11d . . . .

16 bolts (33 m) Climb an outside corner until it's possible to head left to a three dimensional crux. If you've got a 70-m rope, don't stop at the first anchor—there's great stipple climbing above. *(Andy Genereux, 1991)*

33 Sunshine Boys 5.11d . . . .

13 bolts (28 m) Start on *Sun City*, but continue straight up where that route veers left. A couple of committing moves with hard-to-locate feet lead rightward. Once above the hanging corner, beautiful stipple climbing leads to the top. Be gentle with the hollow flake. *(Andy Genereux, 1992)*

Entrance Wall

This vertical wall gets higher as it stretches upstream. Although it's nowhere near as spectacular as Raven's Nest Buttress, there are some great routes on this section of wall. Routes are listed from left to right.

34 Demon Stone 5.11c . . . .

6 bolts (13 m) Start on the left side of the corner and climb onto an arête. Veer left in order to pull over the bulge on the way to the anchor. *(Andy Genereux, 1992)*

35 The Hummingbird Arête 5.12a . . . . .

5 bolts (13 m) Start in a corner and head for a black arête, which is where the fun begins. Too bad it wasn't longer. *(Andy Genereux, 1992)*

36 Bookworm 5.10a . . . .

3 bolts + gear (14 m) Clip one bolt on the way to a big corner where you'll need to fiddle in some small gear. At the top of the corner, traverse left to an anchor on the ledge. *(Andy Genereux, 1992)*

37 Advanced Education 5.11b . . . . .

7 bolts (30 m) From the anchors of *Book Worm* (or *Hummingbird Arête*), trend left under a roof and corner

ENTRANCE WALL

before climbing up an orange, lichen-covered slab to a diagonal break. Rest and continue to anchors over the top of the wall. Lower twice to descend. (*Andy Genereux, 1992*)

38 Higher Learning 5.11c . . . .

6 bolts + gear (18 m) Climb *Book Worm* to the top of the corner before continuing straight up past a small roof to a cruxy bulge. (*Andy Genereux, 1992*)

39 Open Book Exam 5.12a . . . .

10 bolts (23 m) Head for an open-book corner in the yellow rock without getting suckered into climbing straight up the corner. Finish up black rock to anchors over the top. (*Andy Genereux, 1991*)

40 Why Shoot the Teacher? 5.11c . . . . .

8 bolts (20 m) Follow black rock to blue streaks and good holds. Tricky near the start. (*Andy Genereux, 1992*)

41 Learning the Game 5.11d . . . .

7 bolts (19 m) Enjoy great climbing up a beautiful grey streak. (*Andy Genereux, 1992*)

42 Educational Process 5.10b . . . .

7 bolts (16 m) Start in yellow rock and follow a weakness leftward before heading up a blank slab to a blue streak. (*Andy Genereux, 1992*)

43 Quantum Physics 5.11b . . . .

5 bolts (13 m) Start in yellow rock, climb over a small roof into a seam and pull onto a ledge. From here, surmount a roof to reach the anchor. (*Andy Genereux, 1992*)

44 Midterm 5.10d . . . .

5 bolts (13 m) Start in front of a small cave (it's easier than it looks). Pull into a small corner before continuing straight up and over a diagonal break. (*Andy Genereux, 1992*)

45 The Accidental Tourist 5.11a . . . .

5 bolts + gear (35 m) Start just right of a small cave and climb toward a diagonal break, which leads leftward to the *Higher Learning* anchor. It's best to clean this one on a toprope. (*Andy Genereux, 1992*)

46 Entrance Exam 5.10a . . . .

4 bolts (11 m) Start just left of a mossy corner. Follow good, juggy stone to anchors. (*Andy Genereux, 1992*)

Raven's Nest Buttress

The massive, towering wall of Raven's Nest Buttress offers a one-of-a-kind pump found nowhere else in the Bow Valley. Most of the holds have been heavily buffed by eons of raging water and are now smooth, open-handed slopers that glare at you from base to summit. The noise of the creek makes communication difficult, so have belay commands worked out before leaving the ground. Routes are listed from left to right.

47 Sewersidal Tendencies 5.11c . . . . . .

6 bolts (15 m) This pitch is located at the top of the gully and starts just to the right of a water-polished groove. A steep start leads to vertical terrain. (*Andy Genereux, 1994*)

48 Cerveza Sundae 5.11d . . . .

7 bolts (15 m) Survive two roofs before following a corner on the left to anchors at the lip. (*Andy Genereux, 1994*)

49 Brewmeister 5.11d . . . .

6 bolts (15 m) Climb past the *Cerveza Sundae* roofs on the right before angling left into a small, yellow corner. Shake out and surmount a lip to gain the anchor.
(*Andy Genereux, 1994*)

50 Problem with Guinness 5.11a . . . . . .

7 bolts (15 m) Start just left of a short drop-off halfway up the gully. Follow blocky pinches, sidepulls and edges to chain anchors. (*Andy Genereux & Jon Jones, 1987*)

51 Mephisto 5.11c . . . .

7 bolts (15 m) Start in the same spot as *Problems With Guinness*, but meander right up smooth, white rock, generally staying left of the bolt line. (*Andy Genereux, 1990*)

52 Abracadabra to a Bitter End 5.11b . .

13 bolts (26 m) Climb a left-facing corner and gun for the left side of a featureless face. At the top, veer left through a series of blocky roofs to finish on anchors at the top of a short corner. (*Unknown*)

53 Alacazam 5.11d . . . .

11 bolts (26 m) This is an outstanding pitch of climbing—maybe the best of its grade in the canyon. Climb *Abracadabra to a Bitter End* to the top of the featureless face before continuing straight up through blocky roofs on small holds. Finish in the alcove above.

(*Andy Genereux, 1994*)

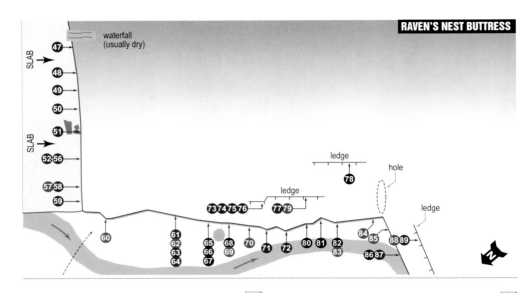

RAVEN'S NEST BUTTRESS

54 Abracadabra 5.11d ☐

12 bolts (28 m) Climb *Abracadabra to a Bitter End* to the top of the featureless face before veering right via a jug. Once under the big triangle-shaped roof, catch your breath before launching over the lip on the left and into the crux. *(Andy Genereux & Jon Jones, 1988)*

55 Sleight of Hand 5.10c ☐

7 bolts (16 m) Climb a large, left-facing corner and veer right into a smaller corner system. From the top, follow a system of flakes rightward to the anchor. *(Jon Jones, 1990)*

56 Sleight of Abracadabra 5.11d ☐

13 bolts (28 m) Climb *Sleight of Hand* to the last bolt before continuing straight up to join *Abracadabra*.
(Unknown)

57 Hey Presto 5.10b ☐

8 bolts (16 m) Start to the right of a corner and climb a discontinuous groove using slopers, edges and the odd "thank god" jug. Finish at the *Sleight of Hand* anchor.
(Jon Jones, 1990)

58 Before Your Very Eyes 5.11a ☐

13 bolts (24 m) Continue past the *Hey Presto* anchor. Head a bit to the right before following a blue and black streak to the anchor. *(Jon Jones, 1994)*

59 Magic in the Air 5.11b ☐

10 bolts (25 m) Start at the bottom of a gully and follow smooth, blocky stone with great jugs and perfect edges to a crux pulling through an overhang. *(Jon Jones, 1990)*

60 Merlin's Laugh Left 5.10b ☐

13 bolt (29 m) Start up a large corner at the left end of the wall and climb a right-trending ramp above. From the top, trend slightly right before tackling a series of overlaps capped with a tricky mantle. A long draw on the sixth bolt will help reduce rope drag. *(Jon Jones, 1991)*

61 Merlin's Laugh 5.11a ☐

11 bolts (29 m) A hard boulder problem start leads to surprisingly pumpy climbing. Join *Merlin's Laugh Left* halfway up the right-trending ramp. When your feet are at the second bolt, look carefully for the third, which is hidden from view. *(Andy Skuce & Jon Jones, 1987)*

62 Merlin's Laugh P2 5.10b ☐

6 bolts (12 m) Continue above the anchor of *Merlin's Laugh*. Lower twice to get down. *(Jon Jones, 1989)*

63 The Magus 5.11b ☐

12 bolts (29 m) After the first two bolts of *Merlin's Laugh* continue straight up to a smooth, V-shaped notch. From the top, traverse left to a hard-to-read grey streak and a no-hands rest. Trend a bit to the right to a hidden bolt before finishing up on good holds. Very high quality. *(Peter Arbic, 1992)*

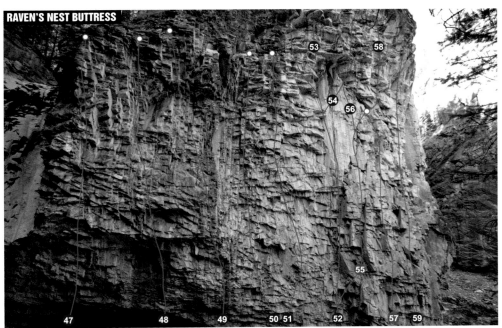

RAVEN'S NEST BUTTRESS

64 The Magus P2 5.11b . . . .

5 bolts (12 m) Continue above *The Magus* to the *Merlin's Laugh P2* anchor. Lower twice to descend. (*Peter Arbic, 2001*)

65 The Short Sword 5.11d . . . . .

9 bolts (20 m) After the second bolt, head left via some great, smooth, open-handed holds that will make your forearms burn. At the second-to-last bolt, climb right into *Caliburn* and a hard crux before the anchor. (*Keith Pike, 1988*)

66 The Sword in the Stone 5.12c . . .

11 bolts (23 m) Prepare for a stout boulder problem directly above the *Short Sword/ Calibrun* anchor. (*Keith Pike, 1988*)

67 Calibrun 5.12a . . . .

9 bolts (20 m) This fantastic route requires a nice blend of technique and stamina to succeed. The holds feel positive, but the open-handed nature of the climbing keeps the pump constantly on the horizon. (*Jon Jones, 1992*)

68 The Warlock 5.12a . . . .

7 bolts (17 m) Begin this classic just left of a large corner. Big moves between generally good holds leads to a fat undercling. A great crux on pumpy holds is followed by a traverse right and the anchors. (*Andy Genereux, 1991*)

69 American Standard 5.13b . . .

10 bolts (26 m) After the *Warlock's* crux, continue directly up into some amazingly technical climbing on slopers. A crimpy crux leads to a sporty finish up a small corner. The texture of the holds inspired the name—it's a toilet bowl company. (*Todd Guyn, 1992*)

70 Coprophobia 5.10c . . . .

7 bolts (15 m) This route follows a small, broken corner feature just right of a larger corner to an arête above. The boulder problem at the last bolt will slow you down. (*Jon Jones, 1987*)

71 Sidekick 5.11b . . . .

7 bolts (17 m) Climb the steep arête just right of *Coprophobia* with difficulty. Move left to join that route for the finish. (*Jon Jones, 1994*)

72 The Sorcerer's Apprentice 5.11c . . . .

8 bolts (20 m) This pumpy route has an alarming amount of open-handed grips. (*Andy Genereux, 1989*)

RAVEN'S NEST BUTTRESS

73 The Illusionist 5.11c ....

11 bolts (22 m) From the belay, trend left through a low crux to a stance below a tufa-riddled roof (you'll know it when you see it). Surmount the roof and finish up a right-facing corner to anchors at the top of the wall.

(*Andy Genereux, 1989*)

74 Witches Brew 5.11b ....

8 bolts (22 m) From the belay, climb up and right until it's possible to traverse left across a small slab. Continue up to the same tufa-riddled roof and trend left into a blue streak. Follow it to a somewhat-dirty, left-facing corner and the anchor at its end. (*Andy Genereux, 1991*)

75 Hocus Pocus 5.11c ....

11 bolts (25 m) This route is best done in two pitches due to problems with rope drag, but can be done as a single, quality pitch with careful management. From the belay, trend slightly right up a short corner before climbing straight up to an anchor above a ledge. Follow a blue streak into a right-facing corner and finish with a tree anchor over the top of the wall. (*Andy Genereux, 1989*)

76 Stolen Thunder 5.11c ....

11 bolts (23 m) Climb up a small, yellow corner just right of a blue streak to a no-hands rest. Trend left to a hard crux that gains the anchor. A variation from the no-hands rest follows two bolts rightward over the lip of a roof to an anchor. (*Andy Genereux, 1992*)

⑦ Prince of Darkness 5.11b . . . . . . 🔲

5 bolts (10 m) This fun, little pitch brings you to an anchor on a ledge. From here, head right and then straight up, avoiding the roof on the right. *(Andy Genereux, 1987)*

⑦ Nothing Up My Sleeve 5.12b . 🔲

9 bolts (17 m) From the belay, follow a left-trending crack with good handholds and poor footholds to finish at the *Stolen Thunder* anchors. This is the best of the upper pitches. Get up there and try it! *(Andy Genereux, 1991)*

⑦ The Enchantress 5.10c . . . . 🔲

11 bolts (27 m) From the belay, traverse right before heading up an airy corner on jugs to an anchor at the top of the wall. *(Andy Genereux, 1987)*

⑧ The Lizard 5.12b . . . . 🔲

5 bolts (21 m) This pitch is difficult right from the start and doesn't relent until after the crux at the end of the overhang. Continue to anchors on the ledge above.
(Simon Parboosingh & Joe Buszowski, 1990)

⑧ The Gizzard 5.12b . . . . 🔲

7 bolts (12 m) A boulder problem ends at a big hold above the second bolt. Pumpy climbing above leads to anchors in the overhang. *(Todd Guyn & Joe Buszowski, 1992)*

⑧ Wizard 5.12a . . . . 🔲

6 bolts (21 m) Start at the base of *Cup O' Joe*, but trend left for three bolts before climbing straight up to finish on the *Lizard*. *(Andy Genereux, 1987)*

⑧ Cup O' Joe 5.13b . . . . 🔲

5 bolts (12 m) Small crimps up a blank shield of rock lead to a stout boulder problem punching through the big roof. *(PREP: Joe Buszowski; FA: Todd Guyn, 1995)*

⑧ Open Project . . . . 🔲

⑧ Open Project . . . . 🔲

⑧ Shadow of a Thin Man 5.12a . 🔲

4 bolts (14 m) Crimp and sidepull up the grey wall to anchors over the ledge. *(Andy Genereux, 1991)*

⑧ 110° in the Shade 5.11b . . . . 🔲

4 bolts (14 m) Start on *Shadow of a Thin Man*, but follow the right-hand line of bolts just left of a yellow streak. Finish at a shared anchor. *(Andy Genereux, 1990)*

⑧ Dirty Trick 5.10c . . . . 🔲

4 bolts (15 m) From the anchors of *Shadow of a Thin Man*, traverse left into a dirty, gaping crack and follow it to anchors on the face above. *(Andy Genereux, 1990)*

⑧ No Sloppy Seconds 5.11b . . . . 🔲

5 bolts (15 m) Continue above *Shadow of a Thin Man* (or *110° in the Shade*) to anchors above the next ledge. Dirty. Rarely gets done. *(Jon Jones, 1990)*

© GERY UNTERASINGER

Chad Perkins on The Sword in the Stone (5.12c)

THE CAVE

37 routes ←5.10 5.11 5.12 5.13→

This area encompasses six different crags scattered across either side of Carrot Creek, all of which are located upstream of Raven's Nest Buttress. The routes range from technical, crimpy and vertical to pumpy and absurdly steep. The most visited wall is, without a doubt, the Cave.

Conditions: If it's too cold in the mouth of the canyon, venture upstream and the temperature will start to rise. The walls on the left side of the creek get plenty of sun and offer a pleasant change from the perpetual shade of the Raven's Nest Buttress, and the walls on the right side of the creek are tucked back into the trees, far from the water's chilling effect. If these options fail, check out the sun trap known as the Cave, which is too hot for most of the summer, but is perfect in the spring and fall, as well as on clear, mild winter days.

Approach: From the Raven's Nest Buttress Sector follow a trail upstream via several creek crossings.

Small Wall

This diminutive crag is located just upstream of the Raven's Nest Buttress. Although it's short, the climbs are good. Routes are listed from left to right.

① Small Fry 5.10c . . . .

3 bolts (12 m) This is the left-most route. Blocky grips lead to slopey holds at the crux. *(Jon Jones, 1991)*

② Think Tall 5.10c . . . .

3 bolts (12 m) A bulge at the start gives way to easier climbing and a crux before the anchor. *(Jon Jones, 1991)*

③ Vandals in Babylon 5.10c . . . . . .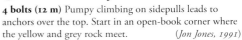

4 bolts (12 m) Pumpy climbing on sidepulls leads to anchors over the top. Start in an open-book corner where the yellow and grey rock meet. *(Jon Jones, 1991)*

④ Small Is Beautiful 5.10c . . . .

3 bolts (11 m) This is a nice, albeit short, route with some cool flowstone above a triangle-shaped roof. *(Jon Jones, 1991)*

⑤ Grime and Punishment 5.9 . . . .

4 bolts (11 m) Trend right past a small ledge to avoid two small roofs on the right. *(Jon Jones, 1991)*

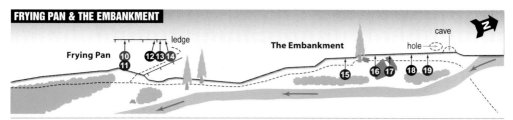

FRYING PAN & THE EMBANKMENT

Wall of Jericho

This is another small wall tucked away in the trees on the right side of the creek. Continue along the trail from Small Wall and climb over a large, uprooted tree to reach the crag. If you come to a creek crossing, you just missed it. Routes are listed from left to right.

6 Equinox 5.10c ....

5 bolts (9 m) This is the left-most route. Chossy rock down low leads to better rock above. *(Jon Jones, 1991)*

7 Fall Guy 5.11c ....

4 bolts (10 m) Big spans between big holds lead to a couple of juggy underclings. Continue straight up using a hard-to-locate edge hidden amongst a plethora of sloping holds. *(Jon Jones, 1991)*

8 Silent Scream 5.11c ....

4 bolts (10 m) This fun, steep line forges up the blunt nose. Big moves on jugs lead over roofs. *(Jon Jones, 1991)*

9 The Phoenix 5.11a ....

3 bolts (9 m) From the top of a short corner above a diagonal break, launch up the overhang. *(Jon Jones, 1991)*

Frying Pan

This is a small shield of perfect rock perched on top of a rotten wall that is just upstream of the creek crossing at the Wall of Jericho. It features great technical climbing and a rock-solid guarantee (well, almost) that you'll be alone. Scramble up a right-trending ramp until you can make a couple of exposed leftward moves onto a ledge. Routes are listed from left to right.

10 Breakfast in America 5.10c ....

4 bolts (11 m) This is the left-most line off the left-hand belay stance. Head up a small, left-facing corner to the face above. It's harder than it looks. *(Jon Jones, 1993)*

11 Have a Nice Day 5.11b ....

4 bolts (11 m) This is the right-most line off the left-hand belay stance. Two horribly slopping dishes lead to a cool series of moves and a huge jug. Some more trickery leads to easy terrain and the anchor. *(Jon Jones, 1993)*

12 Toast 5.12a ....

5 bolts (11 m) This is the left-most line off the right-hand belay stance. Big moves between underclings and sidepulls lead to a great crux on the beautiful face. *(Jon Jones, 1993)*

13 Sunny Side Up 5.11a ....

5 bolts (10 m) This is the middle route off the right-hand belay stance. Follow a wide, yellow streak to the base of a hanging corner. A few tricky moves through the corner lead to anchors above. *(Jon Jones, 1993)*

14 Easy Over 5.10c ....

4 bolts (11 m) This is the right-most route off the right-hand belay stance. Head right around the corner before continuing upward on big blocky holds to anchors, with a crux in the very middle. *(Jon Jones, 1993)*

The Embankment

This crag is located on the same cliff line as the Frying Pan, but upstream about 30 m. It features great stone and edge climbing. Routes are listed from left to right.

15 No Place for a Limp Wrist 5.11a ....

4 bolts (9 m) This is the first route left of a tree that has a boulder leaning against it. Use the corner out right to get started before moving left onto the face to reach a break above. The crux is powerful and unusual. *(Jon Jones, 1993)*

16 It's Not the Length that Counts 5.11a ....

4 bolts (10 m) This is the first route right of a tree that has a boulder leaning against it. Follow a thin yellow streak up a small, right-facing corner to a tough couple of moves at the top. *(Geoff Powter & Jon Jones, 1992)*

14

10 11 12 13

4th class approach

FRYING PAN

15

large hole

16 17   18   19

THE EMBANKMENT

⑰ Digital Stimulation 5.11b . . . .

3 bolts (10 m) This great pitch links two crimp rails to a right-handed slap for jugs at the end. *(Jon Jones, 1992)*

⑱ Short, but Stiff 5.12b . . . .

3 bolts (9 m) The name sums it up. Difficult underclings lead to the crux: a couple of poor edges with less-than-desirable footholds. *(Jon Jones, 1993)*

⑲ Last Gasp 5.11b . . . .

4 bolts (10 m) Start on the right end of the wall next to a large hole. Enjoy nice climbing on the clean face using underclings and sidepulls. *(Jon Jones, 1992)*

> **Interesting Fact**: The Graffiti Wall has an interesting name story. Before Carrot Creek was a climbing destination, a local fellow was told there was good fishing to be had in the creek. After making a long bushwhack into the canyon with gear in hand, he quickly realized there were no fish. Furious at being sandbagged, he scribbled a strongly-worded note onto the canyon wall. The first part of the note which contained the sandbaggers' name has long since disappeared, but the final sentiment remains and reads: "should be put into a cannon and shot to hell". Look for it.

The Cave

This perfect sun trap is located on the left side of the creek and has a good concentration of 5.12 to 5.13 routes that are perfect on cold, early- and late-season days. The winter is an option as well, if the sky is clear and the mercury hasn't dipped too low. Routes are listed from left to right.

⑳ If Tuzo and
Heidegger Had Kinder 5.11d . . . .

7 bolts (15 m) Start at the base of the scree slope below a yellow corner. A funky crux around the fourth bolt is followed by pumpy climbing out the roof. Be careful of the hollow-sounding block left of the fifth bolt. *(Shep Steiner, 1994)*

㉑ Liar 5.13a . . . .

7 bolts (16 m) Start three metres uphill of the previous route. Sustained climbing leads to a powerful and compact boulder problem out a two-tiered roof. *(JD LeBlanc, 1994)*

㉒ Anti-Oedipus 5.12a . . . .

6 bolts (15 m) Climb up a short pillar and follow edges to the right end of a big roof. Pumpy climbing with big moves leads over the roof to a sporty finish above the last bolt. *(Shep Steiner, 1994)*

㉓ The Allegory
of My Sore Back 5.11c . . . .

5 bolts (15 m) Start up a corner above the rock platform

THE CAVE

in the scree slope. This climb is missing a few hangers because of a big loose block, which needs to be trundled off. (*Shep Steiner, 1994*)

24 Open Project . . . . ☐

25 Elmer Fudd P1 5.12c . . . . 📷 🐾 ✏️ ☐

10 bolts (14 m) Start just outside the left end of the cave. Big, powerful moves between flat holds give way to more technical climbing and a pumpy finish. (*Joe Buszowski, 1994*)

26 Elmer Fudd P2 5.12d . . . . 🪨 ☐

15 bolts (26 m) Clip a long draw on the anchor and continue up a technical wall to a hard and committing crux before the anchors. (*Joe Buszowski, 1994*)

27 Mouthful of Freddie 5.13b . . . 📷 ✏️ ☐

11 bolts (25 m) With the bolt at the lip pre-clipped, walk downhill and start on *Elmer Fudd*. Trend right along a pumpy arête, which leads to a big scoop with a large roof above. Climb the right side of the scoop past project anchors to a bolt in the roof. Once in the corner above the roof, a funky crux awaits. (*Todd Guyn, 1997*)

28 Open Project . . . . ☐

**29 The Last
Boy Scout** 5.13c . . . . 📷 🐾 ✏️ ☐

12 bolts (14 m) This beautiful line follows a blue streak up the 45° wall. Stick clip the second bolt and begin relentless climbing with hard clips that leads to a rest above the lip. Easier climbing follows to a heartbreaker crux right under the anchors.
(*PREP: Simon Parboosingh; FA: Scott Milton, 2000*)

30 Open Project . . . . ☐

31 Carnivore 5.12d . . . . 🐾 ✏️ ☐

8 bolts (15 m) This is the steepest route in the cave and starts in the very back. The hardest moves are found in the first half, but the redpoint crux comes after the lip where the pump becomes too much to handle. (*Todd Guyn, 1993*)

32 Open Project . . . . ☐

33 Doppio 5.13b . . . . 🐾 ✏️ ☐

5 bolts (12 m) Start just inside the right end of the cave. Sustained power climbing leads to a crux just before a rest. Finish up with the crux of *Black Coffee*.
(*PREP: Joe Buszowski; FA: JD LeBlanc, 1994*)

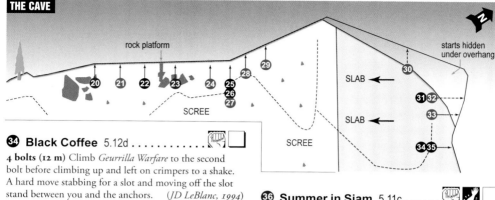

THE CAVE

rock platform

starts hidden under overhang

SLAB ←

SCREE

SLAB ←

SCREE

34 Black Coffee 5.12d . . . .

4 bolts (12 m) Climb *Geurrilla Warfare* to the second bolt before climbing up and left on crimpers to a shake. A hard move stabbing for a slot and moving off the slot stand between you and the anchors. (*JD LeBlanc, 1994*)

35 Geurrilla Warfare 5.12a . . . .

5 bolts (9 m) Start just outside the right end of the cave. Powerful climbing tackles the blue streak. (*Jon Jones, 1993*)

Summer in Siam

This eye-catching, blue-streaked wall across the stream from the Cave has two great lines well worth checking out. To reach it, continue upstream from the Cave to the next bend in the creek. Cross the creek and follow the cliff line into the trees to the base of the climbs. Routes are listed from left to right.

36 Summer in Siam 5.11c . . . . .

12 bolts (30 m) The left-hand route features great sustained climbing up a slightly-overhanging face. Trying to find the correct holds in the bubbly rock is bound to get your forearms throbbing *before* the crux above the small roof. The chain anchor at five metres is meant to facilitate descending with a 50-metre rope and is probably no longer needed. (*Jon Jones, 1992*)

37 Whistling in the Dark 5.11a . . . . .

10 bolts (28 m) This is a superb route on great stone. Once you've clipped the second bolt, climb back down and backclean the first bolt. The crux comes pulling over the roof down low, but don't be fooled, the rest of the route is sustained on perfect edges of all sizes. (*Jon Jones, 1992*)

THE CAVE

We have a long history of climbing in the Canadian Rockies and the narrative likely started with the First Nations (their artwork may still be seen on canyon walls), but has grown to include a vast array of individuals with marked differences in background and style. Local outfitters, Swiss guides, hippies, professionals, athletes and all forms of "Young Turks" have left their mark on the imposing limestone walls. You can call it alpinism, sport climbing, bouldering, trad climbing, or adventure climbing, but in the end it's all the same—we all just want to have fun and come home with a special experience.

If I look back over the past 30 years of climbing in the Bow Valley, it is the people I remember most, not the climbs. I can recall laughing my ass off, fighting with friends, the shared brotherhood on any given day and the great loss when one of the clan did not make the journey home. The cast of characters has been ever changing, but the motives and inspiration have always remained the same. Every climber has their own unique story to tell, and this, not the climbs, is what helps build the climbing culture in any given area.

What makes climbing in the Bow Valley so special? It's most definitely a blend of unique and interesting people, and the spectacular mountains in which they all live. This rugged landscape of peaks, valleys and canyons fill the view, and their complexity leads to a constant state of exploration, the search for the next great climbing theatre. Have we found Shangri-La? In my mind's eye, we have not yet discovered the true centerpiece of sport climbing in the Bow valley, but it's out there. Discovery won't be easy, though. The walks will likely be long and the conditions harsh, but in the end the rewards will overcome any short-lived hardships.

In the meantime, revel in the varied climbing options and the world-class views. Be true to the adventurous nature of the area and fully explore the valley to find the crag that puts a smile on your face. And don't get so focused on the climbs that you forget to take in the amazing surroundings that make this place truly special. It's a mighty world we live in—have a look around and the experience will find you.

Todd Guyn on House of Usher at Raven's Crag.

MARC BOURDON ON "CARN...FEATHER MAP...S, 5.?01"

CHAPTER 11

BLACK FEATHER CANYON

Black Feather Canyon, which is only two metres wide at its narrowest point, is one of many small drainages that feeds the Cascade River, and subsequently Lake Minnewanka. The lake is nestled between tall peaks and its emerald waters provide a striking contrast to the darkly forested slopes on either side. The network of scenic trails that surround the shores are substantial, and provide recreational opportunities for hikers, sightseeing tourists and mountain bikers alike. The climbers' approach utilizes these trails, and begins with a pleasant stroll along a flat, lakeside path before heading upstream along the Cascade River.

The canyon itself consists of solid, grey limestone walls that range in angle from slabby to slightly overhanging. The stone is clean and smooth, a testament to the powerful scrubbing forces of the waters that used to surge through this gorge. The majority of the routes are in the 5.10 to low 5.12 range, and the orientation of the canyon allows climbing in both the sun and the shade. This canyon is also home to one of the most bizarrely featured patches of rock in the Bow Valley, aptly dubbed "the brain". Look for it.

CONDITIONS

The climbing season in Black Feather Canyon ranges from late spring to early fall, with warmish weather being most desirable due to the chilly nature of the narrow gorge. Seepage is rarely much of an issue on the various walls, although the routes around *Mind Bender* will likely seep early in the season and after significant rainfall. The canyon doesn't offer much shelter from the rain, so you might want to head elsewhere if storms are in the forecast. The creek running through Black Feather Canyon is usually no more than a small trickle, but during the spring (and after heavy rainfall), runoff can turn the drainage into a raging torrent. The narrowness of the canyon can make it virtually impossible to navigate when it's in this state.

Brain rock

APPROACH

From Canmore: Drive west on the Trans-Canada Highway and take the first, signed exit for Banff/Lake Minnewanka. Turn right, follow signs to Lake Minnewanka and park.

From Lake Louise: Drive east on the Trans-Canada Highway and take the second, signed exit for Banff/Lake Minnewanka. Turn left, follow signs to Lake Minnewanka and park.

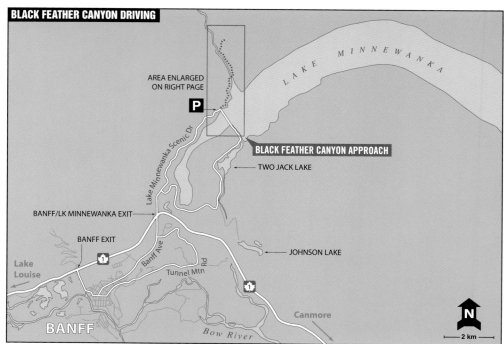

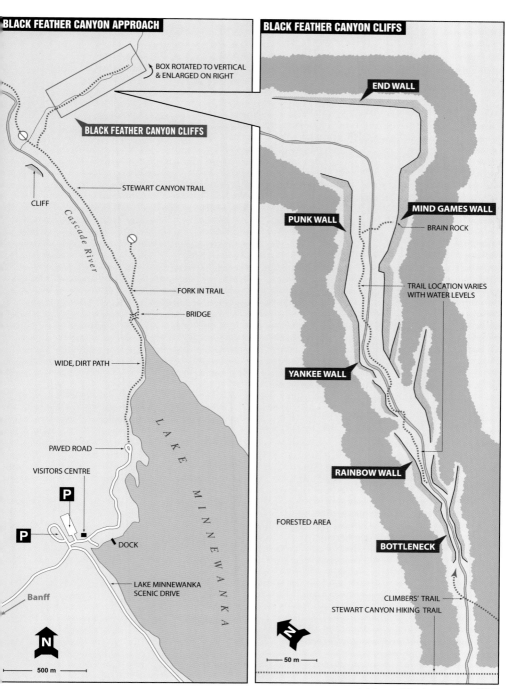

BLACK FEATHER CANYON APPROACH

BOX ROTATED TO VERTICAL & ENLARGED ON RIGHT

BLACK FEATHER CANYON CLIFFS

STEWART CANYON TRAIL

CLIFF

Cascade River

FORK IN TRAIL

BRIDGE

WIDE, DIRT PATH

PAVED ROAD

VISITORS CENTRE

P

P

DOCK

LAKE MINNEWANKA

LAKE MINNEWANKA SCENIC DRIVE

Banff

N

500 m

BLACK FEATHER CANYON CLIFFS

END WALL

PUNK WALL

MIND GAMES WALL

BRAIN ROCK

TRAIL LOCATION VARIES WITH WATER LEVELS

YANKEE WALL

RAINBOW WALL

FORESTED AREA

BOTTLENECK

CLIMBERS' TRAIL

STEWART CANYON HIKING TRAIL

N

50 m

From Banff: Drive out of town along Banff Avenue, eventually passing under the Trans-Canada Highway. Continue following this road to Lake Minnewanka and park.

Hiking: Walk along the paved road (closed to traffic) toward the lake. Stay to the left, passing the boat dock on the right, and follow the paved road all the way to its end. Continue along a well-worn dirt trail that contours above the lakes' edge, eventually reaching a bridge that crosses the Cascade River.

Cross the bridge and follow the trail leftward to a signed fork (about five minutes from the bridge). Take the left fork, which follows the Cascade River upstream. About 12 minutes from the signed fork, the trail climbs slightly uphill, across the river from a large, vertical black wall with some prominent yellow and white streaks. The climbers' trail branches right from the main trail just beyond the black wall. Hike for one minute on the climbers' trail, before dropping into the creek bed, which is the mouth of Black Feather Canyon. About 30 metres upstream is the first route, which will be on the left.

If you miss the turnoff onto the faint climbers' trail on the way in, the main hiking trail crosses the creek just beyond. Simply follow the creek drainage directly up to the crags. It's not as direct an approach, but is straightforward nonetheless.

end of paved road

dirt trail to bridge

trail intersection sign
(5 min beyond bridge)

trail to Black Feather Canyon

Approach photographs *Top to bottom: The start of the hiking trail at the end of the paved road; the left-hand fork after the bridge crossing; the vertical, black wall opposite the right-hand turn onto the climbers' trail.*

ENTRANCE SECTOR

12 routes ←5.10 5.11 5.12 5.13→

This group of crags includes the Bottleneck, Rainbow Wall, and Yankee Wall. Each cliff contains a few decent routes, but these are usually neglected for the more popular climbs on the Punk Wall and Mind Games Wall, which are located at the end of the canyon.

Approach: When hiking upstream, these are the first cliffs encountered on the left, just beyond the point at which the canyon significantly narrows.

Bottleneck

This is the first wall encountered on the left after entering the narrowest part of the canyon. There are only a handful of routes, but the cooler temperatures may be a relief if it's too warm upstream at the other walls. All the routes are located on the left side, and are listed from left to right. No photograph or topo available.

1 Bottle Depot 5.10b . . . .

3 bolts (7 m) This pitch is located about 30 metres upstream from the mouth of the canyon. A short boulder problem leads through some interesting rock. (*Unknown*)

2 Corkscrew 5.10a . . . .

5 bolts (9 m) Start 10 metres right of the previous climb. A small bulge at the start gives way to a short section of face climbing before the anchors. (*Unknown*)

3 Open Project . . . .

No bolts. Only the anchors are currently in place.

4 Canyon Filler 5.9 . . . .

8 bolts (17 m) This pitch is located left of a wide streak of green moss. Negotiate past the second bolt, with difficulty, where more plentiful options for both handholds and footholds start to appear. (*Kelly MacLeod, 2003*)

5 Put a Cork in It 5.10a . . . .

5 bolts (11 m) Start right side of a wide streak of green moss. Abundant holds dissipate near the top. (*Unknown*)

RAINBOW WALL

ramp

8

Rainbow Wall

This crag is on the left, just beyond the end of the Bottleneck wall and gets filtered, midday sun. It's beautifully striped with only a couple of routes, but is bound to see more development in the future. Routes are listed from left to right.

6 Open Project . . . .

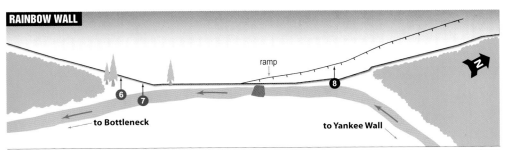

RAINBOW WALL

ramp

6

7

8

to Bottleneck

to Yankee Wall

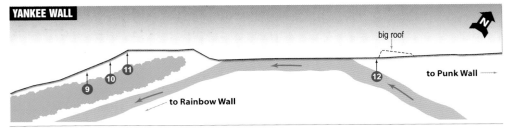

YANKEE WALL

big roof

to Punk Wall →

to Rainbow Wall

7 **Open Project** . . . .

8 **Minniewanker** 5.12c . . . . .

8 bolts (26 m) Scramble up a right-trending ramp to reach the base and then tackle a beautiful orange streak out the middle of the wall. Long draws on the first two bolts will reduce rope drag. *(Ross Suchy & Simon Meis, 2006)*

Yankee Wall

This short, slabby crag is five minutes upstream of the Rainbow Wall and is located in a corner on the left side of the creek. Routes are listed from left to right.

9 **Going South** 5.10a . . . .

5 bolts (12 m) This short, slabby route tackles a series of small overlaps. *(Kelly MacLeod, 2003)*

10 **American Pie** 5.10d . . . .

5 bolts (12 m) Several small cruxes revolve around more small overlaps. *(Kelly MacLeod, 2003)*

11 **Utah Boys Go Wild** 5.8 . . . .

5 bolts (15 m) Climb a corner on good holds. This pitch tends to be a bit dirty and may have water seepage during rainy months. *(Kelly MacLeod, 2003)*

12 **A Yankee at Large** 5.10c . . . . .

5 bolts (14 m) This pitch is 20 metres right of *Utah Boys Go Wild*. Start immediately left of a roof at one metre. A technical start leads to slopers and sidepulls. The anchor is just above the horizontal break. *(Unknown)*

YANKEE WALL

MAIN SECTOR

38 routes   ←—5.10 5.11 5.12 5.13—→

This zone is the main attraction at Black Feather Canyon and features the Punk, Mind Games and Exit walls. These cliffs boast a solid collection of quality routes, ranging in difficulty from 5.10 to 5.12d, and provide sun or shade due to the east and west orientation of the parallel walls. If you are too hot or too cold, just change sides. Poor conditions won't be a viable excuse if you pitch off your project.

Approach: These cliffs are found about five minutes upstream of the Yankee Wall, where the canyon starts to widen. Punk Wall is on the left and the Mind Games Wall is on the right. Exit Wall is located a bit farther upstream behind a stand of trees, on a small slope where the creek takes a hard left.

Punk Wall

This cliff is located on the left side of the canyon. It has a great collection of 5.10 to 5.12 routes and boasts all-day sun. The routes have a good diversity of holds and moves, that together create fun and interesting climbs. Routes are listed from left to right.

❶ X-Ray Spex 5.10b . . . . ☐

4 bolts (14 m) From the top of a dirt hill left of a long, vertical crack, climb directly up compact grey rock to a high anchor. *(John Martin, 2004)*

❷ Le Ritz 5.9 . . . . ☐

4 bolts (14 m) Climb a faint, blue streak. *(John Martin, 2004)*

❸ Ripchord 5.10c . . . . ☐

4 bolts (15 m) Start one metre right of a long, vertical crack. Follow a discontinuous yellow streak to the anchor. *(John Martin, 2004)*

❹ A Simple Plan 5.10c . . . . ☐

4 bolts (14 m) Start one metre right of a roof at four metres with white rock below. Buckets and edges lead all the way to the anchor. *(John Martin, 2004)*

❺ London Burning 5.10d . . . . ☐

8 bolts (19 m) Work your way up shallow, right-facing corners to a small, yet tricky bulge on excellent rock. Continue straight up to anchors just right of a right-facing corner. *(Chris Miller, 2004)*

PUNK WALL

large crack →

11

8

3 - - - - - - - - - - - - - - 4 5 6 7 - - - - - -
ledge

9

10

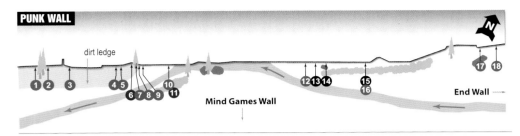

PUNK WALL

dirt ledge

Mind Games Wall

End Wall →

⑥ Never Mind the Bollocks 5.11b . . . . . ☐

8 bolts (19 m) Follow a faint, yellow streak on the left side of a corner. Share the anchor with *London Burning*.
(*Jon Jones 2007*)

⑦ Anarchy in the U.K. 5.10c . . . . ☐

11 bolts (19 m) Start directly below a corner on the right end of a dirt ledge. Climb the corner and trend rightward to another corner. From its top, climb right then back left before finishing straight up. (*Chris Miller, 2004*)

⑧ Holiday in Cambodia 5.10b . . . . ☐

8 bolts (22 m) This fantastic route has great holds, great movement and outstanding rock. To start, traverse right off a dirt ledge below a short corner, to the base of a yellow streak. Follow it to the anchor. (*Chris Miller, 2004*)

⑨ Holiday in Cambodia Direct 5.10b . . ☐

9 bolts (22 m) Start just right of the base of the dirt ledge and climb into *Holiday in Cambodia*. (*Unknown*)

⑩ Sister Ray 5.10c . . . . ☐

11 bolts (27 m) Great climbing on edges and sidepulls leads to pumpy climbing up an overhanging arête.
(*John Martin, 2004*)

⑪ Minor Threat 5.11a . . . . ☐

12 bolts (27 m) Climb *Sister Ray* to the third bolt before trending right on perfect edges to a technical corner and the anchor. (*Jon Jones, 2007*)

⑫ Open Project . . . . ☐

This appealing, powerful-looking line may yield a good route in the future.

⑬ Carnal Prayer Mat 5.12b . . ☐

12 bolts (30 m) Start up a shallow groove (it's easier than it looks) before launching through a series of small overlaps up high. Tough for the grade, but not to be missed by those that are capable! (*Peter Arbic, 2003*)

⑭ Tonto and the Lone Ranger Fist Fight in Heaven 5.12d . . . . . . ☐

13 bolts (29 m) A tough, low-percentage throw right off the ground leads to easier, but still-tricky climbing into a V-shaped notch. Navigate around some bird crap to reach the base of the roof. (This is the only "crappy" part of the route, no pun intended.) Take a couple of deep breaths before powering through a hard-to-read roof sequence.
(*Peter Arbic, 2003*)

⑮ Vanilla Guerrilla 5.12a . . . . . . ☐

11 bolts (35 m) Climb through a scoop and onto a vertical face. Trend left to anchors under the roof. (*Todd Guyn, 2008*)

⑯ Closed Project . . . . ☐

PUNK WALL

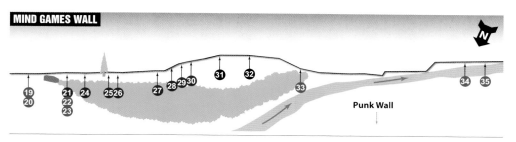

MIND GAMES WALL

Punk Wall

⑰ Open Project . . . . ☐

⑱ Open Project . . . . ☐

Mind Games Wall

This must-visit wall is located on the right side of the canyon and contains one of the most unique sections of rock in the Bow Valley. The majority of the routes require a nice blend of power and technique, and feature sequences that are rarely straightforward. The wall only gets sun in the evening. Routes are listed from left to right.

MIND GAMES WALL

⑲ Forbidden Terrace 5.10a . . . . ☐
8 bolts (20 m) Follow a juggy seam before trending right to a corner. Finish above a small roof. (*Kelly MacLeod, 2001*)

⑳ The Dagger's Edge 5.10d . . . . ☐
17 bolts (40 m) From the anchor of *Forbidden Terrace*, climb the moss just to the left to gain a ledge. Good edge climbing leads to some fun sidepulls on the way to the anchor. Lower twice to get down. (*Kelly MacLeod, 2001*)

㉑ Mochaccino 5.11a . . . . ☐
9 bolts (20 m) Follow brown hangers to an anchor just below a midway ledge. A couple of tricky moves at the start lead to easier climbing and a final crux that exits out of a small, left-facing corner. (*Kelly MacLeod, 2001*)

㉒ Ride 'em Cowboy 5.10d . . . . ☐
18 bolts (40 m) Continue past the anchor of *Mochaccino* to a ledge. Insecure climbing on slopers weaves around the left-hand line of bolts. You might wish you stopped at the first anchor.
(*Kelly MacLeod, 2001*)

㉓ Ormac 5.10a . . ☐
17 bolts (40 m) Continue past the anchor of *Mochaccino* to a ledge. More insecure climbing on slopers weaves around the right-hand line of bolts. Again, you might wish you stopped at the first anchor. (*Kelly MacLeod, 2001*)

㉔ Frappuccino 5.11c . . . ☐
7 bolts (19 m) Start just left of a right-facing corner that divides the yellow rock from the grey rock.
(*Kelly MacLeod, 2001*)

㉕ Tree Enema 5.11b . . . .

8 bolts (18 m) Start at the base of a right-facing corner that divides the yellow rock from the grey rock. Climb up the corner, and step left to a roof move. The cost of failure is… well, I think you know. (*Kelly MacLeod, 2001*)

㉖ Edge Grinder 5.11c . . . .

8 bolts (18 m) Start two metres right of the corner. From the ledge above the third bolt, interesting holds take you to the top of a right-facing corner. (*Kelly MacLeod, 2001*)

㉗ Snake Bite 5.11b . . . .

7 bolts (16 m) Start just left of a thin, blue streak that flows halfway down the wall. Prickly climbing down low leads to a powerful, underclings finish. (*Kelly MacLeod, 2001*)

㉘ Mind Games 5.11c . . . .

7 bolts (15 m) Climb the left side of the awesome brain-like rock. Finish below the roof at the top of the wall. The crux is right before the anchors. (*Kelly MacLeod, 2001*)

㉙ Mind Bender 5.11d . . . .

9 bolts (17 m) Tackles the center of the brain-like patch of rock. Follow a blue streak up a small arête to anchors in the right-facing corner above. (*Kelly MacLeod, 2001*)

㉚ Brain Dead 5.11d . . . .

10 bolts (18 m) Climb the right side of the brain-like patch of rock before following a narrow vertical slot over a series of small roofs. (*Kelly MacLeod, 2001*)

㉛ Buddy's Route 5.12b . . . .

7 bolts (14 m) This cool looking line forges up the overhanging blue streak to bona fide tufas at the break. A thin and technical crux leads through an otherwise blank-looking section of rock. (*Kelly MacLeod, 2002*)

㉜ Kick Me Down 5.12b . . . .

6 bolts (15 m) Start in front of a small pod at one metre. Slightly chossy rock leads to difficult climbing up the overhanging arête above. (*Jeff Relph & Paul McSorley, 2002*)

㉝ Featherweight 5.10a . . . .

5 bolts (10 m) Start on the right end of the wall. Climb a slab with an overhanging corner at your back. (*Al Ducros, 2001*)

㉞ Chutes and Ladders 5.7 . . . .

8 bolts (15 m) Juggy slab climbing leads up the face right of a corner sporting a hole. (*Al Ducros, 2001*)

MIND GAMES WALL

28

pod

29

30

31

32

END WALL

cave

36 37

38

㉟ Tip Top Toe 5.10b . . . .

9 bolts (15 m) A tricky start gives way to easier climbing and a final crux near the anchor. (*Al Ducros, 2001*)

End Wall

This diminutive crag is located at the end of the canyon behind a stand of trees at the top of a small slope. Currently, it contains only projects in various stages of completion. Routes are listed from left to right.

㊱ Closed Project . . . .

㊲ Closed Project . . . .

㊳ Closed Project . . . .

Ross Mailloux on Kick Me Down (5.12b).

CHAPTER 12

TUNNEL MOUNTAIN

Quick access combined with a sizable collection of nice 5.10 climbs makes the backside of Tunnel Mountain Banff's go-to crag when time is at a premium. The area's three walls all face east and receive morning sun, which makes for a comfortable start on a chilly day. The climbing tends to be thin and technical, favouring good footwork and balance as opposed to brute strength. If you are hoping to improve your face climbing skills, Tunnel Mountain is a great place to practice.

MICHELLE KOLLMUSS ON TROUBLE IN PARADISE 5.10c

CONDITIONS

Since the walls at Tunnel Mountain are on the slabby side, they offer no protection from storms and get wet very quickly during rainfall. However, a lack of major drainage features or seep streaks allows the rock to dry quickly once the rain has stopped, making this area a good post-storm choice. The climbing on the various walls occurs on the lower portion of much larger cliffs, so rockfall is always possible and helmets are highly recommended. Take particular caution at the Scoop area, as there are popular multi-pitch routes that climb directly above the wall which have loose debris on the belay ledges. Also, hikers who have reached the summit on Tunnel Mountain occasionally have the urge to throw rocks off from the top, unaware of the activities going on below.

APPROACH

Tunnel Mountain has two different parking options depending on where you plan to climb. For the Scoop and Industrial Playground, park in the north lot, and for the Black Band, park in the south lot.

From Banff: Both parking lots are easily reached from downtown Banff. Which route you choose, will depend on your specific location. Use the driving map of Banff to make your plan.

From Canmore: Drive west on the Trans-Canada Highway toward Banff. Take the first Banff exit and turn left onto Banff Avenue. Just after passing the "Welcome To Banff" sign, turn left onto Tunnel Mountain Road and follow it past campgrounds and scenic overlooks. At a cluster of hotels, turn left onto Tunnel Mountain Drive. For the Industrial Playground and the Scoop, park on the side of the road near a grassy clearing on the left (about 100 m from the last turn), being careful not to block access to any gates. For the Black Band, continue along Tunnel Mountain Drive. Just after passing the Banff Center, turn left into a scenic overlook and park. This driving route may seem indirect, but downtown traffic in Banff during the summer can be horrendous and is well worth avoiding.

From Lake Louise: Drive east on the Trans-Canada Highway toward Banff. Take the second Banff exit and turn right onto Banff Avenue. From here, follow the Canmore directions outlined above.

Hiking: See each area for specific directions.

TUNNEL MOUNTAIN OVERVIEW

THE SCOOP

INDUSTRIAL PLAYGROUND

BLACK BAND

TO P

P

GRASSY CLEARING

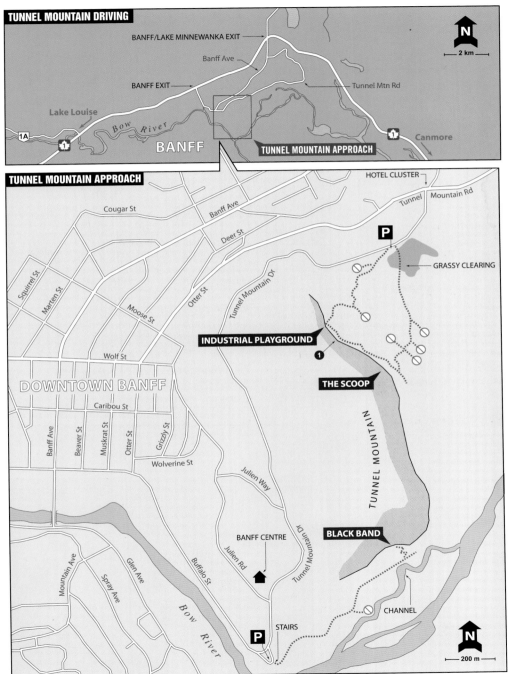

TUNNEL MOUNTAIN DRIVING

BANFF/LAKE MINNEWANKA EXIT

Banff Ave

BANFF EXIT

Tunnel Mtn Rd

Lake Louise

N

2 km

1A

Bow River

BANFF

Canmore

TUNNEL MOUNTAIN APPROACH

TUNNEL MOUNTAIN APPROACH

HOTEL CLUSTER

Tunnel Mountain Rd

Cougar St

Banff Ave

Deer St

P

GRASSY CLEARING

Squirrel St

Marten St

Moose St

Otter St

Tunnel Mountain Dr

INDUSTRIAL PLAYGROUND

1

Wolf St

THE SCOOP

DOWNTOWN BANFF

Caribou St

Banff Ave

Beaver St

Muskrat St

Otter St

Grizzly St

TUNNEL MOUNTAIN

Wolverine St

Julien Way

BLACK BAND

Mountain Ave

Glen Ave

Spray Ave

Bow River

Buffalo St

Julien Rd

BANFF CENTRE

Tunnel Mountain Dr

CHANNEL

P

STAIRS

N

200 m

BLACK BAND

17 routes   ←5.10 5.11 5.12 5.13→

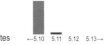

If unfiltered morning sun combined with beautiful views of Mt. Rundle and the Bow River sounds appealing, then check out the Black Band. This crag is very scenic, but the routes will demand your full attention due to their slabby and technical nature. Pitch length's range from 15 to 38 metres so a long rope is a must, as are strong fingers and a solid belief that your shoes will stick to the small footholds.

Approach: From the trail at the back of the parking lot, descend a short section of stairs before turning left and following a well-worn path that leads downhill through the trees. After reaching the bottom of the hill, go left at a Y-junction. The trail flattens out and weaves through larger trees to a point where a channel of the Bow River (which is sometimes dry) makes a sharp bend and comes quite close to the trail. At this bend, look for a climbers' trail that branches left into the trees and heads up the scree slope to the base of the wall.

Black Band

Routes are listed from left to right.

① Rocket Surgery 5.9 . . . .
6 bolts (15 m) Start five metres uphill from an aspen tree. Climb over a series of white overlaps and finish with some cool knobby holds on the black slab. (*John Martin, 2007*)

② Welcome to the Jungle 5.10a . . . . .
8 bolts (19 m) Start just left of a big, right-facing corner. Sidepulls in the white rock lead to fun slab climbing above. (*John Martin, 2006*)

③ Dab Hand 5.10a . . . .
9 bolts (23 m) Start just right of a big, right-facing corner. Enjoy fun climbing on big jugs down low, crimps up high, and two roofs in between. (*John Martin, 2006*)

④ Number One Stir Fried 5.10a . . . .
10 bolts (26 m) Nice edge climbing leads to a few small roofs. Finish with more fun edges. (*Al Ducros & Pierre Giguerre, 2000*)

⑤ Walk the Line 5.10b . .
9 bolts (26 m) Climb up a small, flakey, left-facing corner. Crimps at the top will cause hesitation before cruising easier moves that lead to a small roof. A larger roof above protects the anchor.
(*Chas Yonge & Chris Perry, 2006*)

⑥ The Missing Link 5.10a . . . .
10 bolts (28 m) Climb to the top of a small, left-facing flake. Continue straight up on edges to a tricky move near the top. (*Al Ducros & Deborah Ashton, 2000*)

⑦ Farrago 5.9 . . . .
8 bolts (25 m) Start just left of a bush growing out of the wall. Climb up a small, left-facing corner and into a small, right-facing corner above. (*John Martin, 2006*)

⑧ Who's Afraid of the Black Bear? 5.10a . . . .
10 bolts (31 m) This fun route takes a plumb line up the face on flakes and edges just left of a tree on the wall. It's just possible to get down with a 60-metre rope, but tie knots in the ends to be safe. (*John Martin, 2006*)

BLACK BAND

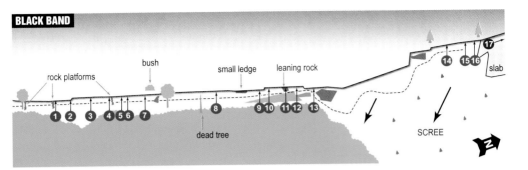

BLACK BAND

rock platforms • bush • small ledge • leaning rock • slab • SCREE • dead tree

⑨ The Force 5.8 . . . .

7 bolts (33 m) This route climbs the face just right of a tree on the wall. Flake climbing down low leads to a big, diagonal break at the base of a right-facing corner. A healthy spacing between bolts will keep you on your toes! It's just possible to get down with a 60-metre rope and a bit of easy downclimbing, but tie knots in the ends to be safe. *(Al Ducros & JP McCormid, 2002)*

⑩ Fifth Business 5.10d . . . . . .

13 bolts (35 m) Climb just left of a small, pointy roof at five metres, heading for a large rock scar. Very thin and technical climbing completes the pitch. A 70-metre rope is required to descend. *(John Martin, 2007)*

⑪ One Brick in the Wall 5.10c . . . .

14 bolts (38 m) Climb just right of a small, pointy roof at five metres. Sustained edges lead straight up between two large rock scars. Lower twice to get down.
(Al Ducros, Deborah Ashton & JP McCormid, 2002)

⑫ Saving Grace 5.10c . . . .

15 bolts (38 m) Start one metre left of a small, left-facing corner and climb through a large rock scar on the right. This will warm you up for the sustained edge climbing above. *(John Martin, 2007)*

⑬ Dude 5.8 . . . .

8 bolts (18 m) Start in front of trees growing next to the wall. Follow a fun, flakey crack to an anchor below a small roof. *(John Martin, 2008)*

⑭ Clean Slate 5.10b . . . .

12 bolts (33 m) Start below a ledge at four metres. Good, balancey climbing on edges leads to a mid-height roof. Easily pull the lip before getting completely stymied as to how best to reach the anchors. *(Chris Perry, 2009)*

⑮ Pentimento 5.10a . . . .

10 bolts (29 m) Fun, sustained climbing on excellent rock leads to anchors under a roof. Good footwork will be of great benefit. *(Chris Perry & Chas Yonge, 2008)*

⑯ Sunburn 5.10c . . . .

8 bolts (29 m) This is a great route up fantastic stone. Start just left of a tree and a bush. *(John Martin, 2008)*

⑰ Camino del Sol 5.11c . . . .

This is a 3-pitch route that has good, varied climbing. The pitches are 5.10c (11 bolts), 5.11c, (11 bolts) and 5.9 (6 bolts). *(John Martin, 2007)*

BLACK BAND

SCOOP AREA

23 routes ←5.10 5.11 5.12 5.13→

Upon first gazing at the less-than-vertical walls of the Scoop, you might assume the climbing is going to be a cruise. Think again. The clean, black and grey face is devoid of jugs, incut edges and large footholds. You'll need good technical skills and trust in your rubber to inch up to the various anchors.

Conditions: The slabby routes at this crag get wet quickly when it starts to rain, but also dry quickly afterward, especially with a little wind. The wall sees sun from morning until early afternoon, but the best conditions for sticking to the slippery edges and footholds is in the cool, afternoon shade. Be extra cautious of rockfall from above. Multi-pitch climbers and hikers have been known to trundle rocks onto unsuspecting climbers below.

Approach: From the back of the flat, grassy clearing next to the parking area (on the left-hand side of the road while facing Tunnel Mountain), pick up a good trail that leads into the forest. Trend left and hike past two Y-intersections, taking the right-hand option each time. At a four-way intersection, go straight through and up a steep incline that leads to the wall. The trail reaches the cliff at the bottom of a small hill on the right. At the top of the hill is the Scoop Area. To reach the Industrial Playground, follow a trail rightward along the base of the wall for five minutes.

Scoop Area

Routes are listed from left to right.

❶ Sweet Nothings 5.11a . . . . .

5 bolts (13 m) A few positive holds start the pitch, before the climbing turns grim. *(John Martin, 2008)*

❷ Stranger than Fiction 5.11a . . . .

5 bolts (14 m) Climb the left side of a short, hanging pillar. Pure friction lies above. *(John Martin, 2006)*

❸ Stick to What? 5.10c . . . . .

4 bolts (12 m) Climb the right side of a short, hanging pillar to a few friction moves above. *(John Martin, 2006)*

❹ Science Friction 5.10c . . . .

5 bolts (11 m) Smear up a left-trending groove to anchors above the final bolt. *(John Martin, 2006)*

❺ Harvest 5.10c . . . .

10 bolts (25 m) This is the second route left of a large tree growing on the left side of a scoop. Enjoyable climbing up clean, grey stone ends at an anchor below a patch of white rock. *(John Martin, 2005)*

❻ Heat 5.10b . . . .

6 bolts (17 m) Start just left of a large tree growing on the left side of a scoop. Follow decent edges directly up the wall. *(John Martin, 2005)*

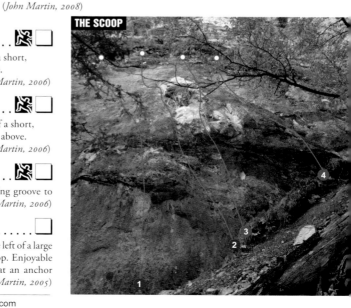

THE SCOOP

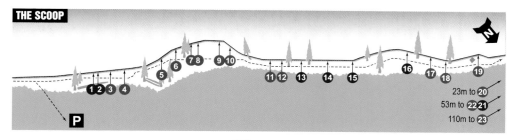

THE SCOOP

7 Los Pinos 5.9 . . . .

9 bolts (26 m) Start just right of a large tree growing on the left side of a scoop. Begin up a short, left-trending ramp and finish straight up on edges with a couple friction moves to keep the climbing interesting. Los Pinos is the official residence and office of the President of Mexico. *(John Martin, 2005)*

8 Scoop Route 5.10a . . . .

8 bolts (27 m) Start at the base of a short, left-trending ramp. Climb straight up the middle of a scoop utilizing edges, pinches and slopers. A lone bolt lurks above the anchor. Ignore it and lower off. *(Greg Golovach, 1996)*

9 Slice of Life 5.10c . . . .

8 bolts (21 m) Start off a small, vegetated ledge at the base of a scoop. Work up the steep, right side to the fifth bolt and trend right onto the face. *(John Martin, 2005)*

10 Strike Out 5.10c . . . .

9 bolts (24 m) Ascend a steep slab on edges just right of a scoop. *(Greg Golovach, 1996)*

11 Sweet Spot 5.10d . . . .

8 bolts (22 m) Slab climb to a high first bolt. Continue past a small, white roof to blocky pinches and cool chert edges. *(John Martin, 2005)*

12 Velocity 5.10d . . . .

10 bolts (26 m) This great route has a short-lived crimp crux at the fourth bolt that is followed by balancey edge climbing to the anchors. *(John Martin, 2006)*

13 Delta Vee 5.11a . . . .

10 bolts (26 m) This quality pitch starts between two large trees. A short crux at the fourth bolt is followed by excellent climbing to the anchor. *(John Martin, 2006)*

THE SCOOP

⑭ Deep Six 5.11b

10 bolts (24 m) Balancey moves lead to a thin crux and then easier, but still-involved climbing above. This pitch is landmarked by a small roof at the fifth bolt. (*John Martin, 2006*)

⑮ Steady as She Goes 5.11a

9 bolts (22 m) Start to the left of a small tree growing next to the wall. Balancey and thin. (*John Martin, 2006*)

⑯ High Hopes 5.11a

15 bolts (30 m) A low crux is followed by nice, sustained climbing and a final tough section past a small roof near the top. (*Chris & Ian Perry, 2008*)

⑰ Closed Project

⑱ Open Project

This is a line of hanger-less studs located behind a tree.

⑲ Ballista 5.10c, A0

Bolts (206 m) This is a fun, adventurous route that is popular on sunny weekends. All you need is a helmet, a 60-m rope, a few shoulder-length slings and 13 quickdraws. Rappel the route to descend. (*Chris Perry, 2006-2007*)

Pitch 1 (5.10a, 13 bolts, 30 m) Climb left of a corner before moving left around a roof and up to a belay ledge.
Pitch 2 (5.8, 7 bolts, 25 m) Head up and left before swinging back right to a large belay ledge right of a tree.

Pitch 3 (5.10c, 9 bolts, 25 m) Smeary and balancey moves lead to a belay at the base of a corner.
Pitch 4 (5.10a, 9 bolts, 25 m) Fun climbing up the corner leads to another big belay ledge.
Pitch 5 (5.10b, 8 bolts, 25 m) Slab and face climbing leads to the base of the chert bands.
Pitch 6 (5.9, 11 bolts, 28 m) Enjoy fun chert knob climbing. Traverse hard right and break through a roof section to a large belay ledge.
Pitch 7 (5.8 A0, 7 bolts, 20 m) A little bobbing and weaving leads to a three-bolt section of aid. Use your shoulder-length slings.
Pitch 8 (5.10a, 8 bolts, 28 m) Face climbing leads to a corner and the top of the route.

⑳ Safe Haven 5.10c

6 bolts (11 m) This fun route follows a crack up an overhanging wall. Clean it on a toprope. (*Greg Golovach, 1996*)

㉑ Tree Hugger 5.11d

6 bolts (21 m) Climb up a tree with a curved trunk and step onto the wall. Work up a scoop utilizing a bare minimum of decent features. (*Greg Golovach, 1996*)

㉒ Stumped 5.10b

6 bolts (18 m) This sporty route lacks many positive holds, unfortunately. (*Greg Golovach, 1996*)

㉓ Open Project

A rope hangs on a steep, white wall, 60 m up the hill.

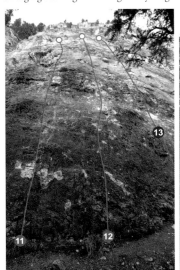

THE SCOOP

INDUSTRIAL PLAYGROUND

30 routes ←5.10 5.11 5.12 5.13→

This sub-90°, grey limestone wall hosts a good collection of thin, technical routes that are tucked away in the trees. At this crag, a good, intricate face climbing background will be of much more use than a winter of endless laps on the campus board.

Conditions: This cliff takes longer to warm up, because trees at the base filter the morning sun.

Approach: Follow a well-worn trail that parallels the road leading toward Tunnel Mountain. At the first Y-intersection, go left. Continue hiking straight before climbing a small incline. Turn left and arrive at an intersection with a small, flat clearing. Follow a trail leading uphill (not downhill) at a steady incline to the Industrial Playground. To reach the Scoop, follow the trail leftward along the base of the wall for five minutes.

Industrial Playground to

Routes are listed from left to right.

❶ Brace Yourself 5.11b . . . .

7 bolts (23 m) This pitch is located 110 metres left along the trail from the Industrial Playground. Start off a boulder and climb to a high first bolt at the top of a black slab. Tricky climbing through small, right-facing corners leads to a roof. Follow a blue streak above to the anchor. *(Unknown)*

❷ Look Mom, No Hands 5.9 . . . .

7 bolts (17 m) Traverse left for three bolts before climbing straight up. *(Kelly MacLeod, 1998)*

❸ Funky Town 5.11d . . . .

Start off a small, right-trending ramp. Climb straight up and over a small overlap (5.8, 6 bolts, 17 m). Continue upwards (5.10d, 7 bolts) and finish with the crux pitch (5.11d, 10 bolts). *(Kelly MacLeod & Josee Larochelle, 1998)*

❹ Norwegian Blue 5.10a . . . .

3 bolts (10 m) This short, slabby face climb is landmarked by a short seam below the anchor. *(John Martin, 2008)*

❺ Pinin' For the Fjords 5.11a

3 bolts (11 m) This technical, slabby face climb starts just left of a tree growing by the wall. If you can get to the first bolt, the rest will be a breeze. *(John Martin, 2008)*

INDUSTRIAL PLAYGROUND

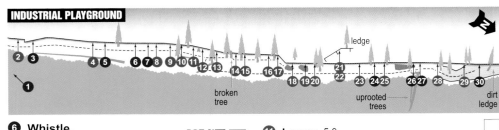

INDUSTRIAL PLAYGROUND

ledge

broken
tree

uprooted
trees

dirt
ledge

6 Whistle, Whistle, Click, Click 5.11b . . . .

5 bolts (17 m) Start three metres right of a tree growing next to the wall. It's all in the feet! *(Unknown)*

7 Steel Bananas 5.11a . . . .

6 bolts (17 m) Follow brown hangers over a tiny roof and join *Whistle, Whistle, Click, Click* to finish. *(Unknown)*

8 The Nanny 5.10c . . . .

7 bolts (17 m) Climb the left side of a shallow scoop to a small overlap. Finish on thin chert bands to the left of a left-facing corner. *(Kelly MacLeod, 1998)*

9 Party Hoppin' 5.10b . . . .

7 bolts (19 m) Climb the right side of a shallow scoop via edges and sidepulls to a small roof. Vertical climbing gains the anchor. *(Kelly MacLeod, 1998)*

10 Screamin' Toad 5.10b . . . .

7 bolts (19 m) Start just left of a tree growing against the wall. Crimp up a slabby face and climb over a small roof toward a larger roof. Solve the roof sequence and gun for the anchor. *(Kelly MacLeod, 1998)*

11 Lenny 5.9 . . . .

8 bolts (19 m) Start right of a tree growing against the wall. Fun climbing leads up a small, left-facing corner to a roof. Good holds lead over the right side. *(Kelly MacLeod, 1998)*

12 Burly 5.10c . . . .

9 bolts (19 m) Start just right of a small, left-facing corner. Climb over a small roof at the first bolt. Slabby face climbing leads to another roof at the top. *(Kelly MacLeod, 1998)*

13 Digitalized Chaos 5.10a . . . .

7 bolts (16 m) Start in front of a tree growing two metres back from the wall. Climb over a small, low roof and up. The anchors are near a small tree on the wall. *(Unknown)*

14 Rogue Wave 5.10c . . . .

8 bolts (19 m) Climb through a large, white rock scar to a small roof. A short, in-your-face crux gives way to easier climbing above. *(John Martin, 2007)*

15 Charlatan 5.10b . . . .

9 bolts (28 m) A short slab leads to a cruxy vertical face. Excellent slabby face climbing through thin chert bands finishes the pitch. *(John Martin, 2007)*

INDUSTRIAL PLAYGROUND

⑯ Femtograms 5.10b . . . . □

9 bolts (22 m) Start below a small roof at five metres. Slabby face climbing leads to a roof encounter. (*John Martin, 2007*)

⑰ The Cat Came Back 5.10b . . . . 🔲

8 bolts (21 m) Start below a small, mossy, left-facing corner with a tree growing out the top. Climb up to and through a small corner and finish with some slabby face climbing. (*John Martin, 2007*)

⑱ Calypso 5.10b . . . . 🔲

7 bolts (21 m) Start below a white rock scar. Climb up and over a small roof, with a short wide crack above it, and onto the clean face above. (*John Martin, 2008*)

⑲ Castilleja 5.10c . . . . □

8 bolts (21 m) Start two metres right of *Calypso* below a white rock scar. Work up small edges avoiding the roof on the right. Join *Calypso* to finish. (*John Martin, 2008*)

⑳ Die Laughing 5.10b . . . . □

11 bolts (18 m) Start below a large, plant-filled, left-facing corner. Prepare for steep slab. (*John Martin, 2008*)

㉑ Pushing the Envelope 5.10d . . . . . □

10 bolts (29 m) Scramble up a mossy ramp to a small stance and the first bolt. Follow a seam, with difficulty, to a small ledge below a roof. Crank the lip and then relax with great edge climbing on chert bands. (*Kelly MacLeod, 1998*)

㉒ Lick the Stamp 5.10d . . . . □

10 bolts (29 m) Climb *Pushing the Envelope* to the

fifth bolt and trend right over a roof. Finish straight up through chert bands. (*Kelly MacLeod, 1998*)

㉓ Rest In Pieces 5.10d . . . . □

11 bolts (29 m) This route is located just right of a tree growing out of the wall. Easy climbing down low leads to a tricky overlap, which is followed by fun edge climbing through chert bands. (*John Martin, 2008*)

㉔ Evanescence 5.11a . . . . □

12 bolts (27 m) Start in front of a tree growing against the wall. Head for a short, left-facing corner with a thin crack above it. (*John Martin, 2008*)

㉕ The Promised Land 5.10d . . . . □

10 bolts (27 m) Start just left of a tree growing against the wall. Climb up and over two roofs to edges above. (*John Martin, 2008*)

㉖ The Third Degree 5.11a . . . . □

12 bolts (27 m) Start in front of a clump of trees growing next to the wall and below a V-shaped notch. Climb to the top of the notch before trending slightly left past a small ledge. (*John Martin, 2008*)

㉗ Chertsicle 5.11a . . . . 🔲🔲

13 bolts (27 m) Start one metre right of a V-shaped notch. Climb past a short, left-facing corner on the right to a very thin crux above. Fun edge climbing through chert bands leads to a final, high crux. (*John Martin, 2008*)

㉘ Carry On Runstible 5.10b . . . . □

11 bolts (28 m) Start below a tree growing out of the wall above a roof. Fun climbing leads up a small, left-facing corner and flake above. (*John Martin, 2008*)

㉙ Elysian Fields 5.10c . . 🔲

11 bolts (23 m) Start just left of two trees growing next to the wall. After climbing over a low roof, enjoy easier moves that end at a high, slabby crux. (*John Martin, 2008*)

㉚ B52 5.11a . . . . □

9 bolts (26 m) Start just right of two trees growing next to the wall. A low roof leads to easier climbing capped by a high crux. (*John Martin, 2008*)

INDUSTRIAL PLAYGROUND

CHAPTER 13

RAVEN'S CRAG

Raven's Crag is a small, overhanging wall of high-quality limestone that's streaked with various shades of light blue and grey. The cliff is perched on the northwest end of Sulphur Mountain in a very scenic setting that overlooks the townsite of Banff. The number of climbs is minimal, but a few of the pitches are outstanding, especially *Telltale Heart* (5.13a), which is one of the best of the grade in the Bow Valley. The routes range in style from long, slightly-overhanging crimping marathons to steep, gymnastic cave routes, and all but one were established by a single person, Peter Arbic. If you want to climb in a pretty setting that stays cool and is almost guaranteed to be deserted, then Raven's Crag is a great choice.

TAKESHI ABE ON TELLTALE HEART (5.13D)

CONDITIONS

16 routes ←5.10 5.11 5.12 5.13→

Since Raven's Crag sees virtually no sun, seepage and runoff can be a real concern. The routes need plenty of warm, sunny weather to dry, so it's best to be patient and wait for a period of stable conditions before venturing up to the cliff. Be sure to pack your parka and warm hat because this zone can get cold. It's best to wait for warm, summer days if you don't want to suffer too much.

APPROACH

From Banff: Drive south on Banff Avenue and cross the Bow River. From the traffic lights at the end of Banff Avenue, turn right onto Cave Avenue and follow it all the way to the Cave and Basin parking lot at the end. Park here.

From Canmore: Head west on the Trans-Canada Highway. Take the first Banff exit and turn left onto Banff Avenue. Follow this street all the way through town and over the Bow River. From the traffic lights at the end of Banff Avenue, turn right onto Cave Avenue and follow this road all the way to the Cave and Basin parking lot at the end. Park here.

Access Note

Raven's Crag sits above an animal wildlife corridor that is closed to all public traffic. Any attempts to approach the cliff through this corridor could seriously jeopardize future access and land you a hefty fine. On the way back down from Raven's Crag, you may notice a trail heading straight down the forested hill. This is the old approach trail that was used before the wildlife corridor was established. It is now closed.

Hiking: From the parking lot, follow a wide, paved path past the Cave and Basin National Historic Site toward Sundance Canyon. After about eight minutes, the path will follow a gradual decline and bend to the right. At this point, go left onto a wide horse trail that leads uphill. When the horse trail starts to gradually level off (approximately 4 minutes from the paved trail), look for a faint trail on the left that heads toward the ridge. (Be vigilant and use your watch as this trail can be a bit tricky to find the first time.) Follow this faint trail up the ridge and past the odd cairn to the base of a cliff band that stretches to the left. Hike leftward along the cliff base to reach Raven's Crag.

4 minutes to climbers' trail

horse trail

paved path

WARNING/AVIS

Bear in area
Travel with caution

Ours dans le secteur. Avancez prudement

NPC/PNC

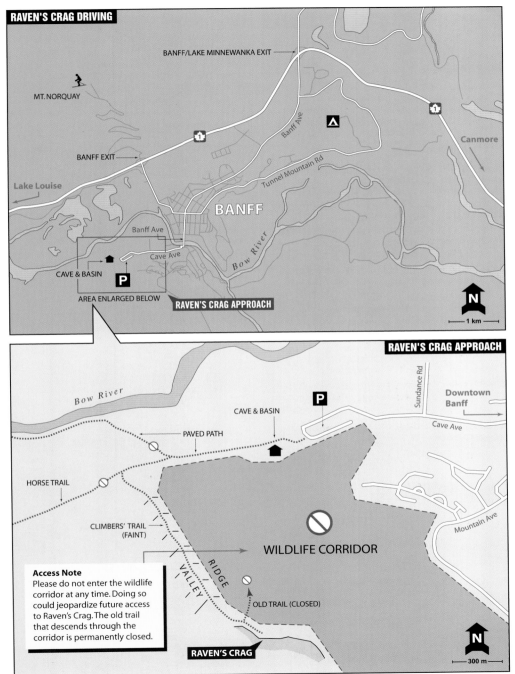

RAVEN'S CRAG DRIVING

MT. NORQUAY

BANFF/LAKE MINNEWANKA EXIT

Canmore

Banff Ave

BANFF EXIT

Lake Louise

Tunnel Mountain Rd

BANFF

Banff Ave

Cave Ave

Bow River

CAVE & BASIN

P

AREA ENLARGED BELOW

RAVEN'S CRAG APPROACH

N

1 km

RAVEN'S CRAG APPROACH

Bow River

Sundance Rd

Downtown Banff

CAVE & BASIN

P

Cave Ave

PAVED PATH

HORSE TRAIL

Mountain Ave

CLIMBERS' TRAIL (FAINT)

WILDLIFE CORRIDOR

Access Note
Please do not enter the wildlife corridor at any time. Doing so could jeopardize future access to Raven's Crag. The old trail that descends through the corridor is permanently closed.

VALLEY

RIDGE

OLD TRAIL (CLOSED)

RAVEN'S CRAG

N

300 m

Raven's Crag

Routes are listed from left to right.

❶ The Raven 5.10d

Although the stone and climbing on this route are both excellent, the somewhat bold nature of the pitches and the requirement for two ropes to descend has caused it to fall into obscurity, which is a pity. From the cave, follow a trial leftward along the cliff base to a small ledge and the start of the route.

Pitch 1 (5.10d, 10 bolts, 48 m) A high first bolt is followed by technical climbing past well-spaced bolts, which aren't always in the best locations. From the last bolt, traverse right around a corner and follow a left-trending ramp for quite a distance to a hidden anchor above.
Pitch 2 (5.10c, 10 bolts, 25 m) Trend right from the anchor. Technical climbing between well-spaced bolts leads to a rappel anchor. Bring two ropes. (*Troy Kirwan, 1992*)

❷ The Hermit 5.13b

10 bolts (12 m) Start on the right-hand side of the cave by the "J.E.B." graffiti. Climb straight up to holds that lead rightward out the cave. Although it's relatively short, this route it packs a punch! (*Peter Arbic, 2001*)

❸ One Robe, One Bowl 5.12c

7 bolts (12 m) Start just to the right of the mouth of the cave. Big moves lead out the roof to a shared finish with *The Hermit*. (*Peter Arbic, 2001*)

❹ Nevermore 5.12b

21 bolts (36 m) This pitch is high on the cliff and follows a very attractive grey corner feature that's begging to be climbed, however it's necessary to negotiate a fair amount of loose and dirty rock to get started. If you decide to embark on this adventurous journey, climb straight up from a small cave at ground level. Pass two rusted anchors on the right (your only chances to retreat) en route to the striking corner and groove above. (*Peter Arbic, 2001*)

❺ Overlooking Paradise 5.12d

7 bolts (13 m) The first crux requires a blend of technique and power to overcome. The second crux requires nothing but brute strength. (*Peter Arbic, 1994*)

❻ House of Usher 5.12a

7 bolts (11 m) Start below a hanging, left-facing corner capped by a small roof. (The piece of the corner that's missing is the coffin-sized block behind you). Climb to a small ledge at three metres before moving left into a hanging corner and up. (*Peter Arbic, 1995*)

❼ Open Project

The continuation of *House of Usher*.

❽ Tales of Mystery 5.12d

7 bolts (13 m) Start on *House of Usher*, but trend right at the second bolt through several bulges using hard-to-locate holds. Finish with a tricky move to the anchor. (*Peter Arbic, 2001*)

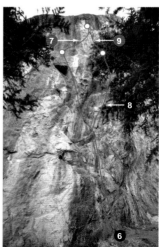

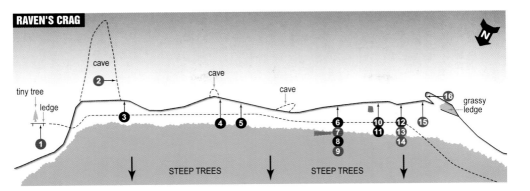

RAVEN'S CRAG

cave
cave
cave
tiny tree
ledge
grassy ledge
STEEP TREES   STEEP TREES

---

⑨ Open Project . . . .

The continuation of *Tales of Mystery*.

⑩ The Masque P1 5.11d . . . . . .

7 bolts (11 m) A hard opening move gains a crack in a left-facing corner. From the third bolt, step left and execute cool moves between jugs that lead to a power-draining crux. *(Peter Arbic, 1992)*

⑪ The Masque P2 5.12d . . . .

13 bolts (17 m) Continue past the anchor by launching directly into a crux that utilizes small crimpers. This is followed by sustained climbing that leads to a powerful and technical crux that guards the anchor. *(Peter Arbic, 2001)*

⑫ Telltale Heart P1 5.11d . . . .

6 bolts (11 m) Starts two metres left of a pod-filled corner. Fun edge climbing punctuated by nice buckets leads to a difficult anchor clip using small edges. *(Peter Arbic, 1992)*

⑬ Telltale Heart P2 5.13a . . .

16 bolts (29 m) Continue past the anchors and skip a rusty, quarter-inch, self-drive bolt below the roof. Once above the roof, never ending technical difficulties await. Absolutely classic! *(Peter Arbic, 1995)*

⑭ Open Project . . . .

Branch right from *Telltale Heart* near the top.

⑮ Open Project . . . .

Chain hangers mark a path up the pod-filled corner to finish on the first anchor of *Telltale Heart*.

⑯ Open Project . . . .

The overhanging prow will produce a striking testpiece someday.

RAVEN'S CRAG

CHAPTER 14

LAKE LOUISE

Perched next to the beautiful, aqua-marine waters of Lake Louise is what many consider to be the crown jewel of Bow Valley sport climbing, the crags at the "back of the lake". This body of water is world famous and rests in a deep, bowl-shaped valley that is framed by massive, ice-encrusted peaks that tremble under the weight of the enormous glaciers which ooze down their slopes. Bulletproof walls of purple and orange quartzite frame the lakes' distant shores and are littered with near-perfect holds, ranging in size from half-pad crimpers to jugs that may swallow your entire hand. The climbing on these sheer faces is both physical and technical, and the tall, slightly-overhanging walls demand considerable stamina.

Many routes on the cliff band are classic, and would be considered so almost anywhere in the world. And while the majority of the climbs are bolted, traditionally protected masterpieces lurk between the hangers, including the Path (5.14a), one of Canada's hardest gear routes. So, if you decide to visit the Lake (a must, really), don't just pack quickdraws—throw a rack in your pack to truly enjoy all the special experiences this area has to offer.

CONDITIONS

With an elevation of over 1,600 m, the crags at Lake Louise fall within a sub-arctic climatic zone classification and have one of the shortest climbing seasons in the Bow Valley (early June to mid-September). What should you expect while climbing here? Typically, the mornings are frosty, but are often followed by slightly warmer conditions throughout the day, except during the warmest weeks of the year when the midday sun can be uncomfortably hot. The walls primarily face east or south and receive plenty of solar radiation, except during early or late season when the high mountain peaks block most of the low-tracking rays. Rainfall isn't a big issue, because the overhanging nature of the crags keeps many sectors dry, even during moderate storms. But all nuances aside, this area is typically quite cold, so warm clothing is *always* recommended, even during the peak of summer.

Access Notes

Lake Louise sits inside Banff National Park and a valid park pass is required for any activities within its boundaries. Park passes can be obtained at the park gates or at the Banff and Lake Louise information centers. If you can't find the time to get a park pass, you can always get one from the check point that is in regular operation during the summer at the entrance to the parking lot! Also, please note that dogs must be leashed at all times.

APPROACH

From Calgary/Canmore/Banff: Drive west on the Trans-Canada Highway toward Lake Louise. Take the Lake Louise/Bow Valley Parkway exit and turn left onto Lake Louise Drive. Follow this road all the way to the Lake Louise parking lots.

Hiking: Lake Louise has, by far, one of the simplest approaches in the Bow Valley. From any of the parking lots, follow paths toward the Chateau Lake Louise (you'll likely have to dodge and weave through a throng of trigger-happy tourists). Once in front of the Chateau, follow the wide, lakeside path along the right-hand shore of the lake for about 30 minutes to a small uphill section locally referred to as "Heart Attack Hill". At the top of this hill is Trailside Wall and the route *Aeroflot*.

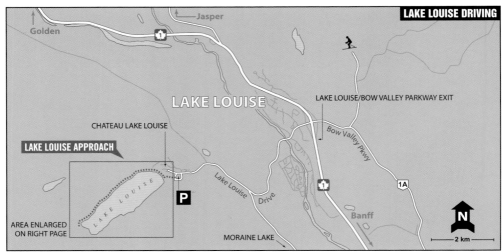

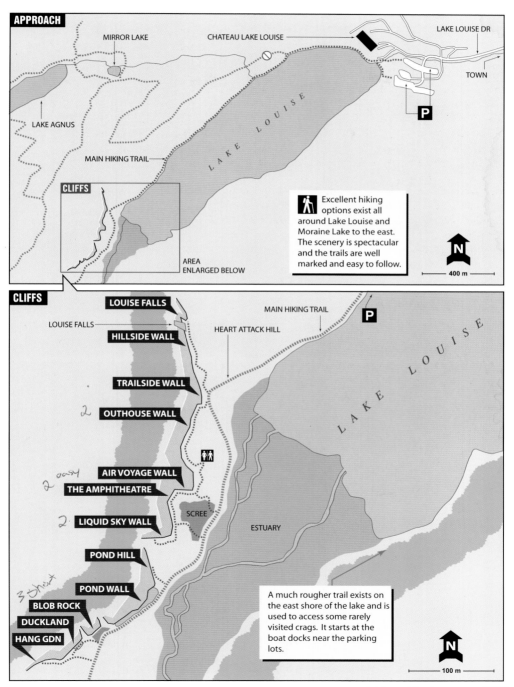

APPROACH

MIRROR LAKE

CHATEAU LAKE LOUISE

LAKE LOUISE DR

LAKE LOUISE

TOWN

P

LAKE AGNUS

L A K E   L O U I S E

MAIN HIKING TRAIL

CLIFFS

AREA
ENLARGED BELOW

Excellent hiking options exist all around Lake Louise and Moraine Lake to the east. The scenery is spectacular and the trails are well marked and easy to follow.

N

400 m

CLIFFS

LOUISE FALLS

LOUISE FALLS

MAIN HIKING TRAIL

P

HILLSIDE WALL

HEART ATTACK HILL

L A K E   L O U I S E

TRAILSIDE WALL

OUTHOUSE WALL

AIR VOYAGE WALL

THE AMPHITHEATRE

LIQUID SKY WALL

SCREE

ESTUARY

POND HILL

POND WALL

BLOB ROCK

DUCKLAND

HANG GDN

A much rougher trail exists on the east shore of the lake and is used to access some rarely visited crags. It starts at the boat docks near the parking lots.

N

100 m

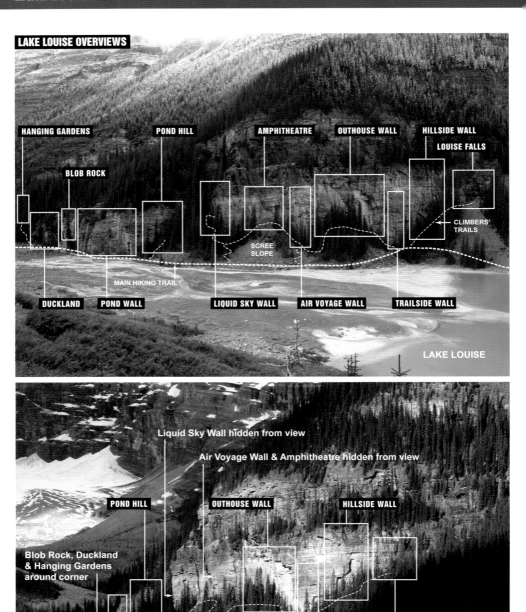

LAKE LOUISE OVERVIEWS

HANGING GARDENS
POND HILL
AMPHITHEATRE
OUTHOUSE WALL
HILLSIDE WALL
LOUISE FALLS
BLOB ROCK
CLIMBERS' TRAILS
SCREE SLOPE
MAIN HIKING TRAIL
DUCKLAND
POND WALL
LIQUID SKY WALL
AIR VOYAGE WALL
TRAILSIDE WALL
LAKE LOUISE

Liquid Sky Wall hidden from view

Air Voyage Wall & Amphitheatre hidden from view

POND HILL
OUTHOUSE WALL
HILLSIDE WALL

Blob Rock, Duckland & Hanging Gardens around corner

MAIN HIKING TRAIL

POND WALL
TRAILSIDE WALL
LOUISE FALLS

LAKE LOUISE

OUTHOUSE SECTOR

62 routes ←5.10 5.11 5.12 5.13→

The Outhouse Sector is one of the busiest areas at Lake Louise, and is usually the first spot that climbers choose to drop their packs. The climbing spans the spectrum from 5.4 to 5.14, but the majority is in the 5.10 to 5.11 range, perfect for most visitors. As an added bonus, there are some fun, two-pitch routes at this cliff that have truly spectacular views of the lake.

Conditions: This sector is one of the first to receive morning sun, and keeps it until early or mid-afternoon. The Outhouse wall stays dry during rainstorms due to the large overhang and capped roof above, but the other walls are all are vertical and quickly get wet. Regardless, they tend to dry fast once the storms have passed.

Approach: After successfully hiking all the way to the top of "Heat Attack Hill", you'll be directly in front of Trailside Wall. To reach Outhouse Wall, follow a trail up a small incline on the left. To reach Hillside and Louise Falls, follow a trail up the treed hillside on the right.

Louise Falls

This is a rarely visited wall, but has some nice easy routes and a couple of steep, physical climbs worthy of the trek up. Routes are listed from right to left.

❶ Zen Arcade 5.11c . . . .

6 bolts (15 m) Hand jam up to a chockstone horn and then work the arête until it's possible to move left onto the face and clip the third bolt (ignore the bolt up and to the right). Finish up *Lords of Karma*. (*Karl Krause, 1993*)

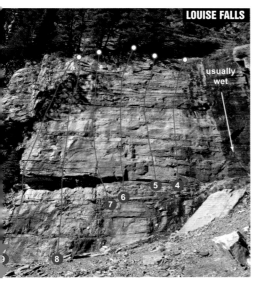

LOUISE FALLS

usually wet

❷ Lords of Karma 5.11d

6 bolts (14 m) This is the middle route and the best of the three. Start left of the first bolt and traverse right on a rail. Big moves off flat holds will tire you by the time you reach the anchor. Watch the easy, but run-out moves between the third and fourth bolt. (*Karl Krause, 1993*)

**❸ Crank if
You Love Jesus** 5.11b . . .

4 bolts (15 m) This is the left-most route. A powerful start is followed by big reaches that lead to parallel cracks. From the top of the cracks, trend up and right to the anchor. (*Karl Krause, 1993*)

❹ Louise Sticks It 5.6 . . . .

4 bolts (20 m) Work up the slab using edges and horizontals. (*Jon Jones, 1999*)

❺ Cruise Control 5.5 . . . .

2 bolts + gear (24 m) Climb the seam feature that has two bolts at the start. (*Unknown*)

❻ Midget's Mantle 5.6 . . . .

4 bolts + gear (25 m) Start just right of a small, vegetated corner. Climb over a couple of ledges and then up the face to a crux near the anchor. (*Barb Clemes, 1986*)

**❼ Please Don't
Step on the Flowers** 5.6 . . . .

3 bolts + gear (25 m) Start up a small, vegetated corner. Climb over a couple of ledges before following a thin crack to the anchor. (*Jon Jones, 1999*)

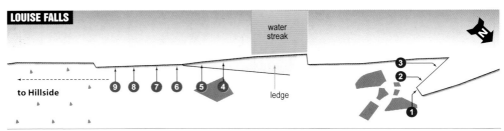

LOUISE FALLS

water streak

to Hillside

ledge

 Pinguicula 5.6 . . . .

2 bolts + gear (20 m) Pull a roof using a big, wedged flake. Trend slightly left and finish at the *Ryan's Eliminate* anchor. (*Jon Jones, 1999*)

 Ryan's Eliminate 5.5 . . . .

3 bolts + gear (20 m) Climb over a roof, up an arête and along a face. The first clip is high for 5.5. (*Jon Jones, 1999*)

Hillside Wall

This rarely-crowded crag has a nice collection of two-pitch routes that provide a bit of exposure and nice views. Routes are listed from right to left.

 The Escalator 5.8 . . . .

Pitch 1 (5.8, 5 bolts, 15 m) Start near the top of a hill, just below a large log leaning against the wall. A fair amount of run-off keeps this pitch dirty.
Pitch 2 (5.8, 13 bolts, 29 m) This long and fun pitch is the reason for enduring the first. Big buckets lead to a crux near the top. (*Greg Golovach, 2007*)

 Tombstone 5.10a . . . .

Pitch 1 (5.9, 6 bolts, 18 m) This is a good pitch with nice climbing, but tends to stay dirty due to run-off.
Pitch 2 (5.10a, 12 bolts, 26 m) Good, positive holds lead to a fun roof encounter and a crux in the orange rock above. (*Greg Golovach, 2003*)

 Traffic 5.10a . . . .

Pitch 1 (5.9, 5 bolts, 19 m) Start by pulling over a roof on jugs. Climb a juggy flake and finish with positive edges.
Pitch 2 (5.10a, 12 bolts, 27 m) This might be one of the best 5.10a pitches in the area, but you wouldn't know it because of the lack of traffic. Stellar rock, stellar holds, and stellar moves. (*Greg Golovach, 2003*)

 Lumberjack 5.10c . . . .

Pitch 1 (5.10b, 9 bolts, 28 m) Nice, rambling climbing

leads to a grassy ledge and a crux pulling into a flake over a roof (smooth footholds). The anchors is above the tree.
Pitch 2 (5.10c, 11 bolts, 26 m) If you can climb the grade, this pitch is a must-do! (*Greg Golovach, 2003*)

 Fiddler on the Roof 5.9 . . . .

6 bolts (19 m) This nice pitch follows a left-trending arch. Airy for 5.9. (*Karl Krause, 1999*)

⑮ Under Cover 5.10c . . . .

This is a good three-pitch outing with a lot of interesting climbing that isn't typical of the area. Start off a dirt ledge. If your mindful of rope-drag on the first pitch, you can

HILLSIDE WALL

log leaning against w

roof

1st pitch o #13 out of view

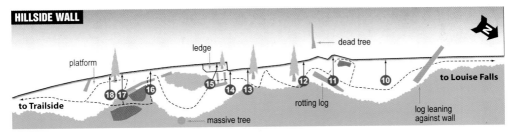

HILLSIDE WALL

platform — ledge — dead tree — to Louise Falls — to Trailside — rotting log — massive tree — log leaning against wall

18 17 16 15 14 13 12 11 10

link the first two pitches together. Rap twice to get down.

Pitch 1 (5.8, gear, 17 m) Trend left up a flake to the base of a roof. Climb around it and up a left-facing corner.
Pitch 2 (5.10b, 6 bolts, 10 m) Climb up a right-facing corner before angling rightward over a blank slab.
Pitch 3 (5.10b, 2 bolts + gear, 21 m) This interesting pitch features climbing that is atypical for Lake Louise. Stem up a gaping chimney and over a roof. Easier climbing leads to a bigger roof. Make a couple of airy moves out the roof to anchors above.　　*(Greg Golovach, 2001)*

16 The Incredible Talking Woman 5.10c . . . .

8 bolts (22 m) Sustained, thin face climbing leads to easier climbing and a slight crux getting to the last bolt. Project bolts lead above the anchor. *(Greg Golovach, 2001)*

17 Heart of Darkness 5.10c . . . .

Pitch 1 (5.10b, 14 bolts, 38 m) This great pitch starts with technical, thin face climbing which fades to cruisy jugs that lead to the base of a corner and arête. Spectacular and exposed arête climbing finishes the ascent. To lower to the ground, clip into the fifth bolt and re-lower through a quick-link.
Pitch 2 (5.10c, 5 bolts, 12 m) A cruxy opening trends right to easier climbing and the anchor. You'll need two ropes to reach the ground.　　*(Karl Krause, 1999)*

18 Darkness at Noon 5.10a . . . .

Pitch 1 (5.10b, 5 bolts, 35 m) This route is rarely done. Hunting around for the fixed pitons that comprise the majority of the protection is mentally taxing with a building pump.
Pitch 2 (5.10a, 6 bolts + gear, 40 m) The extension goes to the top of the wall. Happy pin hunting! You'll need two ropes to descend to the first pitch's anchor.
　　(Peter Arbic, 1992)

Trailside Wall

This is the first wall you'll see after cresting "Heart Attack Hill". There aren't many routes, but they're all of excellent quality. Routes are listed from right to left.

19 Aeroflot P1 5.11b . . . .

7 bolts (23 m) Climb the face left of the corner to a high first bolt. From the small roof, multiple options will likely create confusion. After solving the puzzle, enjoy fun flake climbing to an anchor below a roof. *(Mark Whalen, 1988)*

20 Aeroflot P2 5.11c . . . .

15 bolts (43 m) This extension is decent and worth a look. A long draw on the sixth and twelfth bolts helps with rope drag, and a few pieces of gear may be useful to tame the gaps between bolts. Lower twice.　　*(Mark Whalen, 1988)*

21 Stage Fright 5.11d . . . .

14 bolts (32 m) This fantastic route has four distinct cruxes, each more interesting than the last. Begin off a boulder leaning against the wall. *(Dave Thomson, 1999)*

TRAILSIDE WALL

Outhouse Wall

20 23 25 24 22 21 19

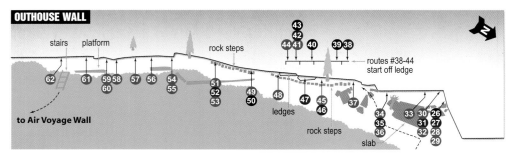

OUTHOUSE WALL

stairs | platform | rock steps | routes #38-44 start off ledge

to Air Voyage Wall

ledges | rock steps | slab

⑳ Rubber Lover 5.11c . . . .

5 bolts (11 m) This popular climb may seem short compared to many of the routes at Lake Louise, but it still packs a punch. You've been warned! (*Marc Dube, 1988*)

㉓ Criterium 5.12a . . . .

14 bolts (31 m) This fantastic extension to *Rubber Lover* has an early crux pulling over the small roof, but a mile of sustained sidepulls and underclings keeps the outcome in question until the very end. (*Bruce Howatt, 1988*)

㉔ Standing Ovation 5.10b . . . .

Gear to 4 inches (36 m) This fantastic route climbs the left-facing corner right of *Chocolate Bunnies From Hell*. Easy stemming comes to an abrupt end just before the large roof where the holds start to disappear. If you reach the base of the roof, step right and finish straight up. With a 70-m rope, you can just get down, otherwise you'll need to lower twice. (*Louis Babine & René Boiselle, 1979*)

㉕ Chocolate Bunnies from Hell 5.11b . . . .

12 bolts (31 m) This highly-technical route climbs the arête and face that divides the Outhouse wall from the Trailside wall. It will give even the most seasoned veteran a real run for their money. (*Joe Buszowski, 1986*)

Outhouse Wall

This wall is jammed with classics and a good choice for a group with varying skills. If you can, check out the various extensions, which offer great exposure, views and climbing. Routes are listed from right to left.

㉖ Colloidal Impact 5.12b . . . .

9 bolts (22 m) Climb the first three bolts of *Wicked Gravity* before traversing right under a roof to a chain draw and a tough crux. Above, big reaches between large holds lead to the anchor. (*Josh Korman, 1986*)

㉗ Wicked Gravity 5.11a . . . .

8 bolts (21 m) There's nothing wicked about this route, but do pray for a low-gravity day. Start right of the large corner. Absolutely classic. (*Joe Buszowski, 1985*)

㉘ The Path 5.14a . . . . . .

Gear (45 m) This stunning line scales one of the tallest walls at Lake Louise, and is one of Canada's hardest traditional lines. The gear is thin and spaced, and the only ascents to date have been pre-rehearsed. A ground-up ascent is possible, but awaits a bold climber with big guns and gear savvy. From the top of *Wicked Gravity*, creep up a thin face with several tough cruxes, a small roof and a decent horizontal break. Place a final, small cam before making a desperate sequence leftward. Runout 5.12 gains the anchor. Lower twice to descend. (*Sonnie Trotter, 2007*)

㉙ The Great Escape 5.13c . .

Gear (45 m) This is an easier variation to *The Path*. Climb that route to the rest above the small roof. Escape right to the arête. Step around to the slab and follow it to a shared anchor. Lower twice to get down. (*Sonnie Trotter, 2007*)

㉚ Pub Night 5.6 . . . .

Gear (22 m) This fun corner crack tackles the obvious large dihedral on the right end of the wall. (*Unknown*)

㉛ Monkey Lust 5.11b . . . . . .

Gear (15 m) Although this route can be climbed in one pitch from the ground, the difficulties directly above the anchor ledge on *Pub Night* convince most climbers to pitch it out. From the ledge, follow a wide crack on the right face that is difficult much of the way. Pray you don't pump out going for the anchor. (*Joe Buszowski, 1985*)

㉜ Clair's Route 5.9 . . . .

9 bolts (35 m) From the anchor of *Pub Night*, follow good rails until you can reach left to a positive flake that leads to the belay. Fixed pins. (*Clair Israelson, 1980*)

33 Duracell 5.10d . . . .

5 bolts (25 m) Solo easy terrain to a small roof where the bolts begin. A short section of tiny crimps leads to a small ledge and a rightward traverse to the *Pub Night* anchor.
(Blair Wardman, 1988)

34 Top Gun 5.7 . . . .

2 bolts + gear (22 m) Start on a tree stump and climb a crack to a ledge. Easy rambling through good edges leads straight up the seam. *(Peter Arbic, 1986)*

35 Energizer 5.11c . . . .

12 bolts (35 m) From the last bolt of *Duracell*, trend left on easy terrain. Sustained crimping leads to an anchor under a large roof. *(Greg Golovach, 2000)*

36 Flameout 5.10b . . . .

5 bolts + gear (35 m) Continue above the anchor of *Top Gun*. Climb a right-facing corner on mostly positive holds with a few sidepulls thrown in for good measure. A flameout refers to the failure of a jet engine caused by the extinction of the flame in the combustion chamber.
(Peter Arbic & Mischi Boehnisch, 1993)

37 Public Enemy 5.10a . . . .

9 bolts (23 m) This is one of the most popular routes on the wall. Start in a left-facing corner and follow good holds to a crux at the midway roof. A final crux traverses left under the higher roof. *(Peter Arbic, 1991)*

38 Bloodsport 5.11b . . . .

19 bolts (43 m) This amazing line is best climbed in one long pitch from the ground (extend the fourth bolt to keep the rope straight). From the anchors of *Public Enemy,* step right onto the face and cruise positive holds to a good rest before a roof. Reach blindly over the roof and continue up the face above. To descend, lower to the anchors of *Public Enemy* and make a second lower to reach the ground. *(Peter Arbic & Mischi Boehnisch, 1993)*

39 Dirty Dancing 5.12c . . . .

9 bolts (20 m) Climb the face just left of a left-facing corner on the right end of a ledge. A crazy boulder problem surmounts the roof. This sandbag finishes on *Bloodsport*. *(Peter Arbic, 2000)*

40 Snatch 5.12c . . . .

11 bolts (20 m) This route climbs the middle of the face to a vicious boulder problem moving over a roof. The grade might be a tad stiff. *(Peter Arbic, 2002)*

Jesse Huey on Scared Peaches (5.12a).

OUTHOUSE WALL

41 Open Project . . . .

42 Venom 5.11d . . . .

8 bolts (21 m) This stunning line tackles the long, overhanging arête that rises above *Turtle Mountain*. From the belay, follow a flake to the base of a roof, and traverse leftward before gunning up the overhanging arête. If you have enough draws and a 70-m rope, you can climb it as one monster pitch from the ground and lower back to the *Turtle Mountain* belay. Pull the rope and lower again to descend to the ground. *(Marc Dube, 1988)*

43 Elbow Venom 5.12a . . . .

11 bolts (26 m) Climb the *Venom* arête, but instead of clipping the anchor, continue up the left face and make an airy traverse rightward until you can straddle a horn. Shake out and make a move straight up before stepping around to the right side of the arête and the anchor. Rap twice to get descend. *(Unknown)*

44 Ash Wednesday 5.10a . . . . . .

Gear (21 m) This brilliant pitch of gear climbing deserves more traffic. From the anchor of *Turtle Mountain* easy climbing leads up an exposed ramp to amazing holds in a corner crack. Belay up your second before making two rappels back to the ground (use the *Female Hands* anchor). If you have a 70-m rope, you can make it down in one rappel, but you'll have to downclimb the slab—tie a knot in the rope ends! A 5.10a variation climbs the exposed ramp to just above the height of the *Female Hands* anchor. Step left around the corner and finish straight up. *(FA: Rob Robin, 1984; Variation FA: Jim Franken, 1985)*

45 Rolling Stone 5.10c . . . .

2 bolts + gear (23 m) Start up *Purple People Eater* before following a crack up yellow rock. *(Greg Golovach, 1989)*

46 Purple People Eater 5.11c . . .

6 bolts (23 m) Gain a massive jug before working dueling sidepulls to a crux that will pump you out if you can't find the right holds. After getting over the roof, balance up the face before following bigger holds to the anchor. A couple of finger-sized cams might be useful between the first and second bolt. Amazing purple rock! *(Greg Golovach, 1997)*

47 Mardi Gras 5.11a . . . .

8 bolts (23 m) A balancey crux leads up a thin crack to a small roof, which is turned on good holds. Cruise to the anchor. If the runout seems too excessive, skirt over and clip the last draw of *Turtle Mountain*. *(Colin Zacharias, 1986)*

48 Turtle Mountain 5.10b . . . .

7 bolts (22 m) This is a fun route with a few cruxy crimps and a tricky mantle. Clip one bolt on the slab before stepping right onto the overhang prow. *(Mark Whalen, 1992)*

49 Tomcat 5.3 . . . .

1 bolt + gear (22 m) This is a sparsely-protected, left-facing corner just left of *Turtle Mountain*. *(Colin Zacharias, 1986)*

50 Female Hands 5.12b . . . .

6 bolts (28 m) Solo *Tomcat* to the base of the overhanging arête. Traverse right before charging straight up on small edges. The crux comes near the top on crimps so small you'll wish you had smaller hands. *(Joe Buszowski, 1990)*

51 Rain Dogs 5.5 . . . .

1 bolt + gear (22 m) Climb a crack leading through a yellow wall to an arching corner and the hardest moves. Jugs lead over the roof to the anchor. *(Bruce Howatt, 1986)*

52 MK Ultra 5.11a . . . .

5 bolt + gear (37 m) From the *Rain Dogs* anchor, climb through an overhanging corner to a bolt above a purple roof. Powerful moves lead rightward. Place a couple of small to medium cams before reaching bolts that lead to the anchor. To prevent rope drag, it's best to backclean the first bolt in the purple roof. To descend with a 70-m rope, it's necessary to unclip the gear as you lower. Otherwise, lower twice to get down. *(Jeff Relph, 2005)*

53 Surfing on Heroin 5.10b . . . .

3 bolts + gear (37 m) From the anchor of *Rain Dogs*, climb through the overhanging corner to a bolt above a purple roof. Gross rock leads directly up to an anchor comprised of nuts. Not recommended. *(Rob Rohn, 1984)*

54 Blue Valentine 5.7 . . . .

4 bolts + gear (21 m) This is the first route left of two trees growing close to the wall. Climb to the top of a small, left-facing corner. Traverse right before climbing up an orange face. *(Mark Whalen & Karl Krause, 1993)*

55 Swordfish Trombone 5.9 . . . .

4 bolts (10 m) This worthy extension continues above *Blue Valentine* for four bolts of technical crimping up the orange face. Enjoy it as one long pitch or a two-pitch outing. *(Karl Krause, 1993)*

56 Heart Attack and Vine 5.10c .....

6 bolts + gear (35 m) Climb a crack two metres right of a tree growing on the wall. Gain a ledge and an anchor halfway up the wall (a great 5.7 gear route to here). Technical edge climbing leads to the top.
(Karl Krause, 1993)

57 Coroner's Inquest 5.4

Gear (23 m) Climb a wide crack just right of the tree growing on the wall. Finish at the top of a large, left-facing corner. A bit vegetated to start. *(Unknown)*

58 My Little Pony 5.5 ......

6 bolts (16 m) Start just left of a tree growing on the wall. Follow a crack to its end before sauntering up to the anchor on jugs.
(Peter Arbic, 2004)

59 Men with Brooms 5.6 ....

7 bolts (16 m) A series of small slabs leads to a final slab before the anchor. Footwork, people! *(Peter Arbic, 2004)*

60 Graveside Humour 5.4 ....

8 bolts (23 m) Continue above the *Men With Brooms* anchor navigating an orange sea of jugs. This is a fun, two-pitch outing. If you have a 70-m rope, you can climb it as one mega pitch from the ground (16 quickdraws) and still make it back to the midway anchor. Pull the rope and lower once more to the ground. *(Peter Arbic, 2004)*

61 School of Rock 5.7 ......

9 bolts (16 m) This fun route follows a thin seam and crack. *(Peter Arbic, 2004)*

62 Neverland 5.8 ....

7 bolts (16 m) This is the left-most route on the wall and is located where the trail heads down to the outhouse. It's a great climb and features fun, interesting moves. Put your thinking cap on. *(Peter Arbic, 2004)*

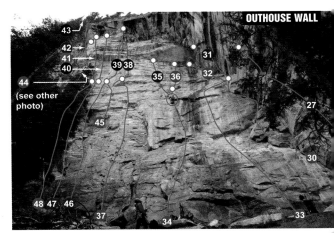

AMPHITHEATRE SECTOR

40 routes ←5.10 5.11 5.12 5.13→

This sector contains the best gear-protected pitches at Lake Louise, as well as a fine collection of classic 5.11 sport routes. The climbing on these walls is generally steep and pumpy, and the cost of failure is obvious—big, clean air. The crimpy *Jason Lives* (5.12d), one of Lake Louise's most sought after test-pieces, takes a steep, direct line up the middle of the impressive Air Voyage wall.

Conditions: The steep nature of these walls allow climbing during light and moderate rainstorms.

Approach: The Amphitheatre Sector is located above the obvious talus slope, which runs alongside the main hiking trail, a couple of minutes beyond Trailside Wall. To reach the base, follow a trail up either side of the talus slope. Alternatively, approach from the Outhouse Wall by following a trail leftward along the base of the cliff band.

Air Voyage Wall

This crag is home to classic gear and sport routes, some of which are simply not to be missed. Routes are listed from right to left.

❶ Exquisite Corpse 5.9 . . . .

Gear (16 m) Follow a splitter finger crack to a high roof. Step right before heading to the anchor. The crux is low.
(Peter Charkiw, 1985)

❷ The Peter Charkiw (I'm not Dead yet) Memorial Route 5.10c

5 bolts (15 m) Unfortunately, this climb is actually as hard as it looks from the ground. Climb to the first bolt from the right and make sure your belayer is being attentive as you move up to the second bolt. *(Unknown)*

❸ DSB 5.9 . . . .

Gear (13 m) Climb the wide crack just around the corner from *Dew Line*. *(Peter Charkiw, 1984)*

❹ DSB Extension 5.10c . . . .

3 bolts (19 m) A glass-like sheet of smooth quartzite stands between you and the anchor. *(Greg Golovach, 1997)*

❺ DEW Line 5.11c . . . .

10 bolts (25 m) One of Lake Louise's most classic lines climbs a beautiful arête. Work up the left side to a high crux. The Distant Early Warning (DEW) Line was a system of radar stations set up in the far north to detect incoming Soviet bombers during the Cold War. *(Jim Sandford, 1988)*

AIR VOYAGE WALL   to Outhouse W

yellow boulder   diving board boulders

rock ledge   rock platform   rock ledge

17 15 13   16 14   12   10 11   6 7 8 9   5

#13 alt start   #10 alt start

to Amphitheatre

❻ Extra Dry 5.9 . . . .

Gear (13 m) Climb a crack to an anchor on a small ledge.
(Bernard Ehmann, 1984)

❼ Manhattan 5.12a . . . .

7 bolts + gear (26 m) Follow a difficult crack above the *Extra Dry* anchor to a cruxy, rightward traverse on crimpers. Finish with the crux of *Dew Line*. *(Colin Zacharias, 1988)*

❽ Where Heathen Rage 5.12c . . . .

5 bolts + gear (30 m) Climb *Manhattan* to the cruxy rightward traverse. At this point, head left before climbing straight up a tough face. A powerful sequence leads through a roof and into a left-trending crack. Exhaust the crack's usable holds before making a rightward move to

the arête. A tough, face climbing variation (5.12c) follows a line of five bolts leftward from the *Extra Dry* anchor before joining *Where Heathen Rage* for the finish.
(*FA: Josh Korman, 1988; Variation FA: Joe Buszowski, 1993*)

⑨ Where Geezas Get Amongst It 5.13a . . . .

6 bolts + gear (45 m) A demanding extension to *Where Heathen Rage* tackles the face just left of the arête. Bring lots of small gear and a strong desire to hang on. (Stay away from the arête for 5.13a.) With a 70-m rope, you can lower onto the pillar at the base, but if you're cleaning gear, lower twice to get down.   (*Ben Firth, 2001*)

⑩ Scared Peaches P1 5.12a . . .

Gear (30 m) One of the most sought-after gear routes at Lake Louise starts just right of a yellow boulder. Strenuous and pumpy moves negotiate a crack system to a redpoint crux in a roof. Once above, do your best to keep the pump at bay. When you find yourself below a bolt, trend left up a crack to the anchor. A 5.12b variation, *Scared Shitless*, is a thin and scary start that follows a left-trending crack into *Scared Peaches* from the diving board boulders on the right.

(*FA: Josh Korman, 1986; Variation FA: Sean Isaac, 1997*)

⑪ Scared Peaches P2 5.12c . . .

4 bolts + gear (42 m) Although originally climbed in two pitches (in the days of shorter ropes), this line is now typically done as a single monster pitch from the ground. The upper half isn't overly difficult, but an accumulating pump keeps it interesting nonetheless. Bypass the first pitch's anchor on the left by continuing directly toward a left-facing corner, which leads to the anchor. If the belayer scales the pillar, it's possible to descend with a 70-m rope, otherwise lower twice to descend, especially if you are cleaning gear.   (*Josh Korman, 1986*)

⑫ Jason Lives 5.12d . . . . . .

6 bolts (15 m) One of Lake Louise's most sought-after testpieces starts with two bolts pre-clipped. Charge up a constantly overhanging wall on small crimpers to a technical crux mid-pitch. If you survive the micro holds, don't get too cocky because a final, pumpy, redpoint crux guards the chains.   (*Marc Dube, 1990*)

⑬ Air Voyage P1 5.10c . . . .

Gear (25 m) You'll get pumped fiddling in gear on this classic, steep wall, despite a plethora of big, rounded jugs. Early ascents began up a crack next to *Jason Lives*, but most now start off a stance next to *Mr. Rogers Smokes a Fat One*.   (*Rob Rohn, 1982*)

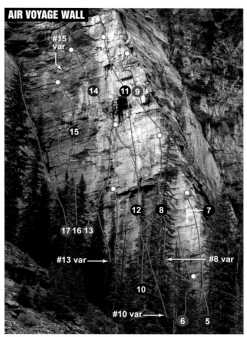

AIR VOYAGE WALL

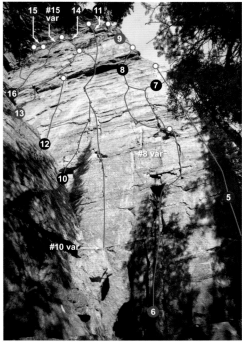

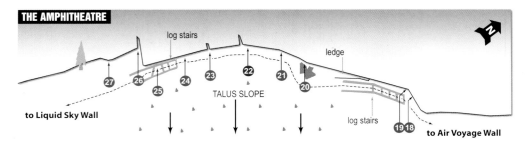

THE AMPHITHEATRE

⓮ Air Voyage P2 5.11c . . . .

Gear (42 m) The continuation trends leftward toward a thin-looking crack. Charge upward, then hang on for the ride to the anchor. A 70-m rope allows a lower to the top of the boulder, but tie a knot just in case! (*Dave Morgan, 1985*)

**⓯ Mr. Rogers
Smokes a Fat One** 5.11b . . . .

11 bolts (28 m) This incredibly pumpy line starts up a crack near the top of the narrow gully. Launch into an endless chain of perfectly-sculpted holds, which are guaranteed to pump you out before reaching the small edges that guard passage to the anchor. A 30-metre, 5.11c variation trends right at the last bolt, adding a bit more pumpy climbing (and one draw) to the pitch. (*FA: Joe Buszowski, 1986; Variation FA: Jon Jones & David Dornian, 1997*)

⓰ Mr. Plod 5.11c . . . .

13 bolts (30 m) This is a slightly harder, pumpier version of *Mr. Rogers Smokes a Fat One*. At the fourth bolt of that route, trend left to a tough crux, which you can sneak by using the corner on the left. Regardless, plenty of pumpy moves lurk above. (*Jon Jones & David Dornian, 1997*)

⓱ Corner Journey 5.8 . . . .

Gear (42 m) This long, fun pitch follows a low-angled corner located at the top of the narrow gully. At the top of the corner, traverse left to the anchor. To descend, rappel twice via the *I Hear My Train A-Comin'* anchor. (*Unknown*)

The Amphitheatre

This wall features one beautiful trad route after another, and has a couple of nice, moderate sport routes thrown in for good measure. The climbs are steep, and present the age-old dilemma of placing minimal gear to save energy versus placing lots of gear in case you do run out of energy. Routes are listed from right to left.

⓲ I Hear My Train A-Comin' 5.10c . .

Gear (21 m) From the base of the log stairs, start up a blunt arête. Follow an easy slab to the base of a crack that leads up the right-hand wall. The crack leads past a small roof to a rightward move to the anchor. (*Rob Rohn, 1983*)

⓳ Long-stemmed Rose 5.10a . .

Gear (35 m) This excellent climb starts in a large, left-facing corner at the bottom of the log stairs. Work up the corner before traversing right at a small roof to the crux. Once you've gained the chimney, amazing jugs lead to the belay ledge. Clip a directional bolt, traverse left to the

THE AMPHITHEATRE

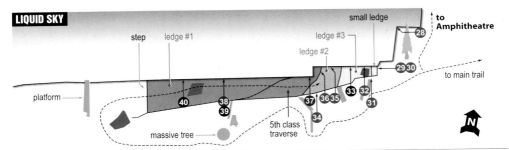

Violet Hour anchor and belay up your partner. Otherwise, lower off and deal with brutal rope drag. (*Rob Rohn, 1982*)

⓴ Crimson Sky 5.10c

Gear (31 m) This high-quality, gear-protected line follows a rightward traverse past a pin. Once around the corner, climb a slab that leads to great jug moves over a roof (be very mindful of minimizing rope-drag to this point). Above the roof, place some good gear—the options get poor in the upper half. (*Scott Flavelle, 1984*)

㉑ Violet Hour 5.10b

Gear (27 m) Climb onto a small pillar, through a cruxy roof and up a crack that features some of the best jug hauling to be found anywhere. This is the most popular gear-protected line at Lake Louise. (*Rob Rohn, 1982*)

㉒ Polio Roof 5.11a

Gear (27 m) Climb out the big roof with a U-shaped hueco at the lip. Share the *Violet Hour* anchor. (*Josh Korman, 1986*)

LIQUID SKY

㉓ Election Night 5.6

Gear (22 m) The wide crack left of the chimney. (*Unknown*)

㉔ Imaginary Grace 5.8

Gear (28 m) This fun route follows a thin crack up the face with a steep, juggy roof at the end. Start off the top of the log staircase. (*Marc Dube, 1984*)

㉕ Imaginary Face 5.9

9 bolts (25 m) This challenging 5.9 requires balance and patience throughout its entire length. Start off the top of the log staircase. (*Mark Whalen, 1994*)

㉖ Propeller 5.7

Gear + 4 bolts (27 m) Climb a wide crack in the big, right-facing corner. (*Unknown*)

㉗ FNG 5.8

10 bolts (25 m) This tricky route starts just right of a small tree growing next to the wall. FNG is military slang for "F_____g New Guy". (*Mark Whalen, 1994*)

Liquid Sky

This secluded wall is tucked away in the trees. The climbing is staged off three separate ledges and the character of the climbs varies from short routes requiring steel fingers and an iron will to long routes that demand endurance. Routes are listed from right to left.

㉘ Manicure Crack 5.10a

Gear (13 m) Climb the corner crack. (*Peter Charkiw, 1983*)

㉙ The Prowler 5.10c

Gear (40 m) Start off a small ledge at the start of *Reclining Pine Short*. Climb out right, onto the face and up. The left-hand variation is 5.11c. (*Dan Guthrie, 1985*)

30 Reclining Pine Short 5.6 . . . . . .

Gear (15 m) Quality climbing follows the corner. Climb past ledge three and onto ledge two. (*Peter Charkiw, 1983*)

31 Youthanism 5.6 . . . .

8 bolts (12 m) Fun climbing ends on ledge three.
(*Mark Whalen, 2001*)

32 Off the Deep End 5.9 . . . .

9 bolts (10 m) Step right off the ledge to start. The exposure hits you instantly. (*Unknown*)

33 Stigmata 5.12c . . . . . .

11 bolts (28 m) A truly desperate, four bolts of face climbing leads to a substantially easier stroll to the anchors. Stigmata are bodily marks, sores, or sensations of pain in locations corresponding to the crucifixion wounds of Jesus, such as on the hands and feet. (*Scott Withers, 1999*)

34 Reclining Pine Direct 5.10a . . . . .

1 bolt + gear (12 m) Start just below a large, log platform. Climb through big horizontal breaks to an anchor on ledge two. (*Joe Buszowski, 1984*)

The next three routes start off ledge number two, which can be accessed by an exposed fourth class traverse or by climbing routes 30 or 34.

35 The Search 5.10b . . . .

9 bolts (23 m) This route is a must-do for the grade. To start, scramble up to the left until it's possible to traverse rightward along good holds level with the first bolt. Enjoy excellent, pumpy climbing on mostly big holds all the way to the anchor. (*Joe Buszowski, 1984*)

36 Reclining Pine 5.9 . . . .

Gear (23 m) Revel in beautiful climbing up the corner crack. Another must-do climb. (*Peter Charkiw, 1983*)

37 Pushin' the Edge 5.11a . . . .

6 bolts (23 m) Climb to a high first bolt. An awesome roof flake leads to a few, steep arête moves that fade to slab before the anchor. (*Colin Zacharias & Chris Miller, 1992*)

38 Liquid Sky 5.11c . . . .

7 bolts (14 m) The crag's namesake and a classic for the grade. From the first bolt, trend rightward over perfectly sculpted holds that slowly suck the life out of your arms. If you've got anything left, a cruxy traverse back left under

a small roof will likely finish you off.
(*Colin Zacharias, Bruce Howatt & David Morgan, 1985*)

39 Mistaya 5.12b . . . .

5 bolts (14 m) Start to the right of a boulder on the ledge. From the first bolt, long moves connect horizontal breaks to a poor shake. Launch into a crimpy crux, which is followed by more long moves. (*Bruce Howatt, 1986*)

40 Love Connection 5.12c . . . . .

8 bolts (16 m) Start left of a boulder on the ledge. After a hard crux at the third bolt, traverse rightward into the crux of *Mistaya*. If you survive it, traverse rightward into the last two bolts of *Liquid Sky* to finish. (*Joe Buszowski, 1991*)

LIQUID SKY

#36 follows corner (hidden from view)

ledge #3

37 35 33

ledge #2

38

40 39

ledge #2

ledge #1

BLOB ROCK SECTOR

58 routes ←5.10 5.11 5.12 5.13→

This sector stretches along the main trail from the beginning of Pond Area all the way to the forest at the end of the cliff band. Blob Rock and Duckland are the main reasons to visit this zone, and feature many great lines from 5.9 to 5.12. Pond Hill, Pond Area and Hanging Gardens also have some nice routes worth checking out, and rarely have any lineups.

Conditions: Sections of Blob Rock and Duckland are climbable in light rain, but the water will work its way down the wall quickly if the rain intensifies. If the weather is cold, Pond Area, Blob Rock and Duckland all receive plenty of sun, which will help warm cold fingers.

Approach: Follow the main hiking trail for a couple of minutes past the talus slope below the Amphitheatre Wall. The Blob Rock sector starts at a pond along the base of the wall on the right side of the trail, which is landmarked by an "End of Nordic Ski Trail" sign. It continues all the way to the end of the cliff band. All the walls, with the exception of the Hanging Gardens, are visible from the main trail.

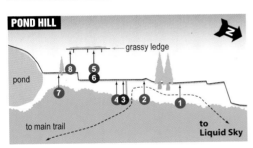

Pond Hill Wall

To get to this cliff, locate a trail that branches into the trees on the right just before the "End of Nordic Ski Trail" sign. Although rarely visited, this crag has several worthy routes, and is a good bet if it's busy elsewhere. Routes are listed from right to left.

❶ Russian Roulette 5.8 . . . . . .

Gear (15 m) That's what you'll be playing if you venture up this line. *(Greg Golovach, 1998)*

❷ Route 36 5.10d . . . .

6 bolts (16 m) This fantastic route is well worth seeking out. The line features beautiful black rock with a great crux sequence. *(Greg Golovach, 1998)*

❸ Eastern Block 5.11d . . . .

10 bolts (21 m) If this route where located at any other wall, it would see much more traffic. Fun arête moves lead to a rightward traverse. Launch up the black face on shrinking edges. Eventually, the edges get almost too small to use. *(Greg Golovach, 1997)*

❹ Just Jazzed 5.10d . . . .

1 bolt + gear (21 m) This decent route involves laybacking and stemming up a left-facing corner. Traverse right near the top to the *Eastern Block* anchor. *(Bruce Howatt, 1984)*

POND HILL

8   6   5

ledge

7   belay anchors

To access the belay ledge for routes 5 and 6, climb the first two bolts of Eastern Block, traverse left to a belay stance and bring up your partner.

5 **Vulcan Princess** 5.10d . . . . . .

6 bolts (13 m) Climb straight up from the ledge to a series of powerful moves that lead over the roof and diagonal seam above. *(Karl Krause, 1992)*

6 **Kobayashi Maru** 5.11c . . . .

7 bolts (16 m) From the small ledge, trend left over a roof, with difficulty, to second roof. Look for a hidden edge, which unlocks the crux sequence. *(Karl Krause, 1992)*

7 **Stubborn Nut** 5.9 . . . .

1 bolt + gear (17 m) Climb a diagonal crack into a left-facing corner, before heading rightward into another corner with a tricky roof. *(Greg Golovach, 1997)*

8 **Genetically Challenged** 5.10d . . .

9 bolts (18 m) This pitch features several cruxes and interesting moves in between. Either access it via *Stubborn Nut* or by gaining the belay ledge. *(Greg Golovach, 1997)*

Pond Wall

The small number of routes at this crag combined with the potential to pull your rope into the pond tends to keep the crowds at bay. If you visit, save it for the end of the day when you can afford to get your rope a wee bit wet. Routes are listed from right to left. (The first five routes are currently unclimbable due to stream flow and have no descriptions.)

9 **Swamp Thing** 5.9 . . . .

Gear (15 m) *(Blair Wardman, 1982)*

10 **Vital Transfiguration** 5.10c . . . .

1 bolt + gear (27 m) *(Sean Dougherty, 1984)*

11 **Swift Flyte** 5.10a . . . .

1 bolt + gear (18 m) *(Peter Charkiw, 1984)*

12 **Filigree and Shadow** 5.12b . . . .

8 bolts + gear (30 m) *(Karl Krause, 1994)*

13 **Goodbye, Mr. Spalding** 5.9 . . . .

1 bolt + gear (25 m) *(Sean Dougherty, 1984)*

14 **Forbidden Fruit** 5.10d . . . .

12 bolts (25 m) This is the right-hand route. Fun moves on good positive holds lead to a slot-crimp crux after the roof. *(Greg Golovach, 1997)*

15 **Original Sin** 5.11a . . . .

11 bolts (23 m) This is the left-hand route and features lots of varied climbing through corners, ledges and roofs. *(Greg Golovach, 1997)*

16 **NFG** 5.10c . . . .

3 bolts (18 m) Start by traversing right above the pond to a dirty corner and ledge. Well-spaced bolts lead to an anchor on a higher ledge. Not good. *(Mark Whalen, 1989)*

17 **The Web** 5.10b . . . .

7 bolts (18 m) Step right onto the face and work up sidepulls and edges to a small roof and the crux. The anchor is on a ledge above. *(Greg Golovach, 1997)*

18 **Way Frizzled** 5.9 . . . .

5 bolts (17 m) From a make-shift stance in the pond, positive holds lead to a high first bolt. More big holds lead over a roof to the crux—working over the smooth bulge. Good fun. *(J. Magnon, 1997)*

19 **10-69** 5.8 . . . .

11 bolts (32 m) This super route has great vertical flow. Enjoy. *(Mark Klassen, 1998)*

20 **Headbanger** 5.10d . . . .

6 bolts (17 m) Delicate face moves lead up a blunt prow to a cruxy roof encounter near the top. *(Greg Golovach, 1998)*

21 **Delirious** 5.9 . . . .

2 bolts + gear (25 m) This pitch is located at the far left end of the wall where the pond ends. Follow a mixture of bolts and gear placements past a black streak, up a flake and over a small roof.   (*Blair Wardman, 1981*)

Blob Rock 🧗 to 🧗 🔭 ☀

There is an odd dichotomy of routes at this crag—steep, physical climbs lurk in the shaded gully on the left side and an edgy face basks in the sun on the front. The wall sits on top of a small scree slope just above the main lakeside hiking trail. Routes are listed from right to left.

㉒ Castle Anthrax 5.9 . . . . . . ☐

9 bolts (22 m) This pitch is located just left of a gnarly-looking chimney and crack. A mindless jug haul peters out around three-quarters height, where you'll have to start thinking.
     (*Blaire Wardman & Mark Whalen, 1991*)

㉓ The Black Knight 5.10a . . ☐

8 bolts (21 m) Follow a groove to a high first bolt on the right. Tricky, puzzle-like cruxes are separated by good shakes.
     (*Mark Whalen & Karl Krause, 1991*)

㉔ Latest Squeeze 5.10d . . . . . . 🪢 🔦 ☐

7 bolts (20 m) Climb *If in Doubt*, but head straight up a black streak to a crimpy crux and hard clip. This is followed by sustained climbing on small edges to the anchor.   (*Jon Jones, 2000*)

㉕ If in Doubt 5.9 . . . . ☐

8 bolts (21 m) Start up a groove, clipping bolts on the left. After the third bolt, trend left onto a big ledge and continue up a corner with ever-increasing exposure. This pitch is best cleaned on toprope.
     (*Pierre Lemire, 1979*)

㉖ Arc of a Diver 5.11c . . 🔗 ☐

5 bolts + gear (20 m) Climb *If in Doubt*, but trend left over *Crowded House* and into a big, left-facing corner. Climb the corner to anchors above.   (*Bruce Howatt, 1984*)

POND WALL

main trail

main trail

BLOB ROCK

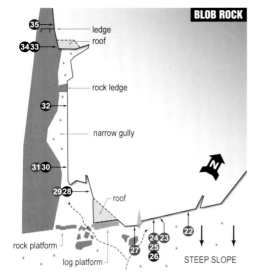

BLOB ROCK

ledge
roof
rock ledge
narrow gully
roof
rock platform
log platform
STEEP SLOPE
N

㉗ Crowded House 5.10c . . . .

9 bolts (19 m) Start just left of a small tree. A powerful opening with a knife-like hold leads to tricky climbing up and over a big ledge. A seriously crimpy crux guards the anchor. *(Peter Arbic, 1997)*

㉘ Sideshow Bob 5.12b . . . . . .

8 bolts (14 m) Share the first two bolts of *Missing Link* before making a tricky, footwork-intense traverse rightward. Charge up the arête to a no-hands rest. From here, traverse left onto the arête and dispatch one final crux before the anchor. *(Peter Arbic, 1999)*

㉙ Whine 5.13b . . . .

11 bolts (20 m) This is one of the hardest routes at Lake Louise. Most of the climbing is reasonable, but getting past the roof stops most in their tracks. Good luck, and if you do it, great job! *(Peter Arbic, 1999)*

㉚ Incomplete 5.12c . . . .

7 bolts (11 m) The most sought-after route on the wall is a steep and pumpy exercise with only a single shake in the middle. Unless you have some incredible lock-off strength, prepare for some big throws. *(Peter Arbic, 2000)*

㉛ Complete 5.13a . . . .

12 bolts (18 m) Continue above *Incomplete* to a thin and technical crux. It's short, so give it all you've got! Traverse right after the last bolt to the anchor. *(Peter Arbic, 2003)*

㉜ Chicks Call Me Daddy 5.11c . . . .

8 bolts (11 m) This is not the prettiest route at Lake Louise, but still offers some good climbing with a powerful crux sequence. *(Peter Arbic, 2002)*

㉝ Exiled 5.12b . . . .

8 bolts (17 m) This fun, challenging route climbs a big roof and overhanging arête. Share the first four bolts of *Unforgiven* before making an exciting traverse out the big roof to gain the arête. The crux comes near the top of the arête. A tricky-to-locate hold forces some to sneak out right in order to get to the anchor. *(Rob Owens, 2008)*

㉞ Unforgiven 5.12a . . . .

8 bolts (17 m) This route tackles the face just left of the overhanging arête halfway up the gully. Start by traversing in from the left and move around the arête to the first crux. Once under the big roof, shake out before launching up the pumpy face above. *(Mischi Boehnisch & Peter Arbic, 1993)*

㉟ Redemption 5.11c . . . . . .

7 bolts (14 m) Scramble all the way up the gully to a small stance below a jumble of large chockstones. Climb straight up. Surprisingly pumpy. *(Peter Arbic, 2004)*

Duckland

This crag features steep routes of the big, blocky variety and is just beyond Blob Rock. It is home to perhaps the most sought-after 5.12a in the Bow Valley, Nobody's Girl. Routes are listed from right to left.

㊱ Age of Electric 5.10b . . . .

8 bolts (21 m) To do this route, start on top of a big block with a belay bolt and scramble to a high first bolt before stepping onto the face. Difficult moves lead through a fractured lower rock band to big, pumpy holds that pave the way to the anchor. *(Greg Golovach, 1995)*

㊲ Cowgirls in the Rain 5.11d . .

8 bolts (21 m) Start on *Wild Frontiers*. Powerful crimps and underclings lead rightward beside a black streak. Finish at the *Wild Frontiers* anchor. *(Peter Arbic, 2000)*

㊳ Wild Frontiers 5.11c . . . .

8 bolts (21 m) Start off a small platform on the right end of the wall. Trend left to a powerful undercling crux that leads to a thin finish. *(Ken Chambers, 1988)*